Swiftly Sterneward

Swiftly Sterneward

Essays on Laurence Sterne and His Times in Honor of Melvyn New

Edited by W. B. Gerard,
E. Derek Taylor, and
Robert G. Walker

UNIVERSITY OF DELAWARE PRESS
Newark

For their generous support, the editors thank the Department of English and Modern Languages at Longwood University and the School of Liberal Arts and Department of English and Philosophy at Auburn University Montgomery.

Published by University of Delaware Press
Co-published with The Rowman & Littlefield Publishing Group, Inc.
4501 Forbes Boulevard, Suite 200, Lanham, Maryland 20706
www.rlpgbooks.com

Estover Road, Plymouth PL6 7PY, United Kingdom

British Library Cataloguing in Publication Information Available

Library of Congress Cataloging-in-Publication Data
Swiftly sterneward : essays on Laurence Sterne and his times in honor of Melvyn New / edited by W. B. Gerard, E. Derek Taylor, and Robert G. Walker.
    p. cm.
  Includes bibliographical references and index.
  ISBN 978-1-61149-058-9 (cloth : alk. paper) — ISBN 978-1-61149-059-6 (electronic)
  1. Sterne, Laurence, 1713–1768—Criticism and interpretation. I. Gerard, William Blake. II. Taylor, Derek (E. Derek) III. Walker, Robert G. (Robert Gary), 1947– IV. New, Melvyn.
  PR3716.S95 2011
  823'.6—dc22   2010050266

♾™ The paper used in this publication meets the minimum requirements of American National Standard for Information Sciences—Permanence of Paper for Printed Library Materials, ANSI/NISO Z39.48-1992.

Printed in the United States of America

Figure 1: *The Woodcutter's House* (or *The Woodcutter's Return*)
Oil on canvas, by Thomas Gainsborough (1727–88)
© Belvoir Castle, Leicestershire, UK/The Bridgeman Art Library
Nationality / copyright status: English / out of copyright

Figure 2: *The Cottage Door with Children Playing* (1778)
Cincinnati Art Museum, Given in honor of Mr. and Mrs. Charles F. Williams
by their children.

Figure 3: *The Cottage Door* (1780)
Courtesy of the Huntington Library, Art Collections, and Botanical Gardens.
San Marino, California.

Figure 4: *Peasant Smoking at a Cottage Door* (1788)
Collection University of California, Los Angeles. Hammer Museum. The
James Kennedy Collection.

Figure 5: *Diana and Actaeon* (c. 1786)
Oil on canvas
158.1 x 188 cm
The Royal Collection © 2010, Her Majesty Queen Elizabeth II

Photographs of "Tristram Shandy, The Quilt" courtesy of Joan New

Contents

Swiftly Sterneward

Introduction

"Attentiveness," claimed seventeenth-century philosopher Nicholas Malebranche, "is the natural prayer of the soul." For more than forty years, Melvyn New has engaged literature with an attentiveness that Malebranche, author of the tellingly titled *The Search After Truth*, would have found admirable. This volume seeks both to celebrate Professor New's achievements and to recommend his practice to present and future scholars.

A balance of passive receptivity and active scrutiny, attention, for Malebranche, encapsulates the rationalist's simultaneously skeptical and faithful approach to the quest for knowledge. Professor New's own search for truth has been similarly grounded in a humble awareness that it will never be found. He once instructed his graduate students in a class on Jewish philosophy to circle the name of every thinker in their course readings about whom they knew little or nothing. The resulting lists functioned not as dead ends, but as warnings; Professor New was inviting his students not to leave their studies, but to join Socrates who, in believing he knew nothing, knew the one thing needful to the life of a scholar. No one can avoid making pronouncements about texts and figures based on secondhand knowledge; the alternative to doing so, as Professor New is quick to point out, is silence. He has continuously challenged himself, his students, and the profession as a whole to proceed as carefully and thoughtfully as possible, always slightly abashed by how careless and thoughtless, despite our best efforts, we necessarily will be.

Professor New became, for those students not intimidated by his reputation for rigor, a model of intellectual life. Teaching his first graduate course at the University of Florida in the late 1960s, he drew a circle on the blackboard and asked how many points lie within the circle? An infinite number. And how many without? Again, an infinite number. The circle's circumference demonstrated the separation of good readings from bad without limiting

the number of either. Throughout his career, Professor New would insist on
the necessity of integrity, both in his teaching and in his writing, and that it
was false—even dangerous—to believe that one person's view is as valid as
another's merely because it is held with equal conviction. "Insipid moral rela-
tivism" was one of his favorite phrases, frequently accompanied by a short
quotation from Yeats: "The best lack all conviction, while the worst / Are
full of passionate intensity." He insisted that his students produce coherent
arguments that respected the text they were treating. A student poorly arguing
the professor's position would be disappointed in the reception accorded his
paper, while a student bold enough to argue well an opposing position would
receive surprisingly good treatment, and a counterargument.

Tracing the roots of a person's intellectual development is an imprecise
task, and many who experienced Professor New in a classroom might well
believe that he was born to teach, but he himself would underscore his
first-rate training. Growing up on Manhattan's midtown east side, he was a
feisty New York Giants baseball fan. Decades later he would joke that his
life peaked with Bobby Thomson's shot heard 'round the world in 1951.
He attended Stuyvesant High School and (a true hometown boy) Columbia
University where, he has admitted, bright students who could do math became chemistry majors and bright students who couldn't do math became
English majors. After serving a two-year stint as a naval officer, he returned
in 1961 to literary studies as a graduate student at Vanderbilt University,
where he wrote his dissertation under the direction of the noted and austere
Pope scholar John M. Aden ("Black Jack," as he was known among Vandy
graduate students). Even though New became a full professor in 1976, only
ten years after joining the Department of English at the University of Florida,
he never lost interest in teaching lower-division courses, nor did he forget
the burden put upon young scholars trying to juggle teaching and publishing, often at levels exceeding those of senior department members. Indeed,
as chairperson from 1979 to 1988, one of his expressed concerns was the
demanding workload facing new PhDs fortunate enough to have landed jobs,
only to discover that they had arrived (as he put it in a memorable neologism)
not in Camelot, but in "Teachalot."[1]

The simultaneous breadth and depth of Professor New's scholarly writings,
which will be addressed below, found its corollary in the range of assigned
reading in a self-designed series of courses. One course included works by
Cervantes, Conrad, Chekhov, Colette, Camus, Coetzee, Cela, Calvino, (Stephen) Crane, and Celan; another class covered Poe, Pushkin, Proust, Peréz
Galdós, Pirandello, Platonov, Paton, Pasternak, and Pynchon. Such "letter
courses" (he constructed similar ones for several other letters as well) did
more than simplify Professor New's book orders; they also illustrated his

conviction that, properly approached, *any* truly enduring work of literature may usefully be read alongside any other. From the outset of each course, Professor New thus staked out implicitly a subtle, and potentially enlightening, argument for his students to consider as the semester unfolded: those unable to find resonance between, say, *Don Quixote* and *The Plague* discovered something not about the insufficiencies of these texts, but about the importance of continuing to develop their own reading skills.

As a scholar, Professor New is best known, of course, for his work on Laurence Sterne. When he toiled over his dissertation in the 1960s, era of revolution and tumult, the world of Sterne criticism was very different from today. Sterne studies slowly had been emerging from the pall of religious heretic and leering sentimentalist cast over the author's reputation by Victorian scholars, thanks largely to the diligence of Wilbur L. Cross and Lewis P. Curtis, who helped focus attention back on the value of Sterne's texts themselves. By the mid-twentieth century, monographs on Sterne had begun to appear, and the moment was ripe for a thoughtful, formative perspective of the sort represented by Professor New's first book, *Laurence Sterne as Satirist* (1969). Here, he framed *Tristram Shandy* not as a novel or a parody of one, but as part of a satirical tradition hearkening back to Jonathan Swift and the Scriblerians, to Robert Burton, to Cervantes, and to Rabelais. Grounding his ideas squarely in close textual analysis, he provided an interpretation that has become foundational for many arguments today, even as Sterne has been treated as a protean author freely adaptable to the varied critical perspectives of Marxists, deconstructionists, and feminists alike.

In a recent conference paper, Professor New said that he "would rather write one good elucidating footnote than almost any other intellectual product I can think of." Although meant partly in jest (his meticulous transcription of Sterne's "Rabelaisian Fragment" from a holograph manuscript [1972] foreshadowed early on his abiding interest in textual editing), Professor New does offer a clue here as to why his stewardship as general editor of the Florida edition of the works of Laurence Sterne has met with such acclaim. Beginning with *Tristram Shandy* (1978, 1984), continuing with the *Sermons* (1996), *A Sentimental Journey and Continuation of the Bramine's Journal* (2002), *Letters* (2009), and concluding with a volume of *Miscellanies* (forthcoming), these nine volumes represent a monumental achievement by any standard. The introductions to these editions and their extensive critical apparatus—appendixes and annotations to satisfy even the most demanding reader—reveal a deft scholarly hand focused intently on the primary tasks of editing, clarification and illumination, but one informed by a spirit of genuine delight-in-discovery. Cleanly and considerately presented in an approachable (and historically accurate) format, each volume works unobtrusively but thoroughly to orient, perhaps to reorient, readers to Sterne's texts.

The connections Melvyn New has discovered between Sterne's writings and their many intellectual influences form the basis not only for the remarkable annotations of the Florida edition but for a host of shorter, often equally eye-opening studies. He has pursued with tenacity Sterne's references to obscure books such as *The Microscope Made Easy* (1970) and *The History of Cold-Bathing* (1997); his mention of the name Deventer in a footnote (1975); his interest in the Cambridge Platonist John Norris of Bemerton (1996); and his allusions to the solemn divine William Warburton (1982), against whom, Professor New proposes, Sterne measured his own (and his forebears') exercise of exuberant wit.

Professor New's various commentaries and collections have earned prominent places on the shelves of Sterneans. His entry on Sterne in the *Dictionary of Literary Biography* (1985) provides a condensed and entertaining overview, while, with its broad textual and critical scope, *Approaches to Teaching "Tristram Shandy"* (1989) offers at once a valuable pedagogical tool and a road map, as it were, for scholars first attempting to make their way through this notoriously challenging text. In a similar mold is his Twayne series study, *Tristram Shandy: A Book for Free Spirits* (1994), where he playfully and purposefully adapts Friedrich Nietzsche's own comments on Sterne's text as invitations to readers interested in attempting a similarly "free-spirited" engagement. Whatever his audience, he has never strayed far from his grounding sense, memorably stated in his introduction to *Critical Essays on Laurence Sterne* (1998), that "[w]hen one begins to confront the human paradox of knowing that truth is unreachable but thinking and speaking and acting as though knowledge moves us toward our goals, one has begun to understand what I believe is the primary crux of Sterne's great fictions."[2]

Professor New's analytical adherence to careful consideration of the text reasonably led him to examine Sterne the priest's adherence to *his* text: the scriptures. He recognized that, as Sterne's primary writing activity during most of his professional life, sermon composition played an important role in the creation of his fictions (1976). Furthermore, while most twentieth-century critics had rejected the notion of Sterne's religious piety—those who considered the sermons at all insisted on reading them as deistic essays, or worse, as hypocritical mouthings of faith—Professor New presented Sterne as a sincere and reasonably orthodox clergyman of the eighteenth-century Anglican faith. This is a point he would make, in various contexts, over and over again (1992, 1993, and especially in his *Notes to the Sermons* [1996]). For instance, by dovetailing Sterne with another Anglican divine-cum-satirist, Jonathan Swift, he connects Sterne to an actual (as opposed to a conjectural) literary tradition. After first comparing the two as fellow preachers with similar theological beliefs (1969), he explores the ways that Swift in *A Tale of a Tub* and Sterne in "Slawkenbergius's Tale" extend their mainstream Anglican perspectives to express concern about the "public danger" of "zeal, dogma, and demagoguery" (1993).[3]

Someone who, in a consideration of the processes of human cognition in reading, argues in a deliberate anachronism for the influence of Proust on Sterne (1988) is not likely to be bothered by novel approaches to literary interpretation. Indeed, Melvyn New has never shied away from assuming unique, sometimes unfashionable positions in the critical discussion of Sterne, even if those positions turn out to be provocative. In one essay, he not only attempts to "rescue Sterne . . . from [the] charge of phallocentrism" leveled by a feminist critic (1990) but also tries "to suggest that he [Sterne] already understood its dangers and was, in his life and writings, exploring ways to rescue himself"; in another, he confronts readerly biases in a playful discussion of how critics and teachers reinforce buried "prejudices and preconceptions" that eventually taint the reading of Sterne by forcing his work into a novelistic, as opposed to a satirical, mold (1991).[4] Perhaps his best-known resistive reading reassesses *Tristram Shandy* as a narrative of "determinateness" (1992) that, rather than adumbrating a postmodern idea of the impossibility of knowing, actually speaks to the genuine and persistent human urge to find truth, which has spawned both the ridiculous and sublime throughout history. But a similarly oppositional approach is evident in his examination of the artwork provided by avant-garde artist John Baldessari for the high-end Arion Press edition of *Tristram Shandy* (1995), where sustained ekphrasis and close textual analysis lead Professor New to ponder whether the ostensibly progressive work of the face-obliterating artist might best be read as "an exercise of authorial power with vengeance."[5]

Not all of Professor New's gauntlets have been thrown down in the service of Sterne. In a study of the role of Providence in eighteenth-century fiction, for instance, he challenged the prevailing critical understanding of the frequency with which "startling coincidences and accidents" surface in novels by the likes of Defoe and Fielding (1976). Where other influential scholars had read such moments as illustrative of "the Christian concept of an active and concerned Providence who interposes in human affairs,"[6] he suggests that the authors of these fictional works were protesting too much—the abundance of such "providential" moments, he argues, reflects instead the degree to which human experience, the very stuff of novels, was ceasing to fit easily into a convenient theological framework. Much the same impulse was evident in a 1995 panel he organized for the conference of the American Society of Eighteenth-Century Studies, where he confronted the pervasive influence of postmodernism on eighteenth-century scholarship, not by rejecting modern philosophy out of hand but by introducing participants to the ideas of a then little-mentioned twentieth-century philosopher, Emmanuel Levinas, who, in acknowledging his indebtedness to Plato, Descartes, and Malebranche, offered something demonstrably relevant to the discussion of an era that did the same. This panel resulted in an essay in which Professor New proffers a Levinasian reading of Sterne's semiautobiographical writings (2001) and in two significant collections on Levinas and eighteenth-century theory for which he served as editor (1999 and 2001).

Indeed, many of us could find a life's work solely in those texts *not* written by Sterne for which Professor New has served as editor or coeditor, or about which he has written critically. In eighteenth-century studies, he has coedited *Mary Astell and John Norris: Letters Concerning the Love of God* (2005), and he is coediting the Cambridge edition of Samuel Richardson's *The History of Sir Charles Grandison*. He has moved into the following two centuries as well, bringing forward the little-known nineteenth-century voice of an Anglo-Jewish lesbian novelist, poet, and essayist with his edition of *The Complete Novels and Selected Writings of Amy Levy* (1993) and offering compelling readings of Orwell (1975), Pynchon (1979), and Mann (in *Telling New Lies* [1992]). In fact, the title of this collection, taken from James Joyce's *Finnegans Wake* ("your wildeshaweshow moves swiftly sterneward"), is appropriate in several ways. Joyce playfully evokes a tradition of eighteenth-century and modern "Anglo-Irish" writers. Sterne, of course, was born in Ireland and Swift was the dean of St. Patrick's. Professor New's early work connected Sterne with Swift intellectually and aesthetically, but, additionally, the nexus between eighteenth-century and modern literature has been one of his abiding objects of study, in widely varying manifestations, throughout his career.

Whatever the venue, nothing Melvyn New has published is devoid of lively argumentative spirit and seriousness of purpose. One need only read through the reviews of scholarship on Sterne, Smollett, or others from any issue of the *Scriblerian* published in the past twenty years to appreciate how faithfully he has borne the mantle of Pope's dictum: "The life of a Wit is a warfare upon earth." His role as reviewer may seem to pale in comparison to his heavy lifting as a Sterne scholar and editor, yet perhaps it is in these briefest of commentaries that his core values shine through most brilliantly. While his relentlessly intelligent, and often acute, reviews have appeared in the gamut of top literary journals, his position as "gatekeeper" of Sterne scholarship for the *Scriblerian* is particularly noteworthy. There, through his scores of reviews, he has shaped a standard of scholarly assessment that values intellectual honesty above all else. In one characteristic critique (1996), Professor New comments that although "Sterne's work is battered" by the essay under review, "what ought to concern us . . . is that a person whose livelihood depends on reading deeply and widely nonetheless allows herself to write in the style to which this essay has been sentenced."[7] Here and elsewhere, one finds Professor New putting into practice his simple and commendable goals as a reviewer, as he himself explains them in a reflective piece (2006): "to discriminate between good scholarship and bad; strong, coherent argumentation, and weak; perceptive commentary and obfuscating."[8]

Through his persistence, insight, and ultimate faith in the value of human artistry, Professor New has transformed—and continues to transform—the landscape not only of Sterne studies, but of literary scholarship itself. He has accomplished the extraordinary, excelling in the large and small, ranging his discussions from punctuation to metacriticism to observations about the profession (sometimes all within the same study). The experience of having returned Sterne securely to the canon, though, has also provided Professor New with the humility of the long view in regard to the omniscience and permanence of any scholarship. He notes, "a lifetime spent with any author tends to convince us that no interpretation, no biography, no critical insight, no editorial practice can or will long endure the critical flux."[9] Nevertheless, one suspects that there always will be a place in literary studies for Melvyn New's "free-spirited" brand of probing, informed, and attentive analysis.

NOTES

1. See Melvyn New, "Research versus Teaching: Once upon a Time in Teachalot," *ADE Bulletin* 89 (Spring 1988): 56–59.

2. Melvyn New, "Introduction: Four Faces of Laurence Sterne," in *Critical Essays on Laurence Sterne*, ed. Melvyn New (New York: G. K. Hall, 1998), 4.

3. Melvyn New, "Swift and Sterne: Two Tales, Several Sermons, and a Relationship Revisited," in *Critical Essays on Jonathan Swift*, ed. Frank Palmeri (New York: G. K. Hall, 1993), 182.

4. Melvyn New, "Job's Wife and Sterne's Other Women," in *Out of Bounds: Male Writers and Gender(ed) Criticism*, ed. Laura Claridge and Elizabeth Langland, (Amherst: University of Massachusetts Press, 1990), 57, and "Swift as Ogre, Richardson as Dolt: Rescuing Sterne from the Eighteenth Century," *Shandean* 3 (1991): 50.

5. Melvyn New, "William Hogarth and John Baldessari: Ornamenting Sterne's *Tristram Shandy*," *Word & Image* 11, no. 2 (April–June 1995): 192.

6. Melvyn New, "'The Grease of God': The Form of Eighteenth-Century English Fiction," *PMLA* 91 (1976): 235.

7. Melvyn New, "(W)holes and Noses: The Indeterminacies of *Tristram Shandy*," *Scriblerian* 29, no. 1 (Autumn 1996): 37.

8. Melvyn New, "Swimming Down the Gutter of Time with Sterne and *The Scriblerian*," *Scriblerian* 39, no. 1 (Autumn 2006): 52.

9. Melvyn New, "Attribution and Sponsorship: The Delicate Case of Sterne," *Eighteenth-Century Fiction* 8, no. 4 (1996): 526.

Selected Publications by Melvyn New

BOOKS

Laurence Sterne as Satirist: A Reading of "Tristram Shandy." Gainesville: University of Florida Press, 1969.

The Works of Laurence Sterne: The Text of "Tristram Shandy." Edited by New and Joan New. Vols. 1 and 2. Gainesville: University of Florida Press, 1978. Reprinted as a limited fine press edition by Arion Press, San Francisco, 1988.

The Works of Laurence Sterne: The Notes to "Tristram Shandy." Edited by New with Richard A. Davies and W. G. Day. Vol. 3. Gainesville: University of Florida Press, 1984.

Approaches to Teaching Sterne's "Tristram Shandy." Edited by New. New York: Modern Language Association, 1989. A volume in the MLA Teaching Masterworks of World Literature series.

New Casebook on "Tristram Shandy." Edited by New. New York: Macmillan, 1992.

Telling New Lies: Essays in Fiction, Past and Present. Gainesville: University Press of Florida, 1992.

The Complete Novels and Selected Writings of Amy Levy. Edited by New. Gainesville: University Press of Florida, 1993.

Tristram Shandy: A Book for Free Spirits. Twayne Masterworks Series. New York: Twayne-Macmillan, 1994.

The Works of Laurence Sterne: The Sermons. Edited by New. Vol. 4, *The Text*; Vol. 5, *The Notes.* Gainesville: University Press of Florida, 1996.

Life and Opinions of Tristram Shandy. Edited by New and Joan New. London: Penguin Classics Edition, 1997. New Penguin edition using the Florida *Text*, annotations based on the Florida *Notes*, with introduction by Christopher Ricks and editor's introduction by M. New. Sixth printing, 2003.

Critical Essays on Laurence Sterne. Edited by New. New York: G. K. Hall, 1998.

In Proximity: Emmanuel Levinas and the Eighteenth Century. Edited by New with Robert Bernasconi and Richard A. Cohen. Lubbock: Texas Tech University Press, 2001.

The Works of Laurence Sterne: A Sentimental Journey Through France and Italy and Continuation of the Bramine's Journal. Edited by New and W. G. Day. Vol. 6. Gainesville: University Press of Florida, 2002.

Mary Astell and John Norris: Letters Concerning the Love of God. Edited by New and E. Derek Taylor. Aldershot, Hampshire, UK: Ashgate, 2005.

A Sentimental Journey Through France and Italy and Continuation of the Bramine's Journal with Related Texts. Edited by New and W. G. Day. Cambridge, MA: Hackett, 2006.

The Works of Laurence Sterne: The Letters. Edited by New and Peter de Voogd. Vols. 7 and 8. Gainesville: University Press of Florida, 2009.

The Works of Laurence Sterne: Miscellanies. Vol. 9. Gainesville: University Press of Florida. Forthcoming.

Sir Charles Grandison. Edited by New, E. Derek Taylor, and Elizabeth Kraft. Cambridge University Press Edition of *The Works of Samuel Richardson.* Forthcoming.

JOURNALS

Emmanuel Levinas and the Eighteenth Century, special issue of the *Eighteenth Century: Theory and Interpretation,* 40 (1999). Edited by New.

"Sterne in Dublin: Five Essays Presented at the Tenth Enlightenment Congress, July 1999." *Shandean* 11 (2000): 28–69. Edited by New.

ARTICLES AND NOTES

"Sterne and Swift: Sermons and Satire." *Modern Language Quarterly* 30 (1969): 198–211.

"Two Notes on Sterne." *Notes and Queries,* n.s. 16 (1969): 353–54.

"Laurence Sterne and Henry Baker's *The Microscope Made Easy.*" *SEL* 10 (1970): 591–604.

"Ad Nauseam: A Satiric Device in Huxley, Orwell and Waugh." *Satire News Letter* 8 (1970): 24–28.

"Sterne's Rabelaisian Fragment: A Text from the Holograph Manuscript." *PMLA* 87 (1972): 1083–92.

"The Dunce Revisited: Colley Cibber and Tristram Shandy." *South Atlantic Quarterly* 72 (1973): 547–59.

"Wordsworth's Shell of Poetry." *Philological Quarterly* 53 (1974): 275–81.

"*Tristram Shandy* and Heinrich van Deventer's *Observations.*" *Papers of the Bibliographical Society of America* 69 (1975): 84–90.

"The Sterne Edition: The Text of *Tristram Shandy.*" In *Editing Eighteenth-Century Novels,* edited by G. E. Bentley, Jr., 67–89. Toronto: Hakkert, 1975.

"Orwell and Antisemitism: Toward *1984.*" *Modern Fiction Studies* 21 (1975): 81–105. Reprinted in *Telling New Lies.*

"Some Borrowings in *Tristram Shandy*: The Textual Problems." Coauthored with Norman Fry. *Studies in Bibliography* 29 (1976): 322–30.

"'The Grease of God': The Form of Eighteenth-Century English Fiction." *PMLA* 91 (1976): 235–44. Reprinted in *Telling New Lies*.

"Nineteen Eighty-Four." *American Speech* 51 (1976): 278–79.

"Gibbon, Middleton and 'the barefooted fryars.'" *Notes and Queries*, n.s. 25 (1978): 51–52.

"Sterne as Editor: 'The Abuses of Conscience Sermon.'" *Studies in Eighteenth-Century Culture* 8 (University of Wisconsin Press, 1979): 243–51.

"Profaned and Stenciled Texts: The Search for Pynchon's *V.*" *Georgia Review* 33 (1979): 395–412. Reprinted in *Modern Critical Views: Thomas Pynchon*, edited by Harold Bloom, 93–109. New York: Chelsea House, 1986; and in *Telling New Lies*.

"Sterne, Warburton, and the Burden of Exuberant Wit." *Eighteenth-Century Studies* 15 (1982): 245–74. SEASECS prize-winning essay; reprinted in *Telling New Lies*.

"Surviving the Seventies: Sterne, Collins and Their Recent Critics." *Eighteenth Century: Theory and Interpretation* 25 (1984): 3–24.

"'At the backside of the door of purgatory': A Note on Annotating *Tristram Shandy*." In *Tristram Shandy: Riddles and Mysteries*, 15–23. London: Vision Press / New York: Barnes and Noble, 1984.

"Laurence Sterne." Entry in *Dictionary of Literary Biography: 18th Century Novelists*, vol. 39, edited by Martin C. Battestin, 471–99. Detroit, MI: Gale Research, 1985. Reprinted in part by Arion Press as part of its limited fine press edition of *Tristram Shandy*, 1988.

"Whim-whams and Flim-flams: The Oxford University Press Edition of *Tristram Shandy*." *Review* 7. Charlottesville: University Press of Virginia, 1985: 1–18.

"Teaching vs. Research: Once upon a time in Teachalot." *ADE Bulletin* 89 (1988): 56–59.

"Proust's Influence on Sterne: A Remembrance of Things to Come." *MLN* 103 (1988): 1031–55. Reprinted in *Telling New Lies* and in *Critical Essays on Laurence Sterne*.

"Sterne and Cowley." *Notes and Queries*, n.s. 36 (1989): 447.

"Modes of Eighteenth-Century Fiction." In *Literature and Criticism: A New Century Guide*, 505–17. London: Routledge, 1990. Reprinted in *Telling New Lies*.

"Job's Wife and Sterne's Other Women." In *Out of Bounds: Male Writers and Engender(ed) Criticism*, edited by E. Langland and L. Claridge, 55–74. Amherst: University of Massachusetts Press, 1990. Reprinted in *Laurence Sterne*, edited by Marcus Walsh, 69–90. London: Longman Critical Readers, 2002.

"A Manuscript of the LeFever Episode in *Tristram Shandy*." *Scriblerian* 23 (1991): 165–74.

"Swift as Ogre, Richardson as Dolt: Rescuing Sterne from the Eighteenth Century." *Shandean* 3 (1991): 49–60.

"Sterne and the Narrative of Determinateness." *Eighteenth-Century Fiction* 4 (1992): 315–29. Reprinted in *Critical Essays on Laurence Sterne* and in *Tristram Shandy: A Casebook*. Oxford: Oxford University Press, 2006.

"Some Sterne Borrowings from Four Renaissance Authors." *Philological Quarterly* 71 (1992): 301–11.

"Swift and Sterne: Two Tales, Several Sermons and a Relationship Revisited." In *Critical Essays on Jonathan Swift*, edited by Frank Palmeri, 164–86. New York: G. K. Hall, 1993.

"'By Way of Commentary': Annotating Sterne's Sermons." *Editors' Notes: Bulletin of the Council of Editors of Learned Journals* 12 (1993): 5–11.

"Teaching *Rasselas* in an Eighteenth-Century Novels Course." In *Approaches to Teaching the Works of Samuel Johnson*, 121–27. New York: Modern Language Association, 1993.

"Classical Allusions in Swift's 'To His Grace the Archbishop of Dublin' and 'The Faggot.'" *Swift Studies* 8 (1993): 106–8.

"Sterne as Preacher: A Visit to St. Michael's Church, Coxwold." *Shandean* 5 (1993): 160–67.

"David Herbert, James P. Browne and Wilbur Cross: Unacknowledged Editorial Debts in Editing Sterne's *Sermons*," *Papers of the Bibliographical Society of America* 88 (1994): 79–86.

"William Hogarth and John Baldessari: Ornamenting Sterne's *Tristram Shandy*," *Word & Image* 11 (1995): 182–95.

"Attribution and Sponsorship: The Delicate Case of Sterne." *Eighteenth-Century Fiction* 8 (1996): 525–28.

"The Odd Couple: Laurence Sterne and John Norris of Bemerton." *Philological Quarterly* 75 (1996): 361–85.

"Sterne and *The History of Cold-Bathing*." *Notes and Queries*, n.s. 44 (1997): 211–12.

"Smollett" and "Sterne" entries in *Britain in the Hanoverian Age, 1714–1837*, edited by Gerald Newman, 664–65, 682–83. New York: Garland, 1997.

"Benjamin Whichcote's Aphorisms and the Importance of Latitudinarianism." *1650–1850: Ideas, Aesthetics, and Inquiries in the Early Modern Era* 4 (1998): 89–103.

"Eighteenth-Century Christianity and Literature: Two Caveats." *Christianity and Literature* 48 (1998): 327–47.

"Something New Under the Sun." Introduction to special issue of the *Eighteenth Century: Theory and Interpretation* 40 (1999): 1–10.

"Three Sentimental Journeys: Sterne, Shklovsky, Svevo." *Shandean* 11 (1999): 126–34.

"Sterne in the Future Tense." *Shandean* 11 (1999): 62–69.

"Sterne, Proust, and Levinas." *Age of Johnson* 12 (2001): 329–60. Reprinted in *In Proximity: Emmanuel Levinas and the Eighteenth Century*.

"John Norris of Bemerton." Entry in *Dictionary of Literary Biography: British Philosophers, 1500–1799*, 291–98. Detroit, MI: Gale, 2001.

"Sterne." Entry in the *Oxford Encyclopedia of the Enlightenment*. New York: Oxford University Press, 2002.

"Sterne." Entry in *Oxford Dictionary of National Biography*. New York: Oxford University Press, 2004.

"Richard Lovell Edgeworth and Laurence Sterne." *Notes and Queries*, n.s. 51 (2004): 417–21.

"The 1773 Edition of *Letters from Yorick to Eliza*: A Facsimile." Coauthored with Peter de Voogd. *Shandean* 15 (2004): 79–105.

"Scholia to the Florida Edition of the Works of Sterne from *The Scriblerian*, 1987–2005." *Shandean* 15 (2004): 135–64. Multiple authors.

"Lisping in Numbers: Some Canonical Statistics for the Present Age." *Scriblerian* 37 (2004): 64–67.

"Ten Letters from Yorick to Eliza: A New Edition." Coauthored with Peter de Voogd. *Shandean* 16 (2005): 71–107.

"Taking Care: A Slightly Levinasian Reading of *Dombey and Son*." *Philological Quarterly* 84 (2005): 77–104. Reprinted in *Levinas and Nineteenth-Century Literature: Ethics and Otherness from Romanticism through Realism*, edited by Donald R. Wehrs and David P. Haney. Newark: University of Delaware Press, 2009.

"A New Sterne Letter and an Old Mystery Closer to Solution." *Shandean* 17 (2006): 80–84.

"Swimming Down the Gutter of Time with Sterne and *The Scriblerian*." *Scriblerian* 39 (2006): 48–52.

"A Note on Clarissa Harlowe's Death." *Eighteenth-Century Intelligencer* 22, no. 3 (2008): 10–11.

"The Shandean and the Schemer: Sterne and James Ridley." *Notes and Queries*, n.s. 56 (2009): 258–59.

"Sterne and the Modernist Moment." In *The Cambridge Companion to Sterne*, edited by Tom Keymer, 160–73. Cambridge: Cambridge University Press, 2009.

"Sterne." Entry in *The Cambridge Companion to English Novelists*. Cambridge: Cambridge University Press, 2009.

"'Read, read, read, read, my unlearned reader!': Five Twenty-First Century Studies of Laurence Sterne and his Works." *Eighteenth-Century Studies* 43 (2009): 122–35.

"Reading the Occasion: Understanding Sterne's Sermons." In *Divine Rhetoric: Essays on the Sermons of Laurence Sterne*, edited by W. B. Gerard, 101–19. Newark: University of Delaware Press, 2010.

"John Carr and Laurence Sterne's Ghost." *Eighteenth-Century Intelligencer* 24, no. 3 (2010): 2–6.

"An Examination of Kenneth Monkman's Attributions to Sterne, 1745–1748." *Shandean* 21 (2010): 42–72.

"A Sterne Holograph." Coauthored with Peter de Voogd. *Shandean* 21 (2010): 81–83.

"Sterne's Bawdry: A Cautionary Tale." *RES*. Forthcoming

"Laurence Sterne's Sermons and *The Pulpit Fool*." *Eighteenth-Century Life*. Forthcoming.

"Anglicanism." In *Contexts of Johnson*. Cambridge: Cambridge University Press. Forthcoming.

Part One

PERSPECTIVES ON THE EIGHTEENTH CENTURY

Chapter One

Alexander Pope, T. S. Eliot, and the Fate of Poetry

Joseph G. Kronick

When we think of Restoration and eighteenth-century writers whose influence T. S. Eliot has acknowledged or whose examples he would emulate,
we are more likely to think of John Dryden than Alexander Pope. Dryden
was the subject of numerous essays by Eliot, Pope of none.[1] Furthermore,
some of Eliot's remarks about Pope indicate that he felt less appreciation
for him than he did for Dryden, despite having written that "the man who
cannot enjoy Pope as poetry probably understands no poetry."[2] This is not
to say that readers have not noted a resemblance between Pope and Eliot.
Ever since the publication of the facsimile of *The Waste Land* manuscripts,
readers have noted the imitation of Pope in the so-called "Fresca passage"
that opened "The Fire Sermon" but that Eliot, at Pound's urging, deleted in
its entirety. Hugh Kenner, like Pound, recognized "Eliot's deficient grasp of
Pope."[3] But this is a mere failure of versification; Eliot's affinities with Pope
lie elsewhere, as Kenner recognized when he linked Eliot, along with Pound
and Joyce, to Pope and Swift as responding to the new world of empiricism,
something that W. B. Yeats was the first to see when he wrote of Eliot in his
introduction to *The Oxford Book of Modern Verse*: "He is an Alexander Pope,
working without apparent imagination, producing his effects by a rejection
of all rhythms and metaphors used by the more popular romantics rather than
by the discovery of his own, this rejection giving his work an unexaggerated
plainness that has the effect of novelty. He has the rhythmical flatness of
the 'Essay on Man.'"[4] Yeats's antipathy for Pope, and Eliot for that matter,
should not obscure his insight into Eliot's affinity with the eighteenth century. In identifying Eliot with Pope, Yeats indicates that the proper way of
poetry—his way—has been lost: "I think of him as satirist rather than poet."
Eliot and other modernists had abandoned what Yeats saw as the source of
poetry—the subject matter he had received from esoteric tradition and the

3

soul, to which sleep and dreams belong. The moderns, Yeats implied, had chosen the soul's antithesis, the self, natural being. Scornful of general ideas and attached to particulars, Eliot exemplifies the materialism Yeats disdained.

Yeats's remarks, idiosyncratic and pointed as they are, indicate that Eliot's poetry of impersonality not merely marks the decline of poetry but constitutes an attack upon it. Yeats lamented, "We are moving away from the Victorians and on towards the modern equivalent of Pope. We are developing a poetry of statement as against the old metaphor. The poetry of tomorrow will be finely articulated fact. T. S. Eliot fascinates us all because he is further on towards their consummation than any other writer."[5] Yeats saw himself as the last romantic, and like the romantics he insisted upon the authority of the poet's vision: the poet's superior knowledge meant that his private vision had public consequences. Eliot rejected the kind of authority to which Yeats laid claim, and he did so in the belief that only when poetry could be held to have epistemological, not visionary, authority could it assert itself in the public realm. This was something he saw was possible for Dryden and Pope, but not for the modern poet.

Like Pope's four-book *Dunciad*, Eliot's *The Waste Land* surveys the fate of poetry in the modern world. Typically, criticism sees both works culminating in apocalyptic visions of the triumph of chaos. It is not unusual for literary history itself to take an apocalyptic form as it recounts the pathway from falsehood to truth, even if that truth rests in a language that recognizes its inability to unite "A heap of broken images."[6] In this schema, whether Eliot is taken as restoring a classical ideal to poetry or struggling with his romantic inheritance, he is the model of the literary self who achieves a kind of unity denied the empirical self—he sacrifices the personal self for the elected self of the poet.[7] As Eliot put it in a 1924 essay on Paul Valéry, "One is prepared for art when one has ceased to be interested in one's own emotions and experiences except as material; and when one has reached this point of indifference one will pick and choose according to very different principles from the principles of those people who are still excited by their own feelings and passionately enthusiastic over their own passions. . . . [I]t is a recognition of the truth that not our feelings, but the pattern which we may make of our feelings, is the centre of value." The self we encounter in the poem is not the product of the originating experience but one "transformed by the poet's superior organization."[8] To speak then of the fate of poetry is to attribute the poet's loss of *auctoritas* and the dissociation of eloquence and wisdom to his becoming a private self and poetry becoming a literary genre.[9] In the aftermath of the battle of the books, the fate of poetry is to be no longer a mode of knowledge ranked alongside or even superior to science, but to become "literature," an aesthetically pleasing mode of writing. The fate of poetry becomes the problem of the literary self, which is not to be comprehended in empirical terms but in terms of modernity, understood as the loss of unified being and exemplified in Eliot's notion of sensibility. If we take the battle of the books as our starting point, then a reading of Eliot in the shadow of Pope reveals the fate of poetry to be a perpetual struggle with its modernity. We have long been accustomed to seeing this struggle as one between tradition and the individual talent, wherein modernity signals the historical conscious-ness of the presence of the past, but we might account for it more accurately by treating the problem of modernity, not as a matter of tradition or canon-ization, but as the determination of the ontological status of poetry itself, a problem that emerged with the battle of the books.

*

Most discussions comparing *The Dunciad* and *The Waste Land* focus on the apocalyptic fourth book of the former and the theme of the decay of "the mind of Europe."[10] These readings cohere around the image of the fallen city and the comparison of a corrupt and dissolute present with a cohesive and orderly past. Indeed, the parallels between the two poems are numer-ous, beginning with the textual difficulties posed by the different editions: both appeared without notes in their first publications and with them in all subsequent editions. Eliot's inclusion of notes came as an afterthought, and he may very well have intended them to be a parody of philological annota-tions.[11] Pope's notes are famously parodic, but the poem itself needed an-notation even for its contemporary audience, as did *The Waste Land*.[12] Most significant, critics have noted the poems' shared concern with the fate of poetry and civilization; both are compendiums of various literary allusions, pastiches, and genres; both have been said to lack narrative cohesiveness; both are set not only in London but in the City, the site of Drury Lane in Pope's day and the financial district in Eliot's; both bear dedications to literary friends who, the poets claim, were responsible for the existence of these poems, at least in their present forms;[13] and both have been con-demned for their obscurities.

These parallels are important, but they point out the distance between the two poets as much as they confirm the close similarities between their two poems. *The Dunciad* was undertaken as part of Pope's and Swift's defense of the ancients against the moderns in the battle of the books, and if we follow the *Dunciad*'s greatest commentator, Pope's satire was not merely settling scores with his enemies, most of whom are of no interest to us today, but was animated, at least in the four-book version, by "the theological metaphor" that the mind of Dulness, "like that of God, will produce a 'word' identical with its source," a "Divinity without a Νοῦσ."[14]

At least this is a view shared by many readers of *The Dunciad* and, we might say, of *The Waste Land* as well, which in place of the goddess Dulness offers fragments and empty voices unable to speak the Word. The idea that Pope's poem of dulness, particularly in its apocalyptic fourth book, is an attack upon the decline of civilization has had many distinguished proponents, including Aubrey Williams, Reuben Brower, Ian Jack, and Alvin Kernan, among others.[15] *The Waste Land* was hailed from its first publication as a vision of the sterility of modern life, but Eliot's famous demurral at a Harvard lecture would undercut all claims for his being the spokesman for the age: "Various critics have done me the honour to interpret the poem in terms of criticism of the contemporary world, have considered it, indeed, as an important bit of social criticism. To me it was only the relief of a personal and wholly insignificant grouse against life; it is just a piece of rhythmical grumbling."[16]

Whatever Eliot's own feelings about the reception of the poem, this private "grouse" became a public statement, whereas Pope's very public grumbling over the state of letters in *The Dunciad* has much of a private character, as testified to by some of his contemporaries. Henry Fielding, in proposing his own prose *Dunciad*, praised Pope for preserving from oblivion the names of the dunces: "He employed a whole Work for the Purpose of recording such Writers as no one without his Pains, except he had lived at the same Time and in the same Street, would ever have heard of."[17] And even then, as Jonathan Swift wrote, in a few years those who live in London would not understand it.[18] This brings us to a central paradox when we contrast the two poems: Eliot's professedly private crisis has been taken for a diagnosis of a collapsing Europe; Pope's private grudge against his largely obscure literary enemies is presented, in the four-book *Dunciad*, as an apocalyptic vision of the collapse not only of the world of letters but also of the nation itself. Or rather, it is a paradox in Eliot, but not in Pope. In his defense of the classics, Pope adheres to the ancient model that links poetry to knowledge and eloquence to wisdom.[19] With the notable exception of Samuel Johnson, Pope is the last poet to write within this tradition rooted in classical rhetoric, with its notion of poetry as a rule-governed art.

According to Douglas Patey, the emergence of aesthetics means that "the experience of beauty is independent of any interest of the *understanding*, any cognitive concern with the object."[20] This shift is accompanied by the separation of sensation from reason. The order of reality is not the object of experience or something we find in the world, but is something constructed in thought. This demarcation between aesthetics and epistemology has been challenged by Paul de Man, who argues that aesthetics is "a phenomenalism of a process of meaning and understanding," by which he means literary understanding "resembles a sense perception."[21] Such a view, which characterizes all hermeneutic theories according to de Man, is mimetic. The alternative to mimesis would be allegory, which, as language, is material or materialistic. Patey charts a course wherein poetry moves from rhetoric, and the certitude of epistemology, to aesthetics and sensation. De Man locates in allegory the movement whereby aesthetic and poetic values part company. The two views are strikingly different except for their similar location of the break between poetic and cognitive values in the emergence of romanticism. Patey, however, sees this as a historical break, whereas de Man challenges this historical schema, which he says is based on the trope of mimesis. My contention is that this break is not so much an event in literary history as it is a constantly recurring feature of literature, coming as it does in the quarrel between the ancients and the moderns. The fate of poetry then is not strictly a historical one in which the rise of romantic subjectivity turns poetry into an increasingly private and personal mode of expression, but is something that adheres to poetry as sensation, which for Eliot is a special mode of cognition without reference. Poetry's loss of its claim to epistemological authority signals the loss of the public role of the poet. Eliot's notion of the "dissociation of sensibility," a separation of intellect and the senses, is but one sign of this. His insistence that the poem must be an objective equivalent to the emotion, something one can *see*, not *feel* or understand, is another. For Pope, on the other hand, poetry remained the prime instrument of knowledge as long as the classical ideal could be maintained: *auctoritas* preserves *humanitas*.

This ideal stands behind Pope's turn to Virgil's story of the removal of Aeneas from Troy to Rome for his account of the removal of dullness from the City to the Court. By means of allusion, he sought to elevate his quarrel with the scholars who had exposed his errors in his *Iliad* and Shakespeare into a vision of the decay of learning and art. Eliot's allusions serve as a screen that translates private grumblings into what Christine Froula, like so many others, has called "a historic monument of literary modernism."[22] Froula argues that Ezra Pound's editing transformed what was a personal and autobiographical poem into a formalist monument of modernism. Her reading would recover from *The Waste Land*'s enshrinement as a modernist "classic" the personal disgust that animates the drafts, making the poem a testament to the poet's suffering during the war years and their aftermath. Such a reading turns against formalism to make *The Waste Land*, like Pound's *Cantos*, "a poem including history," both personal and public. The poem may be personal, but it is not subjective.[23] Froula's reading of the drafts as confessional contrasts sharply with that of Patrick Deane, who argues that Pound's revision turns the poem from classicism to modernist *poésie pure*. In particular, he notes that in deleting the Fresca passage, Pound sought to undo Eliot's allegiance to a neoclassical ethos. Although Deane argues for the importance of personal voice in his examination of the original manuscripts, his notion of the personal is grounded in the eighteenth-century ideal that poetry is a form of knowledge, that is, in the Horatian principle that poetry should instruct as well as delight.[24] His Eliot is closer to Pope, Froula's to Robert Lowell. One looks upon voice as representing *auctoritas*, which carries with it the notion of tradition; the other looks upon voice as the representation of the psyche. Together they point to what divides the two poets: romanticism.

I do not wish to evoke a model of history that accords certain modes of sensibility to certain literary movements or periods. To speak of "fate" is to evoke a sacred idea of history, one in which the poet, if not the world, suffers a loss of what was formally whole or unified. "Fate" is a classical concept set in opposition to the will, and it stands for immutable forces that overtake human endeavors. However, when linked to Christian history, "fate" evokes ends and the manifestation of meaning. When this teleological dimension is transferred to literary history, "fate" almost invariably raises notions of some sort of decline or fall, particularly when linked to romanticism and modernity and the uncoupling of the link between experience and idea, among other figures for an essential unity that no longer exists. Eliot has been understood to have appealed to one such lost ideal, that of European culture, in *The Waste Land*, as well as in "Tradition and the Individual Talent." Pope's art of allusion embraced such an ideal of culture, but allusion in *The Waste Land*, which veers more toward pastiche, merely dabbles with the mock-heroic. Rather than invoke an order that is lost, Eliot treats past texts as materials for experience. Allusions to Shakespeare's Cleopatra at the opening of "A Game of Chess" evoke a style and a sensibility but not a fabled unity of sensation and intellect. The difference in their methods is as much a measure of the distance between Eliot and Pope as it is a sign of the diminished role of the poet after the triumph of the moderns in the battle of the books. Therefore, their uses of the past differ sharply. If we agree with those who argue that Pope's vision of "universal darkness" is counterbalanced by the mock-heroic's form, whereby allusion serves to remind the audience of a still existent, if threatened, order, Eliot's quotations and pastiches do not serve as representations of the ruined city but are explorations of attitudes in verse.[25] In "A Game of Chess" he adheres to Enobarbus's description of Cleopatra in her barge but turns away from its lush eroticism to a kind of verbal profuseness that echoes Keats and even the poets of the nineties. In the Fresca passage his scene is drawn from *The Rape of the Lock*, but rather than rework Pope's verse as he does Shakespeare's, he vulgarizes it, not merely to express disgust with "the hearty female stench," in the manner of Swift, but also to stigmatize a fallen world. Eliot's wit is closer to Webster and Middleton than to Dryden and

Pope. Rather than offer a prophetic vision in the manner of Pope, Eliot looks upon the ruined city as a necessary, fated outcome for a world governed by "Unreal emotions, and real appetite" (*WLF*, 27). He did not write to warn his contemporaries of their fallen state, but, as A. D. Moody so powerfully argues, "to save the self alone from an alien world."[26] *Sauve qui peut.* The best the poet can do, short of dying and thereby gaining new life, is protect himself against the sordid and ugly, and here this requires a comic sense of the gulf separating the self from absolute being.

Pope's comedy is more frequently noted than Eliot's, although Patricia Meyer Spacks manages to miss the humor in both, a result perhaps of both poets' turning their comedic talents on the literary itself in what can only be called virtuosic displays of literariness. *The Dunciad* and *The Waste Land* are works that look like poems but do not read like poems. One is a mock book that risks becoming a cento, a patchwork of quotations, the other a cento that risks becoming a somber poem, were it not for the annotator who tries to convince his readers that it is, indeed, a cento.[27] We are reminded by both poets that literature attains to its status as literature only by virtue of the rules that deem it to be literature. This is why when literature is attacked, it generally is done so in the name of literature; that is, in the name of "true" literature that has freed itself of arbitrarily imposed rules.

Pope's scatology falls within the bounds of literature, but just barely. Ever since Emrys Jones argued in "Pope and Dulness" (1968) that Pope delighted in his dunces, a growing number of critics have found in *The Dunciad* an underlying ambiguity that challenges self-assured readings of it as a defense of civilization against barbarism. Recalling Samuel Johnson's aside concerning "the 'unnatural delight' which the poet of the *Dunciad* took in 'ideas physically impure,'" Jones suggests that Pope is not merely defending cultural standards against the barbarians but is enacting a "psychomachia" in which he tries "to reduce to order, his own feelings," which were more ambiguous than most critics would credit.[28] Noting the influence of Erasmus's *In Praise of Folly*, Jones suggests that dullness, like folly, is not an attribute confined to unscrupulous publishers, pedantic scholars, and hack poets, but "a fundamental principle of being" (131). On the surface, Pope's hostility can hardly be doubted, yet the energy devoted to his subject suggests a fascination with the Grub Street world and an acknowledgment of the "imaginative opportunities" it afforded him (132). Jones's reading reflects a postromantic psychologizing of the poet, and while some may find he goes too far in arguing for Pope's fascination with his subjects, there is much to be said for his thesis that dullness provides Pope not simply with a theme but with a device that in its inclusiveness allows for the creation of a work capacious enough both to contain a world and to destroy it. It is

Jones's yet-to-be fully appreciated contention that "Pope's imaginative desire for completeness, for making an end, is here [in the conclusion] fused with his poetic delight in images of cataclysmic destruction" (154).[29] Not with a bang, but a yawn.

Eliot seems to exude less delight in his apocalypse than does Pope in his. In the draft of *The Waste Land*, Eliot originally wrote, "These fragments I have spelt into my ruins" (*WLF*, 81). In the handwritten manuscript, "shored against" is written above "spelt into," which he leaves uncanceled, as if he were undecided about which to choose. "Spelt" is a form of the past participle of "spell," which commonly means "To denote by certain letters in a particular order," but may also mean "To read (a book, etc.) letter by letter; to peruse or make out, slowly or with difficulty" (*OED*). This last definition, along with "To discover or find out, to guess or suspect, by close study or observation," may reconfirm readings of the poem as an attempt at a diagnosis of the ills of the age. Yet they more accurately reflect the cento-like quality of the poem as repetition, which is reinforced by the subsidiary meaning, "To turn out (literary work or writing) with some difficulty." The poem is a compendium of styles that are just as much facts of culture as are Pope's portraits of Colley Cibber, Richard Bentley, and Jacob Tonson. Finally, "spelt into" suggests the poem is a kind of rune, a spell, meant as much to ward off ruin as to interpret it. Is the poet then a kind of Tiresias or Madame Sosostris, trying to discern in her deck of cards the fate of her customers?

That Eliot might have been offering a kind of critical reflection on his efforts should hardly surprise us, but we might ask ourselves whether he was criticizing the work or interpreting it? The distinction is, as we will see, an important one for Eliot, for the problem of what constitutes literary criticism preoccupied him in much of his prose works, so much so that the goal of establishing a literary criticism lay behind his most famous essays. The question then becomes, is he gathering quotations or interpretations to shore up the ruins of civilization, or is he diagnosing the signs of ruin or even spelling out in these fragments his, and Europe's, rune? If we compare his ending to that of the four-book *Dunciad*, we find that Pope's poem breaks off with a vain invocation to the Muse asking her to tell upon whom Dulness's power has fallen:

> O Muse! relate (for you can tell alone,
> Wits have short Memories, and Dunces none)
> Relate, who first, who last resign'd to rest;
> Whose Heads she partly, whose completely blest;
> What Charms could Faction, what Ambition lull,
> The Venal quiet, and intrance the Dull;
> 'Till drown'd was Sense, and Shame, and Right, and Wrong—
> O sing, and hush the Nations with thy Song!

* * * * * *
In vain, in vain,—the all-composing Hour
Resistless falls: The Muse obeys the Pow'r.
She comes! she comes! the sable Throne behold
Of *Night* Primaeval, and of *Chaos* old!
(B, 4.619–30)

The annotator comments, "It is impossible to lament sufficiently the loss of the rest of this Poem, just at the opening of so fair a scene as the Invocation seems to promise. It is to be hop'd however that the Poet compleated it" (799n). In the self-reflexive ending, the Muse herself succumbs to Dulness and her "uncreating word" (B, 654), but only to confirm the poet's authority as moral voice. Eliot's ending piles up quotations in such rapid succession that it seems to parody the stage directions of Kyd's play-within-a-play in *The Spanish Tragedy*, which inform us that Hieronimo's play "in sundry languages, was thought good to be set down in English, more largely, for the easier understanding to every public reader."[30] No such luck for Eliot's reader. His conclusion is as private as Pope's is public. The final prayer, "Shantih shantih shantih," with its evocation of the desire for undifferentiated being, does not so much set the poet against the world as removes him from it. Spelt or shored, the ruins stand about him.

Literariness, in the form of allusions, self-reflexivity, and textual commentary, can be said to be the subject of both poems. The inclusion of notes in *The Dunciad*, parodic as they are and as necessary as they are to illuminating the obscure identities of the dunces, is a sign that Pope considered his own work to have the status of a classic.[31] If Pope's *Dunciad* was designed to resemble and mock Bentley's and Theobald's editions of Shakespeare and the pretensions of contemporary poetasters, Eliot's notes to *The Waste Land* mock what the poem has become, "official Poetry of a time when poetry is dead, complete with numbered lines and footnotes."[32] In satirizing the textual scholarship of Theobald and Bentley, Pope was insisting that the ideal of correctness lay with the poet, not with editors who defaced the language in the name of *textual* correctness. But for Eliot to satirize the Poem is to suggest that poetry is overburdened not so much by the Tradition but by something quite different—meaning, or the problem of interpretation. This must be distinguished from the difficulties of *The Dunciad*, which are not those of symbolist poetics but of classical tradition and historical reference. Readers who think Eliot's difficulties are of the same order confuse his material appropriation of past texts with Pope's invocation not only of Greece, Rome, and European tradition but also of a moral order that this tradition was thought to embody—until the moderns separated judgment from imagination.[33]

Pope's career began in imitations of English poets from Chaucer to Rochester and Cowley and in translations and paraphrases of the ancients. It ended in the four-book *Dunciad* with imitations of Virgil and Milton, among others. Reuben Brower, whose *The Poetry of Allusion* remains the best study of Pope's art, reminds us that allusion serves as Pope's primary means of asserting the identity between literary culture and public morality. Eliot may very well share Pope's belief that, as Brower puts it, "moral evaluation is inseparable from his historical sense of an inherited culture traceable to Greece and Rome."[34] But recovering such a tradition remains, for Eliot, encumbered by the very thing he would disown but cannot, literary modernity and, along with it, the problem of repetition. Literary imitation was for Eliot a sign of degeneration, while for Pope it was a way to assume authority. Brower writes, "Dryden's most valuable gift to Pope was creation of his generously allusive mode with all of its wider cultural implications" (12–13). In turning to Dryden as his model, Pope was criticizing both Whiggish notions of poetry and Whiggish politics, as did Dryden before him, but in aligning himself with his chosen poetic model, he was asserting himself in the public arena at a time when contemporary poets had "quite consciously removed themselves from the field of public debate." Brower may well have been right in claiming that Pope was perhaps "the last major English poet to feel at home with the whole European and English tradition in poetry," something to which, he notes, Eliot aspired (353), but a comparison of the two will reveal not simply the similar thematic and moral concerns; in addition we discover the very great loss that the modern poet must suffer, that is, the loss of his public role once literature becomes "Literature," something that occurred at the same time the ancients became "classics."

Pope represents the end of the classical tradition with its foundation in rhetoric, which is to say he stands before the precipice of romanticism and the emergence, in the words of Charles Taylor, of "an expressive view of human life," wherein "[f]ulfilling my nature means espousing the inner élan, the voice or impulse." In realizing my nature, I am giving my life "a definitive shape" and not merely "copying an external model."[35] Eliot, on the other hand, rejects not only the romantic notion of inner voice and the expressivist aesthetic, but also poetic hermeneutics. Eliot's disdain for interpretation of poetry is well documented. In "The Function of Criticism," he allows that the only "legitimate" interpretation is one that puts "the reader in possession of facts which he would otherwise have missed" (*SE*, 20). This notion of criticism is of a piece with his idea of classicism and can be attributed to the irreconcilable relation between imitation as mimesis and imitation as quotation and allusion. As mimesis, the poem employs images and dramatic representation to signify the spiritual state of the poet and of present civilization. As quotation, the poem is nonrepresentational and can only repeat as a kind of material memory the texts of the past. The former allows us to read the poem thematically; the latter disrupts a chronological reading that makes modernism the overcoming of romantic subjectivity and a return to neoclassical values. The distance between Pope's sense of himself as a classic and Eliot's treatment of his poem as a Poem, to borrow Hugh Kenner's formulation, can be measured by the degree to which Pope's parodies invoke the authority of the *poet* and Eliot's pastiches serve as evocations of styles, not authority.

Unlike Pope's parodies of Homer, Virgil, and Milton, Eliot's pastiches of Donne, Shakespeare, and others do not so much assert the presence of the past as they manifest the materiality of the poem as quotation. In *The Waste Land*, pastiche transforms the source texts into a new work, as Eliot's famous comment on literary borrowing suggests: "Immature poets imitate; mature poets steal; bad poets deface what they take, and good poets make it into something better, or at least something different. The good poet welds his theft into a whole of feeling which is unique, utterly different from that from which it was torn" (*SW*, 125). The important phrase here is "a whole of feeling," for Eliot thought the poem should not have a "meaning" but should itself produce feeling or sensation, the two words being synonymous for him. In a 1927 essay, he writes, "I would suggest that none of the plays of Shakespeare has a 'meaning,' although it would be equally false to say that a play of Shakespeare is meaningless. All great poetry gives the illusion of a view of life" (*SE*, 115). This illusion may be necessary if the poem is to be understandable, but what the poem should *do* is present a feeling or thought, which is not the poet's but is itself an object. Here we are approaching the "objective correlative."

This mysterious term comes from Eliot's essay on *Hamlet*, in which he argues there must be an "objective equivalent to his [Hamlet's] feelings" (*SW*, 101). Eliot rejects interpretation because it turns the poem into something other than literature: "*Qua* work of art, the work of art cannot be interpreted; there is nothing to interpret" (*SW*, 96). We can criticize the play, and Eliot does—there is no objective correlative. To put it succinctly, if the emotion of a poem is something the reader should *get*, as he states in "Modern Tendencies in Poetry," the emotion must be in "close relation to an object."[36] The audience/reader can only "get" Hamlet's problem if there is an objective equivalent to it. Eliot claims that "Hamlet's bafflement at the absence of an objective equivalent to his feelings is a prolongation of the bafflement of his creator in the face of an artistic problem" (*SW*, 101). This theory makes Hamlet a double of the reader, and of the author. Hamlet's bafflement is Shakespeare's is Eliot's. This displacement of Eliot's bewilderment to the text and its author comes through when he calls Hamlet's puns "a form of emotional relief": "In the character Hamlet it is the buffoonery of an emotion which can find no outlet in action; in the dramatist it is the buffoonery of an emotion which he cannot express in art. The intense feeling, ecstatic or terrible, without an object or exceeding its object, is something which every person of sensibility has known" (*SW*, 102). When Eliot called *The Waste Land* a bit of "rhythmical grumbling" or a "skit," he was playing the buffoon, but readers have preferred to think of him as a man of sensibility who had found an object for his intense feeling. They prefer a romantic to a comic poet.

An exception to the romantic readings of Eliot and Pope as apocalyptic visionaries is Hugh Kenner's. In pointing out the debt to Dryden's "Annus Mirabilis" in "The Fire Sermon," Kenner, as we have noted, dismisses the pastiche of Pope in the Fresca passage, deleted from the same section, but merely comments that Eliot "adopted what he took to be Pope's idiom for a character who invited belittling."[37] It is in his splendid book on the Augustans, *The Counterfeiters*, that Kenner draws a fuller parallel between Eliot and Pope, calling "Swift and Pope, great realists, great modernists," who, like Pound, Joyce, and Eliot, "responded . . . to the new universe of empirical fact."[38] Experience is no longer the vehicle of knowledge; with rationalism and empiricism it comes to mean having a correct representation of things as they are conceived in the mind.[39] There is nothing particularly original in locating modernism in the eighteenth century, as we have seen in our opening quotations from Yeats, but Kenner's equation of modernism with counterfeiting, a phenomenon that reaches its apogee when knowledge no longer depends upon an external order unaffected by time, reconfirms the modernists' poetics of impersonality and the theory of the autotelic text. In place of romantic subjectivism and the divide between the ordinary world and the unattainable Ideal, Kenner proposes a self-reflexivity that sees words existing on the same plain as facts: both await being synthesized into a formal arrangement, whether it be a poem or a city. We are in the realm of *The Waste Land*, where the writer of the poem is an annotator of dead authors and the author of the notes is the creator of something identifiable as a "Poem," a classic, no less, complete with notes and commentary.

According to Kenner, we can be said to know something when we know how it works (and, by extension, when we know how to counterfeit it). Having been defeated in his battle with the scholars over his edition of Shakespeare and his annotations of Homer, Pope achieved victory in imitating a dunce writing and annotating an epic.[40] This notion of imitation reflects the mechanistic world of Descartes and modern science; it is the world in which everything that does not belong to thought is encountered as an object, even our own experiences. It is the vision defended by the moderns in the battle of the books, a battle that Swift and Pope won insofar as they were the better poets but lost insofar as their works, by virtue of their topicality, are reduced to artifacts recoverable by the scholars who have refined the methods of the poets' enemies. With the triumph of the moderns, the world of stable essences, the world of *humanitas* and *auctoritas*, is gone. As Kenner demonstrates in *The Counterfeiters*, once *auctoritas* was lost, *humanitas* was sure to follow. Confronted with the empiricist's world of facts wherein experience is reduced to information, the poet produces counterfeits to save us from a world of empty appearances.

The romantics tried to salvage *humanitas* by basing *auctoritas* not upon a timeless order or eternal truth such as that which sustained the medieval system of learning, but upon imagination and poetic genius. They could not succeed, and so we have the division between the world as experienced and the world imagined; to this division we have given a name, "romanticism," which not only designates a literary and historical period, but a mode of thinking that is, in fact, historical, as Tzvetan Todorov concludes: "One is already romantic if one writes the history of the passage from the classics to the romantics; one is still classical if one perceives the two as simple variants of a unique essence."[41] What Todorov describes as an alternative between history as periodization and change, on the one hand, and as system, on the other, is one that emerges out of the long eighteenth century and the battle of the books. Kenner's account of the emergence of modernism as the disenchantment of the world of authenticity and its replacement by a world of "appearances, imperfectly observed" is but a variant, a highly amusing and insightful one I should add, of romantic historicism and the very dilemma of the divide between the world as perceived (congeries of facts) and an invisible order (the system or rules that bring order to these facts). The eighteenth century and modernists produced counterfeits, "organized modes of unreality," whereas the romantics sought to restore reality.[42]

In this version of the battle of the books, Pope and Swift win, not because they sided with the victorious moderns—they didn't—but because they recognized that the moderns' methods could be imitated and parodied. Virgil can be imitated; he can even serve as a model for a mock-epic, but he cannot be parodied. Pope achieved a similar status; his burlesque of Virgil's *Aeneid* cannot be parodied, either, as Eliot's Fresca demonstrates. Pope's satire succeeds because he recognized that scholars like Theobald and Bentley, in their desire to determine not only what the ancients actually wrote but also what they really meant, denied the universality of the ancients by transforming them into texts in need of restoration.[43] In robbing the ancients of *auctoritas*, Bentley reduced poetry to a text, a copy of an original that remains to be reconstructed. Pope still belonged to a culture that held the imitation of Homer or Cicero to be the essence of education, both intellectual and moral. Philologists and antiquarians not only claimed to have recovered ancient culture, but demonstrated that it was not just different but alien from the modern world and in need of scholarship, not taste, if it were to be understood.[44] Pope, who began training himself as a poet by writing imitations of the ancients, ended his career by imitating the philologists in an epic account—or, rather, by imitating a dunce writing annotations to an imitation of an epic—of the venality of booksellers, the vanity of patrons, and the vacuity of Grub Street poets. If Eliot resembles Pope, he does so by defending the tradition and order with the tools bequeathed by the dunces. *The Waste Land* is a poem written in the aftermath of the emergence of philology, modern science, and empiricism.

Thanks to Bentley and others, we do not look at the poet as "author"—*auctoritas* was abandoned after the ancient texts were subjected to philological scrutiny and historical investigation. "Homer" is found to be not a single person but an assemblage of authors, who were incorrect in their astronomy, geometry, and natural descriptions. Moreover, the world he lived in has vanished; its manners and customs are now foreign and inferior.[45] Instead, we look to the poem and from it infer a poet, whom we then invest with qualities we deem appropriate to one who created such a poem. This had been a governing idea in Kenner's study of Eliot, *The Invisible Poet* (1959), and he not only perpetuated a certain interpretation of the impersonality of the poet as a kind of depersonalization or objectification (one that still remains entrenched despite recent scholarship), he also posited the schism between feeling and thought that critics have come to see as crucial to Eliot's sensibility. If the theory of impersonality has led too many readers to think there is no poet in the poem, this schism has also encouraged readers to find the poet and to place him in a historical narrative where he is exorcizing the late ends of romanticism from his works.

*

Perhaps to say that Pope and Eliot share a common concern with the fate of poetry in a period of decline is to say, if one takes the side of Yeats, that they stand on opposite sides of romanticism, which for him is poetry—if we follow him in "Coole and Ballylee, 1931," poetry began with Homer and closes with himself. If one takes the literary historian's view, it is to say that whereas Pope represents the unity of private and public self that existed before romanticism, Eliot inherited a romantic concept of the divided self that he constantly sought to escape. This struggle with romanticism has, in fact, been central to three of the finest studies of Eliot. A. D. Moody, Ronald Bush, and Ronald Schuchard have all argued that Eliot's career was determined by a struggle to heal the wound incurred by the division between sensation and intellect. Moody characterizes Eliot's career as a struggle to attain the absolute through immediate experience, a struggle that began with his seeking to escape the romantic divide between "a known ideal and a commonplace reality" by assuming a Laforgian pose. Bush reads this conflict more personally as a "split in his psyche between thought and feeling." Finally, Schuchard calls Eliot "a Hamlet of his age, strangely a romantic poet with a classical sensibility," whose "spiritual impulses were desecrated by sexual fantasies."[46] All three critics see Eliot's insistence that "when we are considering poetry we must consider it primarily as poetry and not another thing" (*SW*, viii) both as symptomatic of this divide and as its resolution or cure.

These works represent a significant correction of Eliot the impersonal poet, but in reading him from the perspective of the poet's struggle, in Eliot's words, "to fabricate something permanent and holy out of his personal and animal feelings" (*SE*, 117), they adopt Eliot's views of poetry as a struggle to overcome subjectivity and of modernity as a historical movement that describes the falling away of literature from a genuine state and its circuitous return to an origin, best embodied in works that enact the very movement whereby literature surmounts the divisions that give it its impetus. Such readings enact a desire that is Eliot's own—to break out of literature, out of the negative impulse that led Eliot to poetry itself, toward an ideal that leaves poetry behind.

As appealing as these visions of the redemptive poet may be, they achieve their reconciliation of impulse and art, of self and representation, at the expense of his modernity, which is to say, at the expense of what generates his poetry. I propose that the division they ascribe to Eliot (rightly so, I would add) can be looked upon as a division within poetry between language as event and as entity, or what in Eliot may be seen as the dramatic component and the aspiration of poetry to attain the status of music, which is to say between language as representation and language as pure meaning. If we look upon the division as one that adheres to language, then we recognize that Eliot's poetry belongs to modernity insofar as modernity names the very condition of poetry. In "Lyric and Modernity," de Man describes modernity as "the problematical possibility of all literature's existing in the present, of being considered, or read, from a point of view that claims to share with it its own sense of a temporal present."[47] From this perspective, the problem of modernity can be applied to literature of any period. The "temptation of immediacy" induces literature to erase the past, but in so doing, it rejects what sustains it.[48]

The desire to forget the past and to live unhistorically so as to create life anew expresses a thoroughly romantic topos that would be antithetical to

Eliot's notion of tradition. "Tradition and the Individual Talent" is the most famous of his calls for the poet to know the past, but an earlier version of this argument, a lecture published as "Modern Tendencies in Poetry," reverses the thesis that the truly new work is one in which the past asserts itself:

> The life of our "heritage" of literature is dependent upon the continuance of literature. If you imagine yourselves suddenly deprived of your personal present, of all possibility of action, reduced in consciousness to the memories of everything up to the present, these memories, this existence which would be merely the totality of memories, would be meaningless and flat, even if it *could* continue to exist. If suddenly all power of producing more poetry were withdrawn from the race, if we knew that for poetry we should have to turn always to what already existed, I think that past poetry would become meaningless. For the capacity of appreciating poetry is inseparable from the power of producing it, it is poets themselves who can best appreciate poetry. *Life is always turned toward creation; the present only, keeps the past alive.* (12; my emphasis)

Whereas in "Tradition and the Individual Talent" he spoke of historical sense and the presence of the past in the "new (the really new) work of art" (*SW*, 50), here he warns that the loss of the present and the possibility of action would reduce the past to a kind of lifeless archive, memorials devoid of meaning. The past is dependent upon new creation. His remarks reveal the desire for the poem to be more than an object but to be an act itself, and by this I mean not only the act of writing poetry but the poem as a form of action. Eliot anticipates de Man's point that "considered as a principle of life, modernity becomes a principle of origination and turns at once into a generative power that is itself historical" (*BI*, 150). This paradoxical condition of the self-destroying unity of history and modernity reveals, de Man says, that "literature has always been essentially modern" (*BI*, 151). Eliot, on the other hand, has said that poetry, or that which truly counts as poetry, has been essentially classic.

In "Ulysses, Order, and Myth," Eliot calls "classicism" "a goal toward which all good literature strives, so far as it is good, according to the possibilities of its place and time." Being "classical" can mean "selecting only mummified stuff from a museum. . . . Or one can be classical in tendency by doing the best one can with the material at hand."[49] The choice is between the dry dust of antiquarianism or the belatedness of modernity. Implied in these alternatives is a notion more fully spelled out in his review of Arthur Symons's translation of Baudelaire: the poet who strives for classicism, which means every poet since romanticism, is, as he says of Baudelaire, "born out of his due time."[50] (We should keep in mind his remark that "'classicism' is not an alternative to 'romanticism.'")[51] These statements suggest that classicism, along with his concept of tradition to which it is not always aligned, would constitute a means of overcoming history, but insofar as the work fails to be classical, a fate shared by all modern writing, literature is romantic.

In his late, rather fusty essay, "What is a Classic?" Eliot holds up Virgil as the model by which all poets must be measured. He alone attained the "maturity of mind, maturity of manners, maturity of language and perfection of the common style" that makes a classic.[52] In English literature, these qualities are to be found in Pope, which is not to say, Eliot warns, that the eighteenth century was "the finest period of English literature" or that Pope was the finest poet, but that classical qualities attained by Pope were acquired at too great a sacrifice, which meant a narrowness of mind, a provincialism, and limited sensibility that makes him a classic in English poetry only and not a universal classic, like Virgil (60–61). The universal classic alone tells us what literature is, and without it we "admire works of genius for the wrong reasons—as we extol Blake for his *philosophy*, and Hopkins for his *style*" (71), neither of which, he clearly implies, is literature.

We are now faced with a paradox. Literature is an unattainable ideal in modern languages, but all poems aspire to literature and to "the spontaneity of action," which means being something other than literature. De Man identifies this aporia as constitutive of literature: the poet's awareness that writing depends upon "duration and repetition" "indicates the compulsion to return to a literary mode of being, as a form of language that knows itself to be mere repetition, mere fiction and allegory, forever unable to participate in the spontaneity of action or modernity" (*BI*, 161). In this sense, Pope is modern: he recognized that spontaneity in poetry is an imitation, an effect of the text, hence the attraction of dullness. It represents the perversity of the modern poet's condition: he can achieve spontaneity only in imitation. The superabundant energy of the dunces, represented most vividly in the games of book 2, frees him to do with his models—Homer, Virgil, and Milton—what Bentley had famously accused him of doing in his translation of the *Iliad*: violate them. (Bentley said of Pope's *Iliad*, "It is a pretty poem, Mr. Pope; but you must not call it *Homer*.")[53] Now, Pope can be said to show his fidelity to the ancients by imitating a dunce's version of them. Imitation and spontaneity are joined in a self-destructive union.

The Eliot who calls classicism "*form* and *restraint* in art" and romanticism "glorification of *spontaneity*," has split the inherently paradoxical condition of all literature between two movements or two modes of art (he is not always consistent in describing their opposition as historical in nature or expressive of a sensibility or as literary modes).[54] The question, then, of whether Eliot is the classicist he proclaims himself to be or is the romantic who seeks to overcome romanticism can be answered with a "yes." To declare himself a classicist is to discover he is implicated in "an interdependence between past and future that prevents any present from ever coming into being" (*BI*, 161). He can be classic and he can be romantic, but he cannot be modern. Modernity names the condition of literature as that which can never resolve the paradox of its ontological division between act and entity.

Eliot's attack on modernity's cult of the new as a forgetting of the past repeats the battle of the books. Whereas Pope, in defense of the ancients, attacks the moderns for reducing the past to a body of texts subject to correction and improvement, Eliot turns against the moderns for not reading these texts, or of reading them without a historical sense. In the name of spontaneity the poet produces soulless texts, empty repetitions devoid of contemporaneity. The difference between Pope's and Eliot's relation to the past lies in their attitude toward rhetoric. Whereas for Pope it is the foundation of poetry, for Eliot, like the romantics, it is something to be escaped. In "Reflections on Contemporary Poetry," a series of reviews written for *The Egoist* in late 1917, Eliot warns that the laudable desire to escape the rhetorical cannot be achieved by concentrating, as did the romantics in his view, upon either "commonplace objects" or ideas. The former tend to appear trivial or accidental, the latter are invariably secondhand and, what is worse, vague generalizations.[55] Those writers who attempt to escape rhetoric by striving for a concrete realization of life or by modeling their language after direct speech in a "cry from the heart" end up as rhetorical as Tennyson.[56]

In "Modern Tendencies in Poetry," he offers the alternative of writers who are "much more modern. . . . They wish to evoke an emotion for which they have not found the sensory equivalent. They may *feel* the emotion, but you cannot put mere feelings into language; the thing is to *cease to feel* the emotion, to *see* it as the objective equivalent for it" (16). The error is either to try to deal with emotions directly without the sensory equivalent, as did Shakespeare in *Hamlet*, or to leave them out to deal with the senses, as did Tristan Tzara and the Dadaists. Precisely because emotions are not subject to language, they can be new insofar as they are purely subjective, but to be subjective is to be imitative. Therefore, if the writer is to be new, contemporary, the struggle is to transmute emotion into something objective, something that can be imitated, a poem.

Eliot's solution to the problem of modernity lies in his concept of impersonality; both involve the poet in a struggle with his material, which, in a certain sense, is his experience. In "Tradition and the Individual Talent," Eliot argues against a mimetic notion of expressive emotion, the poem as the objectification of an emotional state. A poem need not make any "direct use of any emotion whatever" (*SW*, 54), and a great poem, like the episode of Paolo and Francesca in Dante's *Inferno*, may employ "a definite emotion, but the intensity of the poetry is something quite different from whatever intensity in the supposed experience it may give the impression of. . . . [T]he difference between art and the event is always absolute" (*SW*, 55–56). The event is always singular, however complex; but the work of art cannot be singular in this sense or else it would be inaccessible. Nevertheless, he claims the poem should be its own reality, but this can be achieved only if the poet has ceased to look upon experience as something in itself, that is, as something private belonging to a personality or self. So he goes on to say, "The point of view which I am struggling to attack is perhaps related to the metaphysical theory of the substantial unity of the soul: for my meaning is, that the poet has, not a "personality" to express, but a particular medium, which is only a medium and not a personality, in which impressions and experiences combine in peculiar and unexpected ways" (*SW*, 56). His dissertation provides a gloss on this puzzling remark: "The soul is so far from being a monad that we have not only to interpret other souls to ourselves but to interpret ourself to ourself."[57] If we take his dissertation as a guide to what he means by "the substantial unity of the soul," we can say personality is not a substance known in the expression, for if the soul interprets itself, there can be no immediate relation between expression and personality; the soul is neither substance, a singular unity, nor the reflexive consciousness but constitutes a third point of view, "a construction based on, and itself transcending, immediate experience."[58] In short, the soul must be felt, which in F. H. Bradley's terminology means being an object for immediate experience, if it is not to "bodily disappear," but of that soul one can say nothing because it is constantly shifting.

Therefore, Eliot concludes that the emotion should have "its life in the poem and not in the history of the poet" (*SW*, 59). The poem is not the event or experience that constitutes its subject matter. Eliot is calling for a poetry that does not merely appeal to the senses but is itself sensation. His notion of the impersonal reflects a belief that emotion is not something expressed but presented to the senses. We are approaching Eliot's notion of the unity of sensibility, "when the intellect was immediately at the tips of the senses. Sensation became word and word was sensation" (*SW*, 129). The implication is that this transfiguration came naturally to Donne, but he seems to posit that it is a historical development in both language and feeling. If the modern poet should fail, his failure lies in confusing poetic emotions with human emotions.[59] There is the emotion of art and the emotion of experience. The "classic" poet succeeds by embodying emotion, but not his emotion, in the poem.

This success, however, comes at a price. Just as the Word made flesh was sacrificed on the cross, so the word made sensation involves a self-sacrifice, "a continual extinction of personality" (*SW*, 53). This is what Valéry achieved in *Le Serpent*: "Like all of Valéry's poetry, it is impersonal in the sense that personal emotion, personal experience, is extended and completed in something impersonal—not in the sense of something divorced from personal experience and passion. No good poetry is the latter; indeed, the virtue, the marvel of Lucretius is the passionate act by which he annihilates himself in a system and unites himself with it, gaining something greater than himself. Such a surrender requires great concentration" ("Method of Paul Valéry," 14). The error of poets who seek the new is not that they seek it in personal experience but that they sacrifice their experiences and emotions to their selves. Had they been true to the letter of their emotions, they would have discovered that "the spirit killeth, but the letter giveth life" ("Poet and Saint," 426). Eliot wrote this the year he was baptized and confirmed in the Anglican Church. Eliot wasn't the first modernist to seek shelter from history by entering the Church, but this was after *The Waste Land*. Pope sought refuge from his worries in his grotto, but this was to create a work of art aside from his poetry, one that was ephemeral because it consisted of living matter, not texts. He created in *The Dunciad* a work that absorbed the ephemera of contemporary Grub Street into a monument of mock philology. As *The Waste Land* manuscripts reveal, Eliot extended mockery of his own emotions into a mockery of letters from the Bible to Baudelaire. In *The Waste Land* and his writings on emotions and thought, and their place in poetry, we are to find what constitutes his modernity and what compels him to disavow it.

NOTES

1. The best known of Eliot's essays on Dryden is his review of Mark Van Doren's *John Dryden* for *Times Literary Supplement*, 1012 (9 June 1921), which was reprinted with "Andrew Marvell" and "The Metaphysical Poets" as *Homage to John Dryden: Three Essays on the Poetry of the Seventeenth Century* (London: Hogarth Press, 1924). All three essays were republished in the first edition of *Selected Essays* (London: Faber and Faber, 1932). Less well known is *John Dryden: The Poet, The Dramatist, The Critic* (New York: Terence and Elsa Holliday, 1932). This book is a revision of three BBC broadcasts first printed in the *Listener*: "John Dryden—I: The Poet Who Gave the English Speech," 5, 118 (15 April 1931): 621–22; "John Dryden—II: Dryden the Dramatist," 5, 119 (22 April 1931): 681–82; "John Dryden—III: Dryden the Critic, Defender of Sanity," 5, 120 (29 April 1931): 724–25. Comments on Dryden appear in many other essays, and a chapter on him, "The Age of Dryden," appears in *The Use of Poetry and the Use of Criticism: Studies in the Relation of Criticism to Poetry in England*, Charles Eliot Norton Lectures for 1932–1933 (Cambridge, MA: Harvard University Press, 1933), 45–57. There are also several mentions of him in *The Letters of T. S. Eliot: Volume I, 1898–1922*, ed. Valerie Eliot (New York: Harcourt Brace Jovanovich, 1988). The first, in a letter of 17 February 1920, to Lytton Strachey, is most striking: "I find that Dryden is a very great man" (367).

2. T. S. Eliot, introduction to *Ezra Pound: Selected Poems*, ed. T. S. Eliot (1928; London: Faber and Faber, 1933), 17–18. In the same piece, he recalls Pound telling him, "Pope has done this so well that you cannot do it better; and if you mean this as a burlesque, you had better suppress it, for you cannot parody Pope unless you can write better verse than Pope—and you can't" (18). In "Andrew Marvell," he calls Dryden "the great master of contempt" and Pope "the great master of hatred." He makes one the imperious judge of his inferiors, the other the vindictive protector of his reputation. "Andrew Marvell" first appeared in the *Times Literary Supplement* (31 March 1921) and is reprinted in *Selected Essays, New Edition* (New York: Harcourt, Brace and World, 1964), 252; hereafter cited in the text as *SE*.

3. Hugh Kenner, "The Urban Apocalypse," in *Eliot in His Time: Essays on the Occasion of the Fiftieth Anniversary of "The Waste Land,"* ed. A. Walton Litz (Princeton: Princeton University Press, 1973), 34.

4. Hugh Kenner, *The Counterfeiters: An Historical* Comedy (1968; repr., Garden City, NY: Anchor Books, 1973); W. B. Yeats, "Introduction to *The Oxford Book of Modern Verse*," in *Later Essays*, ed. William H. O'Donnell, in *The Collected Works of W. B. Yeats* (New York: Charles Scribner's Sons, 1994), 5:190–91.

5. R. F. Foster, *W. B. Yeats: A Life. II: The Arch-Poet, 1915–1939* (Oxford: Oxford University Press, 2003), 419.

6. Paul de Man describes the temporal pattern of literary history as apocalyptic in *Romanticism and Contemporary Criticism: The 1967 Christian Gauss Seminar and Other Papers*, ed. E. S. Burt, Kevin Newmark, and Andrzej Warminski (Baltimore: Johns Hopkins University Press, 1993), 16.

7. A. David Moody argues that "Eliot's poetry is made up out of what the man lived through; but the *poet* we come to know in it is an elected self, a personality deliberately fashioned in the medium of language, and whose only real existence is in the poetry." See *Thomas Stearns Eliot: Poet*, 2nd ed. (Cambridge: Cambridge University Press, 1994), xvii. Although Moody appears to be drawing upon Eliot's statement in "Tradition and the Individual Talent" that "the more perfect the artist, the more completely separate in him will be the man who suffers and the mind which creates," his formulation is closer to the famous opening of Yeats's introduction to the unpublished, collected "Dublin Edition" of his works: "A poet writes always of his personal life . . . he never speaks directly as to someone at the breakfast table, there is always a phantasmagoria. . . . even when the poet seems most himself . . . he is never the bundle of accident and incoherence that sits down to breakfast; he has been re-born as an idea, something intended, complete." *The Sacred Wood: Essays on Poetry and Criticism* (London: Methuen, 1960), 54; hereafter cited in the text as *SW*; W. B. Yeats, introduction for the never-published Charles Scribner's Sons "Dublin Edition" of W. B. Yeats, in *Later Essays*, 204. Eliot's elected self exists solely in the poetry, Yeats's in his character as poet.

8. T. S. Eliot, "A Brief Introduction to the Method of Paul Valéry," in *Le Serpent par Paul Valéry*, trans. Mark Wardle (London: R. Cobden-Sanderson for the Criterion, 1924), 12, 14.

9. In the medieval world, *auctor* designated a writer who possessed authority, *auctoritas*. In A. J. Minnis's account of these terms, an *auctor* was someone who

"'performed' the act of writing" and "brought something into being": "In the specific sense, an *auctoritas* was a quotation or an extract from the work of an *auctor*." Modern writers were not, by definition, *auctors* but gained authority by quoting *auctors*, ancients, and the church fathers. See his *Medieval Theory of Authorship: Scholastic Literary Attitudes in the Later Middle Ages*, 2nd ed. (Philadelphia: University of Pennsylvania Press, 1988), 10, 12. For another historical account, see Trevor Ross, *The Making of the English Literary Canon: From the Middle Ages to the Late Eighteenth Century* (Montreal: McGill-Queen's University Press, 1998), esp. 29–33.

10. See Patricia Meyer Spacks's "Worlds of Unreason: *The Dunciad* and *The Waste Land*," in *An Argument of Images: The Poetry of Alexander Pope* (Cambridge, MA: Harvard University Press, 1971), 84–132; J. S. Cunningham, "Pope, Eliot, and 'The Mind of Europe,'" in *"The Waste Land" in Different Voices*, ed. A. D. Moody (London: Edward Arnold, 1974), 67–85; and J. A. Richardson, *Falling Towers: The Trojan Imagination in "The Waste Land," "The Dunciad," and "Speke Parott"* (Newark: University of Delaware Press / London: Associated University Presses, 1992). Claude Rawson entitles an essay on the *Dunciad* as "Pope's *Waste Land*: Reflections on Mock-Heroic," but he argues that Eliot's satiric voice is more indebted to Swift than Pope, even in the Fresca passage. Moreover, he argues that Pope's use of fragments and broken images are "contained within the larger visible stabilities of the Popeian universe," whereas Eliot is less secure about tradition, and rather than hold up the past as model or order to be contrasted with present decay, he sees the past "as containing the germ of present sickness." Rawson's argument is persuasive. See *Order from Confusion Sprung: Studies in Eighteenth-Century Literature from Swift to Cowper* (London: George Allen and Unwin, 1985), 213, 214. The phrase "mind of Europe" is from "Tradition and the Individual Talent," in *SW*, 51.

11. Arnold Bennett recounts asking Eliot, "'Were the notes to *The Waste Land* a lark or serious? I thought they were a skit.' He said that they were serious, and not more of a skit than some things in the poem itself. I understood him. I said I couldn't see the point of the poem. He said he didn't mind what I said as he had definitely given up that form of writing, and was now centred on dramatic writing." Journal entry for Wednesday, 10 September 1924, in *The Journal of Arnold Bennett* (New York: Literary Guild, 1933), 786. Considering the reputation of Bennett among Eliot's circle, above all Woolf and Pound, one cannot but think that readers such as Bennett were meant not to get the point of *The Waste Land*.

12. Edmund Wilson, however, wrote in his review, "The Waste Land is intelligible at first reading. It is not necessary to know anything about the Grail Legend or any but the most obvious of Mr Eliot's allusions to feel the force of the intense emotion which the poem is intended to convey." "The Poetry of Drouth: T. S. Eliot," originally published in *Dial* (December 1922) and reprinted in Edmund Wilson, *Literary Essays and Reviews of the 1920s and 30s* (New York: Library of America, 2008), 870.

13. See Pope's letter to Swift on 12 October 1728: "The inscription to the Dunciad is now printed and inserted in the Poem. Do you care I shou'd say any thing farther how much that poem is yours? since certainly without you it had never been." And in a letter of the same day to Thomas Sheridan, he writes that Swift "is properly the

Author of the Dunciad: It had never been writ but at his Request, and for his Deafness: For had he been able to converse with me, do you think I had amus'd my Time so ill?" *The Correspondence of Alexander Pope*, ed. George Sherburn (Oxford: Clarendon Press, 1956), 2:522 and 2:523.

14. Aubrey L. Williams, *Pope's "Dunciad": A Study of Its Meaning* (Baton Rouge: Louisiana State University Press, 1955), 158. Williams quotes from the 1743 version, 4.244. Unless otherwise indicated, I will cite from *The Poems of Alexander Pope*, ed. John Butt (New Haven: Yale University Press, 1963), the one-volume edition of the Twickenham text, and I will follow the convention of citing *The Dunciad Variorum* as A and *The Dunciad in Four Books* as B.

15. Donald T. Siebert, Jr., has dubbed those who read the poem as a pessimistic attack on the fate of culture members of "the School of Deep Intent." See his "Cibber and Satan: *The Dunciad* and Civilization," *Eighteenth-Century Studies* 10, no. 2 (Winter 1976–1977): 203–21.

16. Quoted as an epigraph in Valerie Eliot, ed., *The Waste Land: A Facsimile and Transcript of the Original Drafts, Including the Annotations of Ezra Pound* (New York: Harcourt Brace, 1971), [xxxiii]; hereafter cited in the text as *WLF*. The source of the comment is Theodore Spencer by way of Henry Ware Eliot, Jr., which makes it another case of a work by several hands.

17. Henry Fielding, *Covent Garden Journal*, no. 59, Saturday, 15 August 1752, in *The Criticism of Henry Fielding*, ed. Ioan Williams (London: Routledge, 1970), 116.

18. In a letter on 16 July 1728, Swift requested that the notes Pope was preparing after the 1728 edition appeared should "be very large, in what relates to the persons concerned; for I have long observed that twenty miles from London no body understands hints, initial letters, or town-facts and passages; and in a few years not even those who live in London. I would have the names of those scriblers printed indexically at the beginning or end of the Poem, with an account of their works, for the reader to refer to." *The Correspondence of Jonathan Swift*, ed. Harold Williams (Oxford: Clarendon Press, 1963), 3:293.

19. The ancient quarrel between poetry and philosophy is, of course, recalled by Socrates in Plato's *Republic*, book 10 (607b3). For a very good discussion of the emergence of the modern concepts of "aesthetics" and "literature" in the eighteenth century, which fractured "the humanist ideal of a union of wisdom with eloquence," see Douglas Lane Patey, "The Eighteenth Century Invents the Canon," *Modern Language Studies* 18, no. 1 (Winter 1988): 24.

20. Patey, "The Eighteenth Century Invents the Canon," 24.

21. Paul de Man, "Resistance to Theory," in *Resistance to Theory* (Minneapolis: University of Minnesota Press, 1986), 7. For the second quotation, see "Reading and History," in *Resistance to Theory*, 67.

22. Christine Froula, "Corpse, Monument, *Hypocrite Lecteur*: Text and Transference in the Reception of *The Waste Land.*" Originally published in *Text: An Interdisciplinary Annual of Textual Studies* 9, ed. D. C. Greethan and W. Speed Hill (Ann Arbor: University of Michigan Press, 1996): 304–14. Reprinted in *The Waste Land: Authoritative Text, Contexts, Criticism*, ed. Michael North (New York: W. W. Norton, 2001), 276.

23. Leopold Damrosch, Jr., in *The Imaginative World of Alexander Pope* (Berkeley: University of California Press, 1987), makes the distinction between personal detail and subjectivity in his study of how Pope shaped his self-image in his poetry (19).

24. Patrick Deane, "Rhetoric and Affect: Eliot's Classicism, Pound's Symbolism, and the Drafts of *The Waste Land*," *Journal of Modern Literature* 18, no. 1 (Winter 1992): 83, 90.

25. A. Walton Litz has argued "that the essential life of *The Waste Land* does not lie in the obvious contrasts between past and present. . . . The famous description of the modern woman at her dressing table ('The Chair she sat in, like a burnished throne, / Glowed on the marble . . .') is less interesting for what it tells us about Cleopatra and her modern counterpart than for what we learn about Eliot's conception of heroic verse." See "*The Waste Land* Fifty Years After," in *Eliot in His Time*, 37. We might say that Eliot had a greater feel for Shakespearean blank verse than he had for Pope's heroic couplets. The Fresca passage, which is another depiction of modern woman at her toilet, is not only, as Kenner says, built on adjectives ("The Urban Apocalypse," 35), but it departs from Popean satire in its savagery and coarseness, as Rawson points out in noting Eliot's debt to Swift. See *Order from Confusion Sprung*, 186–87n17. Litz's observation holds: the Fresca passage is less interesting for what it tells us about Belinda's modern counterpart, or even Eliot's views on women, than for its illustration of Eliot's conception of heroic couplets.

26. Moody, *Thomas Stearns Eliot*, 111. Moody argues the poem is the culmination of English romantic poetry: "*The Waste Land* put an end to English romanticism by taking absolutely seriously the feelings it had soothed" (109).

27. For Pope's ironic denial that *The Dunciad* is such a patchwork, see the advertisement to *The Dunciad Variorum*: "*The* Imitations *of the Ancients are added, to gratify those who either never read, or may have forgotten them; together with some of the Parodies, and Allusions to the most excellent of the Moderns. If any man from the frequency of the former, may think the Poem too much a* Cento*; our Poet will but appear to have done the same thing in jest, which* Boileau *did in earnest*" (A, 318). The *OED* cites Samuel Johnson's definition of "cento": "A composition formed by joining scraps from other authors."

28. Emrys Jones, "Pope and Dulness." Originally published in *A Chatterton Lecture on an English Poet* (London: British Academy, 1968), 231–63; repr. in *Pope: A Collection of Critical Essays*, ed. J. V. Guerinot (Englewood Cliffs, NJ: Prentice-Hall, 1972), 127; hereafter cited in the text.

29. Donald T. Siebert, Jr., accuses Jones of being "enamored" with Pope's creations. See his "Cibber and Satan," 208. Howard Erskine-Hill has high praise for Jones's article, but he too is critical of it and argues that such a reading does not adequately address the "absolute negativeness of Pope's vision." See his *Pope: "The Dunciad,"* *Studies in English Literature*, no. 49 (London: Edward Arnold, 1972), 66.

30. Thomas Kyd, *The Spanish Tragedy*, 4.4.9, in *Four Revenge Tragedies*, ed. Katharine Eisaman Maus (Oxford: Oxford University Press, 1995).

31. As John Butt points out in "Pope's Poetical Manuscripts," in *Essential Articles on Alexander Pope*, ed. Maynard Mack (Hamden, CT: Archon Press, 1964), 507–8. Originally published in *Proceedings of the British Academy*, 40:23–39.

32. Hugh Kenner, "Eliot and the Tradition of the Anonymous," *College English* 28, no. 8 (May 1967): 562.

33. For a discussion of how the quarrel introduced "the new division of knowledge" into science and the humanities, see Douglas Lane Patey, "Ancients and Moderns," in *The Cambridge History of Literary Criticism*, vol. 4, *The Eighteenth Century*, ed. H. B. Nisbet and Claude Rawson (Cambridge: Cambridge University Press, 1997), 45.

34. Reuben Arthur Brower, *Alexander Pope: The Poetry of Allusion* (Oxford: Oxford University Press, 1959), 352–53; hereafter cited in the text.

35. Charles Taylor, *Sources of the Self: The Making of Modern Identity* (Cambridge, MA: Harvard University Press, 1989), 374–75.

36. "Modern Tendencies in Poetry," *Shama'a* 1, no. 1 (April 1920): 9–18; hereafter cited in the text. According to Donald Gallup in his *T. S. Eliot: Bibliography* (London: Faber and Faber, 1969), the essay was originally delivered as a lecture under the auspices of the Arts League of Service in October 1919 (206).

37. Hugh Kenner, "The Urban Apocalypse," in *Eliot in His Time*, 34.

38. Hugh Kenner, *The Counterfeiters*, xiii.

39. For the remarks on rationalism and experience, I am indebted to Charles Taylor's discussion of Descartes in *The Sources of the Self*, 144.

40. For Pope's failures as scholar and editor, see Joseph M. Levine, *The Battle of the Books: History and Literature in the Augustan Age* (Ithaca: Cornell University Press, 1991), 181–244. Kenner characterizes *The Dunciad* as an imitation of a dunce imitating the epic manner of "Pope's earlier imitations." See *The Counterfeiters*, 84.

41. Tzvetan Todorov, *Theories of the Symbol*, trans. Catherine Porter (Ithaca: Cornell University Press, 1982), 289.

42. Kenner, *The Counterfeiters*, 135.

43. For a good account of Theobald's scholarship and his relation to Pope, see Peter Seary, *Lewis Theobald and the Editing of Shakespeare* (Oxford: Clarendon Press, 1990). A broader history of eighteenth-century editing is available in Marcus Walsh, *Shakespeare, Milton, and Eighteenth-Century Literary Editing* (Cambridge: Cambridge University Press, 1997).

44. Levine, *The Battle of the Books*, 45.

45. I draw upon Levine's account of Homer's treatment at the hands of the moderns in *The Battle of the Books*, 126–32.

46. Moody, *Thomas Stearns Eliot*, 261, 19; Ronald Bush, *T. S. Eliot: A Study in Character and Style* (Oxford: Oxford University Press, 1984), 10; Ronald Schuchard, *Eliot's Dark Angel: Intersections of Life and Art* (Oxford: Oxford University Press, 1999), 20, 3.

47. Paul de Man, "Lyric and Modernity," in *Blindness and Insight: Essays in the Rhetoric of Contemporary Criticism*, rev. 2nd ed. (Minneapolis: University of Minnesota Press, 1983), 166.

48. De Man, "Literary History and Literary Modernity," in *Blindness and Insight*, 152; hereafter cited in the text as *BI*.

49. Eliot, "Ulysses, Order, and Myth," *Dial* 75, no. 5 (Nov. 1923): 482.

50. "Poet and Saint . . . ," *Dial* 87, no. 5 (May 1927): 430; reprinted with some revisions as "Baudelaire in Our Time," in *For Lancelot Andrewes: Essays on Style*

and Order (1928; London: Faber and Faber, 1970). It is worth noting his aside that "one feels that Pope would have better fitted [as a translator of Baudelaire's alexandrines] than Mr. Symons" (430). In the preface to the collection he makes the notorious remark, "The general point of view may be described as classicist in literature, royalist in politics, and anglo-catholic in religion." What critics typically fail to note is that he immediately adds, "I am quite aware that the first term is completely vague, and easily lends itself to clap-trap." The second term, he says, "lends itself to what is almost worse than clap-trap, I mean temperate conservatism; the third term does not rest with me to define" (7).

51. Eliot, "Ulysses, Order, and Myth," 482.

52. Eliot, "What is a Classic?" in *On Poetry and Poets* (New York: Noonday Press, 1961), 60; hereafter cited in the text. This was the presidential address to the Virgil Society, 1944, and was first published in 1945.

53. Samuel Johnson, "Life of Pope," in *Lives of the Poets*, ed. G. B. Hill (Oxford: Clarendon Press, 1905), 3:213n2.

54. Eliot, "Syllabus of a Course," in Moody, *Thomas Stearns Eliot*, 44, 43.

55. "Reflections on Contemporary Poetry" appeared in three consecutive numbers of the *Egoist* 4: no. 8 (Sept. 1917): 118–19; no. 9 (Oct. 1917): 133–34; and no. 10 (Nov. 1917): 151. The phrase in quotation marks is from the first review; the attack on the lack of philosophical depth and originality runs throughout all three articles.

56. "Reflections on Contemporary Poetry," no. 10 (Nov. 1917): 151.

57. T. S. Eliot, *Knowledge and Experience in the Philosophy of F. H. Bradley* (1964; New York: Columbia University Press, 1989), 148. For a reminder about the dangers and difficulties of applying Eliot's philosophy to his poetry, and for some very suggestive applications, see Richard Wollheim's "Eliot and F. H. Bradley," in his *On Art and the Mind: Essays and Lectures* (London: Allen Lane, 1973), 220–49.

58. Eliot, *Knowledge and Experience*, 149. Eliot is quoting from Bradley's *Appearance and Reality* (Oxford: Clarendon Press, 1946), 465.

59. See "Reflections on Contemporary Poetry," no. 9 (Oct. 1917): 133: "A poet like M. de Bosschère is an intellectual by his obstinate refusal to adulterate his poetic emotions with human emotions."

Chapter Two

A Sentimental Journey through Thomas Gainsborough's "Cottage-door" Paintings

E. Derek Taylor

Readers familiar with Laurence Sterne's bawdy prose satire *The Life and Opinions of Tristram Shandy* (1759–1767) surely may be forgiven any misgivings about accepting the author's characterization of his next work of fiction, *A Sentimental Journey through France and Italy* (1767), as "innocent." In a letter on 28 November 1767 to Lord Shelburne, Sterne wrote, "The world has imagined, because I wrote Tristram Shandy, that I was myself more Shandean than I really ever was. . . . If it [*A Sentimental Journey*] is not thought a chaste book, mercy on them that read it, for they must have warm imaginations indeed!"[1] Coming from an author who in *Tristram Shandy* had turned "noses" and "buttonholes" into blushworthy material—and then blamed readers for blushing—such claims of chaste intentions in *A Sentimental Journey* necessarily ring suspect, if not hollow. At times, Sterne seems to have enjoyed encouraging such suspicions, as when, in a letter on 3 December 1767, he characterized the two volumes comprising *A Sentimental Journey* as "a *couple of as clean brats* as ever chaste brain conceiv'd" (8:636). And yet it is difficult to locate any particular signs of like-minded irony in his oft-cited statement of authorial purpose: when Sterne famously insisted to Richard Griffith that he composed *A Sentimental Journey* as his "*Work of Redemption*" (8:627n3), he appears to have meant it. If we cannot take at face value Sterne's claims of innocence for *A Sentimental Journey*, then neither can we discount his characterization of it as a serious-minded work of atonement.

Sterne is nowhere closer to achieving the redemption he claimed he was seeking than in what *ought* to be the final chapter of *A Sentimental Journey*, the tellingly titled "The Grace." In this carefully orchestrated sentimental scene, the members of an extended family of French peasants, having first shared their humble dinner with an unknown and unexpected English visitor ("'twas a feast of love," Yorick muses with satisfaction), break into a series of joyful dances. "I thought I beheld *Religion* mixing in the dance," Yorick hesitantly suggests, at which point his instinctive sensibility is gratifyingly confirmed by the patriarch of the happy family: "all his life long he had made it a rule, after supper was over, to call out his family to dance and rejoice; believing, he said, that a chearful and contented mind was the best sort of thanks to heaven that an illiterate peasant could pay—" "—Or a learned prelate either," Yorick adds, thereby providing a perfectly self-reflexive benediction both to the climactic scene he has experienced and to the work of fiction through which his author (and sometime double) sought to reclaim himself as a moral and sensible man worthy of salvation.[2] As Melvyn New puts it, "In the penultimate chapter of everything Sterne ever wrote," Yorick arrives at an unadulterated moment of physical and spiritual harmony with which "nothing interferes."[3] Sterne has achieved, it would appear, the central insight of his artistry.

Of course, "penultimate" is the operative term here. Sterne elected to end *ASJ* not with "The Grace," but with "The Case of Delicacy," a chapter as sexually suggestive—and, I might add, as funny—as anything he ever penned. Whatever one thinks about the prospects of further volumes—Yorick never makes it to the Italy announced in the full title—it would seem logical enough in a "work of redemption" for Sterne to end the then-current volume with Yorick's satisfying experience of community-as-prayer. Instead, volume 2 of *ASJ* (and thus *ASJ* itself) concludes with a hotel scene awash in throbbing desire and double entendre: stuck together in a single room against their will, Yorick, a French lady "of about thirty, with a glow of health in her cheeks," and a maid "of twenty, and as brisk and lively a French girl as ever moved" (162), negotiate a "treaty of peace" (163) designed to get them through the night without incident or embarrassment. Hours later, insomnia (of a sort) gripping him, Yorick finds that he cannot restrain himself from breaking the third article of the treaty: "that after Monsieur was got to bed . . . [he] should not speak one single word the whole night." "Oh my God!" Yorick exclaims, insisting, in the face of the lady's vociferous protestations, that "it was no more than an ejaculation" (164). As the corking pins holding the curtain that separates Yorick and the lady begin to fall to the ground, and the Fille de Chambre draws near, Yorick attempts to pledge his "word and honour." Stretching his "arm out of bed, by way of asseveration," his hand catches "hold of the Fille de Chambre's / END OF VOL. II" (164–65).

If in "The Grace" Yorick manages to "express the joy of the dance without equivocation or innuendo," as New puts it, just the opposite holds in this final, fragmentary episode.[4] But why would Sterne choose to muddle the redemptive conclusion at which he had seemingly arrived with a bawdy *in*conclusion? For many nineteenth-century readers, among them William Thackeray and Leslie Stephen, the answer was simple: Sterne is at heart incorrigible and thus incapable of controlling his baser impulses. "One grows angry," Stephen wrote, "when he spoils a graceful scene by some prurient double meaning."[5] But perhaps this was the point all along. Elizabeth Kraft has suggested that Sterne's *ASJ* is best understood not as the sentimental "departure" from *Tristram Shandy* for which it is often taken, but rather as an "elaboration" of themes and purposes to which Sterne had long been dedicated: "*A Sentimental Journey* may be a work of redemption," she writes, "but it represents no conversion on the part of its author." In Kraft's view, "[T]he world of *A Sentimental Journey*, like the world of *Tristram Shandy*, is a world of lust and delicacy, riddles and mysteries, desire and sentiment, bodies and souls. . . . Although on the surface *A Sentimental Journey* seems to exchange Tristram's bawdiness for Yorick's acute sensitivity to the feelings of others, the final scene suggests that such sensitivity—the longing for communion with another—is not the attribute of the celibate saint but of the desiring sinner."[6] New would seem to agree with Kraft on this point, at least in part; he points to Sterne's "quick turn" from "heartfelt" sentiment to bawdry as an "ironic strategy that pervades both works."[7] It is important, nevertheless, not to overstate the similarities between *Tristram Shandy* and *ASJ*. As a case in point, it is worth considering how fully inadequate New's assessment of the former would be if applied to the latter: "[T]his is what *Tristram Shandy* is finally about: the triumph of the uncreating spirit in man, the celebration of chaos and confusion, destruction in death. . . . [A]ll the diverse activities of the Shandy household and Tristram's study share in the fundamental movement of the satire from its beginning in birth and creation to its conclusion in dissolution and uncreation."[8]

New himself provides the needful clue to how the two works may be comprehended without collapsing the one into the other—without diminishing, as it were, each work's otherness. "Good authors," he writes in reference to "The Grace," "would have ended the work here, justifiably satisfied with their literary skills; the genius goes on to a final chapter."[9] I would suggest that the "genius" of Sterne's "ironic strategy" in *ASJ* has to do with the fact that, unlike in *Tristram Shandy*, it works not toward corruption or perversion—where Rabelaisian irony renders a particular statement or intellectual position inoperative or foolish—but rather toward complication and dialogue; it is as much a chiasmal strategy as an ironic one. In *Tristram Shandy*, Sterne's quick turns almost always add to the entropy, allowing the author further to elaborate his satiric vision of a sterile Shandean world of broken language and hobbyhorsical delusion. In *ASJ*, Sterne attempts to marshal these quick turns *against* "dissolution and corruption"—to show us that kissing a beautiful woman and bidding "God bless her" really *can* "[amount] to the same thing" (90). To borrow mutatis mutandis Kraft's phrase, Sterne discovers in *ASJ* that he need not falter on the shoals of "celibate saints" and "desiring sinners"—that he can believe, after all, in "desiring saints." How better to describe the composite portrait of Yorick that emerges in the final two chapters of *ASJ*?

In other words, if "A Case of Delicacy" brings readers back to the reality of physical desire and carnal appetite, it also underscores what we should have noticed about the previous chapter— "The Grace," for all its religious implications, was already about full stomachs, satisfied ears, and dancing bodies.[10] And if "The Grace" provides readers a climatic moment of spiritual refinement and physical sanctification, it also prepares us for the final, interruptive conclusion, where an "ejaculation" is both "male sexual discharge" and a "short prayer,"[11] and where a physical reaching across space becomes an emblem for spiritual longing, no matter where Yorick's hand finally lands. Suspended in mutual openness and possibility, each chapter depends upon the other in reciprocal fashion, neither privileged above the other, neither canceling the other out. "The Grace" can no more be separated from "A Case of Delicacy" than can Yorick from the Marquesina di F****; one may as well follow Yorick, then, in admitting the "pleasure" of "the connection" (*ASJ*, 78).

Sterne, I will suggest in what follows, was not the only prominent midcentury artist putting this particular "ironic strategy" to good use in his engagement with sentimental subject matter, nor was he alone in finding in the process a path to redemption, of a sort. In 1765, so the story goes, Thomas Gainsborough, by then a prominent portrait artist making a decent living in Bath, had a chance encounter with Sterne, whose *Tristram Shandy* he so admired that he had named a favorite dog after its title character.[12] "At the request of a friend," Wilbur Cross explains in his 1909 biography, "Sterne sat for his admirer." The resulting portrait, which Cross describes as "perplexing" in its "impression of soberness, almost of melancholy," now hangs at the Peel Park Museum and Art Gallery in Salford. Cross so admired its "highly idealized" presentation of its subject that he included a reproduction as the frontispiece to his biography of Sterne.[13]

It is perhaps unfortunate that, aside from Gainsborough's affection for Sterne's antinovel and his dog named Tristram, almost nothing about the above story is true. There is, in fact, a painting at the Peel Park Museum, but it is neither of Sterne nor by Gainsborough.[14] (It is somehow fitting that the famous portrait of Sterne hanging in the National Portrait Gallery is by Gainsborough's great rival, Sir Joshua Reynolds—and, indeed, Cross changed his frontispiece accordingly in the updated 1925 edition.)[15] Nor did Sterne and Gainsborough, it would appear, have the decency even to meet—though doing so would have provided at least a modicum of biographical cover for the now legion, if generally passing, commentaries linking the two figures. When Cross used the now discredited portrait as his frontispiece, in other words, he was on the wrong side of historical fact—but he was on the right side of long-standing, and continuing, critical consensus. "The most convincing comparison to be made between

Gainsborough and any of his contemporaries—the only one which rings consistently true," as John Hayes puts it in his modern edition of the artist's letters, "is, as Jackson pointed out, with Sterne."[16] Jackson, in this case, is Gainsborough's friend and correspondent William Jackson, who recognized without the benefit of historical hindsight the decidedly Sterne-like quality of Gainsborough's personality, conversation, and writing. The artist "detested reading," Jackson explains, "but he was so like Sterne in his Letters, that, if it were not for an originality that could be copied from no one, it might be supposed that he had formed his style upon a close imitation of that author."[17] Like Sterne, Gainsborough's prose reads as a series of fits and starts—his is "to the moment writing" at its most pure, full of interruptions and witty digressions marked by a proliferation of dashes—and, also like Sterne, Gainsborough had a particular flair for perfectly timed bawdry—as when, in a letter to Jackson accompanying his gift of a harp, the artist concludes, "I'll not take anything for it but give [it] to you to twang upon when you can't twang upon Mrs Jackson."[18] "Brilliant but eccentric . . . too licentious to be published." This is an early nineteenth-century description of, not *Tristram Shandy*, but a packet of Gainsborough's letters—later burned in an unfortunate and fatalistic act of confirmation.[19]

Comparisons between Gainsborough and Sterne have not been limited to their shared style of writing. Indeed, Ronald Paulson contended some thirty years ago, with an eye to *Tristram Shandy* and *ASJ*, that "the literary equivalent" to Gainsborough's artistry "is more easily located than the graphic."[20] More recently, Amal Asfour and Paul Williamson have stressed Sterne's performance in *Tristram Shandy* as a primary analogue for the "painterly wit" evident in Gainsborough's portraiture, and they underscore Jackson's characterization of Gainsborough "in his private life" as a Sterne-like "man of feeling."[21] Michael Rosenthal similarly takes Gainsborough's stated desire "to make the Heart dance" through his paintings as a sign of "his total assimilation into the culture of sensibility" in which Sterne's *Tristram Shandy* was the "key novel" and over which, according to Rosenthal and Myrone, Sterne served as "high priest."[22] Formally, Gainsborough was dedicated to an artistry that "demands our active looking," as Rosenthal puts it; "the graphic equivalent of Sterne's aposiopesis," Paulson contends, "is Gainsborough's dashes and daubs of paint."[23] In a grudging compliment, Reynolds admitted his wonder at the impressionistic effect Gainsborough achieved through his unconventional technique: "It is certain that all those odd scratches and marks, which, on a close examination, are so observable in Gainsborough's pictures, and which even to experienced painters appear rather the effect of accident than design: this chaos, this uncouth and shapeless appearance, by a kind of magic, at a certain distance assumes form, and all the parts seem to drop into their proper places."[24] The "conspicuous artificiality" of Gainsborough's paintings, Ann Bermingham notes, "looked 'odd'" to contemporaries like Reynolds.[25] Much as Sterne incorporates lines, black spaces, and blank pages in his exploration of the "experience of reading," Rosenthal suggests, Gainsborough in his paintings deliberately leaves open a "space for the imaginative and sympathetic engagement of the reader."[26]

Gainsborough made probably his most sustained effort to engage the sympathies of viewers in the series of "cottage-door" paintings, which he began producing in the early 1770s and on which he continued to work until shortly before his death in 1788. As Bermingham puts it in a recent book devoted to these sentimental landscapes, "nowhere is the eighteenth-century way of seeing and feeling more intensely evoked than in Thomas Gainsborough's 'cottage-door' paintings."[27] Rosenthal has suggested that we will better understand the moral economy at work in the cottage-door series if we consider "Sterne's third sermon, 'Philanthropy Reconsidered.'" There, in reference to his own reconstruction of the parable of the Good Samaritan, Sterne writes, "I think there needs no stronger argument to prove how universally and deeply the seeds of this virtue of compassion are planted in the heart of man, than in the pleasure we take" in depictions of it. "We, as polite spectators" of Gainsborough's sentimentalized scenes, Rosenthal suggests, "are confirmed in our own virtue by reacting properly to what Gainsborough shows us."[28] As in Sterne's account, sensibility thus becomes the stick by which the virtue both of artist and of audience may be measured.[29]

The "five major" cottage-door paintings,[30] it is important to note, were not moneymakers; Gainsborough's fascination with and attention to these landscapes was personal in nature. Indeed, he, like Sterne, appears to have been drawn to constructing idealized rural fantasies and to finding solace in imaginatively inhabiting them. For his part, Sterne provides convenient bookends for his love life with two imagined scenes of rural retirement, the first in a letter of 1739–1740 to Elizabeth Lumley, who would soon become his wife. Sterne writes,

> Yes! I will steal from the world, and not a babbling tongue shall tell where I am—Echo shall not so much as whisper my hiding place—suffer thy imagination to paint it as a little sun-gilt cottage on the side of a romantic hill—dost thou think I will leave love and friendship behind me? No! they shall be my companions in solitude, for they will sit down, and rise up with me in the amiable form of my L.—we will be as merry, and as innocent as our first parents in Paradise, before the arch fiend entered that undescribable scene. . . . God preserve us, how delightful this prospect in idea! We will build, and we will plant, in our own way—simplicity shall not be tortured by art—we will learn of nature how to live—she shall be our alchymist, to mingle all the good of life into one salubrious draught.—The gloomy family of care and distrust shall be banished from our dwelling[.] (7:3–4)

In the second, written decades later in a letter on 17 June 1767 to Eliza Draper as part of *The Bramine's Journal*, Sterne, now separated from his wife and near death, once again indulges in a vision (albeit a disturbingly callous one) of escaping to the countryside:

> I have brought y^r name *Eliza!* And Picture into my work—where they will re-main—when You & I are at rest for ever—Some Annotator or explainer of my works in this place will take occasion, to speak of the Friendship wch Subsisted so long & faithfully betwixt Yorick & the Lady of he speaks of. . . . [T]hey caught fire at each other at the same time--& they w^d often say, without reserve to the world, & without any Idea of saying wrong in it, That their Affections for each other were *unbounded*— —Mr Draper dying in the Year *****—This Lady return'd to England & Yorick the year after becoming a Widower—They were married—& retiring to one of his Livings in Yorkshire, where was a most romantic Situation—they lived & died happily—and are spoke of with honour in the parish to this day—[31]

If anything, Gainsborough seems to have been even more invested than Sterne in imagining, perhaps even securing, a permanent rural retreat. "I am sick of portraits and wish very much to take my Viol dam Gam and walk off to some sweet Village where I can paint Landskips and enjoy the fag End of life in quietness and ease," he complained in an undated letter to William Jackson (68). To William Chambers in a letter on 27 April 1783, he explained that if he could only make enough money "in the portrait way two or three years longer," he would "sneak into a cot & turn a serious fellow" (152). As Bermingham notes, Gainsborough's contemporary Uvedale Price had "often remarked in [Gainsborough's] countenance an expression of particular gentle-ness and complacency" whenever the painter encountered "cottage or village scenes."[32] Such idealized affection for natural settings may explain the fact "that some time after moving from Bath to London, Gainsborough purchased a cottage near Richmond Hill."[33]

Gainsborough resisted pure idealization in rendering artistically his own rural fantasies, however; as with Tristram in his encounter with Nannette at the conclusion to volume 7 of *Tristram Shandy*, the male characters in the early cottage-door paintings hover around rustic scenes of consummation that they can never fully join. In the first of his cottage-door series, for instance, *The Woodcutter's Return* (ca. 1772–1773; fig.1), a male figure seems to encroach upon a domain not his own: on the one hand, the light that falls on the central Virgin-esque woman, the children, and the other woman or young lady some-how misses the woodcutter completely—he has yet to emerge from his own be-nighted landscape into the enlightened one of the women and children. Further-more, while the women and children's interwoven poses suggest both leisure and a certain complicity, the man, bent double under the weight of the wood on his back and head, lunges painfully forward in an attitude of labor that cannot but suggest separateness from the lounging comfort of what we assume to be his family (at whose feet, we might notice, he has already deposited one bale of wood). Some critics have found the cottage-door paintings thematically suggestive of an idyllic rural domesticity of which Gainsborough "whole-heartedly approved" and to which he returned time and again for "escape and renewal."[34] Approaching these landscapes as "idealized autobiography," of course, leaves little room for seeing the laboring swain of *The Woodcutter's Return* as anything other than fortunate in his "daily toil," anything other than rewarded by his "family-bond."[35] If we approach *The Woodcutter's Return* without assuming Gainsborough's "whole-hearted" approval, however, we will be hard-pressed to see the male figure as unequivocally fortunate. We might rather find something pathetic in the foreboding darkness of his immediate surroundings, the unwieldy bundle of sticks he bears, and the decidedly large family for which his labor must provide. Asfour and Williamson have suggested that "Gainsborough's cottage-door scenes" contain "the hint of a self-sufficient cottage economy [carrying] overtones of the Horatian *beatus ille*,"[36]—but how many bundles of wood can the laborer carry in a day? How many is enough? While we cannot answer these questions with any certainty, perhaps we can begin to see a Sterne-like tinge of irony in the discrepant possibilities Gainsborough introduces into his sentimentalized scene.

I am hardly the first to notice the rift between the laboring men and genteel women in Gainsborough's cottage-door paintings. John Barrell, in his influential *The Dark Side of the Landscape* (which takes its title from the discrepancy in question), focuses his cultural-materialist eye on the figure to the left in the next of the cottage-door paintings, *Cottage Door with Children Playing* (1777–1778; fig. 2). According to Barrell, the "attractive young ladies" to the right transcend their rural context because, according to the convention, they must. As embodiments of the "new pastoral," which is "essentially domestic," they must have a certain everywoman status in order effectively to represent the "imagined peace of a properly conducted family life." Gainsborough's middle- and upper-class buyers wanted such "domestic pastorals" to supply representational grist, furthermore, for an ideological mill that insisted that the good poor were as well off and as happy as they.[37] Finally, these same buyers needed figures of gentility and leisure with whom they could identify and into whom they could "escape" without really going anywhere. For Barrell, the laboring figure to the left contradicts all that the leisurely figures to the right accomplish—he "blights the landscape,"[38] thwarts the ideal rustic scene. Perhaps most important from Barrell's perspective, his dark presence, when taken in conjunction with the enlightened ladies to the left, "points to a way of apprehending the relations between rich and poor, consumer and producer."[39] In short, the divide between the laboring swain to the left and the leisured ladies to the right is symptomatic of an ideological contradiction, one that insisted both that the poor's work rendered it different from those classes depending on it (hence we do not identify with the "otherness" of the pained drudgery to the left) and that called on the poor to behave as if they were no different from other classes (hence we do identify with the "sameness" of the ladies to the right).

Unless, of course, we find ourselves identifying *with* the laboring male, as his creator seems to have done. Even scholars with evident reservations about biographical approaches to artistic production have found irresistible the "stark contrast," as Asfour and Williamson put it, between Gainsborough's actual domestic situation and the ostensible idealism of his cottage-door scenes.[40] Indeed, in his essay "Spectacles for Republicans," Barrell himself argues that "since Gainsborough's landscape paintings were mostly painted for his own amusement and recreation," it is reasonable to connect his "desire to escape from business . . . and from the whims and importunities of his polite sitters, into an eroticized rustic idyll."[41] Rosenthal likewise believes that Gainsborough likely "saw himself as much a beast of burden as the woodcutter."[42] On this reading, Gainsborough's laborer becomes a fanciful substitute for the painter himself—the woodcutter is to Gainsborough, we might say, as Yorick is to Sterne—while the too-comfortable, overly genteel family unit for whom he works serves as a sardonic version of the painter's "proud and characterful" wife (who insisted she was "a prince's daughter") and of his own "troublesome" daughters.[43]

Certainly, in his letters Gainsborough encourages the association between himself and his fictional male character (much as Sterne did in styling himself Yorick in letters and on the title page of early editions of his published sermons). In a letter of 30 December 1763 to James Unwin, for instance, Gainsborough speaks of his "wife and dear Girls" as being "charmingly well, and what's more (tho' I say it), good in grain" (24). By "good in grain" the painter may mean, as the *OED* defines "in grain," "downright, by nature"—this seems to be the way Christopher Smart uses the phrase in "A Song to David."[44] But Gainsborough may also be playfully conceiving of his labor in terms similar to those operative in the cottage-door paintings; in this case, his efforts, as his faux-coy parenthetical remark suggests, support and enrich leisured dependents who owe to him their abundance of "grain." And like his literally much-put-upon creation, Gainsborough senses that the work he performs on behalf of his family (portraiture, in his case) separates him from rural contentment and beauty that might otherwise be his to enjoy. His exasperation is evident in an undated letter to Jackson written during his final years in Bath (that is, in the early 1770s), a portion of which is quoted above:

I'm sick of Portraits and wish very much to take my Viol da Gamba and walk off
to some sweet Village when I can paint Landskips and enjoy the fag End of Life
in quietness and ease[.] But these fine Ladies and their Tea drinkings, Danc-
ings, *Husband huntings* &c &c &c will fob me out of the last ten years, & I fear
miss getting Husbands too—But we can say nothing to these things you know
Jackson, we must Jogg on and be content with the jingling of the Bel[ls], only
d-mn it I hate a dust, and kicking up a dust; and being confined *in Harn[ess]* to
follow the track, whilst others ride in the Waggon, under cover, stretching their
Legs in the straw at Ease, and gazing at Green Trees & Blue Skies without half
my *Taste* Thats d-mn'd hard. (68)

To my mind, this, one of Gainsborough's more frequently cited complaints,
stands as one of his most puzzling. Where exactly *is* Gainsborough in the
sprawling description that follows the volta-defining "—But"? Is he literally
confined to "the track" alongside his "husband hunting" wife and daughters?
Or is the "I" that "hate[s] a dust" *the same* as the unspecified agent "kicking"
it up, the one "confined *in Harness*," the one set off from the "others" riding
comfortably "under cover"? Certainly, the syntax allows for such a reading,
as ellipses make clear: "I hate a dust . . . and being confined *in Harness*." If
so, this means that Gainsborough, formerly a "good" provider of "grain,"
has now sunk to the status of a drudging horse, stirring up the very dust he
"hates," straining under the weight of the tasteless "others" whose unin-
formed gazing he provides for through his blinder-induced concentration on
the "track" ahead of him—another day, another portrait.

Bermingham notes of this passage that Gainsborough's wife and daughters
stand as "impediments" between the painter and his "sweet Village," but her hint
at a referent for those without "taste" in this passage, namely Gainsborough's
"natural enemies," the "'gentlemen' and the fashionable society they represent"
can, I think, be further refined.[45] Given the artist's sarcastic complaints about
his family just above what I take to be a self-referential horse metaphor, and
given what we know of Gainsborough's conception of his labor in relation to
his wife and daughters, to assume that those "stretching their Legs" behind the
hardworking painter/horse are "gentlemen" would seem to ignore more likely
candidates—Gainsborough does not explicitly mention any "gentlemen" in this
passage, but he does refer to the "fine Ladies" of his family. It is fitting, then,
that Gainsborough would offer a version of this same discrepancy—between
the tramping, dirty, dusty equinal painter and the genteel "Ladies" he feels
separated from but harnessed to—in his cottage-door paintings. The male figure
in *The Woodcutter's Return* may not be a horse, but he, too, for the sake of his
wife and children, must "jogg on."

In the last decade of his life, Gainsborough added two unique efforts to his
cottage-door series; in each case the most significant change involves the male

figure. Where in *Woodcutter's Return* and *Cottage Door with Children Playing* the laboring male is shown as he approaches home, no male at all appears in *The Cottage Door* (1780; fig. 3), while in *Peasant Smoking at a Cottage Door* (1788; fig. 4) the male is represented in a position of relaxation, smoking in apparently contented fashion alongside his wife and children.

John Hayes believes that in *The Cottage Door* Gainsborough achieves his "most majestic statement of [the cottage-door] theme";[46] whatever majesty he achieves is surely related to his decision to elide the problematic male figure of previous efforts. Malcolm Cormack points to the young, fashionable woman and her "chubby" children as "contented images of fecundity,"[47] stressing what Asfour and Williamson describe as the painting's "affinities with soft rather than hard pastoral." The "blessed circle" of nursing woman and healthy children, they suggest, inhabits a landscape fully its own: "in this case there is no male figure to suggest an economic basis for this scene of domestic contentment."[48] Yet even those critics who have stressed the idyllic nature of *The Cottage Door* have sometimes had misgivings. Despite agreeing that "the image does suggest a sentiment for a lost rural ideal," Nicola Kalinsky cryptically concludes that "there is something almost threatening in the enormous size of the turbulent trees and the isolation of the family group."[49] Asfour and Williamson expand on this interpretive line by noting the painting's "darker elements," in particular the potentially discomfiting "narrative possibilities" raised by the situation and setting. "Does the way the woman looks out into the distance," they ask, "suggest an absence? If she is the mother of the children around her, where is their father? Do the dark clouds gathering over the roof of the cottage, and even the possible hint of evening . . . connote an atmosphere of impending disaster?"[50] In other words, however fecund and beatific the grouping of woman and children, no paternal counterpart is, perhaps ever will be, in sight; however fruitful and green the surroundings, the most immediate natural object of setting is "the dead tree arching in from the right foreground."[51]

Perhaps, as Rosenthal has suggested, in refusing to supply *The Cottage Door* with "a male provider," Gainsborough is offering "an invitation to the spectator to fill that role, or to feel virtue in knowing that he (and I am assuming that Gainsborough is appealing to men here), if confronted with such scenes in real life, would behave as charitably . . . as any other person of sensibility."[52] Viewers, in this case, become something like the inquisitive Yorick in his encounter with the woman in the Remise, whose face, Yorick tells us, "wore the characters of a widow'd look . . . but a thousand other distresses might have traced the same lines; I wish'd to know what they had been—and was ready to enquire . . .—'What aileth thee? and why art thou disquieted? and why is thy understanding troubled?'" (*ASJ*, 23). But I wonder if *The Cottage Door* might not just as well be seen as a type of dead end along the lines of Yorick's experience in *ASJ* with the *desobligeant*, the one-person carriage in which Yorick attempts to sequester his guilt after refusing charity to the Franciscan monk. If we allow that the laboring male figure in previous cottage-door paintings represents on some level Gainsborough's imaginative projection of his own condition, it follows that the artist may well have found a measure of satisfaction in depicting a vision of dependents haunted by the possibility that their source of plenty has disappeared—that the woodman will not return, that "I" am on my own now.[53] And yet for Gainsborough, as for Yorick and Sterne, the drive to separate ourselves from community, the masturbatory pleasures of self-indulgence, carry profoundly moral—or immoral—implications. It is surely telling that, having explored the possibility of separation, isolation, and solitude in *The Cottage Door* as a means of resolving the tension generated between the working male and the leisured family unit in earlier paintings, in *Peasant Smoking at a Cottage Door*, which Gainsborough completed in the final year of his life, the painter not only comes back full circle, as it were, by once again including a male figure sequestered by his labor, but elects to go in precisely the other direction—that is, toward the pleasures of leisure and community.[54] It is as if, like Sterne, Gainsborough came to the conclusion that whatever temporary satisfaction we might achieve in living to ourselves, we are invariably "better . . . in a *vis-à-vis*" (*ASJ*, 17).

Critical commentary on *Peasant Smoking* has the strange ring of unanimity about it: here, everyone seems to agree, Gainsborough at last arrives at a satisfyingly comedic conclusion to a series of paintings that had by this point taken on the force of narrative. In this final painting, Rosenthal suggests, the link between the "male provider" and his family unit that had been lost in *The Cottage Door* "is, as it were, restored," and for once, "the family is represented united in repose."[55] "This, the largest of Gainsborough's landscapes, was painted in the last months of his life," Cormack writes; "it is an image of contentment."[56] For his part, Barrell notes that "only in the last and largest of these scenes, *Peasant Smoking at a Cottage Door*, is the burden of labor lifted from the shoulders of the father," who finally is allowed to join "the rest of the family before his cottage" and to share at least "some of the evening light."[57] Asfour and Williamson likewise find that "the dark qualities discernible in *The Cottage Door* are largely absent from the last in the series of cottage pictures, *Peasant Smoking at a Cottage Door*, which takes a more positive view of the values explored in the imagery." Their synopsis of the painting ably captures the consensus view: "Here, with the day's work done, the family enjoys the restful peace of their arcadian home. Watched over by their mother and their dog (whose importance as a link in the chain connecting these people with the natural world should not be ignored), the two older children repeat their evening prayer to their musing

Figure 1.   Thomas Gainsborough, *The Woodcutter's Return*
(ca. 1772–1773)

Figure 2.   *Cottage Door with Children Playing* (1777–1778)

Figure 3. *The Cottage Door* (1780)

Figure 4. *Peasant Smoking at a Cottage Door* (1788)

Figure 5.   *Diana and Actaeon* (ca. 1784–1786)

father who looks heavenward in an attitude that reinforces the basic message of the scene. This is a time of harmony, peace, and contentment for which these simple rustic souls are properly thankful."[58] If Gainsborough manages in *Peasant Smoking* to depict "the perfect microcosm," Asfour and Williamson conclude, it was only by transcending the reality of his own domestic "scenes of strife"; in this respect, the "idyllic holism" of the artist's final cottage-door painting amounts to a crowning achievement of mind over matter—a last, uncompromised effort to "recreat[e] reality in the fugitive realm of the imagination."[59] *Peasant Smoking*, put differently, is Gainsborough's "The Grace."

But as with Sterne's not *quite* last word, *Peasant Smoking* is not, I would suggest, the end of the story—or, perhaps better put, the *whole* story.[60] Sterne's redemptive chapter, we have seen, comes more fully into view in relationship to the deliberately unfinished "A Case of Delicacy"—and the reverse is equally true, for each chapter both comments ironically upon and reinforces thematically the other. Gainsborough's *Peasant Smoking* likewise is better understood, I believe, if we consider it alongside the artist's own "quick turn" away from the cottage-door series: the deliberately unfinished *Diana and Actaeon* (ca. 1784–1786; fig. 5).

It is impossible to know precisely why Gainsborough elected so late in his career to attempt a mythological subject; Jackson explains in his "Character of Gainsborough" that the painter "had no relish for historical painting," and, in his "Character of Sir Joshua Reynolds," suggests that Gainsborough "either wanted conception or taste, to relish historical painting, which he always considered as out of his way, and thought he should make himself ridiculous attempting it."[61] It is equally unclear why he settled upon this particular Ovidian story. In Addison's translation of the critical moment captured in Gainsborough's painting, Diana, having been accidentally glimpsed by Actaeon as she bathes with her nymphs, flings water into the unwitting interloper's face, saying, "Tell, if thou canst, the wond'rous sight disclosed, / A Goddess naked to thy view exposed."[62] As the poem continues, Actaeon, transformed into a deer with "rising" horns on "either brow" (255), becomes the object of the hunt he previously had led; accordingly, he is dragged down and slaughtered by his own hunting dogs—punished, justly or unjustly, for having compromised, if only with his eyes, the "virgin goddess" (310), for having encroached on a feminine domain both enticing and consuming.

Curiously, as Asfour and Williamson note, "Gainsborough's portrayal of the myth diverges in detail, in dramatic emphasis, and in the exact chronology of the events from its Ovidian original." "Gainsborough purges the tale of its wrath and vengeance," they explain, "substituting a distinct gentleness and sensuality of appeal which is quite remote from the violence of Addison's translation"[63]—wherein, to take just one horrific example, the pack of dogs tears at their master's flesh until he "appear'd but one continu'd wound" (291). But while Gainsborough does not capture explicitly the violence that follows this pregnant moment in the story, Actaeon *is already* growing horns as depicted here, even before the water has quite reached him. The painter thus subverts the sinewy beauty of the scene with an explicit hint of future disaster, subtly lodging within the idyllic the marker of the tragic.[64]

Gainsborough's painting has inspired a number of compelling expositions: as an elaboration of the painter's growing interest in voyeurism; as a witty rebuttal of Reynolds' standards for historical painting; as a transcendent work of earnest artistry that is "baptismal in conception."[65] Although its potential relationship to the cottage-door series has gone largely unremarked, there is good reason, I think, to "speculate" with Hugh Belsey about "whether Actaeon, an outsider, represents a development from the woodman made to work hard to fend for the growing demands of his family."[66] After all, as with the cottage-door paintings, Gainsborough elected to produce *Diana and Actaeon* for reasons personal rather than pecuniary, and his work on the painting began in the few years between the two most distinct iterations of the cottage-door theme: *The Cottage Door* (1780), where he had experimented with removing the male figure altogether, and *Peasant Smoking* (1788), where he had allowed him finally to join his family in contentment and solidarity. It is also worth noting that however distinct in subject matter and approach from the cottage-door landscapes, the painting shares with them a pronounced interest in the relationship between male suffering and female allure.

Hayes notes that the dead tree at the heart of *Peasant Smoking* shares similarities to the one dominating the center of *The Cottage Door*,[67] but I think it is instructive, especially in light of *Diana and Actaeon*, to consider carefully the *differences* between the two. Where the tree in *The Cottage Door* shadows the family as a discrete entity, in *Peasant Smoking* the tree so perfectly reflects the position of the man sitting beneath as to be an extension of him. The initial curve of the tree, we might note, conforms precisely to the slope of the man's back and shoulders, while its upward turn mimics his quizzically raised head. Also distinguishing the two trees is the fact that while the *Cottage Door* tree ends its growth in a nonobtrusive, V-shaped split, the *Peasant Smoking* tree is crowned with a pronounced proliferation of branches—branches that, sitting *in perfect symmetry* atop the portion of the tree aligned with the relaxing laborer's head, look remarkably like antlers. Actaeon's "branching horns" have made their way,[68] it would appear, into Gainsborough's last painting, and onto his final depiction of the long-suffering laborer.

From Hogarth, Gainsborough had learned important lessons about how to make "ironic and academically inappropriate pictorial cross-references," and he would have been familiar, Rosenthal notes, with Hogarth's own satiric representations of Actaeon-as-cuckold.[69] Yet the suggestion of horns Gainsborough has provided his woodman in *Peasant Smoking*, it seems to me, stands less as a joke at his character's expense in the Hogarthian model than as a knowing Sternean nod toward the importance, even in our most earnest expressions of ideality, of refusing to pledge full allegiance to our favorite fantasies—of remembering that "there is nothing unmixt in this world" (*ASJ*, 116; and see New's note). Gainsborough's clever allusion to *Diana and Actaeon* thus colors the redemptive implications of *Peasant Smoking*, but it does not cancel them out, anymore than "A Case of Delicacy" nullifies "The Grace." Gainsborough's "ironic strategy" instead invites us to consider the ways that each painting both complicates and enhances the other: if the happy laborer recalls the doomed Actaeon by entering a feminine realm to which he can never fully belong, so too does Actaeon, who courts disaster in the form of an outstretched hand, become a version of the laborer seeking final communion.[70] Sterne knew something about the joys of community and the dangers of outstretched hands, the dangers of community and the joys of outstretched hands. I like to think he would have gotten Gainsborough's joke—and recognized that it was not one.

NOTES

1. *Laurence Sterne: The Letters*, ed. Melvyn New and Peter de Voogd, vols. 7 and 8 of the Florida Edition of the Works of Laurence Sterne (Gainesville: University Press of Florida, 2009), 8:633–34; hereafter cited in the text.

2. *A Sentimental Journey through France and Italy and Continuation of the Bramine's Journal: The Text and Notes*, ed. Melvyn New and W. G. Day, vol. 6 of the Florida Edition of the Works of Laurence Sterne (Gainesville: University Press of Florida, 2002), 158, 159; hereafter cited in the text as *ASJ* followed by the page number.

3. Melvyn New, *Tristram Shandy: A Book for Free Spirits* (New York: Twayne, 1994), 111.

4. Melvyn New, "Job's Wife and Sterne's Other Women," in *Out of Bounds: Male Writers and Gendere(ed) Criticism*, ed. Laura Claridge and Elizabeth Langland (Amherst: University of Massachusetts Press, 1990), 69.

5. Leslie Stephen, *Hours in a Library* (London: Smith Elder, 1907), 4:70; quoted in Ernest Nevin Dilworth, *The Unsentimental Journey of Laurence Sterne* (New York: Octagon Books, 1969), 8.

6. Elizabeth Kraft, *Laurence Sterne Revisited* (New York: Twayne, 1996), 106, 128.

7. Melvyn New, "Laurence Sterne," in *The Cambridge Companion to English Novelists*, ed. Adrian Poole (Cambridge: Cambridge University Press, 2009), 68.

8. Melvyn New, *Laurence Sterne as Satirist: A Reading of "Tristram Shandy"* (Gainesville: University of Florida Press, 1969), 203.

9. New, "Laurence Sterne," 68.

10. "It was a daring thing," Virginia Woolf recognized in her preface to *ASJ* (London: Oxford University Press, 1928), "for a clergyman to perceive a relationship between religion and pleasure" (xvi).

11. New, "Laurence Sterne," 68

12. Gainsborough's painting of his dog Tristram may be found in Michael Rosenthal and Martin Myrone, ed., *Thomas Gainsborough: 1727–1788* (London: Henry N. Adams, 2002), 202. The dog, Rosenthal and Myrone explain, "meant a great deal to Gainsborough and his wife."

13. Wilbur L. Cross, *The Life and Times of Laurence Sterne* (New York: Macmillan, 1909), 341.

14. See Arthur H. Cash, *Laurence Sterne: The Early and Middle Years* (London: Methuen, 1975), 314.

15. Even in the 1909 edition, Cross admits that "the portrait has never been quite identified" (341).

16. John Hayes, ed., *The Letters of Thomas Gainsborough* (New Haven: Yale University Press, 2001), xx; hereafter cited in the text.

17. William Jackson, "Character of Gainsborough," in *The Four Ages* (1798; Bristol: Thoemmes, 1998), 160. This passage is quoted in Amal Asfour and Paul Williamson, "Gainsborough's Wit," *Journal of the History of Ideas* 58, no. 3 (1997): 479.

18. Hayes dates this letter as "probably February 1770" (*Letters*, 71).

19. Hayes, *Letters*, xix.

20. Ronald Paulson, *Emblem and Expression: Meaning in English Art of the Eighteenth Century* (London: Thames and Hudson, 1975), 230.

21. Asfour and Williamson, "Gainsborough's Wit," 486.

22. Michael Rosenthal, *The Art of Thomas Gainsborough* (New Haven: Yale University Press, 1999), 234; Rosenthal and Myrone, *Thomas Gainsborough*, 180.

23. Rosenthal, *The Art of Thomas Gainsborough*, 40; Paulson, *Emblems and Expression*, 230.

24. Quoted in Jack Lindsay, *Thomas Gainsborough: His Life and Art* (New York: Universe Books, 1980), 78.

25. Ann Bermingham, introduction to *Sensation and Sensibility: Viewing Gainsborough's "Cottage Door"* (New Haven: Yale University Press, 2005), 14, 15. It is worth recalling Samuel Johnson's famous mistake in reference to Sterne's conspicuously artificial antinovel: "nothing odd will do long."

26. Rosenthal, *The Art of Thomas Gainsborough*, 240.

27. Bermingham, introduction, to *Sensation and Sensibility,* 1.

28. Rosenthal, *The Art of Thomas Gainsborough*, 204. The quotation from Sterne is on 203–4.

29. Cf. Bermingham's description of Gainsborough's method, whereby "the sensibility of the artist invites the sensibility of the viewer to participate in creating a work of art" (introduction to *Sensation and Sensibility*, 16).

30. Bermingham, introduction to *Sensation and Sensibility*, 1.

31. I am quoting from the edition included in the Florida edition of *ASJ*, 202–3.

32. Quoted in Bermingham, introduction to *Sensation and Sensibility*, 9.

33. Ibid., 9. The above quotations are often cited in studies of Gainsborough, but I borrow heavily from Bermingham's introduction to *Sensation and Sensibility*, 9, in this particular paragraph.

34. Lindsay, *Thomas Gainsborough: His Life and Art*, 171.

35. Anne Birmingham, *Landscape and Ideology: The English Rustic Tradition, 1740–1860* (Berkeley: University of California Press, 1986), 44; Lindsay, *Thomas Gainsborough: His Life and Art*, 171.

36. Amal Asfour and Paul Williamson, *Gainsborough's Vision* (Liverpool: Liverpool University Press, 1999), 186.

37. John Barrell, *The Dark Side of the Landscape: The Rural Poor in English Painting, 1730–1840* (New York: Cambridge University Press, 1980), 70, 69–70, 72.

38. Ibid., 71.

39. Ibid., 72.

40. Amal Asfour and Paul Williamson, "Gainsborough's Cottage-door Scenes: Aesthetic Principles, Moral Values," in *Sensation and Sensibility*, 116.

41. John Barrell, "Spectacles for Republicans," in *Sensation and Sensibility*, 53.

42. Michael Rosenthal, "Gainsborough's Cottage Doors: A Matter of Modernity," in *Sensation and Sensibility*, 83.

43. I am quoting from Asfour and Williamson, "Gainsborough's Cottage-door Scenes," 116, but the artist himself ably captures the unease of the Gainsborough household in a series of letters to his sister, Mary Gibbon, written in the mid-1770s (Asfour and Williamson quote from these letters as well). On 26 December 1775, Gainsborough asks rhetorically, "if I tell you my wife is weak but good, and never much formed to humour my Happiness, what can you do to alter her? If I complain that Peggy is a sensible good Girl, but Insolent and proud in her behavior to me at times, can you make your arm long enough to box her ears for me whilst you live at Bath?" (130). In June 1776, he relates a telling anecdote:

> My present Situation is that of being as much encouraged as the World can bestow, with every success in my business, but in the other scale, counteracted with disobedience Pride and insolence, and eternal Obraidings & reflections—I was induced to try how far Jealousy might be cured by giving into her Hands every Farthing of the Money as I earn'd it, but very soon found th[at] (as a punishment for so unmanly a condescention) instead of convincing, it was a further incouragement to Govern me, and invert the order of Nature in making the Head the foot and the foot the Head. (131)

It is important to note that Gainsborough's perceptions of his domestic situation are hardly "fair and balanced"—he was without question a frustratingly impecunious man, one who was also, as he bragged to John Henderson in a letter on 27 June 1773, "deeply read in petticoats" (116).

44. Smart's poem reads: "Good—from Jehudah's genuine vein, / From God's best nature, good in grain, / His aspect and his heart: / To pity, to forgive, to save, / Witness En-gedi's conscious cave, / And Shimei's blunted dart" (ll. 43–48).

45. Bermingham, *Landscape and Ideology*, 42.

46. John Hayes, *The Landscape Paintings of Thomas Gainsborough* (Ithaca: Cornell University Press, 1982), 155.

47. Malcolm Cormack, *The Paintings of Thomas Gainsborough* (Cambridge: Cambridge University Press, 1991), 132.

48. Asfour and Williamson, "Gainsborough's Cottage-door Scenes," 98, 97.

49. Nicola Kalinsky, *Gainsborough* (London: Phaidon Press, 1995), 96.

50. Asfour and Williamson, "Gainsborough's Cottage-door Scenes," 100.

51. Ibid., 101.

52. Rosenthal, "Gainsborough's Cottage Doors," 87.

53. Of particular interest in this respect is Gainsborough's *The Woodman,* now lost, which the painter completed just before his death in 1788; in it, as Peter Simon's engraving of 1791 suggests, the woodman is utterly alone and seemingly happy.

54. And not without some intellectual effort on Gainsborough's part—Lindsay notes of *Peasant Smoking* that "a study shows that at first the main figure was to be a woodman with a burden of faggots; but instead of showing the man at his toil Gainsborough decided on the moment of happy relaxation" (195).

55. Rosenthal, "Gainsborough's Cottage Doors," 87.

56. Cormack, *The Paintings of Thomas Gainsborough*, 180.

57. Barrell, "Spectacles for Republicans," 53.

58. Asfour and Williamson, "Gainsborough's Cottage-door Scenes," 109, 113.

59. Ibid., 116 and 119.

60. As we shall see, the sequence in the case of Gainsborough is reversed—*Peasant Smoking* was completed after the "quick turn" in question. The effect, I suggest, is nevertheless largely the same.

61. Jackson, "Character of Gainsborough," 159, 179.

62. Paulson, *Emblems and Expression*, 224, suggests that Gainsborough was likely working from Addison's 1717 translation of this section of *Metamorphoses*. I am quoting from the nineteenth-century American edition (New York: Harper & Brothers), book 3, lines 251–52; hereafter cited by line number in the text.

63. Asfour and Williamson, *Gainsborough's Vision*, 228.

64. I am simply not sure what it means to claim, as Kalinksy does, that "there is nothing indicative here of impending tragedy, even though Actaeon has already grown horns" (124).

65. Bermingham, *Landscape and Ideology*, 46–49; Michael Rosenthal, "Gainsborough's *Diana and Actaeon*," in *Painting and the Politics of Culture: New Essays on British Art, 1700–1850*, ed. John Barrell (New York: Oxford University Press, 1992), 172; Asfour and Williamson, *Gainsborough's Vision*, 228.

66. Hugh Belsey, *Gainsborough at Gainsborough's House* (London: Paul Holberton, 2002), 71.

67. Hayes, *Landscape Paintings*, 178.

68. I am borrowing Ovid's description (as translated by Addison) of the suddenly transformed Actaeon (262).

69. Rosenthal, "Gainsborough's *Diana and Actaeon*," 184, 181.

70. Cf. Asfour and Williamson's sense that "The gentleness of Diana's pose [is] more inviting than angered," and that the moment captured by the painting is "a holy occasion, a beatific moment in which water acts as a medium for a spiritual transformation" (*Gainsborough's Vision*, 228).

Chapter Three

Johnson and Moral Argument: "We talked of the casuistical question. . ."

Robert G. Walker

Samuel Johnson's relationship to casuistry is a knotty issue. One may certainly find evidence that his view of casuistry is quite contemporary and identify it with that of the self-proclaimed casuist Nigrinus in *Rambler* 10, who describes himself as "a man grown grey in the study of those noble arts, by which right and wrong may be confounded; by which reason may be blinded, when we have a mind to escape from her inspection."[1] The casuist is criticized in a more serious context in *Rambler* 114, Johnson's powerful argument against the widespread use of capital punishment: "Whatever may be urged by casuists or politicians, the greater part of mankind, as they can never think that to pick the pocket and to pierce the heart is equally criminal, will scarcely believe that two malefactors so different in guilt can be justly doomed to the same punishment" (4:245). Johnson advocates a simple, straightforward, Occam's razor approach to modes of expression in *Idler* 36, telling us "to find the nearest way from truth to truth, or from purpose to effect, not to use more instruments where fewer will be sufficient, not to move by wheels and levers what will give way to the naked hand,"[2] so when he picks up this thread again in *Idler* 70, the casuist is already suspect for unnecessary complication: "In morality it is one thing to discuss the niceties of the casuist, and another to direct the practice of common life. . . . [I]f he, who has nothing to do but to be honest by the shortest way, will perplex his mind with subtile speculations . . . the writers whom [he] shall consult are very little to be blamed, tho' it should sometimes happen that they are read in vain" (220). Were all, or even most, of the other appearances of casuistry in Johnson (and James Boswell's writing about Johnson) of this ilk, there would be no issue. But they are not and there is.

A GOOD CASUIST

To start to untie the knot I begin with Johnson's definition: both the first and fourth editions of his *Dictionary* define *casuistry* as "the science of a casuist; the doctrine of cases of conscience." Two illustrative quotations follow, both from Pope, one of which is clearly pejorative. When Johnson defines *casuist* he expands the root meaning a bit: "one that studies and settles cases of conscience." Here one of three illustrative quotations is pejorative. Johnson's definitions are neutral and his illustrative quotations are balanced between attitudes critical and not critical. The *OED* cites "sophistry" as a synonym and includes in its definition, "Often (and perhaps originally) applied to a quibbling or evasive way of dealing with difficult cases of duty" (s.v. "casuistry"). G. A. Starr properly felt the need in 1971 to rescue the reputation of the term so that its influence on Defoe's fiction could be examined: "Today casuistry tends to be regarded as at best ludicrous, at worst sinister: one must therefore stress at the outset that for all its abuses, casuistry also has its uses, and that moralists have long recognized its potentialities for good as well as evil. In the *Rambler* Johnson acknowledges that casuistry is 'useful in proper hands,' even though it 'ought by no means to be carelessly exposed, since most will use it rather to lull than awaken their own consciences.'"[3] Perhaps the most extensive recent rehabilitation attempt, this time in the realm of ethics rather than literary studies, is the 1988 work by Albert R. Jonsen and Stephen Toulmin, *The Abuse of Casuistry: A History of Moral Reasoning*, which inspired this essay.

While I do not intend to argue that Samuel Johnson's view of casuistry was invariably favorable, I will suggest that his view was as favorable, overall, as that of any prominent thinker since Blaise Pascal's series of tracts, *Les Lettres Provinciales*, begun in 1656, supposedly "demolished the reputation of casuistry for all subsequent generations."[4] Moreover, if we start from this premise, we discover that the tradition of casuistical argument thoroughly imbues many of our favorite "Johnsonian" passages in ways not hitherto pointed out. That contemporary Johnson scholars need to be reminded—if not informed—of the role the tradition of casuistry played in both the content and the form of Johnson's thought is suggested by several recent comments by Nicholas Hudson and Blanford Parker. Hudson sees Johnson following in the footsteps of Matthew Hale, Isaac Watts, and others who argued that charity should be regulated primarily by common sense and that one should, as Hale put it, eschew consulting "with this or that philosopher, schoolman or casuist." He places Johnson among eighteenth-century Englishmen who "energetically assailed" the casuists of the Roman Catholic Church for "the study of problematic issues of conscience" they undertook. Parker concurs: "Pope and his contemporaries share with Johnson a mistrust of metaphysics and theological casuistry."[5] In light of such bald claims, it is well worth recalling the words of Thomas Tyers, one of Johnson's very first biographers, writing for the *Gentleman's Magazine* in December 1784, the month of Johnson's death: "Johnson's advice was consulted on all occasions. He was known to be a good casuist, and therefore had many cases for his judgment."[6] The man who had defined *casuist* as "one that studies and settles cases of conscience" would not have been disturbed in the least by this epithet.

THE CASUISTRY OF LYING

A cartoon in a recent *Wall Street Journal* depicts an assistant interrupting a board meeting and whispering to the person at the head of the table, "Your parole officer is on the phone. Are you in?" The conspicuous corporate chicanery of our times is the obvious occasion for the cartoon, but some of the humor rests also in the implicit contrast between felonious behavior on the one hand and socially acceptable little white lies on the other. "What would Sam Johnson do?" is a question that rarely seems to occur to today's CEO, but we can certainly ask it, and an answer is not far to seek. In the first months of his friendship with Johnson, James Boswell describes the two garrets over Johnson's residence at No. 1, Inner Temple Lane, which served as Johnson's library, chemical laboratory, and hideout. (His living quarters were on the first floor and the garrets up "four pairs of stairs.") Boswell writes,

> Johnson told me, that he went up thither without mentioning it to his servant, when he wanted to study, secure from interruption; for he would not allow his servant to say he was not at home when he really was. "A servant's strict regard for truth, (said he) must be weakened by such a practice. A philosopher may know that it is merely a form of denial; but few servants are such nice distinguishers. If I accustom a servant to tell a lie for *me*, have I not reason to apprehend that he will tell many lies for *himself*?"[7]

Boswell's view, that the "lie" is merely conventional language and harmless to all concerned, is the more modern one, but Johnson's view is far more interesting. The philosopher Johnson mentions could have been any one in a seemingly endless number of casuists debating the morality of lying.

Any attempt strictly to categorize the various subjects most commonly treated by casuistry would be futile, but not surprisingly, casuists often dealt with issues concerning mendacity. We could place the passage just cited in a category titled, "Whether a Servant may lawfully tell a Lye for his Master?" if we wished to quote the question in the words of Defoe's *Little Review*, 6 July

1705.[8] Or we could place it in a broader category of relationships between masters and servants, which, as late as 1841, Thomas De Quincey found the source of "many cases of conscience daily occurring in the common business of the world" and which required the master to make the tough choice between being truthful in giving a displaced servant no character reference, thus "consigning deliberately some young woman . . . to ruin," or being less than candid in providing a reference.[9] De Quincey writes this in an essay entitled by his later nineteenth-century editor, "The Casuistry of Duelling," which highlights the difficulty of categorizing the subject matter of casuistic discussions. When Jonsen and Toulmin selected three "cases" to examine in detail in their multicentury history of casuistry, they chose "the case of charging interest on loans, the case of equivocation under oath, and the case of defense of one's honor" (177). As we shall see, Johnson turns repeatedly to the casuistic tradition and method to discuss issues of truthfulness, sometimes related, as above, to specific social conventions, sometimes related to unacknowledged authorship, sometimes narrowly dealing with traditional casuistic definitions of truth and falsehood in the abstract. He also holds forth on casuistic topics as diverse as hiding accused criminals on the one hand and self-defense on the other, and his discussions frequently spill outside these arbitrary designations, much as De Quincey's was to do in the middle of the next century.

To discuss Johnson on lying is to run the risk of offering old wine in new bottles. It is difficult to think of a topic on which the Anecdotal Johnson is better known than lying, except perhaps dying. The locus classicus may be Johnson's characterizing Warburton's use of "lie" to describe an inaccurate note, as simply an example of Warburton's "warm language"; Boswell, who wanted a condemnation, opines,

> The language is *warm* indeed; and, I must own, cannot be justified in consistency with a decent regard to the established forms of speech. Johnson had accustomed himself to use the word *lie*, to express a mistake or an errour in relation; in short, when the *thing was not so as told*, though the relator did not *mean* to deceive. When he thought there was intentional falsehood in the relator, his expression was, "He *lies*, and he *knows* he *lies*." (*Life*, 4:49)

Boswell is uncomfortable, of course, with Johnson's and Warburton's use of a word implying immoral behavior for what may be an amoral mistake. Contrast the following passage in which Boswell describes Johnson being put on the spot by the author of a translation of *Carmen Seculare* of Horace:

> When Johnson had done reading, the authour asked him bluntly, "If upon the whole it was a good translation?" Johnson, whose regard for truth was uncommonly strict, seemed to be puzzled for a moment, what answer to make, as he

certainly could not honestly commend the performance: with exquisite address he evaded the question thus, "Sir, I do not say that it may not be made a very good translation." Here nothing whatever in favour of the performance was affirmed, and yet the writer was not shocked. (*Life*, 3:373–74)

This typical response is the stuff of the casuistry texts Johnson knew and had thoroughly incorporated into his thinking and behavior.

In the *Abuse of Casuistry* Jonsen and Toulmin devote a chapter to "Perjury: The Case of Equivocation," and, in the course of their broad survey, make several findings that are especially appropriate to the tradition Johnson knew and reflected. St. Augustine took the very hard line that lying could never be morally justified, even in the case of protecting from authorities an innocent man, unjustly condemned, who is hiding in your house. He went on to "distinguish eight species of lying as varying in gravity," as Jonsen and Toulmin explain: "The degree of sinfulness depended on the seriousness of the harm done by the deception and on whether the resulting benefits from the lie accrued to the deceiver himself or to some other party. The malice ranged from the most serious—namely, a lie that leads another to deny religious belief—to the least sinful—a lie that actually helps another without harming anyone but the teller" (196–97). Aquinas largely agreed with Augustine; however, he let the nose of the camel under the tent with this comment: "it is licit to hide the truth prudently by some sort of dissimulation" (197). Raymond of Pennafort distinguished three rather than eight types of lies ("the 'pernicious' lie harms someone without even bringing any benefit to the liar; the 'officious,' or dutiful lie benefits someone other than the liar; the 'jocose' lie does no harm to anyone"), but all were sinful since "the malice of a lie depended not on its consequences but on the very discrepancy between what is in the mind and what is uttered" (197). Various types of behavior began to be discussed and sometimes recommended as ways to avoid sin while not disclosing the information sought by a questioner; these included silence, distracting the questioner, responding in equivocal words, and, most controversial of all, responding with mental restriction.

Mental restriction (or mental reservation, as it was often termed in the eighteenth century) began with the concept that sometimes one was not obliged to answer a question in accord with the questioner's intent, so long as the communication between the responder and God was truthful. Of course, God knows our thoughts, so one could indeed say one (false) thing while thinking another (true) thing. Examples from an early sixteenth-century text suggest this is not so obviously disreputable as a bald explanation implies: "If someone seeking to kill another person asks you, 'did he go this way?' you may answer, 'no, not this way,' meaning 'his feet did not tread the very ground you are pointing at.' If asked about something you are obliged to keep secret, you may say, 'I do not know,' understanding in your mind (*subintelligendo*) 'so that it may be revealed to you.'" But the same source cautions against unwarranted use of this ploy: "it cannot be used in a law court before an authorized judge nor when the questioned person is bound to answer truthfully to a lawful superior" (198). A major backdrop here is the importance of protecting the secrecy of the Roman Catholic confessional, but truth-telling versus preserving a secret remained an issue in Johnson's day in Anglican England. So too was the status of the questioner. Whether or not he had a right to ask his question could determine whether or not one was morally obliged to answer truthfully. This latter point was later formally enunciated by Hugo Grotius—"the obligation to tell the truth was correlative to the right of the questioner to know the truth" (211). Of broad mental restriction, Jonsen and Toulmin point out, "in its simplest form, this kind of dissimulation reflects certain conventions of common speech. 'Is your husband at home?' asks the unwelcome caller. . . . The answer, 'no (not for you)' was, suggested the casuists, understood by people at large" (202). But it was an answer that Johnson did not endorse in this context, as we have already seen.

What Johnson did endorse were many of the typical casuistic subtleties, especially for purposes of evaluating achievement and determining authorship. What Boswell interprets as a momentary puzzlement when the translator of *Carmen Seculare* requests a literary judgment could just as well have been Johnson's weighing the advisability of delivering a rebuke in this social setting to an impertinent questioner. Elsewhere Johnson explained the nuances: "There is a great difference between what is said without our being urged to it, and what is said from a kind of compulsion. If I praise a man's book without being asked my opinion of it, that is honest praise, to which one may trust. But if an authour asks me if I like his book, and I give him something like praise, it must not be taken as my real opinion" (*Life*, 2:50–51). Johnson as literary arbiter is hardly in so difficult a position as a Catholic priest protecting the sanctity of the confessional from officers of the Inquisition, or an English Catholic of the mid-sixteenth century forced to come to terms with the Act of Supremacy (1559) and the behaviors it mandated, or an Anglican of the mid-seventeenth century compelled to negotiate the Puritan Parliament's Engagement Oath, but his choice of language ("a kind of compulsion") suggests a similar seriousness. He was not given to hyperbole but found it natural when dealing with cases of conscience in the area of truth or falsehood. After complaining of the lack of propriety of being shown another translation of Horace, this one by "a young Miss," or the young Miss's mother ("Nobody has a right to put another under such a difficulty, that he must either hurt the person by telling the truth, or hurt himself by telling what is not true"), Johnson continues, "Therefore a man, who is asked by an authour, what he thinks of his work, is *put to the torture* [my emphasis], and is not obliged to speak the truth." Johnson sees a further moral complication in giving a literary opinion of a manuscript and determines it, as a good casuist would, in the direction of doing the least harm to another: "Yet I consider it as a very difficult question in conscience, whether one should advise a man not to publish a work, if profit be his object; for the man may say, 'Had it not been for you, I should have had the money.' Now you cannot be sure; for you have only your own opinion, and the publick may think very differently." When Sir Joshua Reynolds somewhat misses the point and suggests "two judgements; one as to the real value of the work, the other as to what may please the general taste at the time," Johnson answers, "But you can be *sure* of neither; and therefore I should scruple much to give a suppressive vote" (*Life*, 3:319–20).

In an age when some publications were anonymous and others joint ventures, moral issues appeared to Johnson not only in the evaluation of texts but also in the attribution of them. Reynolds tells us, "I once inadvertently put [Johnson] in a situation from which none but a man of perfect integrity could extricate himself. I pointed at some lines in the *Traveller* which I told him I was sure he wrote. He hesitated a little; during this hesitation I recollected myself, that as I knew he would not lye I put him in a cleft stick, and should have had but my due if he had given me a rough answer."[10] Reynolds is aware he has asked a question without having the right to do so and his phrase, "put him in a cleft stick," nicely sums up the position the responder frequently occupies, not just being in a dangerous or tricky place but caught between choices. Fortunately, the situation allowed Johnson to answer specifically and directly and still not harm his friend Goldsmith. Johnson was reputed to have written the entire poem for his (then) unknown friend, so his response to Reynolds was in a sense a defense of Goldsmith: "Sir, I did not write them, but that you may not imagine that I have wrote more than I really have, the utmost I have wrote in that poem, to the best of my recollection, is not more than eighteen lines" (*Life*, 2:6n3).

Reynolds values more highly the intricacies of the casuistic tradition than does Boswell, whose view seems predictably more modern. A subtle sign of this different view occurs in the rendering of the confrontation between Johnson and Donald M'Queen over the authenticity of the works of Ossian. Boswell indeed states that M'Queen had always "evaded" the point of authenticity, but after Johnson challenges M'Queen—"M'Pherson's is not a translation from ancient poetry. You do not believe it. I say before you, you do not believe it, though you are very willing that the world should believe it"—Boswell writes simply, "Mr. M'Queen made no answer to this" (*Life*, 5:240). Johnson's version in his *Journey to the Western Islands of Scotland* seems at first almost identical: "I asked a very learned minister in Sky, who had used all arts to make me believe the genuineness of the book, whether at last he believed it himself? but he would not answer. He wished me to be deceived, for the honour of his country; but would not directly and formally deceive me. Yet has this man's testimony been publickly produced, as of one that held *Fingal* to be the work of Ossian."[11] Johnson carefully establishes his right to ask the question, both because he has been imposed on by M'Queen's "arts" and because M'Queen's opinion has moved into the realm of public "testimony." Here, then, M'Queen's silence will not pass as a tool to avoid lying while at the same time continuing to deceive.

Boswell's more modern view of casuistry shows up as well when he writes about the "Bathurst" *Adventurer* essays. Mrs. Williams has told Boswell that "as [Johnson] had *given* those essays to Dr. Bathurst, who sold them at two guineas each, he never would own them; nay, he used to say he did not *write* them: but the fact was, that he *dictated* them, while Bathurst wrote." Boswell tells us, "I read to him Mrs. Williams's account; he smiled, and said nothing." Boswell seems perturbed by the italicized equivocation and may miss entirely the pun that Johnson surely intended on *own*, for he continues, "I am not quite satisfied with the casuistry by which the productions of one person are thus passed upon the world for the productions of another" (*Life*, 1:254). There follows Boswell's lengthy analogy between children and literary works, with mention of the selling of a Scottish chieftainship and Esau's birthright. This seems rather unconvincing and dull when compared to Johnson's witty, albeit casuistic, statement to Mrs. Williams. Mrs. Williams, by the way, seems to have a bit of the equivocal strain in her as well, as Boswell found out when he questioned her about whether Johnson had written a poem on the death of Stephen Grey: "Sir, (said she, with some warmth,) I wrote that poem before I had the honour of Dr. Johnson's acquaintance." Boswell attempts to verify her statement with Johnson, who answers, "It is true, Sir, that she wrote it before she was acquainted with me; but she has not told you that I wrote it all over again, except two lines" (*Life*, 2:26).

At times the epigrammatic excellence of Johnson can overshadow the surrounding casuistic environment. All students of literature are familiar with the quotation, "Depend upon it, Sir, when a man knows he is to be hanged in a fortnight, it concentrates his mind wonderfully." What may escape us are the threads of casuistry that encircle it. When Johnson disapproves of Dr. Dodd's implicitly claiming authorship of the originating text, "The Convict's Address to his unhappy Brethren," Boswell calls him on it: "But, Sir, . . . you contributed to the deception; for when Mr. Seward expressed a doubt to you that it was not Dodd's own, because it had a great deal more force of mind in it than any thing known to be his, you answered, —'Why should you think so? Depend upon it, Sir . . . '" (*Life*, 3:167). Johnson defends himself first with an argument similar to those used by priests asked to violate the vow of secrecy of the confessional: "Sir, as Dodd got it from me to pass as his own, . . . there was an *implied promise* that I should not own it. To own it, therefore, would have been telling a lie, with the addition of breach of promise, which was worse than simply telling a lie to make it be believed it was Dodd's." He concludes by referring to his manner of diverting the questioner: "Besides, Sir, I did not *directly* tell a lie; I left the matter uncertain" (*Life*, 3:167).

Before leaving the area of attribution, let us consider an instance in the arena of anonymous work. Boswell quotes Johnson on the identity of Junius: "I should have believed Burke to be Junius, because I know no man but Burke who is capable of writing these letters; but Burke spontaneously denied it to me. The case would have been different had I asked him if he was the authour; a man so questioned, as to an anonymous publication, may think he has a right to deny it" (*Life*, 3:376–77). We see the implicit reference to the license to lie under certain types of questioning, although Johnson's "may think" may be telling. We have seen that he preferred other casuistic tools like equivocation or silence. G. B. Hill's note to this passage points toward a recent literary precursor to the "right" Johnson alludes to, namely, Swift's witty defense against Bettesworth. Johnson covers the issue in his "Life of Swift." Swift had satirized the lawyer Bettesworth in four lines of a poem on the Presbyterians in the *Gentleman's Magazine* in 1733. The satire was effective, says Johnson, bringing the lawyer "from very considerable reputation . . . into immediate and universal contempt. Bettesworth . . . went to Swift and demanded whether he was the author of that poem." Swift's answer (as rendered by Johnson) deserves to be quoted at length: "Mr. Bettesworth, . . . I was in my youth acquainted with great lawyers, who, knowing my disposition to satire, advised me, that, if any scoundrel or blockhead whom I had lampooned should ask, 'Are you the author of this paper?' I should tell him that I was not the author; and therefore I tell you, Mr. Bettesworth, that I am not the author of these lines."[12] Swift employs a modified version of a paradox of Eubulides, the self-referential liar, so that his answer will be the same (a denial) regardless of whether or not he was the author. Adding to the delight is that the modification is in the form of legal advice, repeated to "a lawyer eminent for his insolence to the clergy," as Johnson has just put it.

The ninth commandment, "Thou shalt not bear false witness against thy neighbour," is Johnson's text for Sermon 17, which the Yale editors note "combines legal argument and homiletical eloquence." Johnson "deals only briefly with perjury and concentrates his attack on the defamation of which men in society are guilty every day."[13] I hope it is not Zoilistic to suggest that casuistic rather than legal argument is the mode of the sermon, in both the earlier section on perjury and the later one on defamation. The casuist's tendency to categorize is everywhere present, as is the tendency to evaluate the degree of evil in an act by tracing its consequences. Thus a person committing perjury in a literal sense by making false statements under oath in a court of law, "by which the life of an innocent man is taken away, the rightful owner stripped of his possessions, or an oppressour supported in his usurpations," has committed "a crime that includes robbery and murder" (*Sermons*, 182). The inventor and propagator of a defamatory falsehood cannot vindicate himself by alleging that he spread a partial truth: "a calumny, in which falsehood is complicated with truth, and malice is assisted by probability, is more dangerous, but therefore less innocent, than unmixed forgery, and groundless invectives" (184). Ignorance of the falsity of the report one spreads is no excuse, although when we are ourselves deceived by the lie, there is a mitigation: he "who is deceived himself, cannot be accused of deceiving others, and is only so far blameable, as he contributed to the dishonour or prejudice of another, by spreading his faults without any just occasion, or lawful cause. . . . The crime indeed doth not fall under the head of calumny, but only differs from it in the falsehood, not in the malice" (185). Exactly what would constitute a just occasion or lawful cause under which one might properly spread another's faults is an issue Johnson does not specify here, but we shall see him address it later in a very problematic context.

As a final point on Johnson's view of the casuistry of lying, let us recall the classification of lies begun by St. Augustine thirteen hundred years earlier and recounted above. Johnson apparently was working with this idea "jocularly" when he spoke of the license allowable to historians: "There are . . . inexcusable lies, and consecrated lies. For instance, we are told that on the arrival of the news of the unfortunate battle of Fontenoy, every heart beat, and every eye was in tears. Now we know that no man eat his dinner the worse, but there *should* have been all this concern; and to say there *was*, (smiling) may be reckoned a consecrated lie" (*Life*, 1:355). In *Adventurer* 50, devoted entirely to the topic of lying, Johnson puts himself into the casuistic tradition, tongue-in-cheek at first but ultimately to a serious moral purpose: "The casuists have very diligently distinguished lyes into their several classes, according to their various degrees of malignity: but they have, I think, generally omitted that which is most common, and, perhaps, not least mischievous; which, since the moralists have not given it a name, I shall distinguish as the Lye of Vanity." Since "suspicion is always watchful over the practices of interest," most other common lies (for example, "the lye of commerce . . . and the lye of malice") are much more easily detected than the lie of vanity, designed merely for self-exaltation (363).

CASES CONSIDERED

Johnson enjoyed Swift's wit at the lawyer's expense, as we still do today, and his extensive interest in the law was well known, if not well documented, before the publication in 1951 of E. L. McAdam's *Dr. Johnson and the English Law*. Nevertheless, we err if we assume that he refers primarily to a case of law when he uses an expression like "the case would have been different," as he did in the Junius discussion. Jonsen and Toulmin write, "The medieval term for what we call casuistry was 'cases of conscience' (*casus conscientiae*)" (127), and Johnson defined it exactly that way in his *Dictionary* in 1755. I suggest that when Johnson uses the word *case* he recalls more often a casuistic discipline than a legal one. That this presents itself in his periodical essays is not surprising in view of the previous century's progenitor, John Dunton's *Athenian Mercury*, with its original subtitle of "Casuisticall Mercury, resolving all the most nice and curious questions proposed by the ingenious of either sex."[14] Hymenaeus writes to the Rambler, "[I] will lay my case honestly before you, that you or your readers may at length decide it," thus prefacing his detailed narration of failures in courtship (*Rambler* 113, 4:237). In another instance, Myrtilla, at age sixteen years and ten weeks, writes to complain of the "tyranny" of her aunt-governess: "I shall therefore lay my case before you, and hope by your decision to be set free from unreasonable restraints." We smile along with the Rambler, who does not respond, despite Myrtilla's urgent reminder in a postscript: "Remember I am past sixteen" (*Rambler* 84, 4:76–77, 81).[15]

Rambler 81 displays a debt to the casuistic tradition expressed more seriously. The initial topic is "the precedency or superior excellence of one virtue to another," which leads Johnson to the Golden Rule: "Whatsoever ye would that men should do unto you, even so do unto them" (4:60–61). Johnson examines several arguments that have been advanced to suggest that this rule is not so absolute and all-encompassing as its proponents, including Johnson himself, claim: "One of the most celebrated cases which have been produced as requiring some skill in the direction of conscience to adapt them to this great rule, is that of a criminal asking mercy of his judge, who cannot but know that if he was in the state of the supplicant, he should desire that pardon which he now denies" (4:62). Although Johnson does not specify that the criminal is accused of a capital offense, that would make the case most challenging, for the judge could be seen as potentially in conflict with the fifth commandment as well as the Golden Rule. As I mentioned earlier, Johnson was a vigorous opponent of the widespread application of capital punishment in eighteenth-century England, but here he seems to imply support for it under certain circumstances, and by means of familiar casuistic arguments. In discussions of capital cases, the judge was frequently said to be society's sword or instrument of justice, and thus not individually and personally responsible for taking another life. Moreover, the potential harm to society from lack of enforcement was held up as a deterrent to inappropriate leniency. Both ideas appear in Johnson's explanation:

> The difficulty of this sophism [that is, the judge's refusing to grant the mercy he would seek in the criminal's position] will vanish, if we remember that the parties are, in reality, on one side the criminal, and on the other the community of which the magistrate is only the minister, and by which he is intrusted with the publick safety. The magistrate therefore, in pardoning a man unworthy of pardon, betrays the trust with which he is invested, gives away what is not his own, and, apparently, does to others what he would not that others should do to him. Even the community, whose right is still greater to arbitrary grants of mercy, is bound by those laws which regard the great republick of mankind, and cannot justify such forbearance as may promote wickedness, and lessen the general confidence and security in which all have an equal interest, and which all are therefore bound to maintain. For this reason the state has not a right to erect a general sanctuary for fugitives, or give protection to such as have forfeited their lives by crimes against the laws of common morality equally acknowledged by all nations. (4:62)

How firmly Johnson is working in the casuistic tradition becomes even clearer when he discusses another possible objection to the precedence accorded "this great rule": "One occasion of uncertainty and hesitation, in those by whom this great rule has been commented and dilated, is the confusion of what the exacter casuists are careful to distinguish, 'debts of justice,' and 'debts of charity.'" Of these two categories the Golden Rule applies primarily and unquestionably to the former, Johnson continues, but "the discharge of the 'debts of charity,' or duties which we owe to others not merely as required by justice, but as dictated by benevolence, admits in its own nature greater complication of circumstances and greater latitude of choice." Johnson is seemingly willing to accept the distinctions of "exacter casuists," usually made in order to point out that failure to discharge a debt of justice was a sin with a tail (*peccatum caudatum*), that is, it required restoration or restitution. Failure to discharge a debt of charity did not, in part because of the "greater latitude of choice" it involved. The Golden Rule, then, is "not equally determinate and absolute with respect to offices of kindness, and acts of liberality, because liberality and kindness, absolutely determined, would lose their nature; for how could we be called tender, or charitable, for giving that which we are positively forbidden to withhold?" (4:63).

Johnson concludes the essay by cautioning those who would bend the Golden Rule back upon itself and use it as an excuse to act less charitably toward others than they otherwise might. Because of the inherent danger of underestimating what is due another, "it is safest for minds not oppressed with superstitious fears to determine against their own inclinations, and secure themselves from deficiency by doing more than they believe strictly necessary." In circumstances of uncertainty about how charitable one should be, the uncertainty must be resolved by applying the rule of *tutior via*: "it is surely the part of a wise man to err on the side of safety" (4:64).

THE CASUISTRY OF SECRETS AND SEX

Casuistry has much to say, then, concerning how to answer when one is questioned, when it is permissible to respond evasively, and what type of evasion is acceptable. But what does it have to say about volunteering information, especially when such information is entrusted as a secret or when such information might be seen as embarrassing or harmful? In his marvelous discussion of the laws of secrecy in *Rambler* 13, Johnson seems to suggest that casuistry may not be generally useful here even while he indicates an awareness of it: "I am not ignorant that many questions may be started relating to the duty of secrecy, where the affairs are of publick concern; where subsequent reasons may arise to alter the appearance and nature of the trust; that the manner in which the secret was told may change the degree of obligation; and that the principles upon which a man is chosen for a confident may not always equally constrain him." Any and all of these extenuating circumstances could, Johnson suggests, be employed by one who would violate the trust expected of the secret-keeper. But Johnson immediately counters these potentially effective distinctions by ones of his own: "But these scruples, if not too intricate, are of too extensive consideration for my present purpose, nor are they such as generally occur in common life; and though casuistical knowledge be useful in proper hands, yet it ought by no means to be carelessly exposed, since most will use it rather to lull than awaken their own consciences; and the threads of reasoning, on which truth is suspended, are frequently drawn to such subtility, that common eyes cannot perceive, and common sensibility cannot feel them" (3:72–73). Johnson mutes the metaphor of the Cartesian rationalist spinning his spider's web of specious argument from the waste of his entrails, for he does not wish to dismiss casuistry out of hand, as modern commentators frequently do. In fact, in his concluding paragraph, which is somewhat unusual among Johnson's periodic essays in that it actually does conclude most of the issues discussed earlier, Johnson proposes three specific rules concerning secrecy, much in the manner of a Renaissance casuist: "Never to solicit the knowledge of a secret. Not willingly, nor without many limitations, to accept such confidence when it is offered. When a secret is once admitted, to consider the trust as of a very high nature, important as society, and sacred as truth" (3:73).

Situations involving sexual impropriety were as difficult to weigh in Johnson's day as they are today, but for very different reasons. A circumstance very important in eighteenth-century England and virtually nonexistent today is the potentially disruptive effect of promiscuity on inheritance. Indeed, this is the backdrop of the two anecdotes that follow, each illustrating Johnson's working once again in a casuistic fashion. On Good Friday, 5 April 1776, after morning service at St. Clement's, Boswell and Johnson begin talking about Roman Catholicism and then prostitution. Boswell directs the conversation to a different but related topic: "I stated to him this case: — 'Suppose a man has a daughter, who he knows has been seduced, but her misfortune is concealed from the world: should he keep her in his house? Would he not, by doing so, be accessary to imposition? And, perhaps, a worthy, unsuspecting man might come and marry this woman, unless the father inform him of the truth.'" Johnson's answer, at first, is blunt and narrowly legalistic ("Sir, he is accessary to no imposition. His daughter is in his house; and if a man courts her, he takes his chance"), but then it broadens with additional circumstances: "If a friend, or, indeed, if any man asks his opinion whether he should marry her, he ought to advise him against it, without telling why, because his real opinion is then required." So silence or equivocation is not permitted in the face of direct questioning from someone with every right to ask the question, but a narrow response is allowed. Next Johnson moves to the possible moral impact of the father's actions on others within the family: "Or, if he has other daughters who know of her frailty, he ought not to keep her in his house." These circumstantial exceptions aside, Johnson's main argument favors the preservation of the secret: "You are to consider the state of life is this; we are to judge of one another's characters as well as we can; and a man is not bound, in honesty or honour, to tell us the faults of his daughter or of himself. A man who has debauched his friend's daughter is not obliged to say to every body—'Take care of me; don't let me into your houses without suspicion. I once debauched a friend's daughter: I may debauch yours'" (*Life*, 3:18). That we are under no moral compunction to incriminate ourselves is a consistent stance for Johnson. In Sermon 2 he writes, "No man is obliged to accuse himself of crimes, which are known to God alone" (*Sermons*, 20), and goes on to note that the auricular confession required by the Roman church is not essential for repentance in the Church of England.

So a guilty party is not required to accuse himself. But others may accuse, and, in fact, are morally obliged to do so under certain circumstances. When the topic of "making women do penance in the church for fornication" comes up during his travels to the Western Islands of Scotland, Johnson states flatly that this is right, but adds, "as soon as it is known. I would not be the man who would discover it, if I alone knew it, for a woman may reform; nor would I commend a parson who divulges a woman's first offense; but being once divulged, it ought to be infamous." Johnson states the reason as straightforwardly as can be: "Consider, of what importance to society the chastity of women is. Upon that all the property in the world depends" (*Life*, 5:208–9). Five years later in a three-way conversation among Boswell, Johnson, and Mrs. Thrale, Johnson continues to refine the circumstances that would dictate a violation of the laws of secrecy in sexual matters. Boswell suggests that Othello's remark that he was happy not knowing of his wife's infidelity is a "plausible" doctrine, but both Johnson and Mrs. Thrale disagree. Boswell asks Johnson, "Would you tell your friend to make him unhappy?" Johnson replies, "Perhaps, Sir, I should not; but that would be from prudence on my own account. A man would tell his father." Boswell and Mrs. Thrale continue by mentioning the implications for inheritance, and Johnson adds, "You would tell your friend of a woman's infamy, to prevent his marrying a whore: there is the same reason to tell him of his wife's infidelity, when he is married, to prevent the consequences of imposition" (*Life*, 3:347–48).

DUELING AND CASUISTRY

The morality of fighting a duel was a clear and present issue to Johnson, and this was one of two reasons we find him discoursing on the topic. Perhaps the last duel to be fought in Scotland occurred in 1822, thirty-eight years after Johnson's death, and provides an ironic footnote to the subject since Alexander Boswell, James Boswell's eldest son, lost his life therein. Further ironies include the victor's name (James Stuart), his politics (Whig), the cause of the dispute (a political satire penned by Alexander), and the result (Stuart was found not guilty by a unanimous jury). G. B. Hill glosses one of the discussions of dueling in Boswell's *Life* by quoting Horace Walpole's lament that in 1773 "the rage of duelling had of late much revived, especially in Ireland" (*Life*, 2:226n5). But more than the prevalence of dueling occasioned and informed Johnson's thought on the subject. Just as it did for De Quincey in 1841, the subject triggered in Johnson a vein of associated casuistic arguments that extended backward hundreds of years.[16]

Jonsen and Toulmin survey this topic (and its slightly broader variant of taking of a life in self-defense) in a chapter titled "Pride: The Case of the Insulted Gentlemen," and find that "the casus of 'killing for a slap' appeared in the history of casuistry for a brief moment, was entertained as a probable opinion, and quickly vanished" (216). Although this suggests more transience to the topic than it seems to have had, at least so far as Johnson's thought is concerned, their treatment usefully outlines the debate between the Judeo-Christian "absolute prohibition against killing of all kinds" and the Roman law principle that permitted "forceful defense against forceful aggression against one's body" (220). For our purposes, the details and nuances of the debate are highly significant. For example, St. Augustine shows a qualified acceptance of the taking of human life under specific circumstances, including "a soldier or a public official who is permitted to kill in the course of his duties," an idea he further developed within the context of the "just war."[17] Even though he decried vengeance as a motive for killing, Augustine "made room for legitimate self-defense" by speaking of motive (219). In his examination of self-defense, Aquinas introduced into moral literature the doctrine of the "double effect." Here is Jonsen and Toulmin's summary: "A single act . . . may have two effects, one of them intentional and the other going beyond intention. The moral quality of the act depends on the nature of the effect that was intended. Thus the two 'effects' of an act of killing in self-defense are the saving of one's own life and the death of the attacker. Self-defense is legitimate because the defender seeks to save his own life. This is in accord with natural law, in that each thing seeks to preserve itself in being" (221–22). Aquinas prefaced his argument with the text of Exodus 22:2 ("If a thief is found breaking in and is struck so that he dies, there shall be no murder; if the sun has risen on him, there will be murder"). Jonsen and Toulmin point out the long-standing association of this and similar texts to discussions of the morality of killing: "The rabbinic interpretation of Exodus allowed the householder to kill a nighttime intruder because in the darkness of night there was doubt about the intruder's intentions. . . . Roman law also allowed the killing of a thief in the night but not a daytime thief. . . . The canon 'Si perfodiens' also permitted the killing of a nighttime burglar, based on a comment of St. Augustine on the Exodus text" (222). Yet another nuance, and the one that joins views of killing in general with the duel-specific issue of defense of one's honor, was introduced into the debate in the fourteenth and fifteenth centuries, when the social status of the individuals involved began to carry import.[18] A quotation from a seventeenth-century Jesuit casuist suggests the direction the argument had taken: "It is permitted for a gentleman to kill an aggressor who attempts to calumniate him, if the shame cannot otherwise be avoided; similarly, he may kill one who slaps or beats him, then flees."[19]

Johnson's discussions of the morality of dueling, as related by Boswell, may ramble, but they ramble within the traditional parameters defined above. For example, after Boswell has heard the views of Oliver Goldsmith and James Oglethorpe on the subject, and after Johnson has maintained that the question has not been "solved," Boswell presses him to settle "whether duelling was contrary to the laws of Christianity." Johnson's response focuses mainly on the recent increased refinement of society that modern scholars locate from the late Middle Ages onward:

> As men become in a high degree refined, various causes of offence arise; which are considered to be of such importance, that life must be staked to atone for them, though in reality they are not so. A body that has received a very fine polish may be easily hurt. . . . In a state of highly polished society, an affront is held to be a serious injury. It must, therefore, be resented, or rather a duel must be fought upon it; as men have agreed to banish from their society one who puts up with an affront without fighting a duel.

Johnson elaborates the final clause, glancing at the Augustinian position of dispassionate self-defense but also hinging the justification on the avoidance of ostracism: "It is never unlawful to fight in self-defence. He, then, who fights a duel, does not fight from passion against his antagonist, but out of self-defence; to avert the stigma of the world, and to prevent himself from being driven out of society" (*Life*, 2:179–80). A year later Johnson advanced another defense of dueling, again with an Augustinian cast. Boswell writes, "[he] put his argument upon what I have ever thought the most solid basis; that if publick war be allowed to be consistent with morality, private war must be equally so" (*Life*, 2:226).

Ten years later on the occasion of having a "near relative" wounded in a duel in which he ultimately killed his antagonist, Boswell reintroduces the topic. Johnson begins, "I do not see . . . that fighting is absolutely forbidden in Scripture; I see revenge forbidden, but not self-defence." To this Augustinian distinction Johnson adds comments on the mistake of taking the text of scripture too literally, and then leaps to a familiar parallel: "No, Sir, a man may shoot the man who invades his character, as he may shoot him who attempts to break into his house" (*Life*, 4:211). Boswell's lengthy note at this point essentially undercuts Johnson's statement by suggesting it is not "his serious and deliberate opinion on the subject of duelling." He further refers to a passage from his *Journal of the Tour to the Hebrides* where Johnson admits "he could not explain the rationality of duelling" (*Life*, 4:211n4). Boswell could well have quoted Johnson against himself, for in *Idler* 19 we read, "It is common for controvertists, in the heat of disputation, to add one position to another till they reach the extremities of knowledge, where truth and falshood lose their distinction" (59–60).

Against the Johnson carried away by the heat of disputation we must weigh the Johnson advancing interrelated positions from the corpus of an argumentative tradition with which he was both conversant and comfortable. The following passage, although not specifically about dueling, is a beautifully

balanced example of Johnson working within the casuistic tradition, yet coming to a conclusion that suggests there is a germ of truth in Boswell's analysis
as well. One evening Johnson considers traveling to Streatham Park, and his
friend John Taylor dissuades him: "You'll be robbed if you do: or you must
shoot a highwayman. Now I would rather be robbed than do that; I would
not shoot a highwayman." Johnson responds, "But I would rather shoot him
in the instant when he is attempting to rob me, than afterwards swear against
him at the Old-Bailey, to take away his life, after he has robbed me. I am surer
I am right in the one case than in the other. I may be mistaken as to the man,
when I swear: I cannot be mistaken, if I shoot him in the act. Besides, we feel
less reluctance to take away a man's life, when we are heated by the injury,
than to do it at a distance of time by an oath, after we have cooled." The thief
in the night is here a highwayman rather than a housebreaker, but the issue is
the same. Johnson then detours to a path that allows some indirect criticism of
the numerous capital offenses in England at the time, giving Boswell a chance
to introduce the concept of motive into the act of killing: "So, Sir, you would
rather act from the motive of private passion, than that of publick advantage."
Boswell, it seems, knows a bit of Augustine, but Johnson trumps him with
Aquinas's double motive: "Nay, Sir, when I shoot the highwayman I act from
both." Boswell admits rhetorical defeat—"Very well, very well.—There is no
catching him"—yet Johnson continues, "At the same time one does not know
what to say. For perhaps one may, a year after, hang himself from uneasiness for having shot a man. Few minds are fit to be trusted with so great a
thing." Boswell presses for conclusiveness—"Then, Sir, you would not shoot
him?"—but Johnson has none to offer: "But I might be vexed afterwards for
that too" (*Life*, 3:239–40).

THE SERMONS AND CASUISTRY

The difficulty that casuistry has caused the Protestant has been neatly explained by John Henry Cardinal Newman: such books of moral theology
"are intended for the Confessor, and Protestants view them as intended for
the Preacher."[20] Since all of Johnson's sermons were written to be preached
(albeit by someone else) and since they all, consequently, participate fully
in what the Yale editors have called "the central *homiletical* tradition of
established Christianity" (*Sermons*, xli; my emphasis), it may be surprising
to find in them many traces of the casuistic tradition. Johnson admonished
us that we need more often to be reminded than informed, and certainly he
felt that the role of the speaker from the pulpit was to exhort proper behavior rather than establish moral subtleties: "It is therefore no less useful to

rouse the thoughtless, than instruct the ignorant; to awaken the attention, than enlighten the understanding" (*Sermons*, 5). In another sermon Johnson makes a similar point when he writes, "For few men have been made infidels by argument and reflection; their actions are not generally the result of their reasonings, but their reasonings of their actions." In the next sentence, moreover, he suggests how argumentation may even become deleterious: "Yet these reasonings, though they are not strong enough to pervert a good mind, may yet, when they coincide with interest, and are assisted by prejudice, contribute to confirm a man, already corrupted, in his impieties, and at least retard his reformation, if not entirely obstruct it" (*Sermons*, 54). Nevertheless, even in the sermons we come upon occasional passages that an awareness of the casuistic tradition can enlighten; some have been mentioned earlier and there are more.

In Sermon 3 Johnson's topic is the fear of God. The third paragraph begins, "On the distinction of this fear, into servile and filial, or fear of punishment, or fear of offence, on which much has been superstructed by the casuistical theology of the Romish church, it is not necessary to dwell. It is sufficient to observe, that the religion which makes fear the great principle of action, implicitly condemns all self-confidence, all presumptuous security" (*Sermons*, 30). The Yale editors note Johnson's tendency to contrast negatively the Roman with the Anglican Church, an emphasis somewhat different from Boswell's. They find a source in Aquinas for the distinction of types of fear, and they point out that John Rogers, whom Johnson had read and quoted in his *Dictionary*, had made a similar distinction in one of his sermons (30n5–6). But the passage clearly indicates Johnson's awareness of another thread in the casuistic cloth, even while suggesting when casuistic distinctions are "not necessary." A fear of God, regardless of its type or source, is for Johnson of overarching importance in moving man toward his salvation. Here, then, specific casuistic arguments are passed over because they would not further the specific purpose of the sermon.

In another sermon Johnson states that "it is indeed very hazardous for a private man to criticise the laws of any country" (*Sermons*, 279), but that does not stop him from doing so, in what the Yale editors call "the vivid and untypically long illustration . . . of the orphan and the perjuring guardian" (273n9). They may well be correct in spotting a parallel in subject matter to the treatment of Richard Savage by his mother, but the form of this illustration owes much to the casuistic pattern of piling on extenuating circumstances, or chains of cases of increasing complexity, or both, for a case under consideration. Johnson begins by contrasting the application of the death penalty to both a parricide and a petty thief who had "taken from a stranger, a small piece of money." We find this argument frequently in Johnson's writings, but note what comes next: "Let us suppose yet farther that [an indifferent specta-tor] saw the guardian of an orphan called before the courts of justice for the violation of his trust, that he heard him charged with oppression and with fraud, oppression aggravated by proximity of blood, and fraud heightened by that confidence which enabled him to commit it." The victim of a heinous crime, the murdered father, has given way to the surrogate father-criminal who steals not from a stranger but a blood relative, and presumably a virtu-ally helpless one. Mere restitution does seem an inadequate punishment for a guilty verdict, certainly in comparison with "him who for stealing a single piece of money was sentenced to dye" (278).

Jonsen and Toulmin have written that "gradual movement from clear and simple cases to the more complex and obscure ones was standard procedure for the casuist; indeed, it might be said to be the essence of the casuistic mode of thinking" (252). Johnson does not disappoint, as he adds yet another crime to the rap sheet of the guardian, that of employing "hired witnesses to support his usurpations and secure his robberies from detection." Johnson's third-person observer, just two paragraphs earlier described as "indifferent" and, we assume, calmly disinterested, has been transformed greatly:

> [W]ould not the stranger pant to see the accomplices of wickedness brought to their trial, would not his heart glow with impatience, for vengeance against wretches, who had in the highest and most emphatical sense, taken "the name of God in vain". . . to give credit to a lye, a lye intended only for the support of villany, of villany heightened by perfidy and cruelty; and when he saw them pun-ished only with ignominy, which they very little regarded, would he not wonder that they found greater indulgence than he that steals a sheep? (*Sermons*, 278–79)

Here the casuistic mode of thinking that builds simple cases into complex ones is not working at cross-purposes with the homiletic purpose of the sermon; instead it contributes to the observer's (and perhaps the preacher's) justifiable righteous indignation.

A CONCLUDING CASE

When I first noticed what I have argued is a strong connection between John-son's thought and traditional casuistry, I was unaware that Cardinal Newman had made the same observation, implicitly, in *Apologia Pro Vita Sua* (1865). "I cannot think what it can be," he writes, "which keeps up the prejudice of this Protestant country against us, unless it be the vague charges which are drawn from our books of Moral Theology" (208–9). Despite his disclaimer that "casuistry is a noble science, but it is one to which I am led, neither by my abilities nor my turn of mind" (264), in the discussion that follows (including a note, really a small essay, titled "Lying and Equivocation"), Newman rehearses most of the casuistic topics we have just reviewed. Although his discussion is at times delightful (for example, after his definition of *evasion* he notes that "the greatest school of evasion . . . is the House of Commons" [265]), for our purposes it is of interest mainly for the identification of Johnson as a major participant in the English casuistic tradition. Newman begins, "Great English authors, Jeremy Taylor, Milton, Paley, Johnson, men of very different schools of thought, distinctly say, that under certain extraordinary circumstances it is allowable to tell a lie. . . . Johnson [says]: 'The general rule is, that truth should never be violated; there must, however, be some exceptions. If, for instance, a murderer should ask you which way a man is gone.'" (209) Newman returns to Johnson later, telling us much more about the mid-nineteenth-century view of Johnson's personality than anything else: "As to Johnson's case of a murderer asking you which way a man had gone, I should have anticipated that, had such a difficulty happened to him, his first act would have been to knock the man down, and to call out for the police; and next, if he was worsted in the conflict, he would not have given the ruffian the information he asked, at whatever risk to himself" (268). The great Victorian editor of Johnson and Boswell, George Birkbeck Hill, quotes Newman's second passage at even greater length in a note glossing Johnson's discussion of this "case" in Boswell's *Life*, but, not surprisingly, does not mention the first passage (*Life*, 4:305n3).

I have not sought specific sources for Johnson's casuistic ideas for two reasons: first, I have often been tracing a mode of thought rather than a specific idea; and second, the tradition is so broad and Johnson's reading so wide that such a hunt for sources could well have proved either highly speculative, or futile, or both. Newman mentions Johnson in the same breath as Jeremy Taylor, whom the Yale editors of Johnson's sermons list as one of six major influences on the style and substance of those texts. Two others they name, Richard Baxter and Robert Sanderson, like Taylor, were authors of famous works of casuistry. According to the admittedly incomplete Sale Catalogue, Johnson's library contained Taylor's and Baxter's works, as well as casuistic tomes by Francisco Suarez, St. Jerome, and Hugo Grotius.[21] In addition, Johnson stated his admiration for the writings of Sanderson and Samuel Pufendorf, both relatively contemporary sources of casuistic thought, and his knowledge of classical and early Christian sources like Aristotle, Cicero, Augustine, and Aquinas needs no demonstration.[22]

An examination of the lengthy paragraph in Boswell that Newman highlights will serve as an appropriate conclusion for this essay. It is a purple passage from the *Life of Johnson*, and perhaps one that we can view in a somewhat altered light after what has been presented above. Boswell introduces a topic as follows: "We talked of the casuistical question, Whether it was allowable at any time to depart from Truth?" Newman's statement of Johnson's response is condensed but accurate: generally truth is inviolate but exceptions exist; for instance, if "a murderer should ask you which way a man is gone, you may tell him what is not true, because you are under a previous obligation not to betray a man to a murderer" (*Life*, 4:305). Johnson's mind naturally moves to a variation on what Jonsen and Toulmin have called "the classical case about the immorality of lying up to the time of Kant: An innocent man, who has been unjustly condemned, is hidden in your house. May you lie to the authorities who come to arrest him?" (196). St. Augustine took a very rigorous line and forbade a lie in this case, but subsequent casuists (for example, Raymond of Pennafort) sought a way to modify Augustine's position; moreover, the details of the case often changed, as in the example cited earlier of the Dominican Sylvester Mazzolini of Priero writing, "If someone seeking to kill another person asks you, 'did he go this way?' you may answer, 'no, not this way,' meaning 'his feet did not tread the very ground you are pointing at.'"[23] By the way, Johnson's version (lying to the murderer) conveniently avoids a difficulty that Augustine's version (lying to the authorities) would present, for presumably the authorities have the right to ask such questions.

Boswell persists with the casuistical question but now turns the discussion somewhat when he asks, "Supposing the person who wrote *Junius* were asked whether he was the authour, might he deny it?" As we have seen above, Johnson earlier had dealt with the question of authorship of the Junius letters by accepting Burke's "spontaneous" denial and shifting to the issue of the prerogative of the questioner. Here his treatment is more detailed and deserves to be quoted at length, not only for its intricacies but also because of what we will now recognize as the general source of those intricacies:

> If you were *sure* that he wrote *Junius*, would you, if he denied it, think as well of him afterwards? Yet it may be urged, that what a man has no right to ask, you may refuse to communicate; and there is no other effectual mode of preserving a secret, and an important secret, the discovery of which may be very hurtful to you, but a flat denial; for if you are silent, or hesitate, or evade, it will be held equivalent to a confession. But stay, Sir; here is another case. Supposing the authour had told me confidentially that he had written *Junius*, and I were asked if he had, I should hold myself at liberty to deny it, as being under a previous promise, express or implied, to conceal it. Now what I ought to do for the authour, may I not do for myself? (*Life*, 4:305–6)

Here, as Johnson strings case to related case, we see mention of two of casuistry's commonplaces: the conflict between secret-keeping and truth-telling, and the methodological means of avoiding lies through silence and evasion.

The final turn in the discussion is Johnson's doing, in a passage partly informed by the casuistic tradition and partly by his own immediate personal circumstances: "But I deny the lawfulness of telling a lie to a sick man for fear of alarming him. You have no business with consequences; you are to tell the truth. Besides, you are not sure what effect your telling him that he is in danger may have. It may bring his distemper to a crisis, and that may cure him. Of all lying, I have the greatest abhorrence of this, because I believe it has been frequently practised on myself" (*Life*, 4:306). In both *De Mendacio* (AD 395) and *Contra Mendacium* (AD 422), St. Augustine had glanced briefly at the issue of lying to or attempting to withhold the truth from a very ill man, although the news in his examples was the death of the man's son, not the seriousness of his illness. Augustine's hard line on the culpability of lying under even these circumstances is identical to Johnson's. Both adhere to the premise that it is wrong to do evil in the hope that good will come from it. Although Johnson states somewhat wistfully a possible physical benefit from a dose of the truth, it is not too great a surmise to read in these lines the potential downside of a dying man being deluded into thinking he had plenty of time to attain the requisite state of grace necessary for his salvation. Boswell dates this conversation on 13 June 1784, and Johnson, who had been ill for some time, was dead exactly six months later.

NOTES

1. Samuel Johnson, *The Rambler*, ed. W. J. Bate and Albrecht Strauss, vols. 3, 4, and 5 in the Yale Works (New Haven: Yale University Press, 1969), 3:55; hereafter cited in the text.
2. Samuel Johnson, *The Idler and The Adventurer*, ed. W. J. Bate, John M. Bullitt, and L. F. Powell (New Haven: Yale University Press, 1963), 112; hereafter cited in the text.
3. Starr, *Defoe and Casuistry* (Princeton: Princeton University Press, 1971), 1–2. See my discussion of *Rambler* 13, below.
4. Jonsen and Toulmin, *The Abuse of Casuistry: A History of Moral Reasoning* (1988; 1st paperback ed., Berkeley: University of California Press, 1989), 238; hereafter cited in the text.
5. Hudson, *Samuel Johnson and Eighteenth-Century Thought* (Oxford: Clarendon Press, 1988), 165–66; Parker, *The Triumph of Augustan Poetics: English Literary Culture from Butler to Johnson* (Cambridge: Cambridge University Press, 1998), 234n10. Jack Lynch found Johnson "impatient with what he regarded as casuistry" in the online text of his paper delivered at the Johnson Society of the Central Region in 2001, but excised the comment from the subsequently published version, "Samuel Johnson, Unbeliever," *Eighteenth-Century Life* 29 (2005): 1–19. Tom Keymer correctly recognizes, in my opinion, Johnson's understanding of the "double face" of

casuistry; see *Richardson's "Clarissa" and the Eighteenth-Century Reader* (Cambridge: Cambridge University Press, 1992), 88–89.

6. Tyers, "A Biographical Sketch of Dr. Samuel Johnson," cited from *Johnsonian Miscellanies*, ed. G. B. Hill (1897; New York: Barnes and Noble, 1966 and 1970), 2:366; hereafter cited as *Miscellanies*.

7. *Boswell's Life of Johnson*, ed. G. B. Hill, rev. L. F. Powell (Oxford: Clarendon Press, 1934–1964), 1:436; hereafter cited in the text as *Life*.

8. Cited by Starr, *Defoe and Casuistry*, 210n39.

9. Ibid., 47–48. De Quincey's essay first appeared, without a title, in *Tait's Edinburgh Magazine* (February 1841).

10. Leslie and Taylor's *Life and Times of Sir Joshua Reynolds* (1865), 2:458; cited from *Life*, 2:6n3.

11. Samuel Johnson, *A Journey to the Western Islands of Scotland*, ed. Mary Lascelles (New Haven: Yale University Press, 1971), 118.

12. "Swift," in Johnson's *Lives of the English Poets*, ed. G. B. Hill (Oxford: Clarendon Press, 1905), 3:43–44.

13. Samuel Johnson, *Sermons*, ed. Jean Hagstrum and James Gray (New Haven: Yale University Press, 1978), 181; hereafter cited in the text as *Sermons*.

14. See Starr, *Defoe and Casuistry*, especially 9–33.

15. Of course, the casuistic situation in Johnson's periodic essays did not always involve the word "case." See *Idler* 13 and *Idler* 55, where the correspondent lays before the periodical writer a "controversy" and a "complaint," respectively, but with the same expectation of a moral judgment or moral advice. And the word "case" can be used in its narrowly legal sense, as in *Idler* 54, where Sukey Savecharges presents her case "in as juridical a manner as [she is] capable" (168).

16. Johnson seems not to have been influenced by the most prominent antidueling view in eighteenth-century letters, that of Samuel Richardson's *Sir Charles Grandison* (1753), where the hero not only repeatedly refuses to duel but also explains his position at great length.

17. Jonsen and Toulmin, *Abuse of Casuistry,* 218–19, quote from Augustine's *Letters*, letter 47, "Ad Publicolam." Recall Johnson's views of the judge's role as expressed in *Rambler* 81, discussed above.

18. Jonsen and Toulmin here rely on and agree with Shaun J. Sullivan, *Killing in Defense of Private Property* (Missoula, MT: Scholars Press for the American Academy of Religion, 1976), 27.

19. The words of Martin Becanus, as quoted by Jonsen and Toulmin, *Abuse of Casuistry,* 226, who point out that Becanus's view was censured by the theology faculty of Louvain, a censure upheld by Pope Innocent XI.

20. Newman, *Apologia Pro Vita Sua*, ed. David J. DeLaura (New York: W. W. Norton, 1968), 208–9; hereafter cited in the text.

21. Donald Greene, *Samuel Johnson's Library: An Annotated Guide* (Victoria: University of Victoria, 1975).

22. Johnson counted Pufendorf among "the great writers on law" and recommended his "Introduction to History" (*Life*, 2:430, 4:311). Sanderson was praised by Johnson for his letter writing, and G. B. Hill's explanation is interesting: "Bishop

Sanderson, I suppose, was selected on account of 'his casuistical learning' and of 'the very many cases that were resolved by letters,' when he was consulted by people of 'restless and wounded consciences'" (*Miscellanies*, 2:130n2). Hill is quoting from Izaak Walton's *Life of Dr. Sanderson*, which was in Johnson's library (Greene, *Samuel Johnson's Library*, 115). For more on Sanderson's importance as an English casuist, see Camille Wells Slights, *The Casuistical Tradition in Shakespeare, Donne, Herbert, and Milton* (Princeton: Princeton University Press, 1981), 43–59, and passim.

23. Jonsen and Toulmin, *Abuse of Casuistry*, 196–98; Mazzolini's work is *Summa Sylvestrina* (1516).

Chapter Four

Slavery in *Roderick Random*

Taylor Corse

> To remove *Negroes* then from their Homes and Friends, where they are at
> ease, to a strange Country, People, and Language, must be highly offend-
> ing against the Laws of natural Justice and Humanity; and especially when
> this change is to hard Labour, corporal Punishment, and for *Masters* they
> wish at the D——l.
>
> —John Atkins, *A Voyage to Guinea, Brazil, and the West Indies*

This passage comes from John Atkins, a surgeon (like Tobias Smollett) in
the British navy, who wrote candidly and vividly about the slave trade in
A Voyage to Guinea, Brazil, and the West Indies (1735). Atkins describes
a specific expedition in 1721 sponsored by the government to restore "the
Credit of the *Royal African Company*" (1). It was an eye-opening experience
for Atkins, who would accuse his countrymen of engaging in a trade "which
has subjected [Negroes] to the Condition of Slaves, little better in our Plantations, than that of Cattle" (178). Atkins is useful to historians because of the
wealth of ethnographic information he provides about the peoples and places
of West Africa, as well as for his sharp and critical assessment of the business of slavery. He also serves as a useful foil to and gloss upon Smollett,
who wrote his own fictional account of the slave trade in *The Adventures of
Roderick Random* (1748).

In chapters 65 and 66 of *Roderick Random*, Smollett informs us that
Roderick and his uncle Captain Bowling, after cruising along the coast of
West Africa, "purchased four hundred negroes," transported them across the
South Atlantic, and then proceeded to sell them in Buenos Aires.[1] Smollett
offers precious few details about this expedition, except to mention that a
number of slaves died in transit and that Roderick was forced to get rid of his
"disagreeable lading of Negroes" (410). As a result of his lucrative venture,

73

Roderick estimates that he was wealthy enough (in his own words) "to purchase a handsome sine-cure upon my arrival in England, and if I should find
the Squire as averse to me as ever, marry his sister by stealth; and in case
our family should encrease, rely upon the generosity of my uncle, who was
by this time worth a considerable sum" (410). The subsequent reunion with
his father brings all this, and more, to pass, including the restoration of his
estate in Scotland. This episode raises important questions. Did Smollett, like
Atkins, regard the traffic in human lives as a social and moral evil? If so, does
the money Roderick earned from his African adventure cast a shadow on his
triumphant return to England? What exactly did Smollett know about slavery in the 1740s and about the dominant role of Great Britain in this global
market? What could he reasonably expect his readers to know? Furthermore,
what have literary critics had to say about these issues?

In general, scholars have paid little attention to Roderick's slaving voyage. Jerry Beasley, in his excellent study of Smollett's fiction, completely
ignores the slave-trading episode in his chapter on *Roderick Random*. Aware
that readers have found the conclusion to the novel (after Roderick has been
released from prison) abrupt and unconvincing, Beasley argues that Smollett achieves satisfactory closure by means of theology and romance: "having punished Roderick, Smollett goes on to rescue him by the Providential
agency of Bowling, at last giving him a father, his beloved Narcissa, and
a return to his ancestral estate—as if to say that, for the lonely, battered
individual, there can be no redemption except by the miracle of benevolent
intervention."[2] This agreeable interpretation accounts, I think, for many features of the ending: its rapid tying up of loose ends, its neat distribution of
justice and mercy, its placing of the picaresque hero in a stable setting (idyllic
Scotland) where chance and change can jostle him no further. Certainly, the
topsy-turvy world of *Roderick Random* abounds, in Smollett's own words,
with many "strange vicissitudes of . . . fortune" (427) and "amazing stroke[s]
of providence" (416). Roderick owes his success, however, not only to the
"miracle of benevolent intervention," but also to his own exertions in the
mundane business of slavery.

A few critics have commented on this aspect of the novel: James Carson in a
fascinating article on Smollett and Africans, and Aileen Douglas in her book on
Smollett and the Body. Carson disposes of the slaving episode in one sweeping
sentence, where he condemns Smollett for betraying "a callous disregard for
the material realities of the middle passage and plantation slavery."[3] Carson is
echoing the earlier verdict by Paul-Gabriel Boucé, who noted the "total absence
of pity for the black slaves bought and resold at the end of *Roderick Random*."[4]
Douglas, in her two paragraphs on the subject, remarks perceptively that "in
the complacency of Roderick's narrative we can still discern a more disturbing,

sensational account. After all, the ship also has its plague, and it has its quota of involuntary passengers."[5] Douglas also notes that the "casual care with which Roderick tells us his adventure [i.e., investment] was 'laid out chiefly in gold dust' seems an attempt to distance himself from the questionable basis of his wealth" (66). Thus, one critic finds brutal insensitivity to the conditions of slaves, whereas the other sees something more—signs of conflict in the telling of the story that disturb its placid surface.

I find Douglas's comments more helpful than Carson's mainly because she takes into account some of Smollett's narrative details. Consider, for example, the matter of "gold dust." Surely, as Carson suggests, this is a "distancing" device, the implication being that Roderick is somewhat less culpable than the others because they are trading slaves, whereas he, ostensibly, is trading gold. Yet even this insight, valid though it is, calls for correction. Later in the same paragraph, Roderick reports, with evident self-satisfaction, that we "sold our slaves in a very few days, and could have put off five times the number at our own price" (410). Significantly, he makes no mention of the "gold dust" from Guinea that was to be traded at Buenos Aires, and his initial investment of four hundred pounds eventually yields a profit of "three thousand more" (426). So, while one gesture seems to distance Roderick "from the questionable basis of his wealth," another gesture reveals him as an eager participant, fully complicit in the business of slavery.

Furthermore, what are we to make of the frank admission at the beginning of chapter 66: "Our ship being freed of the disagreeable lading of Negroes, to whom indeed I had been a miserable slave, since our leaving the coast of Guinea, I began to enjoy myself, and breathe with pleasure the pure air of Paraguay" (410)? The language here is instructive. Roderick plays with the paradox of role reversal: the master presents himself as a temporary slave who wins his own personal freedom from the drudgery of caring for these "disagreeable" creatures. Ironically, their misery makes him "miserable"; and perversely, he lays claim to sympathy that, by all rights, ought to belong to them. Roderick's attitude reflects, I think, the conflicted mentality of many slaveholders. Eugene Genovese documents in his magisterial work, *Roll, Jordon, Roll* (1974), especially in his chapter "A Duty and a Burden," the common complaint of masters who lament "the miserable occupation of seeing to negroes, and attending to their wants and sickness."[6] Roderick bears witness to the same mentality, which perhaps grows out of Smollett's experience as an owner of slaves on his wife's plantation in Jamaica.[7]

Though Smollett does not present directly the "material realities of the middle passage and plantation slavery," he does conform his narrative to the generally known facts of the slave trade as it was practiced in the early eighteenth century. Like most such voyages, Roderick's follows the established pattern of the trading triangle. This "classic journey," writes Hugh Thomas, was "probably responsible for three-quarters of all the voyages." The traders "began in Europe, picked up slaves in Africa in exchange for European manufacturers, carried the slaves to the Americas, and then returned to Europe with certain typical American goods which slaves would probably have helped to harvest."[8] Smollett, however, particularizes Roderick's journey in several ways, some of which typify the pattern outlined above and some of which make this a special "fictional" case.

One surprising feature is the air of mystery and secrecy that surrounds the voyage, whose intent and destination Captain Bowling is "not at liberty to discover" (398). Even late in the novel, Roderick is reluctant to "disclose the whole secret of my last voyage" (427), an indication of the shame he may feel in telling the truth about it to his close friend, Banting. After liberating Roderick from debtor's prison in Marshalsea, Bowling engages his nephew to serve as ship's surgeon under his command, but only when the ship is under way does he explain the purpose of the journey: "The ship, said he, which has been fitted out at a great expence, is bound for the coast of Guinea, where we shall exchange part of our cargo for slaves and gold dust; from thence we will transport our negroes to Buenos-Ayres in New-Spain, where (by virtue of passports obtained from our own court, and that of Madrid), we will dispose of them and the goods that remain on board for silver, by means of our supercargo, who is perfectly well acquainted with the coast, the lingo, and inhabitants" (407). Bowling explains it was by "instructions" of the owners that he was forced to keep this information secret from Roderick and, presumably, the rest of the crew. Roderick accepts the explanation without question, but we may well wonder why. In 1750, Parliament declared it "lawful for all His Majesty's subjects to trade and traffick to and from any port in Africa" (Thomas, 265). Before that date, however, Englishmen were not permitted to engage in trafficking and trading slaves without special permission or license. This was the prerogative of two corporations, the South Sea Company (chartered in 1712) and the Royal African Company (chartered in 1672). Technically, therefore, Roderick and Bowling are "interlopers," that is, independent traders who (after 1698) had to pay "an *ad valorem* tax of 10 percent on all exports to Africa" (Thomas, 205). To avoid this penalty, the shipowners maintained the greatest secrecy; if word got out to the authorities, penalties could include seizure and confiscation, not to mention a heavy fine. Interlopers also ran the risk of being put "to Slavery if taken by the *Spanish Guard le Costa*" (Atkins, 157). In other words, Roderick's voyage is an illegal operation. That they must "smuggle the rest of [their] merchandize" (Smollett, 410) reinforces this point. The "passports" obtained from the courts of England and Spain allow passage from one dominion to another, but not traffic in slaves from Africa.

Though their operation is clandestine, Roderick and Bowling are following the long-established practice of other *"private Traders"* who, according to Smollett's contemporary, Thomas Astley, "are better able to supply the *American* Plantations with Negroes, because they can certainly fit-out their Ships cheaper than the [Royal African] Company; especially from the Out-Ports."[9] The interlopers also enjoyed the advantage of a sophisticated networking system. As Astley observes, they "carry-on a constant Intercourse of general Trade with the *British* Plantations; and have settled Correspondents there, of Relations, Friends, and Partners: Who will be more careful to do them Justice, as well as more punctual in making Returns, than the Company can expect from any of their Agents" (160). Captain Bowling is an experienced hand in these matters, and the novel shows how smoothly and efficiently he manages his and Roderick's affairs. Except for an outbreak of fever, everything goes without a hitch.

Smollett's narrative both reveals and conceals a great deal of information about the British slave trade. In all likelihood, Roderick's cargo was a typical one, consisting of cloth (woolen and cotton), metals (copper, brass, and iron), shells (especially "cowries," a common form of currency in Africa), beads (made of amber, glass, or coral), alcohol (brandy and rum), tobacco, muskets, and gunpowder. Detailed invoices of these and other items can be found in the contemporary travel narratives of John Atkins and Thomas Astley. All of these commodities, in particular cloth, were greatly prized by West Africans (Thomas, 319). Smollett hints at his knowledge of this fact when he refers to the "European bale goods" (410) that comprise part of the ship's cargo. West Africa was an important outlet for textiles from northern Europe—including England, Holland, France, and Germany. Smollett's reference indicates his sharp, if understated, awareness of the complex economics involved in this business.

One important factor was "insurance." Captain Bowling reminds his crew, when they are accosted by an apparent enemy ship, not to panic, for "my whole cargo is insured" (408). This was a standard precaution: "all ships were insured, often internationally" (Thomas, 312). Insurance took other forms as well. Slave ships also had to be armed to defend themselves from pirates, privateers, foreign vessels, and commercial rivals. Bowling's unusually large ship (it has room for one hundred crew and four hundred slaves) is "mounted with twenty nine-pounders" (398)—a fair amount of firepower, but not enough to match a major warship. The ship's surgeon was a vital member of such expeditions. He was expected, of course, to treat the diseases and injuries that invariably befell the men on these perilous voyages; however, he also played a more valuable role, namely, in the selection of slaves. "Indeed, his was the decisive voice in advising captains whether or not to buy" (Thomas,

395). According to one English witness, "our surgeon examined them [the slaves] well in all kinds to see that they were sound in wind and limb, making them jump, stretch out their arms swiftly, looking in their mouths to judge of their age" (quoted by Thomas, 395). Roderick tells us that Bowling "proposed that I should sail with him in quality of his Surgeon" (400), a position for which he had ample training and experience. Though Smollett does not say so, we can assume that Roderick would have performed these services as part of his normal duties, as well as to protect his financial investment.

Smollett's account of Roderick's voyage, cursory though it is, betrays familiarity with the basic facts of the European slave trade. His journey falls into four stages: (1) cruising the coast of West Africa; (2) sailing across the South Atlantic (the infamous Middle Passage); (3) selling the slaves in Buenos Aires; and (4) returning to England with profits in the form of hard currency and other merchandise. Of the first stage Smollett writes: "In less than a fortnight after, we made the land of Guinea, near the mouth of the river Gambia, and trading along the coast as far to the southward of the Line as Angola and Bengula, in less than six months disposed of the greatest part of our cargo, and purchased four hundred negroes, my adventure having been laid out chiefly in gold dust" (409–10). In one concise sentence, Smollett supplies the bare outlines of a fairly generic eighteenth-century slave-trader's voyage. For centuries, the land of Guinea had been synonymous with slaves and gold. As John Atkins notes, "By *Guinea* here, I mean all *Negro-land.* . . . The Name . . . imports *hot and dry*, and its Gold gives Name to our Coin" (38). Like other traders, Roderick travels from one stretch of West Africa, the river region of Gambia, to the southernmost trading point, Benguela, in present-day Angola. Presumably, his ship made frequent stops at numerous ports along the way, which accounts for the length of the process, inasmuch as four to six months was a normal trading period at this time. Four hundred slaves, however, was an extraordinarily large number to purchase, since the average load for an English ship at the end of the eighteenth century was about two hundred and thirty (Thomas, 411). This heavy cargo may indicate "tight packing." But we also have to keep in mind the exceptional size of Bowling's ship, which held one hundred sailors (the typical crew was about thirty). Since this is a onetime, make-or-break venture for Bowling and Roderick, they have clearly planned to take in as many slaves as possible. The large round numbers (four hundred and one hundred) also give a sense of myth and wonder to the voyage.

Smollett glosses over the second part of the journey in a sentence whose jaunty tone belies one dreadful event that took place en route to Buenos Aires: "Our compliment being made up, we took our departure from Cape Negro, and arrived in Rio de la Plata in six weeks, having met with nothing remarkable in our voyage, except an epidemic fever, not unlike the jail distemper, which broke out among our slaves, and carried off a good many of the ship's company; among whom I lost one of my mates, and poor Strap had well nigh given up the ghost" (410). Carson is wrong to say that Smollett completely ignores the "material realities of the middle passage," for he clearly alludes to the most common danger that devastated men and women on these crossings, namely, "epidemic fever." Dysentery, smallpox, and scurvy indiscriminately attacked slaves and crew alike. Smollett does not supply numbers, just a general figure ("a good many"), but historians reckon that "deaths were rarely less than a fifth of the crew, sometimes more," and the mortality rate for slaves averaged about 9 percent on English ships (Thomas, 311, 424). A six-week crossing from Africa to South America was quite normal in the eighteenth century. Indeed, Smollett seems to stress throughout this episode the normality of Roderick's voyage, in which "nothing remarkable" occurred. The "remarkable" could have included such commonplace events as suicide among the slaves, violence, brawls, and rebellion, not to mention storms and pirates. Smollett, it should be noted, does not individuate any of the slaves' deaths, but he does single out the loss of one of his crew (a surgeon's mate) and the near loss of Roderick's companion Strap.

Why does Smollett provide such a vexingly brief account of the Atlantic crossing? Douglas suggests an aesthetic reason: "we remember the illnesses and suffering of which he earlier gave us such a detailed account" (66). Douglas implies that it would be an artistic blunder to revisit such scenes of horror at the end of the novel when Smollett is preparing Roderick (and the reader) for a happy conclusion. Perhaps, yet Roderick himself makes an explicit connection with those graphic accounts of illness and suffering when he likens the fever to the "jail distemper," thus reinforcing the analogy between one form of human degradation and another. Apparently Roderick does not perceive the irony of this situation—and Smollett has good reason not to press the issue. If Roderick is going to be redeemed as a hero, he must be presented in the best possible light: hence the erasure or withholding of damaging material.

In any event, Smollett moves rapidly to the next stage of the journey: "Having produced our passport to the Spanish governor, we were received with great courtesy, sold our slaves in a very few days, and could have put off five times the number at our own price; being obliged to smuggle the rest of our merchandize, consisting of European bale goods, which however we made shift to dispose of at a great advantage" (410). Elated by his good fortune, Roderick has but one regret—they could have turned an even greater profit by selling "off five times the number at our own price." For Roderick, these slaves are merely "merchandize" and "goods" (and a little later "lading");

he makes no effort to humanize them in any way. Yet Roderick must have tended to some of these slaves in his capacity as ship's surgeon; that is why he had taken such pains to purchase medicines and other pharmaceutical supplies "sufficient for a voyage of eighteen months" (400). The congratulatory and callous tone of Smollett's narrative can be better understood when placed in a broader historical context. Britain was the dominant power in this business. "Between 1740 and 1750, her ships probably took to the Americas over two hundred thousand slaves: far more than any country had carried in any ten years before" (Thomas, 264). It seems to me that Roderick and Bowling are fairly representative figures in this vicious scramble for wealth and status. They are delighted with their brilliant success, even if it comes at the expense of others. Indeed, they give it not a second thought.

Furthermore, there is little evidence of strong antislavery feeling in Britain during the 1730s and 1740s. Refuting earlier views by Knapp and Boucé, Carson demonstrates convincingly that Smollett came "to espouse abolitionist sentiments" in his later career, during the 1760s and 1770s (491). But what about the young Smollett, who at the age of twenty-six wrote *Roderick Random*? He seems to have been no more enlightened than most of his contemporaries. *The Gentleman's Magazine*, a fairly reliable barometer of current opinion, published a total of four articles in fifteen years (1730–1745) on the slave trade, only one of which is decidedly abolitionist in tone. Written by a certain Mercator Honestus, this essay roundly condemns the "*Guinea* Trade" for its violation of mankind's "natural Right to Liberty," for its exploitation of African children, for the "hard Usage that Negroes meet with in the *West Indies*," and for the "base Usage" they suffer "amongst those (tho' very improperly) called Christians."[10] One such editorial does not constitute a reform movement; in fact, vigorous public debate on the issue did not really begin until after 1750. This view is supported by recent scholars such as Vincent Carretta, who finds that "before the 1760s, published opposition to slavery or the slave trade was occasional rather than consistent."[11]

Smollett, however, could have read two influential contemporary accounts that I have already mentioned: John Atkins's *Voyage to Guinea, Brazil, and the West Indies* (1735), and Thomas Astley's famous compilation, *A New General Collection of Voyages and Travels* (1745). Both documents provide hard facts about the African slave trade—its commercial attractions, its perilous costs, and its brutalizing effects on everyone involved in the business. We learn, for instance, that the price of a woman slave in Sierra Leon is fifty gold bars or the equivalent in merchandise: "1 Piece of Planes, 7 77lb. Kettles, 3 Pieces of Chintz, 1 Piece of Handkerchief Stuff' (Atkins, 163). It is an ironclad rule, moreover, "*to keep the Males apart from the Women and Children, to handcuff the former; Bristol Ships triple* [*sic*] *such as are sturdy, with Chains round their Necks*" (173). Frequently, Atkins (as well as Astley) registers a high degree of moral outrage, which is all the more impressive coming from someone who had been a successful trader himself: "[Slaves] are sold in open Market on shore, and examined by us in like manner, as our Brother Trade do Beasts in *Smithfield*; the Countenance, and Stature, a good Set of Teeth, Pliancy in their Limbs and Joints, and being free of Venereal Taint, are the things inspected, and governs our choice in buying" (179–80). No such outcry can be heard anywhere in the pages of *Roderick Random*, though there is plenty of satiric indignation leveled against other forms of injustice (the English navy, debtors' prison, anti-Scots prejudice, and so on).

On the subject of slavery, Atkins is the complete antithesis of Smollett, but his *Voyage* is useful precisely because it provides the sort of material that the novelist could have taken advantage of—if he had wanted to. Smollett, however, was not interested in pursuing this other perspective in *Roderick Random*. Roderick's brief experience as a slave trader is just one interlude in a picaresque novel crowded with colorful and diverse adventures. Quite clearly, Smollett knew what he was doing. He could have made this episode highly sensational, but chose not to; instead, he downplays it almost to the point where readers can overlook the "questionable basis" of his hero's wealth and prosperity. Smollett tells his audience just enough about the slave trade to incite some curiosity and some uneasiness, but not enough (apparently) to spoil vicarious enjoyment of Roderick's good fortune and "true happiness on earth" (435). Secure at last on his ancestral estate, Roderick and his family seem both isolated and insulated from the harsh realities and vagaries of human experience. Life is no longer cruel and unpredictable. We should not forget, however, that this happiness derives, in part, from the misery of others, as Roderick himself attests: "I calculated the profits of my voyage, which even exceeded my expectation" (410). The foreign "profits" of West Africa have made possible the domestic bliss of "Random" Hall.

More than thirty years ago, Raymond Williams documented the human costs of building country houses such as Penshurst, Appleton, Blenheim, and Stow. Random Hall may not be conceived on the same grand scale as these other noble seats, but its prosperity (even its very survival) depends on "exploitation of a most thoroughgoing kind."[12] Williams, of course, is writing about agricultural labor and the virtual serfdom of those who worked the land in rural England of the seventeenth and eighteenth centuries. Roderick Random owes his "flourishing condition" (433) to exploitation of an altogether different kind—the selling of four hundred men and women into perpetual slavery. Even though this is a once-in-a-lifetime-get-rich-scheme, it connects the social economy of Scotland (heralded by joyful peasants, gracious gentry, a generous laird and his bonny bride) with the brutal overseas plantations of

Brazil. At this late date, it is impossible to tell whether or not Smollett wanted his readers to make the connection between these two sections of the novel. It does not take long, however, to go from one episode to the other—a reading distance of twenty pages or so. Smollett even tells us, at the beginning of the final chapter (sixty-nine), that Uncle Bowling refused to join the family on their homecoming journey, "being resolved to try his fortune once more at sea" (432). If we remember that Bowling gets his fortune, in large part, from trading slaves, then this becomes yet another narrative link. The connection with slavery persists all the way to the end, and it tarnishes, at the very least, the pastoral ideal embodied in the last word of the novel: "felicity." Given the general apathy of Great Britain in 1748, one can safely assume that the moral insensitivity of Roderick is probably shared by Smollett himself and his culture at large.

NOTES

Epigraph is taken from John Atkins, *A Voyage to Guinea, Brazil, and the West Indies* (1735; London: Frank Cass, 1970), 178; hereafter cited in the text.

   1. Tobias Smollett, *The Adventures of Roderick Random*, ed. Paul-Gabriel Boucé (New York: Oxford University Press, 1981), 409–10; hereafter cited in the text.
   2. Jerry C. Beasley, *Tobias Smollett, Novelist* (Athens: University of Georgia Press, 1998), 67.
   3. James P. Carson, "Britons, 'Hottentots,' Plantation Slavery, and Tobias Smollett," *Philological Quarterly* 75 (1996): 473; hereafter cited in the text. For another brief mention of Roderick and slavery, see James G. Basker, "Smollett's Racial Consciousness in *Roderick Random*," in *1650–1850: Ideas, Aesthetics, and Inquiries in the Early Modern Era* 6 (2001): 77–90.
   4. Paul-Gabriel Boucé, *The Novels of Tobias Smollett* (London: Longman, 1976), 277.
   5. Aileen Douglas, *Uneasy Sensations: Smollett and the Body* (Chicago: University of Chicago Press, 1995), 66; hereafter cited in the text.
   6. Eugene D. Genovese, *Roll, Jordon, Roll: The World the Slaves Made* (New York: Random House, 1974), 80.
   7. Lewis M. Knapp, *Tobias Smollett: Doctor of Men and Manners* (Princeton: Princeton University Press, 1949), 326–28.
   8. Hugh Thomas, *The Slave Trade: The Story of the Atlantic Slave Trade; 1440–1870* (New York: Simon and Schuster, 1997), 303–4; hereafter cited in the text.
   9. Thomas Astley, *A New General Collection of Voyages and Travels* (London, 1745), 2:160; hereafter cited in the text.
   10. "A Letter to the Gentlemen Merchants in the Guinea Trade," *Gentleman's Magazine* (July 1740): 10:341.

11. Vincent Carretta, *Equiano the African: Biography of a Self-Made Man* (Athens: University of Georgia Press, 2005), 238. Carretta also notes that "sporadic attacks on the trade or institution appeared in print from the late seventeenth century on, but they were apparently discreet comments unconnected to each other" (238). According to Linda Colley and other historians, the abolitionist movement reached its full swing after the American Revolution. See Colley, *Britons: Forging the Nation, 1707–1837* (New Haven: Yale University Press, 1992), 352.

12. Raymond Williams, *The Country and the City* (New York: Oxford University Press, 1973), 37.

Chapter Five

The Printing and Publication of Three Folio Editions of George Lyttelton's *To the Memory of a Lady Lately Deceased* (1747–1748)

James E. May

George Lyttelton (1709–1773) was awarded a critical preface in Samuel Johnson's *Lives of the Poets* for verse in which there is "nothing to be despised, and little to be admired." Johnson notes that Lyttelton lived "in the highest degree of connubial felicity" with his wife, the former Miss Lucy Fortescue of Devonshire, who bore him three children, until she "died in childbed."[1] Christine Gerrard, in her entry for the *Oxford Dictionary of National Biography*, notes that Lyttelton married Lucy Fortescue (1717/1718–1747) "on 15 June 1742" and "was devoted to her," and that her "early death, on 19 January 1747 at the age of twenty-nine, while giving birth . . . was a tremendous blow" to him. At the end of October 1747, Lyttelton published a long elegy to his wife, *To the Memory of a Lady Lately Deceased: A Monody*, with nineteen irregular stanzas printed on five folio sheets. Gerrard calls this Lyttelton's "most famous poem," noting it "has a simple directness which transcends its literary conventionality."

There were three folio editions (or issues), two dated 1747 and a "second edition" dated 1748 (all printed by Samuel Richardson for Andrew Millar).[2] In addition, the poem was reprinted in octavo by George Faulkner in Dublin during November 1747, an extract of more than half the poem appeared in the *British Magazine*'s "Supplement for the Year 1747" (for volume 2, February 1748), and Andrew Millar brought out a rare octavo in 1755.[3] There is no fine-paper issue identifying the first edition, all folios having the same unmarked paper, nor do any copies in the public domain appear to be presentation copies. The problem of determining the order of the two 1747 folios has received two different hypotheses and may sustain more, for the text does not descend on a linear path through the three folio impressions. The "1748" edition probably was not published after both 1747 folios. The complexity of shared type among the three editions allows a demonstration of the value of

analytical bibliography, calls into question the accuracy of mechanical collation in identifying resetting, illustrates the use of stored type, and reveals the
author's unusual involvement in the publications.

William Todd first called attention to the two 1747 folios (with very similar title pages) in 1950, identifying the *Daily Advertiser*'s notice on 1 December of a "Second Edition" as calling for an edition "hitherto unrecorded,"
which he linked to an "edition . . . not so designated on its title-page."[4] Todd
wrongly observed that it is "Reset throughout" and "may be distinguished
from the first only by the points listed below" (274–75). Overlooking most
textual variants, Todd identified the two 1747 editions by the length of a title
page rule, a catchword with and without a comma, and the presence or absence of indentation for two lines (4.11 and 11.18, at B2/3.16 and C2^v/8.18).
Todd concluded that the folio with the catchword error and without the lines
indented to reflect "similar rhymes" (in fact, indentations indicate lines of
fewer than ten syllables) showed "signs" of being "a reprint carelessly composed and hastily printed to meet the demand for copies" (275). Although
anyone who has done much collating would find nothing markedly careless in
a fifteen-page resetting with two errors, there are other compositorial errors in
1747A. As Todd shapes the problem, priority is decided by whether we infer
from incorrect readings in 1747A and correct in 1747B that 1747B later corrected 1747A's readings or that 1747A was carelessly produced after 1747B,
after Lyttelton had ceased to read proof. But the printing and publication
history is more complicated than Todd conceived it—for one, the printing
and publication orders might not be the same, if only for some of the sheets.

David Foxon, identifying a "second edition" dated 1748, reversed Todd's
order, for he found a greater resemblance in the "1748" edition (Foxon's
L339) to the more correct 1747 edition (L338) than to the incorrect.[5] Foxon
recognized that the less correct 1747 edition (Foxon's L337; my "1747A")
cannot have come between the more correct edition (my "1747B") and the
1748 edition, for he defined the 1748 as "a reimpression" of 1747B "except
for sheet C which corresponds to L337" (1747A). The English Short Title
Catalogue (ESTC) employs Foxon's ordering and the signature positions that
he relies on to distinguish the editions. From his own comparison of the typesettings relative to the head- and direction-lines, Foxon incorrectly thought
that the 1747B was a resetting of 1747A "except for sheets B and E." Foxon
only glanced at typographical similarities that require much fuller attention,
for typesettings shared by the three editions and peculiar to each preclude any
straightforward transmission (the three are not in a son-father-grandfather
relationship), but let us stick with the publication history for the moment.

Whatever sequence is offered for these three publications must be related
to an advertisement record that is more complicated than Todd and Foxon

have noted. Todd and Foxon both cite as the first advertisement that in the *Daily Advertiser* on 30 October (for A. Millar and sold by M. Cooper). Repeated through 12 November, it differs only in accidentals and abbreviations from another run on 30 October in the *General Advertiser*. The edition was also advertised as "This Day" published in the *London Evening Post* of 29–31 October and its next two issues. The second edition was first advertised over two weeks before the notice of December 1 that Todd discovered and Foxon repeated: the *Whitehall Evening Post* on 12 November, the *Daily Advertiser* on 14 November, and the *London Evening Post* on 14–17 November announced the publication of the "second edition." A renewed campaign started in early December, with the *Daily Advertiser*'s advertisement on 1 December, its first since 14 November (unchanged, from stored type), and a newly set advertisement—without an edition statement—in the *General Advertiser* on 2 December 1747. Then, after about five months without regular (perhaps any) newspaper advertisements,[6] on 27 and 28 May 1748, the *General Advertiser* carried Millar's announcement for "This Day . . . The Third Edition," and advertisements for the "Third Edition" followed beginning on 1 June in the *Daily Advertiser*. If we assume the folio dated 1748 appeared in May 1748, this advertisement record can support Foxon's ordering of the less correct edition first, followed by the more accurate 1747 edition in November, and the edition dated 1748 third in late spring 1748. However, it is impossible that the 1748 edition was printed four to six months after those of 1747, for it shares with the 1747 editions not only its paperstock but most of its typesettings, some on every page being shared with either 1747A or 1747B, usually but not always within a new skeleton and with slight textual alterations. Typesettings shared by 1748 with 1747B include the half title and title, with large type pieces that would not likely be stored long.

If we hypothesize that the 1748 "second edition," though printed in the fall, was not demanded until May 1748, we might suppose Millar, instead of just sending a waste sheet of the new title to the newspapers, or Lyttelton himself, perhaps with some pride, reported the more accurate edition count. Lyttelton apparently self-published the poem and may well have handled the advertisements: he was not prone to sell copyrights, neither 1747 edition is present in most deposit libraries, and Millar's general advertisements listing many publications at this time do not include the Lyttelton monody. In any case, if the May 1748 advertisements had spoken of the edition's being the "second edition," we might confidently suppose it was the 1748 "second edition"; the identification could be argued as likely even if there were no edition statement at all. But the description of the publication as a "third edition" raises the question whether one of the 1747 editions was not now put on sale—perhaps 1747A or 1747B because it was last printed or, even if first printed, the 1747A because it was less correct and so held off until all the more correct were sold.[7]

Furthermore, George Faulkner's Dublin edition (Foxon L340) throws a wrench into Foxon's order of editions. Faulkner's octavo, announced published in his *Dublin Journal* of 24–28 November 1747, clearly descends from either the more correct 1747B or the 1748 edition, as is indicated by variant readings. In the table of variants, we also see that the *British Magazine* (printed no later than January) also took the 1747B or the 1748 folio as printer's copy, but that Millar's 1755 octavo followed the less correct 1747A:

A2 [title page motto, l. 1]: *Te* 1747A 1755] *Te, 1747B 1748 D1747*
A2: *Catherine-Street 1747A*] *Catharine-Street 1747B 1748*
B1 [head title, l. 4]: Lately *1747A 1748 D1747 1755*] lately *1747B*
C1/5.18: antient *1747A 1748 1755*] ancient *1747B D1747 BM*
D1ᵛ/10.8: Gale. *1747A*] Gale, *1747B 1748 D1747 1755* [1747A errors]
D2/11.7 [14.7]: Elegant *1747A 1755*] elegant *1747B 1748 D1747*
E1/13.CW: Another,] ~, *1747A* [no CW error in *1747B 1748*]
E1ᵛ/14.15 [18.18]: His *1747A 1748 1755*] his *1747B D1747 BM*
E1ᵛ/14.18 [18.21]: his *1747A 1747B D1747 BM 1755*] His *1748*

This list does not include readings in the octavos and the *British Magazine* that vary from all three folios. Any absence of readings for the *British Magazine* text indicates lines not reproduced. In addition, there are the indentations to 4.11 and 11.18, noted by Todd, as well as another to the second line of stanza 1, occurring on B1/1.2, B2/3.16, and C2ᵛ/8.18 (with only eight, six, and eight syllables); those more apparent, on B2 and C2ᵛ (that in B1.2 is obscured by the ornamental initial in line 1), are properly indented in all editions but 1747A and 1755.[8] Setting these differences aside, variants among the folios total eleven accidentals, twelve if we include the catchwords: three involve indentation, three punctuation (A2, D1ᵛ, and the catchword on E1), four involve case (B1, D2, E1ᵛ, and E1ᵛ), and two involve spelling (A2, C1). Whether Lyttelton revised the text to produce a more correct 1747B edition or whether the press carelessly printed 1747A in a hurry after Lyttelton stopped inspecting the press, one can, as Todd did, distinguish the two editions as the more and the less correct. Except for the spelling "Catherine-Street" in 1747A and "Catharine-Street" in 1747B and perhaps the case difference for the "L" in "Lately" of the head title, the variants could be seen as corrections by 1747B of 1747A, including the change to lowercase on E1ᵛ. The spelling "antient" is not typical even of 1747A, for it and the other editions have "ancient" in the next line (C1/5.19) and at C1ᵛ/6.18. The use of uppercase for "Elegant" in 1747A is arguably inappropriate, for another adjective in the line is in lowercase, although adjectives are in uppercase two and four lines earlier ("Silver Lyre" and "Ambrosial Flowers"). The only obvious blunder requiring correction is the period after the subordinate clause ending "Gale" on D1^v (the only 1747A variant not found in 1755).

The collation indicates the Dublin edition probably took as printer's copy the more correct 1747B edition. The three line indentations at 1.2, 4.11 and 11.18 in 1747B and 1748; the punctuation in the motto; and the five accidental variants in the text distinguishing 1747B from 1747A are all shared by D1747. If 1747A were the printer's copy, we would need to suppose there were nine more variants in D1747 than if 1747B were the copy.[9] The 1748 reprinting is sufficiently accurate that it is possible that D1747 was set from 1748, for only three more textual variants would have been incurred by the Dublin compositor if 1748 were his copy: the spelling "ancient" in place of "antient" (7.11), and the change of the uppercase "H" in "His" at 18.18 and 18.21 to lowercase. Furthermore, D1747 does share with 1748 the uppercase "L" in "Lately" of the head title. But the 1748 edition's publication on 12 or 14 November makes it unlikely that the Dublin edition followed it—the transportation and then printing would take too long, and it seems unlikely that prepublication sheets would have been sent when published copies were available. In any case, as will soon be discussed, the 1748 edition was printed during or on the heels of the 1747B such that, if the 1748 did provide Faulkner's copy, probably the 1747B was ready for publication by October 30.

Todd's note does not refer to the octavo reprinting of the poem in Dublin by George Faulkner, though it is a relatively common edition. Faulkner first advertised the edition in his *Dublin Journal* on the 24–28 November 1747: "This Day will be published by the Printer hereof Price 2d | To the Memory of a Lady lately deceased, A MONODY. . . . By Mr. LYTTLETON."[10] Unlike the London advertisements and editions themselves, this advertisement, for the first time, publicly announces Lyttelton's authorship. The *Dublin Journal* contains many references to Lyttelton in and around November 1747, presumably to attract interest in Lyttelton works published by Faulkner. Faulkner had already this month published Lyttelton's *Observations on the Conversion of St. Paul, In a Letter to Gilbert West, Esq.* (advertised as by Lyttelton and sold by Faulkner in *Dublin Journal*, 21–24 November 1747—A. C. Elias, Jr., observed to me that the advertisement's placement on page 4 suggests it repeats an earlier advertisement). The *Dublin Journal* on 28 November–1 December printed in full "Verses Occasioned by a Poem of Mr. Lyttelton's to the Memory of Capt. Greenville of the Defiance Man of War, who was slain . . . 1747"; the *Dublin Journal* on 8–11 December offered "a more correct version" of this poem to Lyttelton, subjoining "the verses of Mr Lyttelton which occasioned it." These would only appear in London's *Daily Journal* on 8–12 December and in the *Gentleman's Magazine*'s 1747 supplement published in early February 1748 (17:600), so Faulkner may well have had the copy more directly than from the London papers. The *Dublin Journal* on 1–5 December, while rerunning Faulkner's advertisement for the monody to Lyttelton's wife, reprinted a six-couplet eulogy or epitaph for Lucy Lyttelton (it had appeared in the *British Magazine* of June 1747).[11]

Faulkner's publication on 24 November of an edition copying the 1747B folio argues that the latter was the first London edition published. It is hard to imagine 1747A's publication on 30 October and then 1747B's soon enough after to allow its transportation to Ireland in time for Faulkner to have produced a copy of it by 24 November. One can only hypothesize 1747B's sale as a second edition on 12 or 14 November and Faulkner's use of it as printer's copy if Faulkner obtained sheets from the shop prior to publication, either through Lyttelton's request or surreptitiously. Faulkner's concentration on Lyttelton might make it more likely that Faulkner received a prepublication copy or at least the superior revised text from Lyttelton. It is worth considering too that Faulkner within a fortnight published volumes 1–2 of Samuel Richardson's *Clarissa*, printed from prepublication sheets. Faulkner advertised it as available "This Day" on 5–8 December (*Dublin Journal*), only one week after the publication appeared in London ("This Day" in the *London Evening Post* on 28 November–1 December 1747, and in the *General Advertiser* on 2 December). Either Richardson had a distribution agreement with Faulkner wherein sheets were advanced to Ireland before publication, or Faulkner obtained stolen sheets of *Clarissa* prior to publication. Without Richardson's blessing, Faulkner previously had obtained prepublication sheets of the continuation of *Pamela,* and later he obtained sheets for *Sir Charles Grandison.*[12] Regardless of whatever agreements or thefts were involved in these cases, they indicate the possibility that sheets printed at Richardson's shop were posted to Ireland prior to that edition's London publication. If the sheets of more than one edition had been printed prior to publication, and if Faulkner obtained prepublication sheets, then Faulkner's printer's copy need not have been those sheets first published. Indeed, the sheets employed by Faulkner could have been a mixture of two editions. Thus, we might suppose the head title in the Dublin edition reads "Lately" like 1748 because that was the B sheet sent over; whereas Faulkner's edition has the variant readings of 1747B's sheets C–E because those sheets were sent. But, if Lyttelton sent Faulkner prepublication sheets, then Faulkner's use of the 1747B sheets argues these were perceived as the more correct and were combined to form the first published edition. That Faulkner's copy was not the 1747A sheets is compatible with the conclusion that 1747A was printed after 30 October.

One of two variant readings on the title pages of the London folios may be useful in relating the editions to the dated newspaper advertisements. The 1747A edition (Foxon's L337) has no comma after "*Te*" in the *first* line of the motto; the 1747B and the 1748 have a comma after "*Te*." The motto ("*Te, dulcis conjux, solo te in littore secum* | *Te veniente die, te decedente canebat*") is from Virgil's *Georgics*, book 4, lines 465–66, and the comma after "*Te*" seems the more common punctuation in contemporary editions.[13] The first "*Te*" in the motto is followed by a comma in all the initial advertisements and most that follow: *General Advertiser*'s settings of 30 October–11 November, *Daily Advertiser*'s on 30 October–12 November, its setting for a second edition on 14 November and 1 December (from stored type), and its setting for a third edition on 1 and 4 June 1748; the *Whitehall Evening Post*'s on 12 November for the second edition; and the *London Evening Post*'s on 29–31 October through its revised setting for the second edition on 14–17 November. If, as sometimes happened, the title pages were sent to the newspapers to provide the text of the advertisements, then the uniform use of a comma after "*Te*" in the first advertisements indicates that 1747B was first published. Almost certainly the 1748 edition with the comma after "*Te*" and the label "second edition" was the "second edition" offered in mid-November. Even if the advertisement bubble in early December was not for the 1747A, it is certainly the edition most easily identified with advertisements in May 1748. The 1747A is the only edition not certain to have been launched by advertising in October and November. Its title page fits the later advertisements. The first "*Te*" in the motto is not followed by a comma in the *General Advertiser* on 2–3 December (newly set, without edition statement) and on 27–28 May 1748 (newly set, with "Third Edition"). The 1747A edition without a comma after "*Te*" is more likely than the 1748 edition to have been that published in conjunction with advertisements in May 1748 announcing a "Third Edition," because it has no edition statement. Contrary evidence, however, is offered by the *Daily Advertiser*'s continued use of the comma in advertisements for all three editions, from late October through June,[14] but that particular compositor could have set copy from the old advertisements, not from a new title page.

Although variants in the Dublin edition and paratextual considerations suggest 1747B was first published, followed by the "second edition," we cannot further conclude safely this was the order of impressions. Let us examine the typesettings themselves for what can be inferred about the order of impressions. Both 1748 and 1747A share most of their type with 1747B, and although Foxon was right to observe that 1748 shares most of sheet C with only 1747A, it does not share all of it, and 1747B also shares some typesetting in C with 1747A, as well as some only with 1748. All three editions share most of the type set for sheets B and E and some of that set for sheets C and D. Type is shared exclusively by 1747A and 1748 (but not 1747B) throughout two-thirds of sheet C, and exclusively by 1747B and 1748 (but not 1747A) on C2^v and in four-fifths of sheet D.

In observing typesettings shared and separately set, I have relied on transparency overlays and the examination of most copies for the presence of identifiably damaged type; in many cases whole lines that appear identical with transparencies (and so would on a collating machine) in fact contain distinct type, identifiable from cracks, cuts, dents, and nicks not shared.[15] Because the shared settings frequently involve only groups of lines on a page, not even pages, and the three impressions share most of all the page-settings but the half title, title page, and two pages on the inner forme of D, we cannot hypothesize concurrent printing of multiple settings except on those four pages. Rather, we must presume that type was stored with the expectation that demand would require one or more reimpressions, but someone redistributed at least part of sheet C prior to the second impression and also type for the other sheets prior to at least the third impression. The fullest resetting occurs in C and D, the middle of the text, and not B and E; whereas, we would expect the first printed and redistributed formes would be those for sheet B.[16] Unless composition began in the middle, the sheets were not impressed in the order composed because some received press corrections. Another possible conclusion is that during the reimpressions of Lyttelton's poem, type was imperfectly stored such that some resetting was always required. And, presumably, very evidently damaged type pieces were on rare occasions replaced during the resetting.[17]

The editions 1747A and 1747B, the two most different, have the following shared and separate settings of type:

Sheet A has separate settings, encouraged by the reuse of large-font letters for half title and title page on opposites sides of sheet A and also for the head title on B1. In 1747A the same four-line large-font title appears on A1, A2, and B1.

Sheet B shares typesetting but for resetting in the head title and second line on B1, the presence or absence of indentation in B1/1.2 and B2/3.16, separate skeletons (i.e., different head- and direction-lines), stanza numbers, and several isolated letter pieces (e.g., B1.5, B1.13, B1^v.16).

Sheet C has separate settings except for at least three words in line C1.20 or all that line, lines C1^v.7-12, 16, and several words in or all line C2^v.2.[18] Thus, the distinguishing variants involving spelling at C1.18 ("antient" vs. "ancient") and the line indentation at C2^v/8.18 occur in separate settings.

Sheet D differs entirely on the inner forme (D1^v–D2), D1.1–15, and D2^v.1–5, 16–17, and 18 after the third word. Within sheet D, 1747A and 1747B only share D1.16–21 and D2^v. 6–14, some of 15, and 19–21 (demonstrated by multiple pieces of type in all but D2^v.10). Thus, the punctuation variant at D1^v.8 (after "Gale") and the case difference at D2.7 ("Elegant" vs. "elegant") occur where separate settings occur.

Sheet E has a largely shared text but all skeletons, stanza numbers, "FI-NIS," and ornament differ. The typesettings not shared in the text are complex and indicate the inadequacy of judgments based solely on mechanical collation:

E1: differing in some type pieces in line 1, the wrap of line 2, and type pieces uniquely broken in 1747B in lines 8 and 16 (while transparencies show different alignments for lines 10–11 and 14–16, broken type pieces show that at least most of lines 1–3 and 9–17 are shared);

E1^v: differing fully in lines 18–22 and with at least some type pieces substituted in lines 11, 13, 15, and 17 (conversely, broken type pieces are shared in lines 1–4, 7, and 9–17, and matching transparency overlays suggest lines 1–12, 15 before and after the variant "His," 16, and the end of 17 are shared). Note that accidental variants occur in lines 15 and 18.

E2: differing in isolated letter pieces, perhaps words, in lines 1, 4–6, 8, and 11.[19] This suggests that differences occurred during the substitution of lost pieces. Transparency overlays of E2 differ by about half an "n"-width in lines 1, 5–6, and 11, and there is more leading between lines 13 and 14 and between 15 and 16 in 1747B/1748 than in 1747A; broken type pieces are shared by all three editions in lines 1(2–3 [pieces]), 2(2), 7(2), 8(3), 9, 10(2), 11(3), 12(2), 13(3), 14(2), and 16(3).

Aside from sheet A, 1747A is most unlike both 1747B and 1748 in sheet D, where it has a separate setting for all the inner forme. I would judge from copies of at least 1747B that the inner forme was printed first and outer last for sheets B–D and the reverse for sheet E, where only the inner has two pages of type. This fits the conventional practice of the period according to Philip Gaskell.[20] Thus, we should not be surprised that in sheets C–D more resetting occurred on the inner forme pages than the outer forme. (The fact that redistribution of type occurred prematurely for multiple sheets might suggest that multiple sheets were impressed on the same day.)

Most noteworthy about the typesetting shared by 1747A and 1747B is that almost all of it is also shared with 1748. Most of the typesetting shared by the 1747A and 1748 editions in sheets B and D–E is also shared with 1747B. However, in sheet C (as in isolated letter pieces of sheets B and E), 1747A and 1748 share typesetting not found in 1747B: all C1/5 except line 20 shared by 1747B; all the text and probably stanza numbers on C1^v/6 but not footnotes and skeleton (also 1748 may have different damaged type pieces from 1747A in lines 13 and 17: "a" in "what" and "n" in "in"); all the text and stanza number on C2 but not the skeleton; and lines 1–7, 13–14, and 19–23 on C2^v. Insofar as 1747B and 1748 are more separate impressions and issues than separate editions, it is surprising that so little type set for sheet C is shared by 1747B and 1748. Yet even in sheet C some type is shared by 1747B and 1748 but not shared by 1747A.

Without regard to the skeletons, the 1747B edition shares with 1748 most of sheets A–B, lines in C shared by all three editions as well as eight lines on C2^v not shared with 1747A, and virtually all of D–E; 1747B and 1748 do not share the revised lines in the title page and head title (A2, B1), and any of C2/7. Copies 1747B and 1748 have identical settings for the half title (A1) but differ on the title page only as was necessary to insert "The SECOND EDITION" after the motto and alter the date (lines 1–8 and the imprint except for the date are shared). On B1, the head title is not shared by 1747B and 1748 even before the variant at "Lately" in line 4.[21] The 1747B and 1748 impressions share the same text throughout sheet B but not the same skeleton, though stanza numbers on B1, B1^v, and one of two on B2 are identically placed. Still, in 1747B and 1748 the bracketed paginations are not identical, and the signature on B1 and the catchwords of B1 and B2–B2^v are separate settings in all three editions.

Foxon wrongly implied that 1748's sheet C solely follows 1747A's. As noted above, 1747B and 1748 share some type in C1.20, C1^v.7–12 and 16, and C2^v.2 also shared by 1747A, but they also share type set for C2^v that is not shared with 1747A in lines 8–12 and 15–18 (excluding a few isolated letter pieces broken in either but not the other, as in lines 10 and 17), lines that closely match on transparencies. Thus, 1748 does not share 1747A's indentation variant in C2^v/8.18. Some broken type pieces on C2^v are unique to each edition,[22] but clearly the set of type in 1748 is an intersection of those sets of type found in 1747A and 1747B. No type for sheet C is shared by 1747A and 1747B that is not also in 1748.

In sheet D, 1747B and 1748 have the same settings, including both skeletons (all page numbers and catchwords and also the signature) as well as the stanza number on D2^v (the same nicked "X" occurs in "XVI"), but they were not a single impression, for there are at least different placements of the stanza numbers on D1 and the first number on D2 and different isolated type pieces (e.g., on D1^v/10.11, "B" in "Bough" severely bent and cut at 5:00–6:00 only in 1747B; and on D2^v/12.10 the "M" in "Mutual" deeply nicked atop the second stroke only in 1748). Both issues share the risen "C" in "Could" in line 4 of D1^r/9, and the same injured or misshaped left brackets in the headlines of D1^v and D2^r. The 1747B and 1748 issues also share the skeleton and nearly all the text setting for the inner forme of sheet E (E1^v–E2). All they do not share is the capitalization of "His" in E1^v.15 and E1^v.18 and isolated type on E2 shared by 1748 only with 1747A (lines 1 and 4) or uniquely broken in 1747B.[23] The editions have the identical settings on E1^r, including the stanza numbers, signature, and catchword, except that the bracketed page number is in a different position (and the space within brackets is narrower in 1747B).

As we draw conclusions from the typographical evidence, we need to remember that our conclusions focus on the order of printed sheets. We cannot even assume that sheets B–E of the 1747B and those of 1748 were all printed with the intention that they would form the editions they form, for they may have been sorted into issues after printing. The 1748 shares variant readings in sheets B, C, and E with 1747A, and, arguably, was viewed as less correct than 1747B. Accordingly, the sheets of 1747B and 1748 might have been divided as unrevised and revised sheets, with the second, or more correct, sheets going into the first edition published. That in no known case is a sheet proper to one edition found in one of the other two is also noteworthy, given how closely in time all three impressions occurred and the editions were published, and given that they were published on the same paperstock. Care must have been taken to avoid such intermingling. This is especially remarkable for 1747B and 1748 since their shared skeletons in sheets D and E indicate these sheets were printed at approximately the same time. Richardson's pressmen did not normally store the head- and direction-lines with the text's type. Furthermore, sharing identical settings on A1 and—but for edition statement and date—on A2, the A sheets of 1747B and 1748 were also printed at approximately the same time. Since the sheets of both issues were printed by early November (such that two weeks later one set was in Faulkner's hands and the other published as the second edition), only the 1747A could have been printed or published after mid-November.

In the transmission of text through the three editions, figured as X-Y-Z, the 1747 folios must be X and Z, and the 1748 must be the intervening Y. This is indicated by three considerations. First, in no sheet is broken type shared only by 1747A and 1747B, to the exclusion of 1748, suggesting that in the transmission, 1747A and 1747B were never beside each other, regardless of which was first printed. Yet, second, there is evidence that transmission occurred exclusively between 1747A and 1748 and between 1747B and 1748. Uninterrupted and exclusive transmission between 1747B and 1748 is obvious in sheets A and, from shared skeletons, sheets D and E (especially in D where 1747A has the inner forme entirely reset). In the B sheet 1747B and 1748 alone have line indentations on both inner and outer formes. As for the transmission between 1747A and 1748, 1747A shares with 1748 the page settings for C1 of the outer forme where 1747B is all but one line reset and for C2 of the inner forme where 1747B is fully reset. Furthermore, sheet E has isolated type shared between 1747A and 1748 to the exclusion of 1747B (for example, E2.1 and E2.4—see note 19). Finally, some lines of type are shared by all three editions in all formes but sheet A and the inner side of sheet D, ruling out concurrent impressions for all but those three formes, and, since 1747A's settings entirely differ there from 1747B–1748, we know that no compositor drew on two prior settings to produce those three. It follows that the 1748 "second edition" lies between the two 1747 folios.

Consider what sequences of impressions can explain the three page settings for C1^v, where 1747A and 1748 share all the text setting but not the skeleton, stanza numbers, and footnotes, and all three editions share lines 7–12 and 16. If 1747A was printed first and then 1748 second aided by standing type for lines 1–18 but not the footnotes, the third compositor, for 1747B, found type still standing for lines 7–12 and 16. If 1747B was printed first and then 1748 or 1747A second (though that 1747A was second is unlikely since no type is shared it exclusively with 1747B), the second compositor would complete the page setting while using seven lines still standing from 1747B and leave a full text setting except for notes and skeleton to be reused by the compositor for the third impression. Only someone's ignorantly distributing type intended to be stored can explain why 1747B only shares seven lines with 1748 when those two impressions, to judge from sheets A, D, and E, came very soon after one another. Nonetheless, we can explain the differences on C1^v by supposing the printing sequence was either 1747A-1748-1747B or 1747B-1748-1747A. However, several sequences do not work, such as 1747A-1747B-1748 and 1748-1747B-1747A. If 1747A came first, 1747B cannot have come second and then 1748 third, for the 1747B compositor only used lines 7–12 and 16 of 1747A while the 1748 compositor found the remaining lines of 1747A's page setting still available, re-embedding 7–12 and 16 into what was not used from 1747A by 1747B. For much the same reason, 1748 could not have been printed first followed by 1747B and then 1747A.

In addition, the typesettings on C2^v/8 are least plausibly explained by supposing the printing of both 1747A and 1747B prior to or after 1748. On C2^v all editions share only line 2; 1748 shares exclusively with 1747A type-settings for lines 1–7, 13, the beginning of 14, and 19–23; and 1748 shares exclusively with 1747B typesettings for lines 8–12 and 15–18.[24] If 1748 came first, we need imagine whichever compositor came second taking roughly half of his lines from 1748 (1–7, 13–14, 19–23 for 1747A or 2, 8–12 and 15–18 for 1747B) and then the third compositor receiving only line 2 from the second setting but also finding in storage half the type for the page from the first setting, type never used in the second. If 1747A or 1747B were the first and second settings, whichever compositor came second would employ only line 2 from the first setting, yet 1748's compositor, coming third, would find roughly half the first page setting unused by the second compositor but still available. For instance, the 1748 compositor would find only lines 2, 8–12, and 15–18 left if 1747B was the second impression but coincidentally find the very lines not left by 1747B (1, 3–7, 13–14, and 19–23) were left standing from 1747A. There could not have been full separate settings of 1747A and 1747B for the 1748 compositor to work with since the settings for 1747A and 1747B share the same setting of line 2. No least-effort principle can explain C2^v. Presumably a second compositor set part of sheet C in duplicate when a new order came from Lyttelton or the earlier typesetting was not found.

Accepting the likelihood that 1748 was the second impression of sheet C, we may find on C2^v some modest support for supposing 1747A printed last. If the order was 1747A-1748-1747B, 1748's compositor would have put to use fourteen lines it shares with 1747A but then passed on to 1747B only nine lines including line 18 newly set and indented, or, if the order was 1747B-1748-1747A, the 1748 compositor would have reused ten lines 1748 shares with 1747B but then reset and passed on to 1747A fourteen lines. In the 1747B-1748-1747A ordering, line 18 would be indented in the first and second editions because 1747B's compositor saw it indented in the manu-script and 1748's compositor received it indented; then 1747A's compositor would mistakenly reset the line without the indentation and the insufficient correction more likely in a third impression failed to discover the mistake. If 1747A had been the first printed and was set from manuscript, the omitted indentation would involve an error not only by the author or compositor but by the corrector of a first edition setting. If 1747A was last printed, there is only one mistake, and that could easily result from spacing lost in type in-completely stored in a tray.

One variant inviting a close look at typographical evidence is the upper-case "Lately" in 1747A and 1748 and the lowercase "lately" in 1747B within the fourth line of the half title ("A LADY Lately Deceased"). This is the only instance in sheet B where 1748 shares a variant with 1747A but not with 1747B. Was it a deliberate correction and does it suggest anything about the order of impressions? The answers require a discussion of sheet A, for all three editions share some type in the large-font lines 1–4 of the half title and/ or the title page with the head title on B1. Copy 1747A has the same setting for these lines on all three pages, and, hence, may have an uppercase "L" in "Lately" on B1 in consequence of reusing type set up for the A sheet. Copy 1747A's head title setting differs from those in 1747B and 1748 except per-haps in the final three words of line 4, where damaged type pieces recur in all editions.[25] In addition, damaged "M" pieces are shared by the three editions if in different positions.[26] From type shared by 1747A with 1747B and 1748, we can conclude that no two settings of A1–B1 were concurrently impressed or stored fully. The reuse of large type pieces on these three pages explains why the large type pieces for the head title were not shared by 1747B and 1748. (It also suggests that Richardson's shop had a shortage of large-font letters.)

Reflecting an economy of effort, 1747B and 1748 fully share a setting for A1 and are probably the same impression (transparency overlays are identical and what broken type they have is shared). They also share the setting of A2 but for changes required to add the edition statement and alter the date. (Some of the same type appears in both half title and title page, particularly in line 4 where they share the same "A" in "A" in addition to the two pieces also in 1747A, but the "M" pieces differ, with the thrice broken first "M" in "Memory" on A2 not appearing on A1.) Copies 1747B and 1748 do not share the same setting of the head title, not only differing in line 4 ("Lately" in 1747B and "lately" in 1748) but also having different "M" pieces in "MEMORY" of line 2 (1748 has an unbroken first "M"). Copy 1748's half title and head title share the four-line title setting. Copy 1747B's title page and the head title share some of the same setting (such as the second "M" in "Memory"; the alignments of lines 1–3 are shared) but differ in more than the presence on B1 of a lowercase "l" in "lately" and that line's spacing (different initial "M" pieces occur in "Memory," both with three cuts, but A2's has a break in the left foot and B1's has a break atop the third stroke). We can explain in two ways why 1747B and 1748 do not share the same setting of the head title nor sheet B's skeletons but do share sheet B's text settings: (1) 1748's B sheet was printed; then the half title of 1747B and 1748 using type from 1748's head title on B1; then, inserting the broken first "M," 1748's title page; then, following revision, 1747B's title page; then, following alteration of the four-line title, including the change to "lately" and the insertion of a different badly injured first "M," 1747B's B sheet; or (2) 1747B's sheet B was impressed; then, with one bad "M" replaced by another and with "Lately" now capitalized, the title page of 1747B; then, after changing the date and adding the edition number, the title page of 1748; then, removing the injured first "M," the half title of both issues; and then the B sheet of 1748. The second hypothesis seems much more likely: it involves the removal of the bad first "M" in "Memory" before printing the half title; it supposes the first edition to be published was printed first, thus the first edition's title before the press variant second's; and it allows the lowercase "lately" in the first-impressed 1747B setting of B1 to follow from the manuscript. Moreover, this sequence assists the hypothesis that 1747A was printed last, for it allows 1747A's uppercase "Lately" on B1 to derive from 1747A's following 1748 or even re-employing some type in 1748's head title. Also, 1747A's failure to indent lines B1.2 and B2.16 seems less likely to arise from a flawed manuscript or the faulty correction of proofs than from quads falling out of stored type (much of the typographical substitution in shared settings occurs at the start and end of lines, such as the final letter in line 5 of B1). The indentation of B1.2, given the large-font "A" in B1.1, would have been more easily overlooked setting copy from a printed text (Todd missed it) than from a manuscript. But, to return to the case variant in the head title, it does not necessarily involve a correction the way variants on E1^v do, for 1747B and 1748 have different settings, and 1747A and 1748 may have "Lately" capitalized because type was carried over to save work. (And the case difference, if recognized, could have been welcomed for suggesting that 1748 was truly a new edition, as could different skeletons in later formes of 1747B and 1748.)

Of the textual variants, most significant are the variant readings on E1^v.15 and E1^v.18 where a possessive adjective refers to God: 1747B (like D1747) has consistently lowercase, 1748 has consistently uppercase, and 1747A has uppercase in line 15 but lowercase in line 18 (aside from 1755, it is the only one of six settings in 1747–1755 treating them inconsistently). Since 1747B and 1748 have an otherwise identical setting for this entire page, either 1747B's "his" or 1748's "His" is a deliberate correction of the other. Given the reference, uppercase may seem on the whole more normative, especially where, as here, no capitalized words precede and follow, but below in line 19 ("Would thy fond Love his Grace to her controul") the possessive for "God's" is in lowercase in all editions, even if capitalized words flank it. Several dozen adjectives can be found capitalized in the folios, yet the handling of "His" and "Her" suggest the norm was to capitalize only nominal use, not adjectival (e.g., B1^v/2.12–13). No convincing case can be made from other passages for Lyttelton's final intention at E1^v.15 and E1^v.18. If 1747A was produced first, 1748 inherited as part of the lines 1–17 shared with it the uppercase "His" in line 15; in resetting as was necessary lines 18–22, 1748's compositor merely regularized the adjectival pronoun three lines below. Then the 1747B compositor, coming third, deliberately changed "His" and "His" to lowercase without making any other alteration. If 1747B came first, providing 1748 with the entire page of preset type, 1748's compositor deliberately capitalized the modifier. Then the 1747A came third, letting stand the uppercase "His" in line 15 but failing to regularize with capitalization the possessive modifier in line 18. In either scenario, the compositor of 1747A inconsistently treats parallel words. If 1747A came first, the inconsistency can be explained as following from the authorial manuscript; if 1747A came after 1748, the inconsistency can be explained as a careless regularization of adjectives and pronouns into lowercase, which commonly happens in reprint editions (such as in both the Dublin 1747 and the *British Magazine* reprintings).

Although one can call 1747B the "more correct" edition and 1747A the "less," as the inconsistent use of "His" and "his" on E1^v in 1747A indicates, the presence of correct and incorrect readings arises from the reuse or failure to reuse available type, in part subject to accident. As noted, the uppercase "Lately" on B1 of 1747A and 1748 may result from the reuse of type from sheet A. Issues 1747B and 1748 share the correct punctuation in D1^v/10.8 and the lowercase "e" in "elegant" of D2/11.7 because they share the entire forme. Similarly, 1747B and 1748 share the punctuation in the catchword on E1 and the proper indentation of short lines at B2/3.16 and C2^v/8.18 because they share these line settings. Thus, too, 1747A and 1748 share the archaic spelling "antient" at C1/5.18 because they share type at that point.

One final kind of argument can be made by focusing on damaged type pieces, those that are replaced prior to reimpression and those that are damaged during an impression. At E2.11 an obviously broken long "s" in "Rise" occurs in 1747A but not in 1747B and 1748, though the line setting otherwise seems the same in all editions (all share three broken letter pieces). I tracked this letter closely, hoping to find that it broke during a press run and so could be evidence of the order of editions. In the fifteen extant copies of 1747A, it is cut short at 12:00, but it is not cut in the twenty-four extant copies of 1747B nor in the twenty-seven copies of 1748. Since no copy of 1747A has the letter unbroken, it remains possible that 1747A was set first and the piece replaced in later resetting. However, in sheet E, an identifiable type piece seems broken worst in 1747A, indicating it was printed last: in E1^v.15 the "O" in "Or" at 12:00 has a dent or crack downward to the left in 1747B (CaOHM CLU-C CSmH CU-B EU[2] InU MH NIC NjP NN-B O[2] OClW PSt TxU) as it does in most copies of 1748 (CU-B InU IU L[2] NcD NIC NSbSU O Owo ShU TxHR TxHU TxU; dented only in LSU MH ViNO), in both producing a tongue of ink downward to the left; all copies of 1747A have the widest cut seen in other editions and most have a wider cut along the same diagonal (CaAEU CU-D DLC ICU IU L MH NIC O PSt TxU WU). One strong confirmation of the greater injury to 1747A is that those copies at libraries with 1747B and/or 1748, after direct comparison, all show the letter piece in 1747A broken widest (IU L O NIC PSt).

From type pieces broken during an impression, the evidence is mixed but at least for sheet C points overwhelmingly toward 1747A's following 1748. In sheet C, eight identifiably broken pieces of type appear more injured in 1747A than in 1748. Of these, three identifiable pieces of type appear to break in 1748 and to suffer only the fullest deterioration in 1747A, providing evidence that sheet C of 1747A was printed after that of 1748. In C1/5.16, the "o" in "Hoar" at 11:30–11:45 is not injured in some 1748 (Cp L1 LSU NcU NIC NSbSU), is shaved thin and/or nicked but probably continuous in others (IU NcD Ne TxHR TxHU ViNO), and is cracked in others but never cut wider than in any 1747A (E[2] InU L2 Owo ShU TxU); whereas, it is cut wide at 11:30–11:45 in all 1747A examined for it (CaAEU CU-D DLC ICU IU L NIC O PSt TxU WU) and in all but CaAEU and PSt the cut is wider than in the 1748 copy at InU, with the widest cut of any 1748 copies. In C1.17, the "o" in "You" is uninjured in some 1748 (CaOHM CU-B E[2] InU TxU) but cut at 11–12:30 in most 1748 copies (not as wide as 1747A: LSU TxHR TxHU; as wide as 1747A: Cp IU L[2] MH NcD NcU Ne NIC NSbSU O Owo ShU ViNO); it is cut wide in all 1747A examined for it (CaAEU CU-D DLC ICU IU L MH NIC O PSt TxU WU). Less convincing but noteworthy is that in C1.8, the "W" in "Where" is cut in the lower half of the second stroke in 1747A (CaAEU CU-D ICU IU L NIC O PSt TxU), but it is uncut in some 1748 (E[2] InU IU L[2] LSU NcD TxHR ViNO) and cut or cracked in others (NIC NSbSU TxHU TxU and probably NeU and Owo).

Four other identifiable type pieces shared by 1747A and 1748 apparently become broken in 1747A. In C1.2, the "w" in "own" is distinguishable by a dent from the right and break in the middle of the second stroke of both editions' copies, but it has the fourth stroke also cracked in some copies of 1747A (CaAEU CU-D IU Pst TxU) or nicked (ICU NIC; not injured in L). In C1.11, "L" in "Love" has a thin horizontal stroke headed downward in both editions; in all 1748 copies seen, the bottom right serif has the normal upward serif, but in 1747A the serif is a small tooth in L O and PSt, has almost no upward movement in CaAEU CU-D ICU NIC TxU, and is entirely missing in IU. In C2^v.13, the "a" in "Wealth" has a dot centered in the bottom loop in all copies of both editions; it is uncut in all copies of 1748 seen but cut at 9:00 in 1747A copies CU-D ICU L NIC PSt and cut fairly wide in CaAEU IU and TxU. In C2^v.5, the "e" in "Manners" is nicked or bubbled at 7:30 in 1748 (apparent in most copies, such as CaOHM InU IU LSU NcD), but in most 1747A copies it has in addition to this flaw a cut at 5:00 in the upper circle of 1747A (CaAEU CU-D ICU IU L NIC O PSt TxU).

Prior to or soon after the first edition's publication, Millar or, more likely, Lyttelton called for the press variant second edition to be set up with the date "1748," expecting sales would require a second edition in or after December, with the edition number and 1748 date insisting on the poem's popular success and the edition's currency. This "second edition" was almost certainly the second published, on 12 or 14 November to judge from advertisements. Sheets A and D–E of the 1748 edition were "in the press" at the very same time as at least those sheets of 1747B, which cannot be said of any sheets of 1747A. Thus, of the two editions dated 1747, only 1747B can be safely assumed to have been printed prior to the work's publication on 30 October. Since the Dublin edition published by 24 November took as printer's copy sheets of 1747B (though possibly several of 1748), the 1747B is more likely to have been the first published. That the *British Magazine* was set from

1747B or 1748 increases the likelihood that 1747A was not yet published. Similarly, since the 1755 octavo took 1747A as its printer's copy, 1747A was more likely the last published and, since not fully sold off, more likely to be turned over to compositors for resetting. That only fifteen copies of 1747A are extant in libraries, whereas twenty-four and twenty-seven are for 1747B and 1748, suggests that 1747A was published third, in a smaller run, when consumer demand was falling off.[27] That copies of 1747B and 1748 are extant in comparable numbers (the greater number of the first edition predictably in private hands will even out their numbers) and share the half title and some skeletons raises the possibility that they were part of a divided order to the press. But, given their differences, unless the appearance of separate editions was desired, probably the press was only told to expect the possibility of a second edition.

Lyttelton could have decided to print a more ambitious impression after the printing of sheets now in 1747A had begun—perhaps flaws in what had been printed only encouraged that decision. And any sheets of 1747A first printed were presumably insufficient to have been used for the sheets of 1747B or 1748. But some sheets of 1747A, the A sheet for one, could have been impressed before those of the 1747B and 1748 editions. This would explain why 1747A and 1748 bear the titles they do and neither is called the third edition. It is possible that sheet C was being composed but was abandoned when 1747B and 1748 were undertaken (hence the confused double settings in sheet C). The E sheet of 1747A might have been printed first if what is now the E sheet of 1748 was printed second and then held off for a more correct sheet E of 1747B. If other sheets of this aborted first impression had been printed, textual revisions might have led to some being discarded for fully reset sheets. However, in the face of all these contingencies, it is safer to conclude that the title pages are misleading and that 1747A was called for in smaller size to meet lessened demand in late 1747. If we suppose sheets of 1747A were first printed prior to publication and thus that all three impressions occurred prior to publication, we cannot easily explain the amount of type not shared by 1747A with 1747B–1748. As discussed above, the failure to indent lines in sheets B and C of 1747A is more easily explained by those sheets' having been set from standing type rather than from manuscript. We have reviewed typographical and textual evidence that 1747A's sheets B, C, and E were probably printed with type stored from 1748, to which settings they are more closely linked than to those of 1747B. Probably more time elapsed between the impressions of 1748 and 1747A than had between those of 1747B and 1748, not so much that most type was no longer in storage but enough that authorial involvement ceased and the press was less vigilant. There is a higher ratio of errors in lines set solely for 1747A than in those set for 1747B. If 1747A followed the other two impressions, sixty-three lines were reset on C2ᵛ, D1–D2ᵛ, and E1ᵛ. In them occur the indentation error at C2ᵛ.18, the punctuation error at D2.7, the uppercase "Elegant" at D2.7, and the inconsistent use of lowercase "his" at E1ᵛ.18. By contrast, in the sixty-six lines unique to 1747B (19 lines on C1, 11 on C1ᵛ, 23 on C2, and 13 on C2ᵛ), the compositor only varies once from the other two editions, adding the variant "ancient" at C1.18, a regularization agreeing with the spelling in the next line. Thus, we are left with the conclusion that 1747A was printed after 1747B and 1748, and, thus, with another instance of Todd's supposition that succeeding reprints grow incorrect.

NOTES

1. *The Lives of the Most Eminent English Poets; with Critical Observations on Their Work*, ed. Roger Lonsdale (Oxford: Clarendon, 2006), 4:189–90, 4:186.

2. *To the Memory of a Lady Lately Deceased: A Monody* (London: For A. Millar and sold by M. Cooper, 1747, 1747, and, "2nd ed.," 1748); all collate: 2°: *A*² B–E² [$1 signed]; pp. [*iv*] *1* 2–15 *16 blank*. The half title (hft) in all editions reads "[rule] | TO THE | MEMORY | OF | A Lᴀᴅʏ Lately Deceased. | [rule] | {Price One Shilling.}." The title page (A2) for 1747A (Foxon L337) reads: "TO THE | MEMORY | OF | A Lᴀᴅʏ Lately Deceased. | A | MONODY. | [rule] | *Te dulcis conjux, solo te in littore secum* | *Te veniente die, te decedente canebat.* | [rule] | [ornament of seated man fishing toward his right, 51.5 x 60.5 mm.] | [rule] | *LONDON*: | Printed for A. Mɪʟʟᴀʀ, over-against *Catherine-Street* in the *Strand*; | And Sold by M. Cᴏᴏᴘᴇʀ, at the *Globe* in *Pater-noster Row.* | [rule, 38–39 mm. in 1747A; 44–45 in 1747B and 1748] | M DCC XLVII." For simplicity, I refer to these folio publications as "editions," but technically the 1748 "second edition," sharing more than two-thirds of its type with 1747B, is a reissue and reimpression with partial resetting. The two 1747 folios are largely different settings on three of five sheets, involving about half the type set, and so can be called "different editions." All editions have unmarked paper with horizontal chain-lines 27–28 mm. across; tranchefiles 13–14 mm. occur either at the top or bottom, never both, of untrimmed sheets of copies C, CU-B, E1, LdU-B, MH, NN-B, and PSt (whole sheets were cut in half, hence the horizontal chain-lines). All lack press figures. All have cut ornaments belonging to Samuel Richardson: title page vignette of a man fishing (Sale #59; Maslen #288); B1/1: headpiece of face over crossed flower horns, within foliation, 35.5 x 132 mm. (Sale #99; Maslen #018); E2/15: tailpiece, fruit vase, with birds flanking, 44 x 50 mm., two cuts: in 1747A: birds' beaks touching fruit (Sale #75; Maslen #304); in 1747B and 1748: a variant cut with beaks not touching fruit (Sale #74; Maslen #303). William M. Sale, Jr., identified the ornaments correctly in noting only the 1747B and 1748 editions in *Samuel Richardson: Master Printer* (Ithaca: Cornell University Press, 1950), 186, 296, 304, and 314. Keith Maslen similarly fails to note the 1747A folio; he wrongly dates the "second" edition "1747" and indicates his ornament #280 as the

title-page ornament of 1747B: in fact, it is #288 (*Samuel Richardson of London Printer: A Study of his Printing based on Ornament Use and Business Accounts* [Dunedin, NZ: English Dept., University of Otago, 2001], 104). The records on RLIN and OCLC do not faithfully distinguish copies of the two 1747 editions. All copies in the public domain have been examined and are listed below. Library abbreviations are those in the *National Union Catalogue* and David Foxon's *English Verse, 1701–1750* (Cambridge: Cambridge University Press, 1975). All measurements are in millimeters.

1747A: Recognized by *"Te"* without a comma following in the first line of motto and the spelling "Catherine" in the imprint. Foxon L337 [Foxon, *English Verse, 1701–1750*, 1:436–37]; ESTC T51302 (wrongly listing copies of 1747B at CaOHM CaOTU CLU-C CU-B MR[2] NIC NN-Berg OClWR TxHR and overlooking copies at CtY-B DLC ICU MH PSt TxU). Copies examined (assume hft [half title] present unless noted): C (7720.a.3; uncut, 366 x 235); CaAEU [U. of Alberta]; CtY-B (Fielding +2a 734d[6]); CU-Davis; DLC (-hft; 4 ll. of MS verse on E2ᵛ); ICU (PR 3543. L8T8 1747; -hft); IU (xq821.L99t; 346 x 221); L (11630.h.34; 339 x 221; rebound by British Library in brown buckram; ESTC copy of record, reproduced on microfilm in *The Eighteenth Century*, reel 1464, no. 19 and on Eighteenth-Century Collections Online [ECCO]); LdU-B ([Brotherton Collection] uncut, 370 x 234); MH (*fEC75. L9994.747t; 342 x 220); NIC (PR3542.L8T6++ 1747; 310 x 212); O (G. Pamph. 1662[24]; 328 x 222; with MS addition on p. 8 regarding final line: "in a subsequent Edition this line is changed to— | Tears from sweet Virtue; source benevolent to All"); PSt ([Penn State U.] PR3542.L8T6 1747Q; 342 x 227; disbound); TxU (Am L999 +L47t; 340 x 222); WU.

1747B: Distinguished by *"Te,"* with a comma in the first line of motto on A2 and "lately" (lowercase) in l. 4 of head title on B1. Foxon L338; ESTC T221490, missing half the copies and wrongly listing ICU, LSU, and a third copy claimed for O—the G. Pamph. 1663[5] copy is Lyttelton's *The Progress of Love, in Four Eclogues* (1732). Not filmed in *The Eighteenth Century*. Copies examined: CaOHM (trimmed small unevenly); CaOTU; CLU-C (uncut, 376 x 242–43; -hft); CSmH; CU-B (pfPR3542.L8T6 1747; 333 x 217; disbound); DFo; EU (2: 1) *S.18.32/12; 310 x 201; +hft; rebound in blue buckram; 2) Q P[amphlets].486/31; -hft; with thirty poems indexed in contemporary MS); ICN (-hft); InU (PR3542.L8T5; 305–8 x 208); L (2: 1) 643.m.16[15]; 342 x 210; hft bound after A2; rebound by BL with other folio poems in half calf with green boards; 2) 840.m.1[21]; 336 x 218; -hft); MH (*fEC75. L9994.747tb; 340 x 218); MR (2: 1) R100161.19; 350 x 220; +hft; rebound with twenty-three other items in marbled paperboards with calf spine; 2) R66851; 280 x 190, severely cropped; -hft); NIC (PR3542.L8T6++; 340 x 226); NjP; NN-B ([Berg Collection] uncut, 378 x 240; no MS notes as called for by ESTC); O (2: 1) G. Pamph 1662[23]; 348 x 224; -hft; in collection of folio poems; 2) G. Pamph. 1666[27]; 320 x 201; -hft); OClWR [Case Western Reserve U.]; PSt (Williamscote Library, PR3542. L8T6 1747a Q; uncut, 370 x 238; with contemporary MS notations by John Loveday: on p. 8, ult. l. crossed out and replaced with "Tears from sweet Virtue's source, benevolent to all"; p. 10.8 [13.4]: "its Western" underlined for replacement with "her gentle" written above; final line of poem with "n" inserted before "e'er"; with commas added in MS on p. 1 after ll. 6, 7, and 9, and after l. 15 on p. 15); TxHR ([Rice

U.] *PR 3542.L8T6; 338 x 220; half title signed "R Eyre"); TxU (Wm L999 +747t; 335 x 208).

1748: Distinguished by "1748" and "second edition"; and "Lately" in uppercase within head title; Foxon L339; ESTC T4628, noting microfilm in *The Eighteenth Century*, reel 6870, no. 9, and reproduction on ECCO, listing a TxHR copy not extant and overlooking copies at CtY (in Miscellaneous Poems 57), O (Vet.A4c.30[5]), and ViNO. Copies examined: Cp [Pembroke College]; CaOHM (disbound; 318 x 209); CtY-B (2: 1) 1978 +331; 300 x 222; disbound; 2) Miscellaneous Poems 57; 271 x 210; -hft); CU-B (fPR3542.L8T6 1748; 340 x 209; rebound); E (2: 1) 7.66; uncut and unbound, 366-68 x 460 across sheet; 2) Nha.E.18/2; 333 x 215); InU (PR 3542. L8T5 1748; 346 x 215); IU (xq821.08 P7514; 338 x 218); L (2: 1) 11630.h.35; -hft; 341 x 217; 2) 11657.m.28; +hft; 322 x 200); LdU-B (320 x 195); LSU; MH (*fEC75. L9994.747tc; uncut, 375 x 230); NcD; NcU; Ne (Literary and Philosophical Society of Newcastle); NIC (Rare PR3542.L8T6+ 1748; 280 x 196; on hft MS "Robt Master | E Coll: Ball"); NPM ([Pierpont Morgan] 77499.32); O (Vet.A4c.30[5]; 340 x 220; -hft); Owo; ShU ([U. of Sheffield] -hft); NSbSU [State U. of New York at Stony Brook] -hft); TxHR (WRC PR3542.L8T6 1748; 337 x 226; disbound); TxHU [U. of Houston]; TxU (Am L999 +747tb; 318 x 202); ViNO [Old Dominion U.] -hft). OCLC lists copies of the 1748 edition with accuracy except for double listing CU-Berkeley. I thank the following librarians for their assistance: Jean Archibald at University of Edinburgh, John Bidwell of the Pierpont Morgan Library, A. Iris Donovan at the Bancroft, Jeannine Green at the University of Alberta, Geoffrey Groom at the Bodleian, Janice Halecki at Old Dominion University, Susan Halpert at the Houghton, Sue Hanson of Case Western Reserve University, Kristen Nyitray of Stony Brook University, Philip Oldfield at the University of Toronto, Julie Ramwell and Thomas Gordon at the John Rylands University Library of Manchester, Meg Rich at Princeton University, Barbara Richards and Jill Rosenshield at Wisconsin University, Jennifer Schaffner at the Clark, John L. Skarstad at the University of California at Davis, Carl Spadoni at McMaster University, Stephen Tabor at the Huntington, and Georgianna Ziegler at the Folger.

3. Dublin: by George Faulkner, 1747; 8vo half-sheet imposition: A^4 B^4; pp. *1-2* 3–15 *16 advt.*; Foxon L340; ESTC T77100, noting twenty-two copies; copies examined: CaOHM, CLU-C, CtY-B, L (1490.r.41; 191 x 118; on ECCO), NIC, TxU. In its "Supplement to Volume 2" (1747), 595–98 (published February 4, 1748, according to the *General Advertiser*), the *British Magazine* reprinted stanzas 1–3, 6–7, 10–11, 12.22–25 (last four lines), 13–16, 18.16–21, and 19.15–20 (last six lines)—for a total of 136 lines (entitled "Extract of Mr. Littleton's Monody to the Memory of his deceased Lady"). These contain no substantive or punctuation variants and almost no accidental variants not related to emphatic accidentals (it places all common nouns and adjectives in lowercase and all italic to roman font). Due to its great fidelity, we can safely conclude it derives from 1747B: it avoids 1747A's indentation errors and has only two punctuation variants if from 1747A, only one if from 1747B or 1748; two spelling variants if from 1747A or 1748, only one if from 1747B. Lyttelton's poem was fully reprinted in 1755 ("Printed for A. MILLAR, in the Strand. | MDC-CLV."); 8vo: A^1 B-C^4 D^1 [$1–2 signed]; pp. [*ii*] *1* 2–17, *18 blank*; press figures: B4/7-3; C4ᵛ/16-6. In the sole copy, located in the Brotherton Collection of the University of

Leeds, there are MS corrections on p. 17 to 19.13: "fleetings" has "s" crossed out in
pen and the final line has "n" added to "e'er" (after "Pow'r"). This edition took 1747A
as printer's copy, for it has "*Te*" without a comma in the motto's first line, uppercase
"Lately" in B1's head title, all 1747A's text variants but the comma after "Gale" at
D1ᵛ.8 of the folios and fails to indent lines 4.11 and 11.18.

4. "Variant Editions of Lyttelton's 'To the Memory of a Lady Lately Deceased,'"
Papers of the Bibliographical Society of America 44 (1950): 274–75.

5. *English Verse, 1701–1750*, 1:436–37. As mentioned above in note 2, William
Sale had noted a second edition the same year as Todd's article.

6. No advertisements for the edition appear between early December 1747 and late
May 1748 in the *Daily Advertiser, General Advertiser, London Evening Post, London
Gazette, Penny London Post, St. James Post, Westminster Journal*, and *Whitehall
Evening Post*. Lyttelton's *To the Memory* was listed under new books in the Novem-
ber 1747 issues of the *Gentleman's Magazine* (17:548), *London Magazine* (536), and
British Magazine (2:517); subsequent editions apparently were not noted.

7. Lyttelton's suppression of an incorrect monody to his wife must be considered possible, for William Zachs indicates that two editions of Lyttelton's lengthy
Dialogues of the Dead were produced for publications by John Murray in 1768,
with Lyttelton's direct involvement (as in the ordering of presentation copies).
These are "two entirely distinct settings," distinguishable by press figures, with the
less correct "reissued in 1774 with an altered title page," apparently a canceled title
page differing only in the date (*The First John Murray and the Late Eighteenth-
Century London Book Trade with a Checklist of His Publications* [Oxford: Oxford
University Press for the British Academy, 1998], 22–23, 265). These editions
are listed as #1 and #2 with the second also listed as #81 under the 1774 date in
the chronological bibliography of Murray's publications (255 and 265). Also, as
Johnson notes in his "Life of Lyttelton" in *Lives of the Poets* (see note 1, above),
Lyttelton incurred extraordinary personal cost ("at least a thousand pounds") for
multiple impressions of his *History of Henry the Second*, needed to satisfy his
desire for an accurate text.

8. In addition, superscript footnote letter "c" before *Anio* in C1ᵛ/6.8 is missing
from all copies of 1748 (probably lost after composing, for footnote letter "d" in the
following line is dropped low in all copies). The half title's rules are 148–49 mm.
apart in 1747A and 158–60 mm. apart in 1747B and 1748.

9. In the Dublin resetting there are five changes to lowercase (four involve pronouns) and two changes to uppercase ("*veniente*" in the motto and "midst" at 13.10).
This pattern suggests that, were 1747A taken as copy, the uppercase "L" in "Lately"
in the head title, the uppercase "E" in "Elegant" at 14.7 and "H" in "His" at 18.20
would have been reduced to lowercase as part of a characteristic change. The other
Dublin changes are: eight changes in punctuation, seven in spelling (including "*canchat*" for "*canebat*" in the motto, the loss of an apostrophe for "Shepherd's" [3.7],
"pours" to "pour" [8.8], the loss of hyphens at 16.11 and 19.17, and "*Appeninus*" for
"*Apenninus*" [13.11]), and three substantive errors: the omission of "*te*" in the motto's
second line, the addition of an incorrect "is" in the footnote to 8, and the reasonable
(still meaningful) substitution of "ne'er" for "e'er" at 19.20.

10. The advertisement, transcribed by A. C. Elias, Jr., was rerun in the next two issues, with the misspelling "canchat," also on the Dublin edition's title page.

11. Entitled "To the Memory of Lucy Lyttelton," the verses follow an epitaph describing her relations, death, and character. These twelve lines are entitled "Verses, Making Part of an Epitaph on the Same Lady" in *The Works of George Lord Lyttelton,* 3rd ed. (London: J. Dodsley, 1776), 3:159, where they differ only in reading "gentlest" before "Female Tenderness" where Faulkner has "gentle." In 1748 Faulkner published Lyttelton's *To the Memory of Capt. Grenville of the Defiance Man of War* (not in Foxon; ESTC T107955) and in 1768–1772, Lyttelton's *The History of the Life of King Henry the Second,* 4 vols. Faulkner's earlier publications of Lyttelton include *The Progress of Love: In Four Eclogues* in 1732 (Foxon, L336); and two editions (or issues?) of *Considerations upon the Present State of Our Affairs, at Home and Abroad* in 1739.

12. T. C. Duncan Eaves and Ben D. Kimpel remark, "The best known bookseller in Dublin, George Faulkner, was able to induce someone to send him copies of the sheets [of the "continuation of *Pamela,*" released in London 7 December 1741] as they were printed off, which he then published for his own benefit" (*Samuel Richardson: A Biography* [Oxford: Clarendon, 1971], 146). They note Richardson had agreed to "furnish the sheets" to the Irish bookseller Thomas Bacon and that "Richardson's reaction does not seem to have been so violent as it was later, when *Sir Charles Grandison* was similarly pirated" (146). Regarding the theft of the last, Richardson detailed his complaints against Faulkner in *The Case of Samuel Richardson of London, Printer, with Regard to the Invasion of His Property in the History of Sir Charles Grandison* (a free handout written in September 1753), later excerpted in the *Gentleman's Magazine* for October 1753, and, after Faulkner's reply, further developed in "Address to the Public" printed in the third edition of *Sir Charles Grandison* (Catherine Coogan Ward and Robert E. Ward, "Literary Piracy in the Eighteenth Century Book Trade: The Cases of George Faulkner and Alexander Donaldson," *Factotum* 17 [November 1983]: 27 and 33). Ward and Ward, as also Eaves and Kimpel, have discussed how Richardson's plan to sell prepublication sheets of *Clarissa* to Faulkner for seventy guineas was disrupted by the purchase of the sheets of the first two London octavo volumes by Peter Wilson and of first two London duodecimo volumes by John Exshaw and Henry Saunders (Eaves and Kimpel, 378). James E. Tierney has noted that Faulkner then failed to "render [to Richardson] his share of the profits of *Clarissa*" ("More on George Faulkner and the London Book Trade," *Factotum* 19 [October 1984]: 9).

13. These line numbers are shared by John Stirling's *P. Virgilii Maronis Opera* (London: Atley, 1741), 139; John Hawkey's Dublin edition (Typographia Academiae, 1745), 86; Thomas Neville's second edition (Cambridge: Woodyer et al., 1774), 218; and Christopher Pitt's translation, edited by Joseph Warton, *The Works of Virgil in Latin and English* (London: R. Dodsley, 1753), 3:378, all employing the comma after the first "*Te.*" In the monody's reprinting within *The Works of George Lord Lyttelton,* 3rd ed. (1776), the motto is expanded to three lines, with the preceding l. 464 added: "Ipse cavâ solans aegrum testudine amorem / Te dulcis conjux, te solo in littore secum, / Te veniente die, te decedente canebat" (3:144). Pitt translated the

three lines, "He on the desart shore all lonely griev'd, / And with his concave shell his love-sick heart reliev'd; / To thee, sweet wife, still pour'd the piteous lay, / Thee, sung at dawning, thee at closing day!" (3:379).

14. No advertisement appears in the *London Evening Post* of May and June 1748. The other title page variant in the London folios involves the more common spelling "Catherine-" in 1747A and the less common "Catharine-" in 1747B and 1748. It is 1747A's spelling that appears in most advertisements (as in the *General Advertiser* on 30 October), but a common street name does not require compositorial fidelity to text the way a Latin motto does (the *Daily Advertiser* employs "Katharine-" with two *a*'s in its advertisements from October through June, and the *London Evening Post* employs "Katherine Street" in its from 29–31 October to 14–17 November 1747).

15. Transparencies suggest, as collating machines would, that on D1/9 1747A and 1747B have identical settings in ll. 1–3, 5–7, 10–11, and 16–21, but only ll. 16–21 are shared to judge from broken type in both: ll. 16(3[pieces]), 17(4), 18(2), 19(3), 20(2), 21. Type broken only in 1747A appear in ll. 5 ("O" in "On," "F" in "Fortune's"), 8 ("b" in "Ambition," "g" in "highest"), 10 (second "a" in "maintain"), 11 ("B" in "But"), 12 ("W" in "Wit"), and 14 ("p" in "pleasing"); type broken only in 1747B and 1748 appear in ll. 1 (second "o" in "Good"), 2 ("S" in "Strong," "d" in "Elevated"), 4 ("C" in "Could"), 6 ("R" in "Regret," "o" in "or," "a" in "Pain"), 8 ("O" in "Or," "r" in "or"), 10 ("s" in "Its," "b" in "by," first "n" in "Vengeance," first "a" in "maintain"), 12 ("p" in "temperately"), 13 ("o" in "inoffensive," second "e" in "inoffensive"), and 15 ("o" in "Bounds"). On C2ᵛ, transparencies suggest that 1747A and 1747B share ll. 4 (except one word), 6–9, 15–16, and 23; yet broken type pieces rule out the possibility that any of these lines have shared settings. One comes to judge cautiously after finding pieces similarly broken on the same page and thus recognizing that Caslon type was prone to break at certain locations (as the loop of the "d" at 12:00, the "e" at 5:00–6:00 in the top loop, or the "M" at the joint of the first and second stroke). Few injuries will be apparent in every copy, for dirt fills in nicks and cuts; conversely, grease and other impediments to thorough inking will make a letter appear broken in one or a few copies when six or more others show it is probably not broken. The ideal marker has multiple breaks, nicks, and/or dents.

16. For example, in the following partly reset works, the resetting does not include the text and skeleton of the final sheet (D) and the text of B inner in the later of two "second editions" of Edward Young's Night I of *The Complaint*, 1742 (Foxon Y25 or Y26); the final three and the first of the eight sheets of Defoe's *A Hymn to Victory*, 1704 (D124); the final two of the eight sheets of Defoe's *True-born Englishman*, 1701 (D157); the first and last of the five sheets of William Pitt's *Canterbury Tales*, 1701 (P428); the last three of six sheets in the second octavo of Alexander Pope's *Dunciad*, 1728 (P766); the last two of four sheets of Pope's *Epistle to Burlington*, 1731 (P910); the last two of the five sheets of the second edition of Pope's *Second Epistle of the Second Book of Horace*, 1737 (P957); the last three of six sheets of Pope's *Sober Advice from Horace*, 1734 (P969). There are exceptions to this pattern in Foxon's catalog, such as P767, but they prove the rule.

17. An example of type evidently broken that was not reemployed for later impressions appears to be the damaged first "M" in "Memory" on the title pages of 1747B

and 1748, not also employed on the half title, though type in l. 4 of the title was. It is much easier to identify type that should have been replaced when reimpressions occurred, such as two pieces shared by 1747A and 1748: in C1.17 the "o" in "You" cut wide at 11-12:00; and in E2.1 the "d" in "Mind" cut 10–12:00.

18. All editions share in C1/5.20 the "h" in "her," "a" in "raptur'd," and "S" in "Spirit"; in C1ᵛ/6.16 the "s" in "search'd," "*R*" and "*o*" in "*Rome*"; and in C2ᵛ/8.2 the "n" in "brighten'd" and "e" in "some." These lines are identical on transparency overlays.

19. These include broken pieces unique to 1747A in ll. 4 ("e" in "enthron'd" cut at 10:00), 5 (4 pieces: "f" and "a" in "frail," "w" in first "how," and first "e" in "insecure"), 6 ("B" of "Bliss"), and 11 (long "s" cut short at 12:00 in "Rise"); broken pieces in 1747A shared by 1748 but not in 1747B in l. 1 (the "n" and "d" and probably the "M" in "Mind") and possibly l. 4 ("h" in "enthron'd"); broken pieces in 1747B shared by 1748 but not in 1747A in ll. 4 ("I" in "In," "n" in "now," and "w" in "with"), 6 (second "s" in "Bliss"), and "S" in "FINIS"; and broken pieces uniquely broken in 1747B in ll. 6 ("r" in "ev'ry" nicked on right side) and 8 ("e" in "Beyond" cut at 5:00). Frequently the damaged type pieces not shared occur at the edges of lines, such as damaged type only in 1747B and 1748 at the start of l. 4 and the end of l. 6 and damaged type only in 1747B in the first word of l. 8.

20. *A New Introduction to Bibliography* (Oxford: Oxford University Press, 1972), 127, noting that K. Povey found 86 percent of sheets printed in 1701–1750 were first printed on the inner forme. Printing second the inner forme of E allowed the side with most type to look the better.

21. Copies 1747B and 1748 have different alignments in the head title relative to the word "OF" and the different letter pieces for "MEM" in "MEMORY."

22. On C2ᵛ/8, broken type pieces unique to 1747A occur in ll. 5, 8–12, and 15–18 (and it alone fails to indent l. 18); unique to 1747B, in ll. 1, 3–4, 6, 8, 13, and 17–23; unique to 1748, in l. 10 ("T" in "Tell," the first letter of the line, nicked underneath the left cross-stroke, which is employed in C2ᵛ.16 by 1747A).

23. For instance, E1ᵛ.21 ("p" in "pure" nicked at 3:00 in circle), E2.6 ("r" in "ev'ry" nicked on right side), and E2.8 ("e" in "Beyond" cut at 5:00).

24. Copies 1747B and 1748, however, do not share isolated broken letter pieces, such as the "T" in "Tell" of l. 10 only broken in 1748 and the third "s" in "Distress" of l. 17 only broken in 1747B.

25. Transparencies of the 1747A settings for ll. 1–4 on A1, A2, and B1 overlay each other with the same alignment, though vertical spacings vary, and damaged type indicates that ll. 2 and 4 are certainly shared: e.g., in l. 2, the first "M" of "MEMORY" is nicked upward from the crotch between the first two strokes and also nicked left into the first ascender; the "O" in "MEMORY" has a white spot at 8:30–9:00; in l. 4, the "A" in "A" has a nick high on the left side; the small capital "A" in "LADY" has a piece of lead sticking out like a finger to the left near the top; the long "s" in "Deceased" is nicked upward at the center of the top end (the second two injured type pieces also occur in 1747B and 1748's title settings).

26. The first "M" in "MEMORY" on A1, A2, and B1 of 1747A is the second "M" in the word on A1 and B1 of 1748 and the second "M" on A1 of 1747B.

27. Although allowance must be made for copies in private hands, the relative scarcity of the 1747A edition argues against its having been the first printed of several prepublication printings, held back as less correct, for Lyttelton in ordering 1747B and 1748 foresaw that demand would justify larger press runs. No copies of any folio edition have been on the auction market in decades or offered by a major antiquarian bookseller in at least a decade.

Chapter Six

Parson Adams's Sermons: Benjamin Hoadly and Henry Fielding

Martha F. Bowden

The joke is, of course, that we never actually see any of Parson Adams's sermons, he having inadvertently left home without them (his wife, a practical theologian, decides that clean shirts will be more useful than nine manuscript volumes of the sermons she hears every Sunday). He reads one before being unceremoniously dumped into a barrel of water by the roasting squire, but the author does not transcribe the text for us. There are, nonetheless, many references to sermons in *Joseph Andrews*, both Parson Adams's own and those of several real preachers of the period.

Of the parson's own sermons, we hear that he is particularly proud of a sermon on vanity, and that he has a standard sermon he uses for weddings, on the text, "Whosoever looketh on a Woman so as to lust after her." He applauds the sentiments of a disguised Roman Catholic priest, and claims to have preached on them often. Of the popular preachers being read in his own day, the notes to the Wesleyan edition are filled with references to Clarke, Tillotson, Barrow, and Hoadly, in some ways a standard pantheon, especially in the latitudinarian tradition in which Battestin places Fielding.[1] The only one of these preachers, however, to which the parson makes particular and approving reference is Benjamin Hoadly. His advocacy of Hoadly comes directly out of a discussion of Whitefield in which he disparages that preacher's theology of faith over works. Martin C. Battestin's article on Fielding's revisions of *Joseph Andrews* demonstrates that a number of those revisions are directly concerned with the sermons, whose numbers varied between three and nine volumes, and are finally established as nine in the fourth edition. The treatment of the missing sermons is expanded in the second edition, and the marriage sermon with its dubious text is a later addition.[2] But the references to Hoadly are in the original.

The choice of Hoadly rather than Tillotson or Clarke is significant for both Adams and Fielding. Tillotson's sermons had already entered into the canon, being widely reprinted since his death in 1694, and even being taught in divinity schools. A surgeon listening to the conversation among a bookseller and Parsons Barnabas and Adams is astonished at the number of sermons the bookseller claims are in print, having himself only read Tillotson: "Five thousand! . . . what can they be writ upon? I remember, when I was a Boy, I used to read one *Tillotson's* Sermons; and I am sure, if a Man practised half so much as is in one of those Sermons, he will go to Heaven."[3] Clarke, a divisive figure despite being Queen Caroline's favorite preacher, had been nonetheless a modest man, who had refused two bishoprics for fear of ripping the church apart over his Arian views. He also was safely dead, and thus ready to be beatified if not canonized. But Benjamin Hoadly was very much alive, and as a result of his 1717 sermon on the governance of the Church, the Canterbury convocation essentially was shut down, and would remain so until the nineteenth century.

Recent work by a number of church historians has revised the standard view of Hoadly. The traditional opinion is summed up usefully by Susan Rutherford, one of his recent apologists: "Contemporary nonjuring, high church and Tory opponents maintained that he was an ambitious, unprincipled opportunist who used the ideas of deists, Socinians and atheists to foster anarchy in the Church of England and rebellions in the state. Although some later commentators have been more objective, many have accepted the view that Hoadly employed the secular reason of the deists to dilute Christianity and undermine the established Church."[4] In this number may be counted B. W. Young, who in *Religion and Enlightenment in Eighteenth-Century England* (1998), describes Hoadly as a schemer determined to advance his own career: he refers to "the near-heterodoxy of an ultra-latitudinarian such as Hoadly, who was widely held, with good reason, to be a Whig opportunist and a blatant clerical careerist."[5] Hoadly's reputation, however, has benefited from changes in church history methodology in the recent past. Jeremy Gregory and Jeffrey S. Chamberlain describe "a revolution in the archives," with the increasing availability of the collections in various repositories, and the publication of many local church records. As a result, the picture of the church in this period has been made more detailed and specific, and scholars are beginning to recognize local and regional diversity that calls into question the monolithic depictions of older studies. It is no longer possible to say that the Church of England in the eighteenth century was either universally neglected or completely vibrant throughout its dioceses, or that it sailed along, unchanged and unchanging, from the beginning of the period to its end.[6]

This newly available material suggests that Hoadly was a conscientious bishop, instead of a bloated pluralist moving from episcopacy to episcopacy in a path that took him farther east with each promotion, from the poverty of a Welsh bishopric to the eventual reward of the princely see of Winchester. His modern biographer, William Gibson, posits him as a victim of nineteenth-century High Church and Tractarian historiography, for many years the dominant voice in our understanding of the period.[7] Gibson overturns the conventional view that Hoadly never went to his diocese in Bangor, whose name he has made notorious for the controversy he began while the incumbent; there is evidence that he was in his diocese in 1719 and kept his house there fully staffed.[8] Philip Jenkins, proceeding under the received opinion of Hoadly's neglect, defends it by describing nonresidence as "typical" of the eighteenth-century Welsh episcopate. Hoadly's successor, Thomas Herring, who was exceptional in his devotion to his charge, nonetheless "admitted that 'Though I love Wales very much, I would not choose to be reduced to butter, milk, and lean mutton.'"[9] Thus, Hoadly's actual attention to Bangor is all the more notable. Hoadly has a reputation for being equally derelict in his next position, the Diocese of Hereford, where he was the bishop from 1721–1723. New evidence, however, has shown that there too he ordained and did a primary visitation in 1722. Because primary visitations (that is, by the bishop and not the local archdeacon) were only expected to be done every three years, and Hoadly was only in Hereford for two, he was not neglectful of his charge. He also was very conscientious in his parliamentary duties at a time when all bishops sat in the House of Lords, but not all of them appeared there.[10]

His most significant episcopacy, and his last, was in the Diocese of Winchester. While William Gibson does not deny that he and his immediate predecessor, Richard Willis, reached out to dissenters, he insists that Hoadly and Willis always worked within the system: "The strategy of Willis and Hoadly was to exploit the episcopal patronage at their disposal to appoint tolerant Latitudinarians to the diocese, who would bring dissenters into the Church. It was an approach that complemented the Whigs' national policy of making loyalty to the Church compatible with support for the House of Hanover."[11] Although his most controversial writings opposed subscription and sacramental tests, he nonetheless insisted that his clergy must subscribe—he even refused his close friend Samuel Clarke a preferment because the latter would not do so. His approach was to encourage dissenters into the fold by emphasizing toleration; he also rejected "the High Church sacerdotalism that placed great weight on the Apostolic Succession and therefore on a monopoly of Anglican ministry. . . . This position was not lost on dissenters. It came close to the dissenters' model of Christian ministry, marked by sincerity of motivation rather than the exclusiveness of an apostolic sacrament." And he was successful—four of the ten dissenters who were ordained in the Diocese of Winchester in the eighteenth century came during his tenure.[12] Of course, this position was also guaranteed to raise the ire of the High Church clergy. That he was quoted by no less an advocate for individual liberty against tyranny than John Adams does indicate his importance in disseminating Locke's views among the American colonists before the revolution;[13] it is an equally clear indication of why he alarmed his contemporaries. In a collection of sermons and tracts published in March 1715/1716 to celebrate his preferment to the see of Bangor, thus before that particular controversy and characterized by Gibson as "a welcome re-statement of the Whig Low Church position on the 1689 Revolution,"[14] he gives evidence of similar ideas. The date is significant for the kingdom as well, as it followed the first major Jacobite Rebellion. When describing four of the sermons in the preface, he emphasizes his objections to the external and regulatory nature of the Church as being in contradiction to the Gospels:

> To these I have *now* added *Four Sermons,* Preached at the same Time: in which I have, at more length, handled the same Subjects; and added what is of great Importance, to take Mens Minds off from all pretenses to that *Incontestable Authority,* and *Imperfect Subjection,* which are the strongest of all *Bars* against Inward, and True, *Religion.* I should be sorry to find that, amongst *Protestants,* it should stand in need of any *Apology,* to refer Men to *Christ* himself, for the *Fundamentals* of *Christ's Religion;* and not to any *Humane Constitution* whatsoever.[15]

Indeed, however much the worthiness of his actions in the episcopate has been illuminated by the current research, no one denies that he was a serious troublemaker.

In the dispute about Whitefield, Parson Adams invokes several of Hoadly's works, including his most notorious sermon. On March 31, 1717, Hoadly, at that time bishop of Bangor, preached a sermon on the text "Jesus answered, My Kingdom is not of this World" (John 18:36). Because he was preaching at the Royal Chapel at St. James's Palace, and his audience included the king, the sermon had a political heft it would not have had in a parish church in the countryside, or even in his cathedral in Wales. He begins by deploring the fact that while the nature of things is "unmoveable," the words that human beings use to describe those things change connotatively; and in matters of religion, language is at its most debased, and results in an "Evil" that must be rectified by a return to originals, in this case the words of Jesus himself. After a short disquisition on the particular evils of enthusiasm, whose proponents have changed the meaning of the love of God from "*keeping his Commandments, or doing his Will*" to "a violent *Passion, Commotion,* and *Ecstasy,* venting it self in such sort of Expressions and Disorders, as other *Passions* do,"[16] he is ready for his central argument.

He equates the term "Church" with the Kingdom of Christ (in itself an interpretation), whose original meaning he believes is, "the Number, small or great, of Those who believed *Him* to be the *Messiah*; or of Those who subjected themselves to *Him, as* their *King,* in the Affair of *Religion*" (10). The first of the two heads of the sermon attacks those who "erect *Tribunals,* and exercise a *Judgment* over the Consciences of Men" as usurping the sole power of Jesus, who "left behind Him, no visible, humane *Authority;* no *Vicegerentes,* who can be said properly to supply his Place; no *Interpreters,* upon whom his Subjects are absolutely to depend; no *Judges* over the Consciences or Religion of his People" (14, 11–12). Such surrogate authority would change the nature of the Church, so that it would become ruled by the men in whom such authority was vested, and thus be their kingdom. The second head claims that if the Church is the Kingdom of Christ, and not of men, then the laws are Christ's as well, and punishments and rewards, being the prerogatives of God, belong to the future world of the Day of Judgment.

While the sermon bears in it many of the hallmarks of anti-Catholic rhetoric—the complaint that worship has denigrated into mere ritual, the assertion that no prelate can claim to be Christ's representative on earth, the attack on the tyranny of zealous church legalists—there is no doubt that the rhetoric was aimed at the Church of England, and it was certainly taken personally by that body. It calls into question the validity of the hierarchy of the Church, its courts, and governance structures. At the time it was preached, the Church was in the midst of one of several controversies about subscription and comprehension—the requirement that all clergy subscribe to the Book of Common Prayer and the Thirty-Nine Articles, and the desire of a number of prominent churchmen, including Hoadly, that the regulation be relaxed to include many fine and upstanding clergy who under the present system were forced into nonconformity. Hoadly concludes with an implicit attack on subscription: "All his Subjects are *equally* his Subjects; and, as such, *equally* without Authority to alter, to add to, or to *interpret,* his *Laws* so, as to claim the absolute Submission of *Others* to such *Interpretation.*" It is better, he claims, to accept the plain word of God in scripture as a source of his laws than "to hunt after Them thro' the infinite contradictions, the numberless perplexities, the endless disputes, of *Weak Men,* in several Ages, till the Enquirer himself is lost in the Labyrinth, and perhaps sits down in Despair, or Infidelity" (30, 31). Gibson enumerates the response to this challenge: "In the ensuing controversy, over 50 writers entered the lists in pamphlets or books. Most of these works had astonishingly big print runs, sometimes over a thousand for individual editions. One account, taken in 1718, lists 41 contributions 'of note,' some with two or three answers to each, and a further twenty-four publications on the matter, in addition to the thirteen works written by Hoadly himself during the furore. In fact hundreds of tracts poured forth during the protracted debate."[17] He also contends that, while Hoadly is generally blamed for the impotence of the Canterbury Convocation for the next century, the Convocation was already in trouble as a body, and that William III had frequently used prorogation as a means of controlling it.[18]

Another work by Hoadly to which Adams appears to refer explicitly is no less controversial than the sermon. When the bookseller who is participating in the conversation about Whitefield asks what Adams's own sermons are like, Adams, with unerring instinct for ruining his own case, describes a position that is the opposite extreme of Whitefield's *sola fide* beliefs: that "a virtuous and good *Turk*, or Heathen, are more acceptable in the sight of their Creator, than a vicious and wicked Christian, tho' his Faith was as perfectly Orthodox as St. *Paul's* himself" (82, 82n2). This statement, Battestin notes, echoes Hoadly's sermon on the Good Samaritan, an especially appropriate allusion given the treatment to which Joseph has been subjected, and no doubt less inflammatory in context than out: the Samaritan is the biblical exemplum of the outsider pointing the way to the righteous. The sermon, however, was not published until 1755, some time after the publication of *Joseph Andrews,* although Hoadly was said to have preached it frequently.[19] But on its own Adams's position suggests a heterodoxy that alarms the bookseller: he declines all interest, because he does not want to publish books that will bring down the wrath of the clergy, who, he implies, might be offended both at the suggestion that they should do as they preach, and that there might be righteousness outside the established church. Adams settles his fate by discounting the influence of a small number of disgruntled clergy to damage the sales of a book, giving as his example the opponents to Hoadly's *Plain Account of the Nature and End of the Sacrament,* "some few designing factious Men, who have it at Heart to establish some favourite Schemes at the Price of the Liberty of Mankind, and the very Essence of Religion" (83). He insists that the peevish attempts of these troublemakers were insufficient to damn the book, of which he himself has a very high opinion. Barnabas, convinced he is in the presence of a heretic as egregious as any of the deists, rings the bell vociferously and requests his bill so that he can get out before the lightning strikes.

Adams's summary of *A Plain Account* is accurate, although naive and lacking in nuance: "A Book written (if I may venture on the Expression) with the Pen of an Angel, and calculated to restore the true Use of Christianity, and of that Sacred Institution: for what could tend more to the noble Purposes of Religion, than frequent cheerful Meetings among the Members of a Society, in which they should in the Presence of one another, and in the Service of the supreme Being, make Promises of being good, friendly and benevolent to each other?" (83).[20] In this description the text sounds innocuous, its only hint of controversy the statement that the proper use of the Eucharist needs to be restored, because it points toward the requirement under the Test Act that those persons taking the oath follow it by receiving communion. It also is accurate in emphasizing Hoadly's insistence that the Eucharist is meant to be a unifying action:

> *Christians*, meeting together for Religious Worship; and eating *Bread* and drinking *Wine*, in *Remembrance* of *Christ's Body* and *Bloud*, and in honour to Him; do hereby publickly acknowledge Him to be their Master, and Themselves to be His Disciples: and, by doing this in an Assembly, own Themselves, with all other Christians, to be One *Body* or Society, under Him the Head; and consequently profess Themselves to be under His Governance and Influence; to have *Communion* or Fellowship with *Him*, as *Head*, and with all their Christian Brethren, as *Fellow-Members* of that same *Body* of which He is the *Head*.[21]

But in fact the book calls into question the Church of England's sacramental theology. From a political standpoint, while there is nothing in the book or Adams's description of it that directly addresses the controversy over the sacramental tests, the statement that the sacrament is significant in part because it is unifying points directly at its requirement as part of the test, a requirement that resulted in polarization; those persons who could not in all conscience receive the Eucharist in the Church of England precisely because they disagreed with its theology in some way were automatically excluded from many roles in civic life.

Not all critics have agreed with Adams that Hoadly's prose is angelic. Leslie Stephen, who admired Hoadly's ideas, felt he committed the ultimate crime of writing badly, something Stephen rarely does: "His style is the style of a bore; he is slovenly, awkward, intensely pertinacious, often indistinct, and, apparently at least, evasive; and occasionally . . . not free from a tinge of personal rancour. . . . The three huge folios which contain his ponderous wranglings are a dreary wilderness of now profitless discussion."[22] Certainly, Hoadly's replies to Atterbury reprinted in 1715 catch hold of a single issue, the question whether virtuous people are happy or miserable, and, terrierlike, shake it until there is little life left in it (or the reader). His favorite criticism of his opponents is that they are begging the question, but he himself is not free from that logical fallacy. On the other hand, his sermons and other writings do exhibit the clarity and careful argumentation that Gibson claims are hallmarks of his style. A reading of his works that includes both sermons and polemics demonstrates why he was admired as a preacher and loathed as a controversialist.

Hoadly's preface to *A Plain Account* also makes the innocuous, or perhaps evasive, case that the book, which takes the form of a series of propositions supported by explanation and scriptural references, grew out of a sermon that he had preached when he was a parish priest in London. He claims that his congregation was unwilling to take their communion for superstitious reasons, and their religion had become a burden to them. The problem was real, and lay in the wording of the Exhortation, the charge required to be read the Sunday before the priest intended to celebrate the Eucharist. With its stern directive to self-examination and its dire warning that those who receive their communion "unworthily"—unprepared and not reconciled to all their friends and neighbors—are in worse condition than if they had never received it, it had been frightening the laity for a century and a half at this point. The preface to the invitation to the General Confession repeats many of the same sentiments: "So is the danger great, if we receive the same unworthily. For then we are guilty of the body and blood of Christ our Saviour; we eat and drink our own damnation."[23] Certainly, the work does contain much to allay these fears; it counsels that while examination of one's entire life may be a salutary exercise, it is not necessary each time one prepares for the sacrament; "worthily" can be understood as reverently and mindfully (as opposed to carelessly or thoughtlessly), thus not suggesting a requirement for a state of spiritual perfection. Hoadly presents preparation as a matter of ascertaining whether the Christian comes to receive communion "not as a Common Meal, or an Ordinary Eating and Drinking; but as a particular *Rite* appointed by Christ." Always an apologist for his own denomination to the outside world, he points out that Anglican practice is preferable to all others by administering both wine and bread directly into the hands of the communicant, thus making it virtually impossible to receive it unmindfully.[24]

These statements do not contain any doctrine that could possibly offend the Church, and no doubt include much that could be useful to Parson Adams, who might well have experienced the same reluctance and superstitions in his own parish. Nor could any Anglican theologian argue against Hoadly's insistence that they should base their beliefs about the nature of the sacrament on a reading of the New Testament. But Hoadly's interpretation of the text does not reflect Anglican beliefs in the period, although it is in line with the Zwinglian theology of many Church of England clergy, including Thomas Cranmer, in the years immediately following the Reformation. His remark that the nature of the Eucharist be read figuratively, not literally, and his emphasis on its being a memorial meal only, without any suggestion of the real presence, was very close to Zwinglian memorialism: "This *Wine* is allowed by All, not to be itself the *New Covenant*; nor to be changed (or transubstantiated) into the *New Covenant*; but only to be the *Memorial* of the *New Cov-*

enant. . . . it follows, by all the rules of Interpretation, agreeably to the Way of speaking throughout the Whole, that the *Bread* and *Wine* are not the Natural *Body* and *Bloud* of Christ, but the *Memorials* of his *Body* and *Bloud*."[25] The word "All" at the beginning of this passage is particularly contentious. The rubrics for the disposal of the remnants of the bread and wine at the end of the service, which differentiate between the consecrated and unconsecrated elements, indicate that the official theological stance of the Church of England, a weighty component of the "All," is rather more complex. The reference to transubstantiation is a useful rhetorical ploy to redirect his attack to the Church of Rome, but does not cover his strict insistence on the memorial nature of the sacrament, the denial of any sacrifice in the celebration, and the declaration that the communion table is only a table, and not an altar, because there is no sacrifice. His insistence that the whole thing is really very simple, while no doubt reassuring to his stated audience (should any such persons read it), must have been infuriating to many of his clerical contemporaries.

And infuriated they were. Susan Rutherford shows, as neither Fielding nor Adams do, that the context for Hoadly's contemporaries included another work, *Objections against the Repeal of the Corporation and Test Acts Considered*, a reply to a pamphlet by the bishop of London, Edmund Gibson. Published in 1736, and thus after the book on the Eucharist but written before it, the text makes explicit what A *Plain Account* implies: that the use of the sacrament of the Lord's Supper as a state-required demonstration of loyalty taken in conjunction with an oath, as both the Corporation Act (1661) and the Test Acts (1673 and 1678) required, was an egregious misuse of a holy thing.[26] Most people were not in favor of repeal at that exact moment, but while Queen Caroline and Walpole and other Whigs believed that the time might come eventually, Thomas Sherlock and Edmund Gibson were staunchly against repeal at any time, present or future. Men like Hoadly, the most liberal of the Whigs, and all Protestant dissenters, however, were staunchly against any kind of test. Thus it was not an issue that manifested a simple Tory-Whig split, if such matters are ever simple, but a fracturing and divisive question.

Hoadly's position aligned him with Protestant Dissent, especially because he objected to the Occasional Conformity Act, which made it illegal for dissenters to communicate in the Church of England if required to do so in order to take public office. The Act excluded this behavior as subverting the intention of the tests, whereas Hoadly in the eighteenth century and dissenters like Calamy and Baxter in the seventeenth believed that the requirements of the tests were oppressive.[27] Walpole, for this reason and because he knew the dissenters tended to be Whigs and he wanted to pacify them, in 1730 invited Hoadly (through Queen Caroline with whom Hoadly was on good terms) to approach the Committee of Dissenting Deputies to explain to them why, despite its sympathy, the government could not eliminate the tests. According to Rutherford, the historical understanding of Hoadly's role as intermediary also requires revision: "It has sometimes been suggested that Hoadly was a political opportunist rather than a man of principle. The evidence does not support this view. The bishop reminded the queen that he had already spoken and written against the Test and Corporation Acts and informed her that he would support repeal whenever it was proposed in Parliament. Nevertheless, he realized that the issue was dividing the Whigs and agreed to speak to the Dissenters."[28] Hoadly suffered the usual fate of people who attempt to mediate between two obdurate groups and was vilified by both sides for failing to support them sufficiently and conceding too much to the opposition. He was in fact effective in quieting dissenting demands for repeal of the Test Act, but was in an "equivocal" position, in Gibson's words: "he was committed to the repeal of the Test Act but sworn to discourage the Dissenters from agitating for it."[29]

Given this fraught context, as well as the Zwinglian character of his theology, it is not surprising that A *Plain Account* caused an uproar, both theologically and politically, although in this case those two matters cannot be considered independently. William Gibson describes Hoadly as a "spent force" by 1730,[30] but he had obviously not lost the ability to inflame his contemporaries. Most respondents to the book did not consider it angelically inspired, but, reading the subtext that was certainly there, as an assault on the tests.[31] In a period that did not hesitate to draw the personal into the political, satirists linked Hoadly's severe lameness with his perceived spiritual crookedness. It is not clear what caused the disability (his son claimed it was the result of smallpox badly handled) but he was forced to walk with assistance—walking sticks in public, crutches at home—and he preached in a kneeling position to avoid standing on his weak legs.[32] His walking stick becomes his identifying characteristic in prints like "The Schismatical *attack of yᵉ* Church, Besieged by yᵉ Ephesian Beast" and "Guess at my Meaning."[33] He is linked in both these prints to Puritans and dissenters: in the first, he is compared to Commonwealth men, and in the second, the books on his shelves include those by Milton, Harrington, Locke, and Hobbes. Gibson quotes "The British Censors," in which Hoadly is also linked to Milton:

> Let Whigs have their will they'd quickly all
> The Apostles writings vote Apocryphal
> That square not with their interest, and instead
> Milton's and Hoadly's to the canon add.[34]

Parson Barnabas joins the company of such commentators as William Warburton in understanding the context of the book; in fact, Barnabas knows only the context: "I never read a Syllable in any such wicked Book; I never saw it in my Life, I assure you" (84). The name is enough for him.

The controversy, both in the countryside of *Joseph Andrews* and in the wider world, is a good example of the complexities of theological disputes. Parson Barnabas has complained against Whitefield, of whom Fielding did not approve, by citing the one tenet with which Fielding was in agreement: "He would reduce us to the Example of the Primitive Ages forsooth! and would insinuate to the People, that a Clergyman ought to be always preaching and praying. He pretends to understand the Scripture literally, and would make Mankind believe, that the Poverty and low Estate, which was recommended to the Church in its Infancy, and was only temporary Doctrine adapted to her under Persecution, was to be preserved in her flourishing and established State" (81). Parson Adams responds with what are apparently Fielding's true objections to Whitefield. He first indicates that he is in agreement with him about the proper role of the clergy, couched in words that echo Hoadly's notorious sermon: "Surely those things, which savour so strongly of this World, become not the Servants of one who professed his Kingdom was not of it." His objections are to Whitefield's emphasis on faith over works, and to his preaching style: "but when he began to call Nonsense and Enthusiasm to his Aid, and to set up the detestable Doctrine of Faith against good Works, I was his Friend no longer" (82). It should be noted, however, that Whitefield joined the majority (against Fielding and Adams, and in agreement with Barnabas, who opposed his theology of orders) in disagreeing with Hoadly's sacramental theology (83n1). While theological controversies in the eighteenth century were undoubtedly polarizing (as they continue to be), it was possible for most Protestants, dissenting and establishment, to be in agreement with many others at least some of the time.

Gibson believes that most purchasers of sermons knew the political affiliations of the clergy whose sermons they selected[35]—they might well be buying both Hoadly and Atterbury, but they knew that the two authors would take no delight in their proximity on the buyers' bookshelves. While Parson Adams seems to be oblivious to the reaction his chosen preacher would receive, we cannot expect the same of Fielding, who was much more knowledgeable and worldly than his character. But even if he did wish to praise Hoadly (and there were many personal and theological reasons why he might), why choose the most controversial of his works? There was much else to choose from: in many of his sermons Hoadly expresses the latitudinarian principles of practical divinity, offering his auditors and readers advice on how to lead a godly life. Gibson's contention in the biography that Hoadly generally espoused a theology that argues for a beneficent God who wishes only for the happiness of his people is borne out in his writing: "I, for my part, was ever ready to contend that the *Christian System of Precepts* carried *Morality* to a greater Heighth and perfection, than unenlighten'd Reason ever did, or ever would have done: tho' at the same time nothing is recommended in it, but what is perfectly agreeable to our best and uncorrupted Reason. And I argue, because it carries its sincere Professors to the greatest heighths of *Virtue*; therefore, doth it tend more effectually to their present Happiness."[36] It was unnecessary for Fielding to choose the sermon that started the Bangorian controversy or the Zwinglian Eucharistic theory, or even the most inflammatory part of a sermon whose subject is a good reflection on the recent action of the novel. Why, then, did he so choose?

The answer may be distributed between Fielding's past and his invocation of Cervantes on his title page. According to Brian McCrae, when Fielding arrived in London in 1724, at the age of seventeen, his journey was much more significant than a trip to the big city. By leaving his grandmother, who had fought for custody of him and his siblings, and reconciling with his father, from whom he had been estranged by the custody suit, he left behind his boyhood and the countryside in which he grew up. McCrae considers him to have made an implicit declaration of independence, choosing an urban life, most of it dedicated to literary projects, rather than a rural existence and the legal career that his grandmother intended for him. He also "accepted a financially uncertain patrimony." [37]

The destination in *Joseph Andrews* may well symbolize a return to that authorial past, as the village could be a recreation of East Stour, complete with its parson, generally identified with William Young, who held the living in Fielding's youth. Young had many of the characteristics of Fielding's cleric, including his classical learning, certain vague habits of mind, and the occasional violent outburst.[38] But if that is the case, the memories of boyhood may not have been entirely sunlit. The fictional trip back to the place of his youth is not without its shadows—Joseph and Adams march straight into "darkness visible," a world where the clergy and courts are corrupt, squires shoot little girls' pets, and the lady of the manor thinks it amusing that the curate is forced to live in squalor because his stipend is so low. Furthermore, when a man suggested to William Young that he was the original of Parson Adams, Young threatened to knock him down, a gesture that considerably undermines the denial it seeks to enforce, bringing to mind as it does the fictional parson's offering to support his friend Joseph, and "clenching a Fist rather less than the Knuckle of an Ox" (67). One wonders with what part of the cleric's character Young did not want to be associated.

The presence of Don Quixote in the wings of the tale gives us a hint as to how to read it; the full title reads, "The History of the Adventures of *Joseph Andrews*, and of his Friend Mr. *Abraham Adams*. Written in Imitation of The

Manner of Cervantes, Author of *Don Quixote*." Adams has many of the physical attributes of the Don, including his scrawny horse, his tattered appearance, and his devotion to peculiar ideas. Simon Dickie shows in the reception
history of the character of Parson Adams that by and large the early readers of
the novel had no trouble with the way in which Adams was treated; he links
this to the enjoyment of practical jokes in the period, particularly among the
elite—a propensity that conduct manual writers frowned upon, needless to
say, but that was otherwise acceptable.[39] In the discrepancy between an apparently admirable character's being maltreated in a way that makes readers
laugh at the scenes, apparently with the encouragement of the author, Dickie
locates an instability in the satiric rhetoric of the text. He appropriately links
Parson Adams's treatment with Don Quixote's, but claims that Quixote "was,
for mid-eighteenth-century readers, not the loveable eccentric or noble ideal-
ist that he subsequently became, but a hilariously deluded old man and the
deserving victim of so much comical mistreatment." Dickie maintains that
this attitude was changing, and that *Joseph Andrews* marks a significant point
in that change.[40]

Whether Quixote was universally held up to be a purely comic character
in the period is certainly a matter for debate. Patricia C. Brückmann's work
on the Scriblerians suggests that they held him in rather higher regard.[41] But
doubtless both he and Parson Adams are ambivalent figures. The Knight of
the Mournful Countenance, much admired for his sweetness of character
and for his admirable principles, is recognizably mad, and his madness is
both induced by and results in misreading; his devotion to romance literature renders him unable to "read" the world around him. He is quite right to
be appalled by the world in which he finds himself; he is mad to think that
the fictions with which he has been entertained in any way represent the
real world, that they can or should be imitated, and that they can provide
him with a means of righting the wrongs he sees. Adams, too, does not read
well, especially the human character. In several places in *Joseph Andrews*,
Fielding points out Adams's inability to read beyond surfaces: he does not
see subtexts, is vulnerable to pranksters, and is completely at the mercy
of hypocrites. Nonetheless, the mistreatment of Adams, while indubitably
part of the comic world (it does not appear to do lasting harm to anything
but his cassock), does not lead us to admire his tormentors any more than
we admire the duke and duchess for their treatment of Quixote and Sancho
Panza. Their pranks and jests at the Don's expense might make us laugh,
but we do not miss them when they disappear from the text. And unlike
Fielding, Cervantes allows his hero to be severely injured and finally killed;
when his grieving friends and relatives surround his bedside, surely we are
there with them.

Adams, while admirable in many ways, is a menace to others, much as the Don is to everyone he meets, from sheepherders, to puppeteers, to the faithful Sancho. For all his parish experience, Adams is unable to live by his own tenets—witness his grief at his son's reported drowning immediately after he has preached stoicism to Joseph—and unfit to lead his young friends into the Miltonic darkness that is the English countryside. He is unable to pay; cannot keep track of his horse; is oblivious to pranksters, hypocrites, and other cheats; and quixotically champions exactly the wrong latitudinarian prelate. Dickie claims that Parson Adams becomes the moral center of the book, but Brian McCrae astutely suggests otherwise. McCrae sees the true center of the book in Joseph's gradual development from student to teacher. It is Joseph who leads his parson safely home, and not the other way around.[42] Young may not have wanted to be associated with a character who so often seemed to be the butt of everyone's jokes, and Adams's ecclesiastical record was not one a country parson would want to emulate.

But there may in fact be two cervantic figures in the text, and it may be the second one from whom Young wished to distance himself. According to Battestin, Benjamin Hoadly and Gilbert Burnet, both bishops of Salisbury in Fielding's lifetime, were the clerics whom Fielding most admired,[43] and there is much evidence that his theological beliefs coincided with Hoadly's brand of rationalist latitudinarianism, as his political beliefs matched both prelates' Whig loyalties. Hoadly was both a part of the past to which Fielding returned and, with his Whig allegiances, a manifestation of the political loyalties he embraced. From 1723 to 1734 Hoadly was bishop of Salisbury, where he did visitations in 1726 and 1729, and was as active as the bad roads and weather, which took their toll on his already fragile health, allowed.[44] He was a friend of Fielding's from the latter's time in Salisbury in the 1730s, and Fielding was even closer to Hoadly's son Benjamin.[45] John Hoadly, archbishop of Armagh, the bishop's younger brother, held various positions in the diocese from 1703 to 1718: he was appointed to a prebendary seat at Salisbury by Burnet, after he defended the latter's book on the Thirty-Nine Articles in 1703. He remained in Salisbury until 1718, when Fielding was eleven, rising in power to archdeacon and finally chancellor. According to Gibson, John was even more radical than Benjamin, and probably influenced his opinion on the tests, having come to the conclusion that the Test Act should be repealed more than a decade earlier than Benjamin did.[46] McCrae asserts that the change in loyalty, from the Tories that Fielding's grandmother's family supported to the Whigs from whom his father received patronage, is related to his reconciliation with his father and the influence of his cousin, Lady Mary Wortley Montagu,[47] but he may have been swayed earlier by the Whig clergy in Salisbury.

His defense of Hoadly, then, can be read quite straightforwardly as a tribute to an old friend, as his portrait of Adams seems to have been. It is also an equally straightforward statement of his political and religious beliefs, and however his political tenets might have been shaped by his alliance with his father, the theological ideas can be traced to his boyhood. But when we reflect on the fact that Fielding has put his defense of that friend in the hands of a man who is rarely heeded and often undermined, we should remember that the novel is described on its title page as being in the manner of Cervantes. Fielding's sympathies with Hoadly could well lead him to see in that belligerent cleric a man who, despite the opposition of his contemporaries, wished to practice what the period called comprehension and we call ecumenicalism. While Christians often invoke unity as a desideratum, they are rarely accommodating enough with each other to put it into practice. Hoadly was faced with a dilemma: a need for competent and committed clergy, and a body of men whom he could not incorporate into his diocese because of their doctrinal differences with his church. In his desire to eliminate sacramental tests and in his belief that, if educated and encouraged, dissenters would be willing to conform, he was in some ways as naive as Parson Adams, who claims that reading about a place is the equivalent to going there, although he did have some success at bring dissenters into the fold, especially in Winchester.

He too, however, was as ambivalent a character as Adams. His determination to promote unity in the Church and to heal the denominational breaches caused at the Restoration is admirable, but his rhetoric was often calculated to destroy concord rather than to create it. Even in his own defense, he was as irascible as Adams, his rhetoric as confrontational as a blow from a fist. The preface to *Sixteen Sermons* skates dangerously close to the apologetics that Fielding found both risible and contemptuous in Colley Cibber:

The only *Inferences* in my own Favor, which I wish to be drawn from what is now published, are, That I never omitted any One public Opportunity, in proper Time and Place, of defending and strengthening the true and only *Foundation* of all our *Civil* and *Religious Liberties,* when it was every Day most zealously attacked; and of doing all in my Power, that All the *Subjects* of this *Government,* and this *Royal Family,* should understand, and approve of, those *Principles,* upon which alone their Happiness is fixed; and *without which,* it could never have been rightly Established, and must in Time fall to the Ground: And also, That I was as ready, whenever Occasion was offered, by the Writings and Attacks of *Unbelievers,* and by the absurd *Representations* of *Others*, to defend a Religion, most amiable . . . in it's native Light, with which it shines in the *New Testament* itself, free from all the *False Paint* with which *Some,* or the undeserved *Dirt* with which *Others,* have covered it.[48]

As with his claim that his views in *A Plain Account* are transparently truthful, his accusation that his opponents are applying paint and slinging dirt is not likely to quell the opposition. Furthermore, despite the work of his most recent apologists, there is no avoiding the contradictions of his own position: while opposed to subscription, he accepted the Thirty-Nine Articles over and over again in order to be sworn into his sees, and required that his clergy do the same in order to receive preferment. He preached against the external hierarchy of the Church, but did not hesitate to benefit by it; he accepted a leading role in a church whose theology he clearly questioned.

Fielding's championing of such a cleric, even long after the controversies in which he had engaged had died away, is a clear indication that his own theology lay on the side of the radical latitudinarians. As a "fictional continuation of the campaign begun in *The Champion* to correct a prevalent contempt of the clergy" (in Battestin's words), he picks an unlikely ally, especially if he is holding up Adams as "the good clergyman, heroically maintaining the true religion in a benighted world badly in need of him."[49] If Hoadly's views on the Eucharist and church governance reflect Fielding's, we would be advised seriously to consider including him with leading dissenters, a place that many commentators then and now believe is the appropriate place for Benjamin Hoadly.

NOTES

1. See Martha F. Bowden, *Yorick's Congregation: The Church of England in the Time of Laurence Sterne* (Newark: University of Delaware Press, 2007), especially chapter 3, "The Company of Preachers: William Rose's *The Practical Preacher* (1762)."

2. Martin C. Battestin, "Fielding's Revisions of *Joseph Andrews*," *Studies in Bibilography* 16 (1963): 86, 98, 88, 100, 116.

3. Henry Fielding, *Joseph Andrews*, ed. Martin C. Battestin, the Wesleyan Edition of the Works of Henry Fielding (Middletown, CT: Wesleyan University Press, 1967), 76; hereafter cited in the text.

4. Susan Rutherford, "Benjamin Hoadly: Sacramental Tests and Eucharistic Thought in Early Eighteenth-century England," *Anglican and Episcopal History* 71 (2002): 473.

5. B. W. Young, *Religion and Enlightenment in Eighteenth-Century England: Theological Debate from Locke to Burke* (Oxford: Clarendon Press, 1998), 32–33.

6. Jeremy Gregory and Jeffrey S. Chamberlain, "National and Local Perspectives on the Church of England in the Long Eighteenth Century," in *The National Church in Local Perspective: The Church of England and the Regions, 1660–1800*, ed. Jeremy Gregory and Jeffrey S. Chamberlain (Woodbridge, England: Boydell Press, 2003), 7, 9.

7. William Gibson, *Enlightenment Prelate: Benjamin Hoadly, 1676–1761* (Cambridge: James Clarke, 2004), 11.

8. Ibid., 138.

9. Philip Jenkins, "Church, Nation and Language: The Welsh Church, 1660–1800," in *The National Church in Local Perspective*, 280. The Welsh dioceses were notoriously impoverished, and were often seen as transitional: "At best, a Welsh diocese was an apprenticeship position that might augur well for one's future career."

10. W. M. Marshall, "The Dioceses of Hereford and Oxford, 1660–1760," in *The National Church in Local Perspective*, 205, 207–8, 209.

11. William Gibson, "'A happy fertile soil which bringeth forth abundantly': The Diocese of Winchester, 1689–1800," in *The National Church in Local Perspective*, 109.

12. Ibid., 110–11.

13. Gibson, *Enlightenment Prelate*, 9.

14. Ibid., 132.

15. Benjamin Hoadly, preface to *Several Tracts Formerly Published: Now Collected into One Volume . . . To which are added, Six Sermons, never before Publish'd* (London, 1715), n.p. Italics reversed.

16. Benjamin Hoadly, *The Nature of the Kingdom, or Church, of Christ: A Sermon Preached before the King, at the Royal Chapel at* St. James's*, on Sunday* March *31, 1717,* 2nd ed. (London, 1717), 3–4, 8–9; hereafter cited in the text.

17. Gibson, *Enlightenment Prelate,* 152.

18. Ibid., 179, 197.

19. Ibid., 277. Arguing for Hoadly's important influence on Hogarth, Gibson writes, "Hoadly emphasized that an honest and sincere heathen was more acceptable to God than a deceitful Christian; and Hogarth depicted this emphatic belief in the external works of charity in the [St. Bartholomew's] Hospital murals" (280).

20. Gibson (ibid., 335n160) calls attention to a passage from *The Pulpit-Lunaticks* (London, [1717]), in which the author, a supporter of both Hoadly and the dissenters, also describes Hoadly as an angel, and "a Bright Luminary of our Church, A Glorious Asserter of Religion and Liberty *and* A Shining Pattern of Piety, Charity, Moderation" (32, italics reversed).

21. Benjamin Hoadly, *A Plain Account of the Nature and End of the Sacrament of the Lord's-Supper* (London, 1735), 58.

22. Leslie Stephen, *History of English Thought in the Eighteenth Century* (New York: Harcourt, Brace and World, 1962), 2:129.

23. *The Book of Common Prayer, and Administration of the Sacraments, and Other Rites and Ceremonies of the Church, According to the Use of the Church of England; Together with the Psalter or Psalms of David, Pointed as they are to be Sung or Said in Churches* (Oxford: John Baskett, 1717), n.p.

24. Hoadly, *A Plain Account,* 71, 91. For students of liturgical history, this point is particularly interesting because it implies that at the administration, the priest handed the chalice to the communicants rather than holding it to their lips, as is the common practice today.

25. Benjamin Hoadly, *A Plain Account,* 17.

26. Rutherford, "Benjamin Hoadly: Sacramental Tests and Eucharistic Thought," 474–75.

27. William Gibson, *The Church of England, 1688–1832: Unity and Accord* (New York: Routledge, 2001), 194.

28. Rutherford, "Benjamin Hoadly: Sacramental Tests and Eucharistic Thought," 476–77.

29. Gibson, *Enlightenment Prelate,* 228.

30. Gibson, *The Church of England*, 92.

31. Rutherford, "Benjamin Hoadly: Sacramental Tests and Eucharistic Thought," 482.

32. Gibson, *Enlightenment Prelate*, 48.

33. British Museum Catalogue Numbers 1502 and 1503, respectively.

34. Gibson, *Enlightenment Prelate*, 113.

35. Gibson, *The Church of England*, 160.

36. Hoadly, "A Second Letter to the Reverend Dr. Francis Atterbury," in *Several Tracts Formerly Published*, 144.

37. Brian McCrae, *Henry Fielding and the Politics of Mid-Eighteenth-Century England* (Athens: University of Georgia Press, 1981), 47.

38. Martin C. Battestin, with Ruthe R. Battestin, *Henry Fielding: A Life* (New York: Routledge, 1989), 189.

39. Simon Dickie, "*Joseph Andrews* and the Great Laughter Debate," *Studies in Eighteenth-Century Culture* 34 (2005): 272–77.

40. Ibid., 301.

41. Patricia Carr Brückmann, *A Manner of Correspondence: A Study of the Scriblerus Club* (Kingston, ON: McGill-Queen's University Press, 1997), 103–7.

42. Dickie, "*Joseph Andrews* and the Great Laughter Debate," 301; McCrae, *Henry Fielding and the Politics of Mid-Eighteenth-Century England*, 108.

43. Battestin, *Henry Fielding: A Life,* 98.

44. William Gibson, *Enlightenment Prelate,* 214–18.

45. Battestin, *Henry Fielding: A Life,* 104.

46. William Gibson, "Brother of the More Famous Benjamin: The Theology of Archbishop John Hoadly," *Anglican and Episcopal History* 75 (2006): 417, 401.

47. McCrae, *Henry Fielding and the Politics of Mid-Eighteenth-Century England*, 9–10, 24–25.

48. Benjamin Hoadly, *Sixteen Sermons Formerly Printed, Now Collected into One Volume, to which are added, Six Sermons upon Public Occasions, Never Before Printed* (London, 1754), viii.

49. Battestin, "Fielding's Revisions of *Joseph Andrews*," 93.

Chapter Seven

Joseph Andrews, Realism, and Openness

Eric Rothstein

Fielding's plays mix realistic portrayal, satiric distortion, and self-conscious theatricality in different proportions. These three elements reassemble in *Joseph Andrews*—but how, since its preface claims it is a just imitation of nature? Well, consider an eighteenth-century model of scientific realism, which comprehends three aspects of perceiving the real world. First is the factual world itself; second, the factual world as both human limits and partial interests filter it (Bacon's Idols of the Tribe and of the Cave); and third, the factual world as the tools we use for truth let us understand it—mechanical instruments, but also categories and conceptual patterns (risking Bacon's Idols of the Marketplace and of the Theater). Accordingly, scientists address the world: they gather projectible particulars, facts that help us model parts of reality and predict their workings. They address human limits and partiality: they value disinterestedness and ways to extend the limits we recognize. And they test instruments and inherited paradigms of knowledge. The instruments of knowledge therefore exist self-reflexively among the heterogeneous inventory of scientific facts.

In *Joseph Andrews* these usages have analogues, all of them establishing Fielding's realism—realism, that is, as scientific realists practiced it, not the realism of Gissing, Hemingway, and Rossellini. Fielding's realistic portrayals bring us the actual world in terms of a hypothesized string of cases, from which we can work by analogy. One checks the accuracy of his hypothesized portrayals by applying criteria of verisimilitude: is this case plausible and projectible? And so with genre: a "just imitation of nature" distinguishes "the comic epic in prose" from romances and burlesques; and for fiction, we measure "justness" by verisimilitude. Once one has the necessary facts, verisimilitude exposes the false pretentions of an imposter to truth, the "Affectation" that Fielding calls "the only Source of the true Ridiculous" (7).[1]

The satire that he imports from his dramatic practice, aiming at the ridiculous, supports, not counters or thwarts, his realism. Naturally, it often flunks the test of verisimilitude, because it echoes the ridiculous "Affectation" that necessarily flunks such a test. Fielding's satire exposes our limits and shames our partiality, rebuking the Idols of the Cave and the Tribe. He mocks rigidity in affected, self-interested, and obsessive people, and shows that rigid, obsessive, often arbitrary social systems—those of the law and of rank, for example—hinder allegedly natural values under guise of preserving them. By way of balance to this strain of satire, Fielding also appeals for our agreement about evidence and values through his gentleman's voice, judicious, without partis pris.[2] These means reinforce his readers' openness to complexity and empiricism.

As to his self-conscious theatricality, the third element Fielding imports from his plays, it displays our tools for truth, the instruments and inherited paradigms of knowledge that let us represent the hypothetically real. Accordingly, *Joseph Andrews* keeps alluding to books and their devices, including its professed model, *Don Quixote*, which yields a whole repertory of such devices in aid of restoring an addled protagonist to a sometimes brutal and unjust, but factual reality. What might be antirealistic elements in a late nineteenth-century author, then, here converge in a realism. The skeptical openness that complements a patient, case-oriented empiricism lets us better imagine and appraise everyday life.

Every distinctive element in *Joseph Andrews*, I suggest, rests on the needs of such complex realism. As a realist, Fielding prompts readers' openness to the world by forcing their openness in reading his novel: they must assimilate a verisimilar, teeming variety of characters, allusions, tones, shifting points of view, distances from the immediate action, and hermeneutic puzzles. His broad range of evaluative references, offered with a variety of ironic inflections, complicates how we appraise the depicted world, as real, narrow or biased in depiction, or affected by literary convention. We collaborate in *Joseph Andrews*. We collaborate too because Fielding leaves unresolved a good many interpretive problems in the novel, forcing us to see supposedly simple issues as complex. Narrative elements in *Joseph Andrews* rarely have univocal meanings, and some stay unresolved. We thereby shuck unthinking, stock responses, even if at last we choose those same responses from among the possibilities. We, autonomously, must decide, or decide not to decide. There's a parallel here to the radical, momentous shift in ethical ideals, during the eighteenth century, from obedience to autonomy.[3] Autonomy in the search for truth marks scientific realism and Fielding's. "Nullius in verba" (take nobody's word for it) was the Royal Society's skeptical motto in the service of experiment. This principle saturates *Joseph Andrews*.

Nullius in verba: obviously one suspects the words of vain and hypocriti-cal characters, in situations where the vanity and hypocrisy come into play. For the ends of this novel, "nullius in verba" plainly suits what Pamela and *Pamela* say. In fact, it also fits other fit-all formulas of exemplarity and stan-dard social categories, whether in the main narrative of *Joseph Andrews* or the interpolated stories. Fielding's own storytelling exemplar, Cervantes, of course, has similar experimental principles: Don Quixote's inherited body of older normative tales, knightly romances, fail him by failing to depict con-temporary reality.

A first case in point is the treatment of the biblical story of Joseph, to which Joseph Andrews recurs, as his supposed sister Pamela recurs to the Bible. Biblical Joseph is sold into Egypt, traditionally the land of bondage, by merchants who find him in a pit after he has been stripped of the coat his father made for him (Gen. 37). After he rejects his master Potiphar's wife's advances, she also strips him of a garment (Gen. 39). This pattern carries over to Joseph Andrews. Gypsies (Egyptians) kidnapped him as a baby. In servitude, he spurns the charms of Lady Booby, his late master's wife, alleg-ing his virtue and citing his "Name's-sake" Joseph's example as well as his sister Pamela's (47, 58). Later, like biblical Joseph, he lies in a pit (a ditch in *Joseph Andrews*) after being twice stripped, first of his livery when Lady Booby discharges him, and then of his borrowed clothes.

But the parallels diverge. For biblical Joseph's distinctive coat of many colors, sign of paternal honors, Joseph Andrews has standard livery. "His" colors belong to the Boobys. Biblical Joseph in Egypt rises as a prophet by glossing symbolic dreams narrated to him. He knows his family. Joseph Andrews never before the end foresees his imminent or eventual future. As to dreams, he sleeps while Wilson mentions a crucial symbol, the strawberry birthmark that would explicate his past. Like biblical Joseph, Joseph Andrews rises socially and rejoins his father, but not because he is "discreet and wise" (Gen. 41:33). He requires errors and coincidences. To cap the reversal, bibli-cal Joseph turns out not even to be our Joseph's true namesake, just as Pa-mela is not truly his sister—"the Lord knows whether he was baptized or no, or by what Name," says Mrs. Andrews (337), who picked "Joseph" for the changeling in her daughter's cradle. Paralleling Fielding's hero and biblical Joseph yields no prophetic knowledge, locating a destiny. The likeness is a chimera hatched from ignorance, Joseph's and ours. It's as "accurate" as, say, Joseph's gaining love because a strawberry birthmark lies on his left breast, his heart, for the strawberry is a fruit legendarily governed by Venus—this is Fielding's sly joke.[4] We readers can guess Joseph's future by glossing symbols, literary devices. But neither Joseph Andrews nor we can do that in real life.

If one hopes to apply the Bible as a large allusive, normative pattern behind *Joseph Andrews*, it suffers serious deflation. What about concentrated, embedded narratives, the three interpolated stories? Each story is keyed to one of the canonical values that underpin Fielding's preface about his own "Species of writing": the Beautiful (false glamour lures Leonora in the first tale to discard solidly British Horatio for flashy, francophoney Bellarmine), the Good (Wilson's narrative of debauchery, disgrace, and lucky rescue), and the True (Paul fibs strategically to Leonard and his wife). Each might be a normative, exemplary tale, as are *Pamela* and the biblical story of Joseph. That is, faulty Leonora gets punished, reformed Wilson gets rewarded, and Paul's deceit is uncovered. Yet each, increasingly in order of the tales, erodes its central value as the tale itself exemplifies it.

Mr. Wilson's tale, the second, occupies the spatial center of *Joseph Andrews* (chapters 3–4 of the third of four books). Wilson sweepingly generalizes his own experience of sin, squalor, frivolity, and pain. His first-person account, with confessional penitence as well as inventoried social indictment, provides a brief, bitter counterpart to the scope and discriminated detail for which Adams has just praised Homer (197–99) and that Fielding himself practices in his comic prose epic. Does Wilson's account also have a moral rationale? If so, why does Wilson gain happiness through happenstance? Having desperately thrown himself "into Fortune's Lap" (218), Wilson exits debtor's prison through winning a lottery, having a serendipitous death occur, and a suddenly introduced heiress's revealing her crush on him. He gains a fortune, all right, and a lady's "Lap," by accident. His rescuer Harriet says she loves him for his "Worth" (223). Worth? His tale has shown us none thus far. Providential grace? Neither Wilson nor his rescuer Harriet mentions that. If one thinks that Wilson catalogs the town's sins to awake our moral vigilance, what does his rewarded appeal to Fortune awake? Shouldn't a normative ethical tale imply, maybe entail, moral responsibility, agency together with awareness?

After fortune grants Wilson liberty and property, he becomes the virtuous, pastoral Wilson we meet. But so? Both Wilson's vice and his virtue (his upright dealing as a wine merchant) punish him in the city. In the country, plus ça change. Vice thrives there—venal, brutal, and deluded characters—just as well as virtue. Symptomatic ills still afflict virtuous, rural Wilson. These may be random from below, in the rootless, classless gypsies' theft of his eldest son, or systemic from above, in the local squirearchy who trample his land and murder his eldest daughter's dog. Fielding embellishes *Joseph Andrews* with a handsome formal arrangement to respond to this high/low pairing: another rootless figure, the nomadic peddler, restores the stolen son to Wilson (338), and that same son, together with Adams, kills two of the squire's dogs

(242). Fielding's readers expect such formal elegance, for his writing never relies on fortune—but where fortune rules, as throughout Wilson's tale, what warrants useful inferences?

These questions gain force because the pattern of fortune carries forward from this central interpolated tale. *Joseph Andrews* ends happily through a flurry of coincidences filched from romance, freeing Wilson's son Joseph from the threats of Bridewell and then bridal ill, incest. Only Fielding's triumphant impudence carries us aloft to rejoice at such strange dei ex machina. Certainly no one, not even the pious pedagogue Adams, invokes anything metaphysically higher than fortune here. This denouement—is it serendipitous support of primogeniture, lucky Joseph as lucky Wilson's heir? We learn of Wilson's own happy fortune after having seen fortune repeatedly succoring Joseph in books 1 and 2—is Wilson his son's narratological heir? Given these options, how, if at all, does the role of fortune in Wilson's story clarify the denouement's ambiguity as literary convention? Does the happy ending, for instance, recall Terentian romance, as in *The Conscious Lovers*; generic satire, as in another active repertory piece, *The Beggar's Opera*; or nose-thumbing escapism, as in *The Author's Farce*? In these last two plays, what pleases us deliberately does not convince us. Does the denouement flip the moralism of *Pamela*, since in Fielding virtue gets rewarded, but not for virtue? Any of these, each with a different "message," would be plausible for Fielding. What conclusions, if any, given several interpretive models, shall we draw about the benefits of being good?

The other two interpolated tales, like Wilson's, deal with spousal relations, deceit, financial disparity, and a protagonist's free choices. The form and problems of each tale differ, however, to suit its focal canonical value, the Beautiful (Leonora's story) and the True (Leonard and Paul's). An idiom of art, drawn from Cervantes and Scarron, suffuses Leonora's tale, with its romance names for English people and its exaggerated love language. The allegedly "saturnine" Horatio, for instance, writes to Leonora about "the extatic Happiness of seeing you" and his "utmost Rapture" (103, 105-6). Its eager teller, an anonymous, otherwise featureless, well-bred lady, pours forth the account, repeating, verbatim, allegedly memorized love letters (105), and, also verbatim, conversations she didn't hear, so couldn't memorize.

The dense detail increases one's sense of her story's finished self-enclosure, its artiness. So does its arbitrariness. Alone among the interpolated tales, it serves no easily discernable thematic or narrative purpose, even though it repeats motifs, such as that of clothes and social identity, from Joseph's current plight. The teller too has no discernable motive, except for gossip, by analogy with "the Ladies of the Town" (125). Two points here: first, the lady's supposedly faithful facts and her cool righteousness make truth and ethics serve romantic "beauty." As a self-justifying entertainment, the tale does not perform the values it ostensibly preaches. Second, if we blame Leonora's infatuation with Bellarmine's fancy foreign dress-up, how can we explain Fielding's imitating a French (or Spanish) mode of embellishment in presenting the tale? How does the mode of Cervantes and Scarron suit a story that tells us, "Buy British"?

Truth, not Beauty, governs the blunt story of Paul and Leonard, which breaks off without closure. It embarks from a young boy's school reader and his Latin rote, auguring didactic business. Sure enough, the chapter title promises "an useful Lesson" (315) from this schoolbook. But what lesson? To keep peace between Leonard and his wife, squabbling, cocksure spouses, their penniless guest Paul ostensibly sides with whichever aggrieved spouse is currently confiding in him. When they discern his strategy, their shared wrath at him at least momentarily reconciles them. What then does truth mean for one's preferred end, be it peace, considerateness, or extrapolative knowledge? Mightn't Paul's partially lying, pragmatic self-effacement—he conceals whom he thinks right—ring truer than the wealthy spouses' literal, polemic truth claims? Does it matter that we never learn Paul's motives for his acts, perhaps benign deceit or maybe sharp self-interest? Do these questions of truth bear upon Fielding's fictional truth and his care for his readers' desires? By this point in *Joseph Andrews*, what truth means in the main plot is messy, and about to become quickly messier as the young protagonists realize their "true" identities. Hence the story of Paul and Leonard here, but it is calculatedly of no help.

In the interpolated tales, then, Fielding troubles the inherited, transcendent norms of the Beautiful, the Good, and the True. That is, he disturbs how one applies them, as he disturbs the application of the biblical Joseph narration. Never rejecting them, he nonetheless complicates and situates their use, fogging them in practice with various kinds of indecision within the sample world of *Joseph Andrews*. He counters stock responses to give us multiplicity, as soon as one gets to real life. Predictably, this questioning and testing also keeps recurring in the body of this novel, especially with immanent norms. By "immanent," I mean those normative, "natural" categories supposedly implicit in reality itself, such as familial classifications and a good many social and biological ones.

Think of "nature" in the incest motif concluding this family-centered novel. Fielding turns the deepest familial taboo into a shell game of identity and belonging. Joseph and Fanny briefly seem to be siblings. They in fact only switch positions in the Andrews family, Fanny moved in, Joseph out. But the switch playfully preserves the sibling incest motif: the gypsies swap baby Joseph for baby Fanny, so that he shows up in her bed—her cradle

(337). Particularly among the multiple familial promotions caused by Pamela's marrying Booby, the incest game stresses how much social artifices riddle the "natural." That "nature" is axiomatic in Fielding's background texts—one is Genesis, so zealous for family and tribal lines, and another, Adams's cherished Aeschylus, where tragedy rises from fractures and negations of family. But when Fielding's wit infects the "natural" of received history, nature's laws look like kissing cousins to writer's license.

Joseph Andrews also toys with male/female boundaries. It starts with the no-double-standard comparison of Joseph and Pamela as guardians of chastity—"Did ever Mortal hear of a Man's Virtue!" cries the variously heated Lady Booby, avatar of her brother B. in *Pamela* (41). Fielding ends by teasing these boundaries in Beau Didapper, so androgynous—male and female didappers (small grebes) have nearly identical plumage: "No Hater of Women; for he always dangled [!] after them; yet so little subject to Lust, that he had . . . the Character of great Moderation in his Pleasures" (312; and see 332–33). Between these brackets Fielding musters up marital arrangements that overlap but not repeat. We see gender role reversal, as with the Tow-wouses, and caricature, as with the Trullibers (84–88, 164–65). Wilson finds "none of my own Sex" more capable than Harriet "of making juster Observations upon Life, or of delivering them more agreeably; nor do I believe any one possessed of a faithfuller or braver Friend" (226). Sex distinctions, like those of family, have enough arbitrary admixture that we cannot take them as simple givens. Fielding additionally scrambles into them a strong dose of social class, which the narrator declares arbitrary (156–58). Since this arbitrary system relies on family and gender groupings, its dubiousness dyes them too.

Family, sex, and social class are real-world facts. We use them to cope with the world and to form the world that we and others cope with. In respect to biology and status, they are sufficiently consistent within the world to be useful. Beyond that, they are not. Again, as with biblical Joseph and Platonic ideals, Fielding does not reject these categories; he teases and disenchants them in practice. He thus questions when and how useful they are, empirically, for ethical or metaphysical judgments, or for begetting norms from facts. I would note that he also does not promote these categories. He ignores the traditional paradigm, in which one blames human lapses for seeming damage to some universal ideal, established by God or Nature, an immanent source of order. A weak, secular form of the paradigm does appear in Fielding's institutional satire: law and medicine remain unshakably honorable, no matter how shysters and quacks disgrace their practice. Their honor can derive from their ideal use, not their metaphysical status. The ideal use of family, gender, and social class, however, differs: given that one cannot trust the empirical results they yield, an ideal use of these categories would have to be tentative and provisional. Significantly, in *Joseph Andrews*, the most admirable characters, as well as faulty ones, exhibit the shakiness of family, gender, and social class.

In tune with a skeptical, pragmatic logic, no character, however admirable, embodies universal ideals or serves as a paragon to establish reliable, real-world norms. The best candidate to be an exemplar is Adams, for *Joseph Andrews* never smirches his personal integrity and the soundness of his impulsive actions. (The sturdy Christian, as approved by Fielding, swings the other fist, not turns the other cheek.) Early on Adams errs merely through preoccupation and naïveté, amusing us and endearing himself by personal foibles. By midnovel, though, he slips further, repeatedly permitting his vanity to blemish him as a clerical source of spiritual wisdom. Over and over, vanity confirms his wrong, dogmatic opinions, products of a blinkered mind, not merely of preoccupation and naïveté. He praises ignorance to preserve boys' innocence (230–31), rebukes grief (264–67), and advocates strict husbandly authority (310–11, 323). As "a great Enemy to the Passions," he "preache[s] nothing more than the Conquest of them by Reason and Grace" (309). He rejects this-worldly pleasure (330) and accepts witchcraft (334). In one episode, he knowingly omits an inconvenient scriptural verse, and cites the Bible selectively: preaching to Joseph a doctrine of resignation, he invokes his namesake Abraham's willingness to sacrifice Isaac, but ignores the story of Joseph's namesake, where Jacob rends his garments and mourns long for his son's supposed death (308; Gen. 22, 37:34). Adams's "bitterest Agony" (309) at the supposed death of his own son Jacky—Fielding's form of "Isaac"—then immediately belies his preachments. At other times his wife and quasi-son Joseph properly correct his foolish "wisdom." Feet of clay are better than a heart of bronze, no doubt, so that flawed Adams does better than other figures of trust in *Joseph Andrews*. Still, especially when he struts as an exemplar, he parodies one.

If Adams's example would inculcate vanity, one source of Fielding's "ridiculous," then the example of Joseph's other beacon, Pamela, could teach the other source, hypocrisy. That is the thrust of Fielding's mock-exposé burlesque *Shamela*. Fielding had broader plans in alluding to *Pamela* in *Joseph Andrews*, though, where all outside aids to proper assessments—biblical Joseph's history, classical (Platonic) norms, "natural" categories (family, gender, class), and literary convention—turn out to be unevenly and variably unreliable. So, more elaborately, this logic includes *Pamela*, a romance that dwells on natural categories. *Pamela* resembles the story of biblical Joseph as a seemingly exact but actually off-kilter exemplary tale, and it resembles the interpolated tales in its dubious relationship to its professed moral.

What *Joseph Andrews* does, in my reading of it, *Pamela* cannot. With its shallow realism and its traditional idea of nature, based on a fixed order, Richardson's novel typically tells readers what they already (should) know. True, at least before Pamela marries B., it adds to our knowledge by using intimacy to explore psychological processes. Yet even Pamela's subjectivity is hardly more than son et lumière for a moral fable, by Richardson's design. His pubescent heroine's actions are so meagerly her own that her eyewitness account of them follows a fixed genre to match a fixed order, a Cinderella tale. Stylistically it pretends to be as new as its heroine is naive, yet it engages its reader through a once-upon-a-time romance plot, based on desire and aversion, featuring kidnapping, captivity, ogres, distraught virtue, a happy ending, and a thin, conventional sense of personal agency. Indeed, for Richardson *Pamela*'s banality beneath the personalized surface helps guarantee its teachings.

Whereas *Joseph Andrews* is self-reflexive about its instruments of truth, its narrators and narrative genres, *Pamela* disallows questioning its instrument of truth, Pamela herself, a single naive voice and consciousness, with one filter for events. Were Pamela's subjectivity to indicate her own agency, as in more realistic fiction, readers could move to real-life inferences about systematic bias and motives. For example, her preternatural literacy might hint at a sophistication that she willingly hides from her parents. Frequently in the eighteenth century, "female reading and idleness, sensual pleasure, and secret intimacy" were linked.[5] Since such speculation would wreck *Pamela* as Richardson intended it, we are invited to look for psyche and blocked from really doing so. We have the illusion of intimacy but no real person with whom to be intimate. This failure of mind or nerve from a realist perspective had launched *Shamela*, which parodies and reveals *Pamela*'s skittish realism along the lines just suggested.

And *Joseph Andrews*? Its realism swallows up Richardsonian romance and romance's counterpart, burlesque, modes that Fielding addresses in his preface. Burlesque appears in *Joseph Andrews* as almost entirely the characters' genre. They burlesque themselves through self-interested pretense, Affectation, "the only Source of the true Ridiculous" (7), when they caricature themselves by their single-minded quest for others' favor, pushed by vanity and hypocrisy. Romance twists in *Joseph Andrews*, by contrast, come from authorial fiat, so-called Fortune. Why? In *Pamela*'s romance mode, the heroine steers with ancestral charts through choppy waves to a port of happiness. Until after her marriage, Pamela must in Richardson's conception stay staunch about an ideal, obedience-based morality, expressed in preestablished codes, biblical or familial. She cleaves to heteronomous behavior, such as also underlies self-burlesque. Fielding is on the other side of the shift in eighteenth-century ethics, mentioned above, from ideals of obedience to an ideal of autonomy. Accordingly, for *Pamela*'s touted ethics of obedience, *Joseph Andrews* substitutes an ethics based on questioning codes and categories. Unquestioning romance in *Joseph Andrews*, as within Wilson's tale and the novel's denouement, then yields interpretive indeterminacy or at least question-raising complexity.

Joseph Andrews recycles burlesque and romance, I have argued, as agents of skeptical realism, to depose Baconian Idols. As to what he sees as the closed, desire-based romance of *Pamela* specifically, Fielding goes further. In two respects he develops and supersedes the limited truths of *Pamela*. His techniques here go well beyond the simpler reversals that import the biblical Joseph story into *Joseph Andrews*. First, Fielding's critique of categories leads him to enlarge on a major point in *Pamela*, the social leveling by which an ex-schoolmaster's poor daughter wins a wealthy squire's hand. As to B., Richardson had hedged *Pamela*'s social leveling, making it partial and anomalous. In addition, B.'s obsessive fascination raises her above his employees, but her captors, Jewkes and Colbrand. She has an uncertain, liminal status. In *Joseph Andrews* Fielding expands on liminal status and social leveling. Through most of the novel, Fielding's unspoiled principals—Adams, Joseph, and Fanny—freely travel as near equals. The men's uniforms, livery and a cassock, typecast them, but beneath those, their fluid, often concealed identities exemplify the "communitas" that the anthropologist Victor Turner relates to pilgrimage and consequent changes in status.[6] Such fluidity enacts an alternative to the rabid hierarchies the travelers encounter.

We have leveling up: by book 4 Joseph's sudden, seeming promotion to B.'s family via Pamela privileges him to box the ear of the "immensely rich" Didapper, so soundly "that it conveyed him several Paces from where he stood" (320–21). We have lateral leveling, not only through on-the-road communitas but also through other narratives. For instance, the interpolated stories create temporarily classless groups of listeners.[7] And we have much, often ominous leveling down, when humans get muddled with other animals. While battling, Adams is soaked with hog's blood that is mistaken for his (120) and the porcine Trulliber later pushes him into a "Hogs-Stye" (163). The travelers are trapped by bird batters (140), confuse sheep-stealers with murderers (192–95), and battle with dogs who have just ripped apart an anthropomorphized hare (236–44). The roasting squire's men compare Adams to a badger and a fox; the narrator calls the squire's huntsmen "Curs" (244–47) and his quack doctor a "mischievous Dog" (249). Adams condemns Wilson's past profligate life as "below the Life of an Animal" (204–5). The motif recurs with Lady Booby's social contempt for Adams—"*Quelle Bête! Quel Animal*" (313)—and the introduction of bird-named Didapper; and thence expands into the denouement, with its extensive familial, social, and personal leveling.

Second, *Joseph Andrews* sublates a theme in *Pamela* of liberty and property—the hardheaded realist's means of secular salvation. Richardson's heroine gains liberty and then a share in B.'s property by reserving her own primal property, her self and body. *Joseph Andrews* distributes Pamela's property, made material and ironic, among the protagonists: her religion in Adams's bundled, unsalable sermons, her ability to turn love into money in Joseph's inalienable golden love amulet, and her allures in both Fanny's chaste body and punning Christian name. (The pun on "fanny" already appears in *Shamela*'s introductory letters.) Pamela's private property, made public through her private letters, buys marriage and status; in *Joseph Andrews*, its public, material form has no exchange value. From that reversal, Fielding's novel reenacts Pamela's doubtful status, captivity, and poverty, now multiplied and differentiated, with her supposed brother Joseph, her actual sister Fanny, and Adams, who as father, schoolmaster, and parson absorbs the roles of *Pamela*'s two good men, Parson Williams and Pamela's ex-schoolmaster father.

Fielding resolves the plot through another itinerant figure engaged by occupation in property transfer, the peddler whose itinerant common-law wife, at one time a predator herself, sold baby Fanny. In fact, the peddler has long been involved with other people's buying and selling men and women, since he was a military recruiter who "struck a Bargain" to cohabit with this wife (324). At last the peddler becomes "an Excise-man; a Trust which he discharges with such Justice, that he is greatly beloved in the Neighbourhood" (344). The relatively recent (1732–1733) Excise Bill controversy had centered on liberty and property: "Excise would extinguish the Englishman's liberty," the press claimed. "His house would be broken open, his wife and daughters violated; robbed without redress, he would be indistinguishable from a Frenchman."[8] The peddler, who steers righteously within a perilous system, then, is the perfect figure to restore liberty and property.

Liberty and property: in *Joseph Andrews* the providential claims in *Pamela* melt into highly temporalized claims on the worldly future, repeatedly and realistically acknowledging the property system. Liberty, the principal characters have or gain; but without exchangeable property, liberty is fragile, illusory. Through their bodily properties, like strength and beauty, the protagonists can act freely only in "low" actions, like brawls, which are as socially egalitarian as their communitas; otherwise they need auxiliaries. True charity sometimes saves them, as when the postilion rescues naked Joseph (53), but more often charity acts through dubious simulacra. Only promissory inferences from his gold piece and white skin get Joseph decent treatment at the Dragon Inn. Borrowing, still further promises in time, redeem his bill and then Adams's horse (100). Later, a squire who knows Lady Booby releases the travelers from a justice who has never "committed a Gentleman" (149); the hostess's bad guess that the wealthy, powerful Trulliber is Adams's blood brother almost redeems the travelers from another inn, though in fact they need the peddler's intervention (169–70); and the inn host who affords them charity, as victims of a practical joke, argues for material trade over spiritual clothing and feeding (182–84). The pattern continues through books 3 and 4 till the property-shifting denouement. As I have suggested through comparing analogous denouements—Wilson's, and those of *The Conscious Lovers*, *The Beggar's Opera*, and *The Author's Farce*—faith in God's immanent hand, like "the Apostolic and feudal role of charity[,] is itself demystified in *Joseph Andrews*."[9] Verbal high jinks show the narrator's hand as the fictional source of charity, while in the narrative, charity repeatedly slides from apostolic *caritas* into its modern, material sense, giving and taking money. That is hardheaded, worldly realism.

Fielding's humor and panache give us enough comfortable distance that we can practice openness and skepticism, following him, without worry about consequences. His variety deprives us from relaxing into formulaic reading, falling back on inversion, deflation, burlesque, or benignly protective imitations of a penumbral Providence. In these ways he elicits from us, apprenticed to him, the practice of skeptical realism—toward the world, our own prejudices, and modes of representation. His skepticism, like scientists', never becomes corrosive or nihilistic; like scientists, he asks and urges us to consider cases, tacitly, as to what explanatory norms or principles do and don't hold, which remain projectible, and why. He does not aim for discoveries, as some scientists did, but for more practical taxonomies, as they also did. Because he controls his world by using worn devices that please but should not convince us, he illustrates a real world whose tightly knotted problems and loose, leaky categories escape control, and yet yield knowledge so that we can cope adaptively with the world as we receive it. These, I suggest, are the aims and means of Fielding's skeptical realism.

NOTES

1. Citations from *Joseph Andrews*, in parenthetical page numbers in the text, come from Henry Fielding, *Joseph Andrews*, ed. Martin C. Battestin, the Wesleyan Edition of the Works of Henry Fielding (Oxford: Clarendon Press, 1967).

2. Steven Shapin has shown how a code of civility, with its gentlemanly, therefore disinterested tone, increased credibility in eighteenth-century scientific discourse. It testified to the writer's keeping to that code, with principles of integrity and honor. *A*

Social History of Truth: Civility and Science in Seventeenth-Century England (Chicago: University of Chicago Press, 1994).

3. This point is made and massively documented by J. B. Schneewind, *The Invention of Autonomy: A History of Modern Moral Philosophy* (Cambridge: Cambridge University Press, 1998).

4. For the strawberry, see Nicholas Culpeper, *The Complete Herbal* (1653; repr., Birmingham: Kynoch Press, n.d.), 247.

5. Roger Chartier, ed., *A History of Private Life,* vol. 3, *Passions of the Renaissance*, trans. Arthur Goldhammer (Cambridge, MA: Harvard University Press, 1989), 147.

6. Victor Turner, *Dramas, Fields, and Metaphors: Symbolic Action in Human Society* (Ithaca: Cornell University Press, 1974).

7. I owe this point to Jeffrey Williams, "The Narrative Circle: The Interpolated Tales in *Joseph Andrews*," *Studies in the Novel* 30 (1998): 473–88.

8. J. H. Plumb, *Sir Robert Walpole*, vol. 2 (Cambridge, MA: Houghton Mifflin, 1961), 251.

9. Michael McKeon, *The Origins of the English Novel, 1600–1740* (Baltimore: Johns Hopkins University Press, 1987), 402.

Chapter Eight

Satire and the Psychology of Religion in Swift and Nietzsche

Frank Palmeri

Although they can both be seen as radical conservatives, it might seem strained to bring together Jonathan Swift and Friedrich Nietzsche as thinkers on religion—the first an orthodox minister of the Church of England, the second the son and grandson of Lutheran ministers and the philosopher who pronounced the death of God. Yet Swift and Nietzsche share extensive and striking insights concerning the psychology of religious behavior, and they employ parallel satiric strategies in exploring and exposing that psychology. Not only does Nietzsche refer to Swift by name four times in *Human, All Too Human* (1878), but both that work and *A Tale of a Tub* (1704) represent most or all believers in the doctrines of organized religions and even more so the founders of such religions as pathologically subject to delusions and self-deception. Using nearly identical formulations, the two works describe such believers and especially their leaders as mad. Although other satires of organized religions such as Hume's *Natural History of Religion* (1757) constitute mediating texts that advance the thesis that most or all popular organized religion is pathological, Swift and Nietzsche conspicuously stress the importance of religious observances as substitutes for or extensions of sexual activities. In addition, both call into question the praise of interiority and of depth of religious feeling; they draw attention to the inescapability and importance of surfaces, exteriors, and masks. It might be objected that as an honest and very public clergyman Swift, unlike Nietzsche, must exempt Christianity from his analyses: however, almost all the figures in Swift's satire in the *Tale* participate in the madness of extremes; only one fleetingly gives evidence of occupying a supposed middle ground of rational belief. In addition, Swift's "Thoughts on Religion" imply that he may not have shared the faith of his coreligionists, but that he regarded freedom of conscience as the impossibility of thinking otherwise than his God-given reason led him to think. On the evidence of his sermons and other writings, he practiced his vocation as a minister largely to ensure social order and to encourage civic and nontheological virtues.

For Nietzsche, the question of the appeal of religion begins with and constantly returns to believers' mental imbalance, their lack of psychological health. The thrills and satisfactions obtained by heightened states of existence help explain the appeal of a religion to those who are most active in its rituals and observances. Offering a capsule history of how one obtains religious authority, Nietzsche writes that "it was noticed that a state of excitement often made the head clearer and called up happy inspirations"; therefore, it was felt that "the extremest states of excitement" would offer the happiest inspirations, "and thus the mad were revered as the wise and propounders of oracles."[1] When such frenzied states are encouraged by coreligionists, then all participants in the community have a motivation to follow and extend their own visions, their own pathologies.

Madness can exert such influence and authority because in Nietzsche's view religions are not founded on reason or measure. Christianity in particular, he says, is based on a "pathological excess of feeling"; the conviction of utter depravity casts one down into the mud, to be followed often by a feeling of salvation that assures one of life in the heavens (*H*, 66). Nietzsche argues that religious systems are projections of the irrational, and that fear even more than hope has served as the prime and continuing motivation for religious beliefs and behaviors. Early humans would have felt the need for the assistance of mysterious forces, unknown and unpredictable, for the success of their undertakings, whether these involved hunting, fighting, or surviving the hardships of weather and environment (*H*, 64). For Nietzsche, "*a religion has never yet, either directly or indirectly, either as dogma or as parable, contained a truth. For every religion was born out of fear and need, it has crept into existence along paths of aberrations of reason*" (*H*, 62).[2]

But it is not only that religions encourage madness in oracles and other authorities; nor do irrationality and pathological excess play a determining role in religious behavior only in foundational times. Madness and excess extend through all strata of believers and throughout religious history.[3] Nietzsche also warns believers not to take the happiness that they derive from their religion as evidence of its truth or accuracy. In this respect, it is in religion as in art, where we sometimes exaggerate the accomplishments of the artist who moves us greatly, although we may later realize that it was our judgment or sensibility that was deficient. "The blessings and raptures conferred by a philosophy or a religion likewise prove nothing in regard to their truth: just as little as the happiness the madman enjoys from his *idée fixe* proves anything in regard to its rationality" (*H*, 85). Beliefs that produce real psychological benefits, including happiness and a sense of security, may have little or no foundation in fact or truth.

For Nietzsche, asceticism constitutes the specific pathology that character-izes almost all religions—a subject that he will consider at length in the final third of *On the Genealogy of Morals* (1887).[4] The ascetic splits himself in two; he holds himself in contempt because of his base physical needs and denies them, yet such an attitude of self-contempt also involves pride in thus being able to triumph over oneself.[5] "Whoever despises himself still respects himself as one who despises."[6] The morality implied by this splitting of the self, this lowering in order to elevate oneself, Nietzsche finds expressed most saliently in the Sermon on the Mount: "man takes a real delight in oppress-ing himself with excessive claims and afterwards idolizing this tyrannically demanding something in his soul. In every ascetic morality man worships a part of himself as God and for that he needs to diabolize the other part" (*H*, 74). One can discern here the defining operation of the superego in Freud's theory: the tormenting of oneself with excessive claims and harsh demands in order to raise up an ideal of moral rectitude.[7]

If the leaders of religions and their followers reveal one kind of internal division through their asceticism, they display another kind through their reli-ance on self-deception. Nietzsche diagnoses in the great deceivers in world history an ability not only to bring others over to their visions and purposes, but even at some point to convince themselves of the truth of what they say. Those who establish new institutions of belief equal or excel the most skilled practitioners of the art in other areas: "the founders of religions are distin-guished from these great deceivers by the fact that they never emerge from this state of self-deception" (*H*, 40).[8] The most effective deceivers succeed in deceiving themselves—and these include the founders of religions.

But more is involved in establishing religions than merely a massive capacity to deceive others and oneself. Founders of religions, according to Nietzsche, observe a certain average or widespread way of life, then formu-late a set of teachings and interpretations of life in accord with that way of life. Thus, Jesus and Paul observed closely the bleak life of virtuous, humble people in the Roman provinces, and placed the highest meaning upon it; Bud-dha observed good, peaceable, and inoffensive people who did not like to work, and promised a world in which one would not have to work if one was good and peaceable. "The religion-founder must be psychologically infallible in his knowledge of a certain average breed of souls who have not yet *rec-ognized* one another as allies. He is the one who brings them together."[9] The genius of the founder consists of being able to formulate his pitch precisely so that it appeals to the self-image and satisfies the basic psychological needs of millions of like-minded human beings.

Frank Palmeri

Nietzsche argues that the founders of religions possess more than a colossal ability to deceive, and more than an ability to tune their message finely to the impulses and presumptions of potential believers. They must also resemble conquerors in being willing to step over established constraints. "The strongest and most evil spirits," he writes, overturn frameworks of behavior and belief, mostly, like conquerors, "by force of arms, by toppling boundary stones, by violating pieties—but also by means of new religions and moralities! In every teacher and preacher of what is new we find the same 'mischief' that makes conquerors infamous" (*GS,* 32). This passage implies a strongly ambivalent attitude toward such conquerors and founders of new religions, toward such innovators and toward innovation in general: on the one hand, they make mischief; they cannot let well enough alone; they found constraining systems whose results Nietzsche deprecates bitterly. On the other hand, these are the strong spirits who can violate pieties and effect a reversal of moral values; their role in the founding of systems of belief has parallels with the task Nietzsche sets himself of renovating European culture after the ebbing of traditional beliefs.

In his later writings, Nietzsche intensifies his focus on the way ascetic practices give power. In the *Genealogy of Morals*, he analyzes asceticism as a strategy that denies life forces in order to sharpen the feeling of being alive. He had already begun the investigation of asceticism in aphorisms concerning sexuality from works leading up to the *Genealogy*. In *Beyond Good and Evil* (1886), he writes, "The degree and kind of a man's sexuality reach up into the ultimate pinnacle of his spirit" (*BGE,* 81). From the nature of his beliefs and ideals, his everyday practices and recurring behavior, one can infer a man's relation to his sexuality, his distance from and disciplining of it; conversely, his sexuality shapes and finds expression in his ideals and beliefs. Such a view of communication between different ranges of human experience brings the processes and products of the lower and the upper body to a single level and tends to eliminate a qualitative distinction between high and low registers.

Similarly, Nietzsche questions the conventional distinction between the inner and outer, the deep and the superficial, and implies both a cutting cruelty in the investigator of depths and insides, and the attractiveness of adherence to surfaces, masks, and roles. He discerns a desire to submit to the "occasional will of the spirit to let itself be deceived. . . . *This* will to mere appearance, to simplification, to masks, to cloaks, in short, to the surface . . . is *countered* by that sublime inclination of the seeker after knowledge who insists on profundity, multiplicity, and thoroughness, with a *will* which is a kind of cruelty of the intellectual conscience" (*BGE,* 160–61). In the preface, he acknowledges that he has been guilty of wrongheaded enthusiasms—for

Schopenhauer, Wagner, the Greeks. But he asks, "how much cunning in self-preservation, how much reason and higher safeguarding, is contained in such self-deception. . . . Enough, I am still living; and life is, after all, not a product of morality: it *wants* deception, it *lives* on deception" (*H,* 6).

Nietzsche's analysis of the psychology of religion, then, focuses both on anonymous believers and on the world-famous founders of religious systems. Diagnosing what he takes to be a pathological state, he stresses the importance of madness and deception in structuring the lives of the religious. Fear is at the origin of religion, which is irrational in its fount and throughout. Observing that the mad are seen as oracles in earlier social formations, he implies that oracles, prophets, and religious authorities are themselves mad. Worship of a powerful and beneficent deity seems to require a derogation of a demonic evil principle, and the world of the believer, especially as his belief moves toward monotheism, tends to be increasingly Manichean. The founders of religion can be ranked among the most complete and successful deceivers in the world, because they even succeed in convincing themselves of the truth of what they teach. Such founding figures have more in common with conquering invaders than they do with obscure, pacific men who do not try to conquer men's minds and turn their lives to the form of their own deluded moral notions. The operations that express intellect and participate in culture are shaped in response to the sexual energies of the believer. Finally, however, all these compromised foundations do not mean that the happiness that religion brings its followers is unreal; the madman may be truly happy in his delusions.

Nietzsche's argument presents a striking similarity of concepts, terms, and analysis to Swift's representation of the psychology of religion in *A Tale of a Tub*, sections 8 and 9 (1704, along with the related vision in "Mechanical Operation of the Spirit," published as part of the same volume). Like Nietzsche, Swift concentrates much of his attention on ancient religions, and both strongly imply continuities between paganism and forms of Christianity. The Aeolists described in section 8 of the *Tale*, who sound like early Greek philosophers, serve as allegorical equivalents for any Protestants who are more extreme than Luther in their rejection of Catholic doctrines concerning free will, transubstantiation, tradition, and the authority of the pope.

It is true that Nietzsche explicitly considers Christians and Christianity in the same category as other religions and their believers, whereas Swift does not usually allow even his insane narrator openly to conflate the entire Christian religion with other religions in the *Tale*. Those who defend the orthodoxy of Swift's beliefs claim, as the author does in the "Apology" (prefixed to the *Tale* in 1710), that he is giving a satirical account only of fanatical extremists, not of those who adhere to the more reasonable core tenets of the religion.

Martin is usually read along these lines as Swift's model of Christian interpretation and practice by contrast with the opposed extremes of Jack (literal-
ist, predestinarian, Calvinist), and Peter (a Catholic with the name of the first
pope given to figurative interpretation, oral tradition, the physical presence
in communion, and his own authority). But Martin is indistinguishable from
his two brothers until he and Jack separate from Peter, and after that, he has
only one short speech in which he defends doing nothing more to remove the
decorations on the coats inherited from their father, for fear of tearing the
fabric itself.[10] This constitutes his only appearance in the *Tale,* a speech of
half a page in a religious narrative of more than fifty-five pages (more than
sixty-five, if one includes the closely related "Mechanical Operation"). By
devoting more than 99 percent of his energy and intelligence in the *Tale* to
the satiric critique of religious behavior throughout the ages, Swift demonstrates that he is less interested in a defense of moderate orthodoxy than he
is in a critique of the psychology of religion. I have argued elsewhere for the
effective absence of Martin from the *Tale,* contending that the text is consistently characterized by the satiric logic of the excluded middle, in which only
extremes but never middle grounds are represented.[11] The general account of
the insanity of human endeavors in the climactic section 9 leaves no room
for a moderate position between the extremes of fools and knaves, deceived
and the deceivers.[12]

The history in section 8 of the Aeolists, who are believers in inspiration,
begins with an account of the workings of oracles, just as Nietzsche considered it important to note the association of oracles and madness. The Aeolists, like the pre-Socratic Greek philosophers, believe in a first principle, and
theirs is wind. In their system of beliefs, all expulsions of wind from above
or below are as sacred as the breath of the nostrils (73–75). Their gods are
the four winds, plus a fifth effluvium that proceeds from underground, and is
conveyed from there to the altar or pulpit, where the organs of female offici-
ants are held to be most fitting for the reception of "oracular *gusts*" because
as they pass through the female "receptacle," they cause "a pruriency by the
way, such as with due management hath been refined from a carnal into a
spiritual ecstasy" (76).

Many times in this account of the Aeolists and other religious enthusiasts,
the author observes the consistency between believers' sexuality and their
religious practices. At another point, the congregation share their divinity in
a parodic communion by forming a circle with mouths affixed to backsides;
each is inflated by his neighbor behind while inflating his neighbor in front.
In the "Mechanical Operation of the Spirit," the author observes the continuities linking Christian worshippers, both early and late, with the ecstatic
worshippers of Dionysus, Osiris, and Bacchus; both pagans and Christians

observe a *"community of women"* (140); that is, they practice a promiscuous sexuality that is either ritually prescribed or is allowed to the pure by their religion. It would be hard to overstate the importance of the connection between sexuality and spirituality to this author. At the end of the "Mechanical Operation," he proposes that "the seed or principle which has ever put men upon *visions* in things *invisible*, is of a corporeal nature," and he observes that "*zeal* is frequently kindled from the same spark with other fires, and from inflaming brotherly love will proceed to raise that of a gallant" (140). The author of the *Tale of a Tub* insists that religious ecstasies can be traced to and arise from the physical and sexual realm; the communication of energies can proceed in either direction—from the corporeal to the spiritual or from the spiritual to the physical. The Aeolists, having risen to what they consider a high conception of the divinity, have also provided themselves with devils, like those who climb mountains to approach closer to the heavens, but then are more terrified of the precipice that opens beneath them (76).

Although he begins his account with religious fanatics and returns to them in the "Mechanical Operation," the author does not confine his argument to the lunatic fringes of religion. Rather he generalizes in section 9 to claim that if we examine "the greatest actions that have been performed in the world under the influence of single men, which are *the establishment of new empires by conquest, the advance and progress of new schemes in philosophy, and the contriving, as well as the propagating, of new religions*; we shall find the authors of them all to have been persons whose natural reason hath admitted great revolutions" (78). Here the satire, which may originally have been directed only against the extremists and enthusiasts, moves outward to encompass successful conquerors, innovative philosophers, and revered religious figures: all have been madmen whose wits were overturned. "For what man in the natural state or course of thinking, did ever conceive it in his power to reduce the notions of all mankind exactly to the same length, and breadth, and height of his own?" (80). Yet this is the plan and purpose of all the founders of new systems in philosophy, religion, and empire. In order for them to succeed, the characteristic string of their understanding must be screwed up and tuned to exactly the right key; if it is then struck in the presence of those of the same pitch or temperament, they will vibrate in sympathy and agreement (81). On the other hand, if the innovator strikes his note among those tuned to a different pitch, they will call him mad, confine him, and keep him on a diet of bread and water (81).

Again, in this ninth section, the author finds that sexuality, or suppressed sexuality, leads to characteristic thoughts and actions in all three of these realms. Offering examples from the military field, the author points out that the semen that causes a "protuberancy" intended for an "absent *female*" may, if not expelled, dry to dust, ascend to the brain, and lead a frustrated king to set about massive preparations for war, sieges, and battles, just as a similar cause will lead a bully to "break the windows of a whore who has jilted him" (79). In another case, the movement proceeds in the reverse direction, and the energies or spirits that led a king to invade, plunder, and massacre, when they descend from the brain to the lower regions, finally take the form of a hemorrhoid (79–80). In both cases, the patient's body needs to be purged of excess vapors.

When the author moves in section 9, his "Digression on Madness," from the realms of conquest and philosophy to that of religion, it is again clear that the terms of his discourse extend far beyond the extreme phenomenon of enthusiasm; rather, they demonstrate that any system of "belief in things invisible" (82) is a product of madness in its founder and his followers. This argument takes the form of observing the universal delight humans take in delusion and self-deception, and by contrast the displeasure that results from discovering that all is not as it appears to be. "How fade and insipid do all objects accost us that are not conveyed in the vehicle of *delusion*! How shrunk is everything as it appears in the glass of nature! So that if it were not for the assistance of artificial *mediums*, false lights, refracted angles, varnish, and tinsel, there would be a mighty level in the felicity and enjoyments of mortal men" (83). The inducements to delusion here take the form of theatrical properties; delusion is understood by analogy with the illusions of art, especially the arts of appearance. These arts of improving nature produce that state of "being well-deceived," which constitutes the author's definition of happiness.

By contrast with the consoling illusions of art and religion, the pursuit of knowledge through scientific probing and observation does not produce pleasing sights of the investigated objects or bodies. Reason arrives like a surgeon, armed with instruments for "cutting, and opening, and mangling, and piercing, offering to demonstrate that [bodies] are not of the same consistence quite through" (83). Swift resembles Nietzsche in noting that investigating the internal composition of living bodies involves the application of serious violence. The model of such experimental observation is the exposure of the body, whether that means the unclothing of the diseased corpse of a male beau or the whipping of a woman, presumably for prostitution: "Last week I saw a woman *flayed*, and you will hardly believe how much it altered her person for the worse" (84). On this understanding of the operations of reason, the most striking example of the truths uncovered by science is the human or animal body écorché: the truth-seeker peels back the exterior skin of the bodies he investigates, as Apollo removed that of Marsyas. If such procedures characterize the investigations of reason, then, at the least, such passages remind us that the outer layer of human beings is not an artificial cover that can be removed like clothing. The satire still works primarily against those, like the narrator, who choose to remain deluded, content with the "serene peaceful state, of being a fool among knaves" (84); however, by critiquing such contented acceptance of superficies, pretenses, and social constructions as natural phenomena, in other words, by such satire of self-deception, Swift places himself closer to the position of the probing anatomist: he recognizes the universal appeal of artistic and religious illusions and the violence often involved in exposing them, yet he continues to expose them.[13] In this, Swift's insights in the *Tale* and the strategy he employs to express them closely resemble Nietzsche's observations and his satiric strategies in *Human, All Too Human*.

At the end of the "Digression on Madness," the author informs us that he was for a time an "unworthy member" of the "honourable society" of Bedlam (85). Thus, he can speak from experience concerning the many qualifications of the mad for employments in the world outside the asylum, as well as the qualifications of those in the world for a place in the asylum. Although formulated in a satiric and ironic register, this admission of his own madness by the narrator of the *Tale* is comparable to Nietzsche's recognition at the end of the *Genealogy of Morals* that, as a philosopher, he too is an ascetic whose pursuit of truth is fueled by self-denial. In the *Genealogy*, the author acknowledges his kinship with those who have been the object of his fierce exposure. In the *Tale*, the author's mask acknowledges his kinship with the objects of Swift's satire, but we may also infer—since he speaks his truth through this mask and notes the truthfulness of masks—that on some level Swift includes himself among the mad, and such self-exposure is not the least of his accomplishments or of Nietzsche's.

It might seem that Swift's conscientious tenure as minister in the Church of England for fifty years, including three decades as dean of St. Patrick's, would not be consistent with the wide-ranging critique of religious psychology that I have argued is a principal implication of the *Tale of a Tub*, or similarly that the sharp satire of freethinkers in the "Argument Against Abolishing Christianity," or even the straightforward statements of position in the "Sentiments of a Church-of-England Man" would not support such an implication. But if one wants to appeal to documents outside the *Tale*, and especially to those not written under the name of a parodied persona, the evidence in fact indicates that Swift may not have been a committed believer in the Thirty-Nine Articles of the Anglican Church, including perhaps some of the most important articles of Christian belief.[14] If we examine the surviving sermons, we find no discussion of spirituality, faith, the depravity of man and the need for salvation, or any theological or Christological doctrines.[15] Instead, the sermons exhort the congregation in clear nonmetaphorical language to perform their social and civic duties, in particular, not to cause unnecessary civil agitations on the

basis of abstruse, undecidable questions of religious doctrine.[16] He opposes
divergences from accepted church doctrine not because they are mistaken, but
because they lead to factiousness, civil unrest, and perhaps violence.[17]

If we examine Swift's "Thoughts on Religion," we find several clearly
stated positions that are consistent with the evidence of the sermons and the
reading of the *Tale* offered here. Swift regards the primary responsibility
of a minister of the Church to be the maintenance of order; he understands
himself to be like a soldier on sentry duty, guarding an outpost against dis-
turbances and rebellions.[18] Second, the issue in the "Thoughts" is not what a
man believes or does not believe, but rather what he says and does: "To say
a man is bound to believe, is neither truth nor sense. You may force men,
by interest or punishment, to say or swear they believe, and to act as if they
believed: You can go no further" (261). We cannot control what we believe,
but we can control what we say and do. God gave each man his reason; one
is not responsible for what one in all good conscience cannot believe, but that
does not entitle one to proclaim one's lack of belief publicly, with the result
of fomenting disagreements and disturbing public order and safety. On this
question, the king of Brobdingnag observes that "a Man may be allowed to
keep Poisons in his Closet, but not to vend them about as Cordials."[19]

We can never know Swift's beliefs and his doubts. But all these positions
in the "Thoughts" and the sermons could be consistent with the views of a
man who did not believe in one or more of the central doctrines of Christianity, but who nonetheless considered that teaching the orthodox version of
those doctrines was essential to the maintenance of civil order.[20] Whatever the
actual state of his beliefs, it is at least interesting that Swift casts the following
thought in such personal terms: "I am not answerable to God for the doubts
that arise in my own breast, since they are the consequence of that reason
which he hath planted in me, if I take care to conceal those doubts from others, if I use my best endeavours to subdue them, and if they have no influence
on the conduct of my life" (262). Indeed, perhaps Swift so fiercely attacked
freethinkers such as Collins, Toland, and others because he shared a lack
of belief with them, but felt convinced that he was exercising the necessary
discipline of keeping his opinions quiet, and that to do otherwise was to give
arguments to rebels and excuses to libertines who scoffed at the law. Such a
cause could also help account for the feeling that many readers have had that
in addition to parodying the voice of the contented, mad, modern author, at
times—indeed, in some of the most important passages in the *Tale*—Swift
also allows the truth of that voice and its positions to be heard.[21] But the
voice of the conservative hierarchical satirist as well continues to be heard
throughout the text. Therefore, as one of its distinctive accomplishments, the
Tale provides a kind of stereophonic record of the positions available for

those thinking and writing at the time, especially two of the most extreme and opposed positions. If Swift expressed his own doubt concerning established opinions and doctrines of the Church, he did so only in the indirect, satiric and parodic forms of the *Tale* and the "Argument against Abolishing Christianity."

We therefore can note that Swift's satiric critique of religious psychology overlaps with that of Nietzsche in all of its essential points. Swift diagnoses the founders of religions as delusional madmen who convince themselves and others of the truth of their visions. They do this by hitting a pitch that their followers respond to mechanically; reason and logic have nothing to do with religious conviction.[22] To the contrary, both founders and believers are motivated largely by fear, and they make sure to provide themselves with a devil who inspires terror as much as their divinity deserves praise. For Swift as for Nietzsche, sexuality plays a crucial shaping influence on the beliefs and practices of religious authorities and believers. Both understand that there is a direct communication, an influence that can flow in either direction, between the processes and products of the lower body and those of the upper, between body and spirit. Religions both proscribe and prescribe definite forms of physical satisfaction, ritual, or recommended ways of stimulating or disciplining parts of the body. Finally, both Swift and Nietzsche maintain that the attractions of religion depend on the pleasures of illusion, and both also place themselves in the position of the cruel and unhappy pursuer of knowledge.

In considering the significance of this extensive correspondence between the two on the subject of religious psychology, we might begin by noting the importance of Hume's *Natural History of Religion* (1757) as a link between Swift and Nietzsche. Indeed, almost all the elements of the analysis that we have drawn out from the work of the earlier satirist and the later philosopher can also be found in Hume's work, although with somewhat changed emphasis. Arguing against the deistic position that all men would be led to believe in a beneficent creator of a harmoniously constructed world, Hume pointed out that early humans would not have been considering the wondrous design of creation but instead would have been driven by fear and hope to seek the help of stronger powers.[23] He examines continuities between pagan religions and Christianity, noting the inconsistency between theological virtues (especially in monotheism) and civic or social virtues. He focuses on the irrationality of belief, and the strong role of delusion in "popular" or organized religions. He observes the oxymoronic yoking of what is highest in aspiration with what can be lowest in actuality, and he concludes by stressing the pathological nature of religious belief and behavior: "Examine the religious principles, which have, in fact, prevailed in the world. You will scarcely be persuaded that they are any thing but sick men's dreams; Or perhaps will regard them more as the playsome whimsies of monkies in human shape" (*NHR*, 184).

These continuities linking Swift, Nietzsche, and Hume bring into view a line of thinkers who with different emphases share most of the essential arguments concerning religious psychology that can be drawn from the works considered here. This line would include Mandeville (*Fable of the Bees* [1715, 1729]), Diderot (*Supplement to Bougainville's "Voyage"* [written 1772]), and Condorcet (*Sketch for a Historical Picture of the Progress of the Human Mind* [1795]). The critique of religious psychology that Swift shares with Nietzsche participates in an Enlightenment anticlericalism and critique of organized religion. Indeed, this critique identifies both Swift and Nietzsche as Enlightenment thinkers in this respect. Nietzsche's repeated citation of Enlightenment figures in general and Voltaire in particular in *Human, All Too Human* signals not only his awareness of this tradition, but also his desire at this point to associate himself and his thought with it (see, for example, *H*, 81–82, 169, 215).

Swift employs the complex ironies and personae of an early modern cultural paradigm in which satire predominates; his indirect tactics allow him to claim in the anonymous "Apology" that he is only satirizing religious deviance. Nietzsche's satiric reversal of traditionally accepted hierarchies of value is more explicit and scientific; he is thinking about what will replace Christianity in Western culture. (Hume mediates between the two in tone and form.) The difference between the use of satire and irony in Swift and Nietzsche corresponds to and indicates the difference between intellectual and formal perspectives that are early modern and early modernist. Although Nietzsche employs sarcasm in *Human, All Too Human* and other works, he very rarely resorts to irony, but rather adopts a more direct mode of presenting his observations and arguments. He objects to irony, in fact, arguing that except in the address of a teacher to a student, irony is a "vulgar affectation": "All ironical writers depend on the foolish species of men who together with the author would like to feel themselves superior to all others. . . . Habituation to irony, moreover, like habituation to sarcasm, spoils the character . . . : in the end one comes to resemble a snapping dog which has learned how to laugh but forgotten how to bite" (*H*, 146–47). Nietzsche seems to have in mind verbal irony more than the complex self-satiric personae that Swift employed to such effect in the *Tale* and elsewhere in his writings; in addition, there seems to be some self-criticism in the derogatory inclusion of sarcasm in this passage. Still, Nietzsche's contemptuous dismissal of irony here indicates that he no longer felt it necessary to use the indirection, disguise, and self-censorship that Swift had adopted for the communication of ideas concerning religion regarded as unsettling and dangerous in his own time.

NOTES

1. Friedrich Nietzsche, *Human, All Too Human: A Book for Free Spirits*, trans. R. J. Hollingdale (Cambridge: Cambridge University Press, 1996), 69; hereafter cited in the text as *H* followed by the page number.

2. On the importance of *Human, All Too Human* as a new departure in Nietzsche's thinking, because its naturalistic derivation of ethics departed from the concerns of his early works but led directly to the later, see Robin Small, *Nietzsche and Rée: A Star Friendship* (Oxford: Clarendon Press, 2005), 56–74. See also Walter Kaufman, *Nietzsche: Philosopher, Psychologist, Antichrist* (Princeton: Princeton University Press, 1974), 181–86.

3. On the religious body as a sick body, see Tim Murphy, *Nietzsche, Metaphor, Religion* (Albany: State University of New York Press, 2001), 81–85.

4. The range of possible interpretations and implications of the *Genealogy* for the history of religion and morals can begin to be investigated through two collections of essays: *Nietzsche, Genealogy, Morality: Essays on Nietzsche's "On the Genealogy of Morals,"* ed. Richard Schacht (Berkeley: University of California Press, 1994), and *Nietzsche's "On the Genealogy of Morals": Critical Essays*, ed. Christa Davis Acampora (Lanham, MD: Rowman and Littlefield, 2006). Also see Gilles Deleuze, *Nietzsche as Philosopher*, trans. Hugh Tomlinson (New York: Columbia University Press, 1983), 143–45.

5. For a recent analysis of ascetic ideals in culture, see Geoffrey Galt Harpham, *The Ascetic Imperative in Culture and Criticism* (Chicago: University of Chicago Press, 1987).

6. Friedrich Nietzsche, *Beyond Good and Evil: Prelude to a Philosophy of the Future*, trans. Walter Kaufman (New York: Vintage, 1966), 81 (no. 78); hereafter cited in the text as *BGE* followed by the page number.

7. See Sigmund Freud, *Civilization and Its Discontents*, trans. James Strachey (New York: Norton, 1989), 83–96.

8. Later on the same page, Nietzsche mentions Swift in the course of explaining why so few people lie in ordinary life.

9. Friedrich Nietzsche, *The Gay Science*, trans. Josefine Nauckhoff (Cambridge: Cambridge University Press, 2001), 211; hereafter cited in the text as *GS* followed by the page number.

10. Jonathan Swift, *A Tale of a Tub and Other Works*, ed. Angus Ross and David Woolley (Oxford: Oxford University Press, 1986), 67; hereafter cited in the text.

11. See my *Satire in Narrative* (Austin: University of Texas Press, 1990), 48–63.

12. The accuracy of this reading of the religious satire based on the published text is borne out by the additional material published in a 1720 edition of the *Tale* as "The History of Martin" (*Tale*, 142–46; and see 226n142), being part of the "Abstract of what follows after Sect. IX in the Manuscript." In the "History," Martin's behavior is not distinguished in any way from that of Peter and Jack: he is not more moderate, and he is just as self-interested and given to alliances with powerful secular authorities. His determination to kill Jack and all of Jack's followers drives him mad and makes him indistinguishable from Peter (146). As for the doctrine and discipline of the

Church of England, which the author of the "Apology" calls the "most perfect of all" churches (2), the "History of Martin" tells how Lady Bess, not only "more moderate" but also "more cunning" (143), inherited the farm from her predecessor, who loved Peter; how she set up her own "Dispensatory" using mostly recipes stolen from Peter; though at the end of her life she was told of the "many defects & imperfections" in her new dispensation, and she was about to begin a new purge of survivors from Peter's time (143–44). Thus, Martin goes as insane as Peter, Jack, and all the other religious leaders described in sections 8 and 9 of the *Tale*, and even Elizabeth's settlement of questions of doctrine and practice is acknowledged to be full of imperfections. There simply is no moderate middle ground available for readers of the *Tale of a Tub*. One may say that Swift only attacks the religious fanatics and extremists, but according to this work, there are none but extremists in religion.

13. On the violence ascribed to the satirist in early modern culture, see Mary Claire Randolph, "The Medical Metaphor in Early Satire," in *Satire: Modern Essays in Criticism*, ed. Ronald Paulson (Englewood Cliffs, NJ: Prentice-Hall, 1971), 135–70.

14. I am not aware that such an argument has been made on the basis of the *Tale* and the "Thoughts on Religion," although several studies of Swift have drawn attention to the paradoxes in his character as thinker and writer. See Peter Steele, *Jonathan Swift: Preacher and Jester* (Oxford: Clarendon Press, 1978); Patrick Reilly, *Jonathan Swift, The Brave Desponder* (Carbondale: Southern Illinois University Press, 1982); and David Nokes, *Jonathan Swift, a Hypocrite Reversed* (Oxford: Oxford University Press, 1985).

15. The surviving sermons constitute a small percentage of the number Swift must have written and delivered, but there is no reason to believe that they are unusual. "On the Trinity" might seem to constitute an exception here. But in this sermon, Swift discusses the triune nature of the divinity only to declare that attempts to provide rational understanding of the doctrine will fail. The teaching is orthodox; that is all one needs to know; any further inquiry is impertinent and out of bounds. Phillip Harth places Swift in relation to a tradition of what he calls Anglican rational religion in *Swift and Anglican Rationalism: The Religious Background of "A Tale of a Tub"* (Chicago: University of Chicago Press, 1961). Harth's erudition has made available to us the sources of much of the thinking that must have been behind the *Tale*. However, Harth does not take into account that Swift is writing satire, as none of the other divines and philosophers were, and Swift's is a particularly fierce and deforming kind of satire. Although More, Tillotson, or Stillingfleet may have made the case for the middle ground of the Anglican way, Swift does not do so in his satire; rather, the extreme opposites he describes repeatedly preclude any middle ground. The universality of the terms in section 9, for example—encompassing *all* founders of religions, philosophical systems, and conquerors—does not leave room for moderate founders of religions, reasonable conquerors, or restrained systemizers.

16. Louis Landa cites two of Swift's contemporaries as having heard Swift himself say that "if he did sometimes exert himself in the pulpit, he could never rise higher than *preaching pamphlets*." *Irish Tracts, 1720–1723, and Sermons*, ed. Herbert Davis and Louis Landa, in Swift's *Prose Works* (Oxford: Blackwell, 1968), 9:98. See also Swift's note to the blank passage where the author of the *Tale* claims to have

explained his theory that vapors cause madness. To the text that reads "*Hic multa desiderantur*," the footnote adds, "it were well if all metaphysical cobweb problems were no otherwise answered" (82).

17. Melvyn New has argued that the sermons of both Swift and Sterne turn away from doctrine and emphasize civic order in response to the English Civil War and the violent religious clashes of the seventeenth century. See "Swift and Sterne: Two Tales, Several Sermons, and a Relationship Revisited," in *Critical Essays on Jonathan Swift*, ed. Frank Palmeri (New York: G. K. Hall, 1993), 164–86.

18. See "Thoughts on Religion," *Irish Tracts, 1720–1723, and Sermons*, 261–64, 262; hereafter cited in the text.

19. Jonathan Swift, *Gulliver's Travels* (London: Penguin, 2003), 122.

20. One of the most recent considerations of Swift's positions on religion, like almost all earlier discussions of the topic, finds no reason to consider Swift heterodox or a nonbeliever in any way. See Marcus Walsh, "Swift and Religion," in *The Cambridge Companion to Jonathan Swift*, ed. Christopher Fox (Cambridge: Cambridge University Press, 2003), 161–76.

21. On the resistance of the parodied voice or language to "the parodying intentions of the other," see Mikhail Bakhtin, "Discourse in the Novel," in *The Dialogic Imagination*, trans. Caryl Emerson and Michael Holquist (Austin: University of Texas Press, 1982), 409.

22. For a closely related argument that Swift is deeply concerned with demagogues and their strategies throughout *A Tale of a Tub*, see Melvyn New, "Jonathan Swift, Thomas Mann, and the Irony of Ideology," in *Telling New Lies* (Gainesville: University Press of Florida, 1992), 163–88.

23. David Hume, *Dialogues and Natural History of Religion* (Oxford: Oxford University Press, 1998), 136, 139–40; hereafter cited in the text as *NHR* followed by page number.

"Tristram Shandy: The Quilt"

"Tristram Shandy: The Quilt"

Part Two

PERSPECTIVES ON
LAURENCE STERNE

Chapter Nine

Gershom Scholem's Reading of *Tristram Shandy*

Elizabeth Kraft

Any student, friend, colleague, or intellectual legatee of Melvyn New will recognize in my title an allusion to his intermittent engagement in the general topic "Sterne and Modernism." In his 1988 essay "Proust's Influence on Sterne: Remembrance of Things to Come," New deliberately—and with characteristic slyness—upends our notion of authorial relations, rejecting traditional "influence study" in favor of a fluid, creative, and evocative enterprise that speaks more fully to the "complexity of the concept of literary tradition." What difference does it make if Proust pored over the works of Sterne, particularly *A Sentimental Journey*, at some point before he sat down to write *À la Recherche du Temps Perdu*? Very little, to New's mind, for he "find[s] almost everything about their techniques quite dissimilar and . . . [does] not believe for a moment that Proust learned anything about literary form or style from Sterne." What does interest New and what provokes his bringing the two authors together in conversation with each other is that the correspondence of their sensibilities on "the very fundamental human problem of male-female relations resulted in some uncanny similarities of images and concepts."[1] Whether or not the eighteenth century influenced twentieth (and now twenty-first) century writers, we who study earlier periods of literature come to those periods first having read the works of our contemporaries or near contemporaries. We (and perhaps more important, our students) see connections that may not exist intentionally, but that are nonetheless valid in terms of the preoccupations of Western culture. Thus is literary tradition written and rewritten by every new generation of readers and scholars who perceive influences where they do not exist in echoes that, in fact, do resonate down the long corridors of time. It is because of our perceptions as readers and scholars that we can validly say that Proust influenced Sterne.[2]

My essay adds a twist to this New-like project in bringing together Gershom Scholem and Laurence Sterne. Scholem (1897–1982) was a near contemporary of Proust (1871–1922), but his academic preoccupations were the history, texts, and traditions of Jewish mysticism, or kabbalah. Robert Alter, in fact, finds that the term "modernist" needs special pleading when applied to Scholem as "there is little indication that . . . [he] took much time off from poring over kabbalistic texts to steep himself in the literature of modernism." Yet, as Alter persuasively argues, there is a reason that Scholem's seemingly narrow (or "esoteric") studies have had such an impact on "international intellectual life over the past several decades," for everywhere in his work one is aware of "the imposing imagination of the deep and dangerous business of life in history."[3] Scholem, like the modernists—and indeed like Sterne, who is, in this trait, like the modernists as well—looks into the abyss of a world that has become radically destabilized and finds there not fear, not annihilation, not emptiness, but a source of strength and knowledge.[4]

Scholem and Sterne seem strangely similar in their willingness to meet the challenges of modernity or the Enlightenment (as the case may be) head-on, but that in and of itself would not be reason to bring the two of them together had Scholem himself not extended an invitation to do so, as it were. In his 1977 autobiographical memoir *From Berlin to Jerusalem*, the scholar of kabbalah invokes *Tristram Shandy*, not as an influence, but as a fond memory associated with his intellectual transition from childhood to maturity:

> Around that time, in September of 1910, I sold all my children's books to a secondhand book dealer on Wallstrasse in a fit of defiance which I greatly regretted later, because I had decided to set up a "real" library. I was greatly interested in history, even before my mathematical inclinations also asserted themselves. The awakening of the latter was due to the influence of my marvelous longtime mathematics teacher, Franz Goldscheider, whose brother was a famous physician. He was the only teacher in my school who meant anything to me. (To him I owe my early acquaintance with Laurence Sterne's *Tristram Shandy*.)[5]

Given this cryptic but pointed reference, we might legitimately wonder why the book is so important to Scholem that he remembers and reveres the teacher who first recommended it.

We may never know definitively what attracted Scholem to *Tristram Shandy*, or why he continued through the course of his long life to find it a meaningful and significant work. That he did so consider it, however, is attested to by the above quotation and substantiated by the fact that he shared his enthusiasm with his friend Walter Benjamin. In 1926, Benjamin writes to Scholem:

Your letter from Safed reached me today via Berlin. I was pleased to receive it for—at least—three reasons. First, you are seeing Safed for yourself—with your own eyes. Second, you are not strictly and without exception adhering to the principle of writing only in response to a letter received. This is the principle we have hitherto observed in our correspondence. Third, at the very moment I was about to start a letter to you, yours arrived. Should this digression and its mathematical character appear to be and strike you as something new in my correspondence, you can attribute it to my immersion in the third book of *Tristram Shandi*. At the same time you will have observed that sooner or later I do follow up on your suggestions of what to read[.][6]

By 1933, *Tristram* had become a byword between the friends, as we see in Benjamin's letter of June 15: "I allowed K.M.'s greetings to take effect on me. The story of her first letter to me seems to be unfolding in the purest *Tristram Shandy* style. With this observation we also best do justice to the utter uncertainty as to whether the letter will ever come into being."[7] Poignantly, the reference to *Tristram* and the whimsical vagaries of social life follows Benjamin's reflections on the direr uncertainties of the times. He reveals that his brother is "in a concentration camp" suffering "God only knows what," though "the rumors about his wounds were exaggerated in at least one respect. He did not lose an eye."[8]

Scholem's response to Benjamin does not include overt discussion of *Tristram Shandy*, yet, clearly, the novel had an impact on both men, who were struggling in the late twenties and early thirties to pursue their own "literary studies"—Scholem's kabbalistic study and Benjamin's "conspicuously European" work.[9] Scholem's path was easier, as he acknowledged, because he found Palestine (later Israel) the perfect location for his own literary and intellectual pursuits. He urged Benjamin to join him, away from the dangers of European life under the various fascist regimes that were sweeping the Continent, but he recognized that Benjamin might have difficulty participating in the Zionist cause and that difficulty, in turn, would "rapidly bring about a morally unbearable state of estrangement" in which work would be impossible and "in which life cannot be sustained."[10] As Scholem expresses himself to his friend, it is clear that he is preoccupied with the difficulties of creation and the dangers of extinction on a number of levels, all of which concern *Tristram Shandy* as well.

What follows is necessarily speculative as I will be treating episodes of *Tristram Shandy* as they may have resonated with a kabblistic scholar of German-Jewish descent living through one of the worst periods of anti-Semitism in a world whose history is replete with such episodes. How did *Tristram Shandy*, an eighteenth-century work authored by a Protestant clergyman, remain dear to one who had every reason to distrust the intellectual and creative heritage of Europe? My speculation is that Scholem had long recognized in *Tristram* a sympathetic imagination committed to life in the world but intrigued and inspired by the world beyond. Further, read with alertness to mention of Jewish culture, religion, and texts, *Tristram Shandy* evidences awareness of and sympathy for the pains of oppression suffered by European Jews as well as surprisingly detailed knowledge of the cultural and religious heritage of the Jewish people.

TRISTRAM SHANDY'S "MYSTICISM"

Bernard McGinn, a scholar of Christian mysticism, has noted a broad appeal in Scholem's presentation of kabbalah. While "Scholem himself made no universal claims for Jewish mysticism" nor did he claim "that Kabbalah was the archetype or inner core of other forms of Western mysticism," nevertheless, "all students of mysticism should read Scholem" in order to "deepen their insights of the dynamics of other mysticisms," dynamics that McGinn explains, drawing on Scholem's "Religious Authority and Mysticism": "'All mysticism has two contradictory or complementary aspects: the one conservative, the other revolutionary'" (or one digressive, the other progressive, we might say). "What Scholem meant by this," McGinn elaborates, "is that the new direct contact between God and human that marks the mystical phase of religion is . . . ineffable." Mystics in all three monotheistic faiths experience both contact with God and a "desire to communicate this to others" in such a way that invariably points to a "'rediscover[ing] of traditional authority.'" In that sense, mysticism is fundamentally conservative. But, "due to the wild card of ineffability . . . mystical preservation of tradition is never mere repetition, but also allows for creative transformations of the inherited amalgam." McGinn concludes, "While Scholem never denied a creative aspect to the more abstract elements of religion, like law and philosophy, it is obvious that he was drawn to the study of mysticism precisely because he saw in it the deepest resource for dynamic change and development within religion."[11]

It would be wrong to say that Sterne was a student of mysticism in the way that Scholem was, but the eighteenth-century writer and clergyman was certainly aware of the Christian mystical tradition, especially, as New has pointed out, as articulated in the writings of the Neoplationist John Norris.[12] While Norris's sermons and other writings cannot be said to partake of kabbalistic learning, their focus is on heaven, the other world—a focus that, for all his immersion in the senses of this world, Sterne ultimately shares and endorses in *Tristram Shandy*. Moreover, while certainly not a spokesman for the historical Sterne, Walter Shandy exhibits a thorough acquaintance with the literature of alchemy, learning he could hardly have without Sterne's awareness. Sterne's obvious willingness to delve into bodies of forbidden or discredited knowledge for creative inspiration probably appealed to the similarly minded Scholem. Further, the focus of such knowledge on the moment and means of human creation resonates with what we have noted to be one of Scholem's concerns. Tristram introduces us to himself as a homunculus who was to have been named "Trismegistus" in Walter Shandy's homage to the hermetic tradition. Although clearly Walter's "natural philosophy" is the object of satire in the early pages of *Tristram Shandy*, the highlighting of the word "*HOMUNCULUS*,"[13] the reference to alchemy, machinery, animal spirits, animation, clockwork, and the like may have, for Scholem, invoked the legend of the golem, a legend that directly addresses the moment of mystical contact between man and God.

While we are accustomed to thinking of the homunculus as that "little man" in the spermatazoon who makes his microscopic appearance in seventeenth-century preformationist theories of reproduction, Clara Pinto-Correia has pointed out that the "leading spermists" of the seventeenth century never used the term and would not have used the term because it "was consistently related to occult sciences and magical formulas": "It would therefore have been impolitic for the spermists to have chosen such a dangerous term when they sought to defend their theories."[14] The homunculus was always a made-man (and the *OED* supports Pinto-Correia, citing Henry More on the "artificial way of making an Homunculus," John Edwards on the "artificial Homunculus," and *Tristram Shandy*, too). Based on her understanding of the terminology involved, Correia thinks that Sterne is presenting Tristram as a being that has not been conceived and born in the usual way. We know from the beginning, she says, that "something is not normal about Tristram Shandy." Then we find out just what that is:

> Chapter six starts with the subtly threatening warning that "in the beginning of the last chapter I informed you exactly when I was born; but I did not inform you how." From here, although the secret is going to be withheld in hallucinogenic convolutions of the narrative, we can see it coming—especially since we have already been informed that his father was somewhat estranged from his mother around the time of his presumed conception. And also because chapter two suddenly interrupts the flow of the story to dwell on the condition of the homunculus in this world—by all accounts, in the author's description, a sad and tormented life.[15]

I doubt any conscientious literary scholar would go so far as Pinto-Correia to suggest even the possibility of Tristram's being made in a metal tub of some sort according to Paracelsus's famous formula;[16] however, most readers would agree that Walter's intentions in the act of making love, as later on in writing his *Tristrapoedia*, are to "make a man," if not an alchemical creation, at least a man that Walter believes he can shape and form by detailed attention to the words and circumstances of the child's early life. Homunculus or golem, Tristram is to be (if Walter has his way) his father's creation, body and soul.

In his *Major Trends in Jewish Mysticism*, Scholem uses the word *homunculus* as a synonym for *golem*, a fact that seems to suggest the connection in his own mind between the figure of Jewish lore and Tristram's early state-of-being:

> It is to Hasidism that we owe the development of the legend of the Golem, or magical homunculus . . . and the theoretical foundations of this magical doctrine. In the writings of Eleazar of Worms . . . discourses on the essence of *Hasiduth* are to be found side by side with tracts on magic and the effectiveness of God's secret names. . . . There one also finds the oldest extant recipes for creating the Golem—a mixture of letter magic and practices obviously aimed at producing ecstatic states of consciousness. It would appear as though in the original conception the Golem came to life only while the ecstasy of his creator lasted. The creation of the Golem was, as it were, a particularly sublime experience felt by the mystic who became absorbed in the mysteries of the alphabetic combinations described in the "Book of Creation."[17]

Scholem wrote and read in at least three languages—German, Hebrew, and English. I do not know whether he read *Tristram Shandy* in English or in the German translation by Johann Elert Bode as Benjamin did.[18] It makes no difference, really, for *homunculus* was retained in the Bode translation, and, indeed, the word was associated with Sterne from the beginning in Germany, *Ueber den Homunculus* being part of the German title of *Yorick's Meditations* published in Frankfurt in 1769.[19]

Of course, Sterne does not hold a copyright on the word *homunculus*. Scholem would have known of the homunculus created by Goethe's Faust, as well as, perhaps, a 1916 German film entitled *Homunculus,* which tells a story very similar to the typical golem tale in which the made-man grows too powerful and must be destroyed. Scholem had very likely encountered the word often in the esoteric reading involved in his study of the history of kabbalah. Yet, given his early love of *Tristram Shandy* and the prominent use of the word in that work, it seems reasonable to conclude that Scholem thought of Tristram when he heard, read, or wrote the word *homunculus*—and given his association of that word with *golem*, it seems fair enough to speculate that Scholem may have seen similarities between Tristram and the *golemim* of kabbalah.

Scholem may have even suspected that Sterne knew the Jewish legend of the golem in addition to the medieval Christian story of the homunculus. While there is no clear evidence one way or the other, it is possible that Sterne was aware of the myth.[20] Knowledge of kabbalah and other forms of Jewish mysticism had flourished in secret societies in Stuart England, as Marsha Keith Schuchard's exhaustive study of Freemasonry during this time has established definitively.[21] That Scotland and northern England remained repositories of such knowledge during the more staid Hanoverian reigns is hinted at by the popular association (which surfaces occasionally—and not necessarily by way of praise) between Scotland and "the Jews."[22] There were also readily available sources in print, such as Johann Andreas Eisenmenger's 1700 *Entdecktes Judentum*, literally, "Judaism Revealed," but translated into English in 1732 as *Rabbinical Literature; or, The Traditions of the Jews contained in their Talmud and Other Mystical Writings*. A new edition had been printed in London in 1748, and had Sterne been interested in doing so, he certainly could have acquired the book and read the following account of the golem:

> The same Treatise (*Yalkut Chadash*) in the Part entitled *Neshamoth*, teaches, that Souls before they come into the World, are cloathed, and appear before Almighty God in the Bodies in which they are to appear in the World. "All the Souls (*'tis there said*) before they come into the World, cloathe themselves in the same Bodies, and put on the same Likeness, in which they are to appear in the World. Every Soul above, before she cometh into the World, cloatheth herself with a Body; and in that Image, or Figure (i.e. *so habited*) she standeth before the Holy and Blessed God. Then doth the Holy and Blessed God adjure that Soul and Body not to sin. And these Things are signified by the Words, *Thine Eyes did see my* GOLEM: That is, my *Golem*, which is the Body, thine Eyes did see when I stood before thee."[23]

Eisenmenger's project was to subvert Jewish authority. He had studied with rabbis under the guise of pursuing conversion to Judaism and had repaid their efforts by writing this "treasure trove of . . . anti-Jewish arguments," which "served as ammunition for antisemitic agitation" well into the twentieth century.[24] Yet, though Eisenmenger's interpretations are invariably perverse and dismissive, his renditions of the texts themselves are not always distorted. If Sterne did read here of the golem, he would have been correctly informed that the figure is invoked both in the Talmud and in Jewish mysticism in order to explore, elaborate, or experience aspects of creation, particularly the moment before bodies and souls are fused.[25] Sterne was perfectly capable of distinguishing the narrow-minded from the exuberant when encountered in the same source, as his relationship with William Warburton suggests. Melvyn New explains that Warburton, as bishop, "preached caution and prudence" to

Sterne, but as author of *The Divine Legation of Moses*, he demonstrated "en-cyclopedic, energetic abundance[,] precisely the fertility and variety Sterne most desired."[26]

Whether or not he knew the golem legend, Sterne teaches in *Tristram Shandy* many of the same lessons to be derived from a close study of the figure. In *On the Kabbalah and Its Symbolism*, Scholem cites several Mi-drashic and Talmudic sources that attribute a golem phase to the creation of Adam.[27] There are several variants of this myth, but most emphasize a delay in the time between God's creating of Adam and his endowing Adam with a soul. In one version of the story, to the golem Adam, God reveals "all future generations to the end of time" (Scholem, 161); in another, God creates Adam before he creates anything else, but hesitates to breathe a soul into him: "If I set him down now," God says, "it will be said that he was my companion in the work of Creation; so I will leave him as a golem, until I have created everything else" (Scholem, 162). In all versions, the golem is both more privi-leged than man and less powerful—all due to the will of his creator. Accord-ing to Scholem, these various Adamic myths attest to the mystical union of body and soul—of course, a preoccupation of Sterne's as well. In one sense, the golem is mere matter, not a being with rights as Tristram insists he, in his homuncular state, is. In another sense, the golem is simply matter wait-ing for a soul, rather than never to have a soul; and while the word "golem" means clod, even the Adamic golem is presented as more than a mere lump of inanimate clay. Though he lies prone, he also sees (Scholem, 162). One Midrash, in fact, portrays this "seeing" in particularly animated terms: "While the first man lay prone as a *golem*, the Holy One showed him each and every righteous man that was to issue from him—some hung on Adam's head, some hung on his hair, some on his forehead, some on his eyes, some on his nose, some on his mouth, some on his ears, some on his teeth."[28]

Around the twelfth century, Scholem explains, the golem is transformed in Jewish learning into an "object of a mystical ritual of initiation which seems actually to have been performed, designed to confirm the adept in his mastery over secret knowledge" (Scholem, 174). Here the focus shifts from God as creator of bodies informed by souls to man as creator of matter capable of movement. One wonders if Scholem might have seen Tristram as an adept performing ritualistic mysteries in order to create his golemim, Walter and Toby, mechanical men animated by hobbyhorses rather than souls. Certainly, Tristram's descriptions of his creative processes emphasize his physical pos-session by forces that act upon him and send him in directions he may or may not plan to go. He writes with frenzied nerves, in hurry and precipitation, with things crowding in upon him, in rash jerks and squirts. Occasionally, he mentions being "relaxed," but usually he is in motion—"so much of motion, is so much of life" (7.13.593)—and the reader is continually reminded that writing for Tristram is a matter of inspiration: "I begin with writing the first sentence—and [trust] to Almighty God for the second" (8.2.656).

One further kabbalistic view of the golem also seems pertinent to Sterne's purpose in *Tristram Shandy*. This is the view of the golem as a moralistic warning against pride. In a thirteenth-century text about the prophet Jeremiah's creation of a golem, this point is clearly made. Jeremiah and his son combine letters according to kabbalistic formulae and create a man on whose forehead stand the words "Elohim Emet" or "God is truth." But this golem takes a knife and scrapes off the aleph from *emet* leaving the word *met* or death, and so the words then signify "God is dead." Jeremiah rends his garments in agony due to the blasphemy of what he now reads and asks the golem why he did such a thing. The golem replies with a parable:

> An architect built many houses, cities, and squares, but no one could copy his art and compete with him in knowledge and skill until two men persuaded him. Then he taught them the secret of his art, and they knew how to do everything in the right way. When they had learned his secret and his abilities, they began to anger him with words. Finally, they broke with him and became architects like him, except that what he charged a thaler for, they did for six groats. When people noticed this, they ceased to honor the artist and came to them and honored them and gave them commissions when they required to have something built. So God has made you in His image and in His shape and form. But now that you have created a man like Him, people will say: There is no God in the world beside these two! Then Jeremiah said: What solution is there? He said: Write the alphabets backward on the earth you have strewn with intense concentration. Only do not meditate in the sense of building up, but the other way around. So they did, and the man became dust and ashes before their eyes. Then Jeremiah said: Truly, one should study these things only in order to know the power and omnipotence of the Creator of this world, but not in order really to practice them.[29,]

To know and not practice the art of creation is to learn the lesson of the golem, even as the mystic seeks God in order to know God, not to become God—or, we might add, even as the writer masters the principles of novel-writing in order not to write a conventional novel. We have creative powers that link us to the divine, but when we invoke them and put them into play, we face the abyss of history and write onto it letters that may prove beneficial, but that may prove destructive as well.[30] The most famous story of the golem is one that Sterne probably did not know—the golem of Prague, created by Rabbi Loew, the Maharal, to protect the Jews during a time of persecution.[31] This golem was a savior for a while, but he turned destructive because he became too empowered, too little subject to the control of his maker. He stands as a lesson in pride and its destructive tendencies. In more than one sense, *Tristram Shandy* teaches the same thing.

STERNE AND THE JEWS

For Scholem, the destructive power of human creativity was everywhere evident in the 1930s as the Nazi state redesigned a world in which there would be no Jews. Sterne's sympathetic treatment of Jewish history and culture in *Tristram Shandy* must have been a powerful source of encouragement during those dark times. In fact, there are moments in the book that Sterne reveals surprisingly intimate knowledge of Jewish life and learning—so intimate that one might suspect him to have had direct acquaintance with Jewish texts and, perhaps, with Jews themselves.[32] In two instances, *Tristram Shandy* offers evidence of Jewish knowledge hard to explain without personal interaction with Jews or Jewish texts. The first is centered on the sympathetic portrayal of Trim's brother Tom.[33] Tom marries the widow of a Portuguese Jew and is taken before the Inquisition and imprisoned in a dungeon. Readers more than likely have varying opinions as to why Tom meets this fate, but close attention to the text reveals that Trim is quite clear about it. It is not because Tom is an Englishman; nor is it because he has married a Jew's widow. It is because of the sausages that he and his wife make and sell: "[M]y brother *Tom* went over a servant to *Lisbon*,—and then married a *Jew*'s widow, who kept a small shop, and sold sausages, which, some how or other, was the cause of his being taken in the middle of the night out of his bed, where he was lying with his wife and two small children, and carried directly to the Inquisition, where, God help him, . . . the poor honest lad lies confined at this hour" (2.17.144). "Some how or other" can be explained. As Trim suggests later on, Tom and his wife do not put pork in their sausages. Why not? Because, one has to assume, they cater to the Crypto-Jewish shoppers, the Marranos, who had undergone mandatory conversion rather than leave Portugal but who still practice their religion in private. Why do Tom and his wife cater to them? My guess is that they are also Jewish—or at least she is, and that means their children are, and for all practical purposes, Tom is Jewish as well. Trim indicates that if "after their marriage . . . they had but put pork into their sausages, the honest soul had never been taken out of his warm bed, and dragg'd to the inquisition" (9.4.742). The option was there, but Tom chose not to take it.

These sausages referred to by Trim (and Sterne) are called *Aiheiras* and are "heavily seasoned sausages (the word derives from *alho*, garlic), still very popular in Portugal. Originally made with chicken, turkey, and partridge, it is said that they were created by *conversos* to give the impression that they ate pork, the main ingredient of Portuguese sausages."[34] Perhaps the sausages were popular enough on their own to account for the "rousing trade" to which Tom is drawn in the first place (9.5.745). But if the popularity was dependent on the absence of pork, the indictment of Portuguese intolerance is profound, as it indicates a rather large population of Judaizing Portuguese who remain loyal to a religion they have been forced to abandon. And if the popularity was not dependent on the absence of pork, why not add it after the marriage and avoid imprisonment? There are surely matters of conscience at stake here. This kind of knowledge and sensitivity, it seems to me, must have come to Sterne through the Sephardic Jewish population of England.[35] The sausage ruse is not the kind of thing an outsider would know; the sympathy for Tom's commitment to the Jewish life he has embraced as a husband or, perhaps, a convert, is not the kind of thing one expects from an Anglican clergyman with no Jewish acquaintances.

Significantly enough, Tom's courtship of the Jew's widow is prefaced by his encounter with a Negro servant, the report of which prompts the discussion between Toby and Trim as to whether or not "a Negro has a soul?" Trim is not sure, but Toby reduces the question to its fundamental essence: "I suppose, God would not leave him without one, any more than thee or me." Trim's response is definitive: "It would be putting one sadly over the head of another" (9.6.747). His implication is that God would not do such a thing. We might, were we to create golemim. But God would not because he creates men and women.

The second instance that seems to reveal Sterne's uncanny knowledge of Judaism occurs in the reference to "Ambition" in chapter 8 of book 9 of *Tristram Shandy*. Toby invokes the word in response to Trim's suggestion that he loves glory more than pleasure: "I hope, Trim, answered my uncle Toby, I love mankind more than either; and as the knowledge of arms tends so apparently to the good and quiet of the world—and particularly that branch of it which we have practised together in our bowling-green, has no object but to shorten the strides of AMBITION, and intrench the lives and fortunes of the *few*, from the plunderings of the *many*—whenever that drum beats in our ears, I trust, Corporal, we shall neither of us want so much humanity and fellow-feeling as to face about and march" (9.8.753). In their notes to the Florida edition of *Tristram Shandy*, Melvyn New, Richard A. Davies, and W. G. Day draw our attention to Sterne's sermon on Herod, which advances the opinion that the Judaean king was driven by ambition and led into unjust wars on that account. In other words, Toby's assertion that wars are waged from motives of "humanity and fellow-feeling" is not to be taken as Sterne's own conviction.

The sermon itself fuses a scriptural passage about the matriarch Rachel with a historical meditation on the character of Herod as presented by Josephus.

The sermon was preached on Innocents' Day, which commemorates Herod's slaughter of the male children of Bethlehem reported in Matthew 2:1–18 (and nowhere else in the Gospels or in independent accounts such as Josephus's *Jewish Antiquities*). Sterne's text is from the end of the chapter, Matthew 2:17–18: "Then was fulfilled that which was spoken by Jeremy the prophet, saying,—in Rama was there a voice heard, lamentation, and weeping, and great mourning, Rachael weeping for her children, and would not be comforted because they are not." He moves immediately from the fact of Rachel's weeping to the place of her burial, asserting that "to enter into the full sense and beauty of this description, it is to be remembered that the tomb of Rachael, Jacob's beloved wife . . . was situated near Rama, and betwixt that place and Bethlehem."[36] New points out that here "Sterne simplifies a standing confusion concerning the location of Rachel's tomb, whether near Ephrathah, identified with Bethlehem (and where Rachel died giving birth to Benjamin . . .) or north of Jerusalem, near Ramah."[37] Christian biblical commentator Matthew Poole, indeed, insists that Rachel's tomb is near Bethlehem and glosses the scripture's reference to Ramah as one that need not "be taken appellatively, as it signifieth a High place, from whence a noise is most loudly, and dolefully heard."[38] Sterne, however, does not call on Christian commentary; instead he moves, unexpectedly, to "Jewish interpreters" who "say upon this, that the patriarch Jacob buried Rachael in this very place, foreseeing by the spirit of prophecy, that his posterity should that way be led captive, that she might as they passed her, intercede for them."[39] While Sterne rejects this "fanciful superstructure" as an example of the "doctrine of intercessions" that strikes him as all too similar to traditions embraced by "Romish dreamers," he is absolutely accurate in his understanding of the oral tradition regarding Rachel's tomb.[40] The "Jewish doctor" who "dreamed" this interpretation was Nachmanides in his commentary on Genesis 48:7 where Jacob says, "And as for me, when I came from Padan, Rachel died unto me in the land of Canaan in the way, when there was still some way to come unto Ephrath; and I buried her there in the way to Ephrath—the same is Bethlehem." Nachmanides focuses on the repetition of "in the way" as "implying in the way her children were destined to pass did she die and there she was buried in their interests, since she had not actually died 'in the way' but at 'Ramah' which is a town in the land of Benjamin and there she was buried, but what the text meant to suggest was that she was buried at a spot where her descendants were destined to pass, when they were *on the way* going into exile. The text does not, however, explicitly refer to future events, but merely alludes to them."[41] Nehama Leibowitz remarks that in this passage "Rachel . . . is pictured as the symbol of the Matriarch of Israel standing by to protect her descendants on their way into exile and interceding on their behalf."[42] Sterne's gloss, and I believe it can be called such legitimately, is slightly different: "the lamentation of Rachael . . . has no immediate reference to Rachael, Jacob's wife, but . . . it simply alludes to the sorrows of her descendents, the distressed mothers of the tribes of Benjamin and Ephraim who might accompany their children, led into captivity as far as Rama, in their way to Babylon, who wept and wailed upon this sad occasion."[43] The mothers he commemorates on Innocents' Day are "mothers of the same tribe" as Rachel. They suffer at the hands of Herod, whose "ambition" leads him to "trample upon the affections of nature" with violence, cruelty, and heartlessness and, though "bred a Jew," to care more about "ingratiat[ing] himself with Augustus and the great men of Rome from whom he held his power" than about the Sanhedrin or his own sons (all of whom he executed).[44]

Sterne's portrait of Herod, as New points out and as Sterne himself tells us, is "derived . . . from Josephus's *Jewish Antiquities*"; however, "the lack of specific verbal echoes" has led Lansing Van der Heyden Hammond to speculate that "some convenient 'intermediary' saved Yorick the trouble of perusing the pages of the Jewish historian for himself."[45] Who or what might this intermediary have been? And could it be the same intermediary that provided access to Nachmanides, gossip about sausages in Portugal, and lore about the golem? Perhaps the esoteric reading that Sterne may have indulged in John Hall-Stevenson's library can explain some of this knowledge, though, as Cash has pointed out with regard to all the "odd lore that went into *Tristram Shandy*," definitive documentation is simply lacking.[46] It seems just as likely to me that Sterne's knowledge of Jewish matters came from acquaintance with a Jew.

We tend to think of the times as totally segregated in terms of race and religion, but, after all, it is in the mid-1750s that, on the Continent, Gotthold Ephraim Lessing and Moses Mendelssohn become friends over a love of chess and a joint interest in the works of Alexander Pope, among other things. Their coauthored *Pope, A Metaphysician* (*Pope ein Metaphysiker*), although published anonymously in Danzig in 1755, was very quickly identified and celebrated as the product of intellectual and aesthetic partnership between Jew and Gentile. During this period, as well, Freemason lodges in London were open to Jewish members as the constitution of the brotherhood required a simple deistic faith, "that religion in which all men agree, leaving their particular opinions to themselves." Though certainly there was some discrimination in practice, there were also occasions on which the stated principle was honored: a Jew applied for membership to a London lodge in 1732 and was accepted.[47]

In other words, while the atmosphere in the eighteenth-century Jewish-Christian world was not completely open, there were occasions for non-Jews to meet Jews. Indeed, as Todd Endelman points out, such occasions for "social contact" were "increasingly common" in the Georgian period.[48] Sterne may have simply been in the presence of Jews from time to time. There is also the possibility, however, that he sought acquaintance in the midfifties, for the heated rhetoric surrounding the passage and then the repeal of the "Jew Bill" in 1753 and the devastation caused by the Lisbon earthquake in 1755 could not have left a sensitive spirit such as Sterne's unmoved.[49] Some of the Jews in eighteenth-century England (indeed the oldest communities) hailed from Portugal and Spain, driven out of those countries by an intolerance that had also, at one time, driven them out of England. Sterne lived in York, after all, site of one of the most tragic incidents of the thirteenth century's wave of anti-Semitism.

All things considered, I think it quite possible that Sterne wrote *Tristram Shandy* (as the Maharal is said to have created his golem) at least partly to combat what he might legitimately fear to be a new instantiation of an age-old antagonism.[50] It is probably too much to attribute to *Tristram Shandy* the atmosphere of openness and exchange between Jews and non-Jews that would characterize nineteenth-century England and Europe, but certainly the novel did its part to open minds and hearts to look for points of connection rather than matters of contention.[51] Nowhere is this tendency more evident than in *Tristram Shandy*'s one direct reference to the Talmud. In paying tribute to Trim for his gloss on the commandment to honor father and mother, Yorick says, "I honour thee more for it . . . than if thou hadst had a hand in the *Talmud* itself" (5.32.471). How has Trim glossed the commandment? By dedicating part of his daily pay to the sustenance and care of his parents—or, in other words, by deed, not creed. Ultimately, here and throughout both *Tristram Shandy* and *Sentimental Journey,* Sterne endorses what Enlightenment Judaism (haskalah) and Enlightenment Protestantism (Anglicanism in particular) will embrace with vigor in the century to come: the important thing is how we behave, not what we believe. Reading, as we must, from the point of view of our own times, we might pause, as we imagine Scholem did, for a sigh of regret that we have so poorly learned this lesson as we proceed thoughtlessly and violently, like *golemim* gone bad, down paths of global destruction upon which our various masters have set us.

NOTES

1. "Proust's Influence on Sterne: Remembrance of Things to Come," *MLN* 103 (1988): 1053.

2. For other of New's meditations on Sterne and modernist writers, see "Three Sentimental Journeys: Sterne, Shklovsky, and Svevo," *Shandean* 11 (1999–2000): 126–34, and "Sterne and the Modernist Moment," in *The Cambridge Companion to Laurence Sterne,* ed. Thomas Keymer (Cambridge: Cambridge University Press, 2009), 160-73.

3. Robert Alter, "Scholem and Modernism," *Poetics Today* 15 (1994): 430, 431.

4. The "abyss" as a source of meaning is, according to Alter, one of the key correspondences between Scholem and the modernists. See "Scholem and Modernism," 432–37. I think anyone reading this essay will concede that the concept is important to Sterne as well. After all, we stare into a black page that commemorates Yorick's death in volume 1 of *Tristram Shandy*, and we confront meaningful gaps, hiatuses, blanks, and silences from that point on. The abyss in Sterne is never a nihilistic fantasy. It is always, as in Scholem, an occasion to seek meaning on a higher—or lower—plane.

5. Scholem, *From Berlin to Jerusalem: Memories of My Youth*, trans. Harry Zohn (New York: Shocken Books, 1980), 33. I would like to thank Alan Levenson for introducing me to Scholem in this context.

6. *The Correpondence of Walter Benjamin, 1910–1940*, ed. Gershom Gerhard Scholem and Theodor W. Adorno (Chicago: University of Chicago Press, 1994), 304.

7. *The Correspondence of Walter Benjamin and Gershom Scholem, 1932–1940*, ed. Gershom Scholem (Cambridge: Harvard University Press, 1989), 60. K.M. refers to Kitty Marx with whom Benjamin would have a flirtatious, Yorick-like, friendship, but at this point, the relationship is fraught with uncertainty.

8. Ibid.

9. Ibid., 66.

10. Ibid.

11. McGinn, "Foreword" to Gershom Scholem, *On the Kabbalah and Its Symbolism*, trans. Ralph Manheim (New York: Schocken Books, 1996), vii, xi–xii.

12. New, "The Odd Couple: Laurence Sterne and John Norris of Bemerton," *PQ* 75 (1996): 361 and 373. For Norris's Neoplatonism and its indebtedness to philosopher Nicolas Malebranche's "complex interweaving of Platonic idealism, Cartesian dualism, and Augustinian theocentricism" into his own "Occasionalism," see E. Derek Taylor and Melvyn New's introduction to their edition of *Mary Astell and John Norris: Letters Concerning the Love of God* (Burlington: Ashgate, 2005), 7–22, 14–15.

13. *The Life and Opinions of Tristram Shandy, Gentleman: The Text*, ed. Melvyn New and Joan New, vols. 1 and 2 of the Florida Edition of the Works of Laurence Sterne (Gainesville: University of Florida Press, 1978), 1.1.2. All references to this text cite Sterne's original volume and book numbers followed by the Florida edition page number and will appear parenthetically in the text.

14. Clara Pinto-Correia, "Homunculus: Historiographic Misunderstandings of Performatist Terminology," Topic 4.1 in *Developmental Biology Online*, ed. Scott F. Gilbert, 9th ed. (http://9e.devbio.com).

15. Ibid.

16. "Let the semen of a man putrefy by itself in a sealed cucurbite with the highest putrefaction of venter equinus for forty days, or until it begins at last to live, move, and be agitated, which can easily be seen. At this time it will be in some degree like a human being, but, nevertheless, transparent and without a body. If now, after this, it be every day nourished and fed cautiously with the arcanum of human blood, and kept for forty weeks in the perpetual and equal heat of venter equinus, it becomes thencefold a true living infant, having all the members of a child that is born from a

woman, but much smaller. This we call a homunculus; and it should be afterwards educated with the greatest care and zeal, until it grows up and starts to display intelligence." Quoted by Pinto-Correia, ibid.

17. Gershom Scholem, *Major Trends in Jewish Mysticism* (New York: Schocken Books, 1995), 99.

18. Scholem and Adorno note that Benjamin's "spelling is a mixture of *Shandy* and the spelling used by Bode in his German translation, *Schandi*." *The Correspondence of Walter Benjamin*, 307n2.

19. I am grateful to John Oberholt of the Houghton Library of Harvard University for checking the Bode translation for me and to Howard Gaskill of Edinburgh University for the information regarding *Yorick's Meditations*. E-mail correspondence with both, via C18-L listserv (to which I am also indebted), 5 March 2010.

20. Emily Bilski notes that Christian authors began publishing accounts of the creation of a golem (specifically Rabbi Eliahu of Chelm's golem) in the mid-seventeenth century, which became the source material for Jakob Grimm's version of the tale that he published in *Zeitung für Eisiedler* (*Journal for Hermits*) in 1808. "The Golem: An Historical Overview," in *Golem! Danger, Deliverance, and Art*, ed. Emily D. Bilski (New York: Jewish Museum, 1988), 13–14.

21. Marsha Keith Schuchard, *Restoring the Temple of Vision: Cabalistic Freemasonry and Stuart Culture* (Boston: Brill, 2002). See also Jonathan I. Israel, *Radical Enlightenment: Philosophy and the Making of Modernity, 1650–1750* (Oxford: Oxford University Press, 2001), 538, 645–50. David S. Katz has also demonstrated that seventeenth-century English "projectors" of universal language were well versed in Jewish mysticism, particularly kabbalah; see his *Philo-Semitism and the Readmission of the Jews to England, 1603–1655* (Oxford: Clarendon, 1982), 71–88.

22. See, for example, *Oppression: A Poem* (London, 1765), which compares the Northern Britons to "the Jews" whose "greatest crime is too partial love" (30) and the *North Briton*, 19 June 1762, in which Scots are compared to "the Jews" in that they "are spread over the face of every country." John Wilkes et al. *North Briton*, 2nd ed., 3 vols. (Dublin, 1763), 1:19. See also Michael Ragussis, "Jews and Other 'Outlandish Englishmen': Ethnic Performance and the Invention of British Identity Under the Georges," *Critical Inquiry* 26 (2000): 773–97, especially 775.

23. Eisenmenger, *Rabbinical Literature; or, The Traditions of the Jews contained in the Talmud and Other Mystical Writings* (London, 1748), 1:269–70.

24. H. L. Strack and Günter Stemberger, *Introduction to the Talmud and Midrash*, ed. and trans. Markus Bockmuehl (Minneapolis: Fortress, 1992), 224.

25. Indeed, as Frank E. Manuel has demonstrated, the late Renaissance had witnessed a "revival of interest in virtually all aspects of Hebraic thought" in the Christian world—kabbalah, as well as ritual law—that continued throughout the eighteenth century. "Christendom's Rediscovery of Judaism," *Bulletin of the American Academy of Arts and Sciences* 40, no. 7 (1987): 17.

26. "Sterne, Warburton, and the Burden of Exuberant Wit," *Eighteenth-Century Studies*, no. 15 (1982): 263. I would disagree with New's conclusion that the one overt reference in *Tristram Shandy* to the *Divine Legation* is a thorough repudiation of Warburton's "ponderous treatise" (273), as opposed to Swift's *A Tale of a Tub*,

the other text with which he compares his own. Indeed, I believe Sterne to be quite serious in seeing all three books as efforts to deflect religious controversy and defuse religious passion.

27. Scholem, *On the Kabbalah and Its Symbolism*, 161–62; hereafter cited parenthetically.

28. Exod. R. 40:3.

29. Scholem, *Major Trends*, 180–81.

30. With "abyss," I echo Alter on Scholem (discussed above). It was also Alter, interestingly enough, who first read *Tristram Shandy* as "a continuous demonstration and celebration of the imagination" that coexists with articulation of "the possibility that the imagination is a cheat, a purveyor of substanceless flimflam." *Partial Magic: The Novel as Self-Conscious Genre* (Berkeley: University of California Press, 1975), 38.

31. It is really difficult to say what people of the past knew and did not know about oral history. We cannot confirm Sterne's awareness of the legend of the golem of Prague because it was not written down until well after his death, around 1835. Moishe Idel, *Golem: Jewish Magical and Mystical Traditions on the Artificial Anthropoid* (Albany: State University of New York Press, 1990), 252.

32. Arthur H. Cash speculates that Sterne was "introduced to Hebrew grammar and logic" at Hipperholme (*Laurence Sterne: Early and Middle Years* [New York: Routledge, 1975], 34). Sterne's acquaintance with rabbinic texts appears to Norman Simms, who has thoroughly considered "Jewishness in *Tristram Shandy*," to be secondhand, through Josephus, John Spencer, and William Warburton primarily ("The Missing Jews and Jewishness in *Tristram Shandy*," *Shandean* 4 [1992]: 139). As will become clear, I am not so sure.

33. While Simms sees this episode as encoding "an almost imperceptible anti-Jewish fantasy," I (and I think most readers) see the portrayal of Tom and the widow as completely sympathetic ("Missing Jews," 139).

34. Eduardo Mayone Dias, "Crypto-Jews in Portugal: A Clandestine Existence," Society for Crypto-Judaic Studies, http://www.cryptojews.com/cryptoJewsinPortugal.htm.

35. On the Sephardim in England at this time, see Simms, "Missing Jews," 137–38; for a full history of eighteenth-century English Jewry, see Todd Endelman, *The Jews of Georgian England, 1714–1830: Tradition and Change in a Liberal Society* (Philadelphia: Jewish Publication Society, 1979). He discusses the Jewish immigrants from Portugal on 167–68.

36. "Sermon 9: The Character of Herod," in *The Sermons of Laurence Sterne: The Text*, ed. Melvyn New, vol. 4 of the Florida Edition of the Works of Laurence Sterne (Gainesville: University Press of Florida, 1996), 81–82.

37. New, *The Sermons of Laurence Sterne: The Notes*, vol. 5 of the Florida Edition of the Works of Laurence Sterne (Gainesville: University Press of Florida, 1996), 133–34.

38. Cited by New, ibid., 134. Poole's two-volume *Annotations upon the Holy Bible* appeared in 1683.

39. Sterne, "The Character of Herod," *Sermons: The Text*, 82.

40. Ibid.

41. Gen. R. 82:10. Nachmanides or Ramban (Rabbi Moshe ben Nachman) was a thirteenth-century commentator, a Spaniard, and, like Maimonides earlier, a physician as well as a rabbi. His biblical commentaries were the first to incorporate the mystical tradition. See *Encyclopedia Judaica*, s.v. "Nachmanides." See also the brief biography at http://www.jewishvirtuallibrary.org/jsource/biography/Nachmanides.html.

42. Nehama Leibowitz, *New Studies in Bereshit* (Genesis), trans. Aryeh Newman (Israel: Eilner Library, n.d.), 541.

43. Sterne, "The Character of Herod," *Sermons: The Text*, 82–83.

44. Ibid., 83, 86–87.

45. Hammond, *Laurence Sterne's "Sermons of Mr. Yorick"* (New Haven: Yale University Press, 1949), 59; cited by New, *Sermons: The Notes*, 133, 137.

46. Cash, *Laurence Sterne: Early and Middle Years*, 194.

47. *Encyclopedia Judaica*, s.v. "freemason." Indeed, wealthy Jewish merchants and patrons of the arts Moses and Solomon Mendez were Freemasons, as was their friend James Thomson. Solomon Mendez provided shelter for Richard Savage during some of his low moments in London. Sterne was not a Freemason, but two Free-masons erected his memorial stone around 1780, inscribed to one whose "keenest Knowledge of Mankind / Unseal'd to him the Springs that move the Mind." Wilbur Cross meets objections to the inappropriateness of the tribute and those who paid it by calling it "a sincere encomium" (*The Life and Times of Laurence Sterne*, 3rd ed. [New Haven: Yale University Press, 1929], 494–95). For Solomon Mendez and Rich-ard Savage, see Richard Holmes, *Dr. Johnson and Mr. Savage* (New York: Pantheon Books, 1994), 3, 175, 215. For Thomson and the Mendez brothers, see James Sam-brook, *James Thomson, 1700–1748: A Life* (Oxford: Clarendon Press, 1991), 168.

48. Endelman, *Jews of Georgian England*, 249–50.

49. I follow Simms here in highlighting these two events as significant for Sterne, both as independent events and as they stood in relation to each other.

50. My argument does not really contradict Simms's perception of an underly-ing, unconscious reflection of certain aspects of an anti-Jewish myth. We agree that "Sterne . . . would not knowingly articulate the racial and social fears encoded" in this myth (Simms, 145). And we also agree that *Tristram Shandy* is directly engaging with various aspects of the "Jewish question." My emphasis on the cultural, intel-lectual, and mystical aspects of Judaism and Sterne's seeming awareness of them as opposed to Simms's emphasis on the ritual and covenantal aspects (circumcision, in particular) result in different readings of Sterne's overall purpose and effect. While Simms sees in Sterne's Jewish themes evidence of "creative misunderstanding," I see (and I believe Scholem saw) intuitive sympathy. See Endelman, *Jews of England*, 44, 50–85, on the role of Anglican clergy in relation to the Jew Bill (bishops in the House of Lords did not oppose it) and on the general philo-Semitism among liberal Anglo-Christians of this time.

51. For the literary effect of such openness—and for the participation of novelists in the consequent rewriting of English national identity in the nineteenth century, see Michael Ragussis's excellent *Figures of Conversion: "The Jewish Question" and English National Identity* (Durham, NC: Duke University Press, 1995).

Chapter Ten

Laurence Sterne, the Apostrophe, and American Abolitionism, 1788–1831

W. B. Gerard

Laurence Sterne is not typically looked upon as an influential figure of the American abolitionist movement of the late eighteenth and early nineteenth centuries. The author of the innovative fictions *The Life and Opinions of Tristram Shandy, Gentleman* (1759–1767) and *A Sentimental Journey* (1768), Sterne spent most of his adult life as a country vicar outside of York, far from London or even from the seaports that might have exposed him first-hand to enslaved Africans or slave traders. He largely tended his rural flock, traveling the rolling landscape around Stillington and Sutton-on-the-Forest for regular services, as well as administering to local births, marriages, and deaths, occasionally making the trip to York to dabble in local politics, and, in his role as prebendary, to preach in its great cathedral. (Equally remote Coxwold, the location of "Shandy Hall," would be added to his living much later.)[1] Moreover, the subjects of his fictions, a peculiar country family and a clergyman on a quest for feeling, seem unlikely to suggest a role for Sterne as an antislavery advocate.

Yet the voice of the vicar of Sutton resonates through American abolitionist discourse between 1788 and 1831. This presence derives from elements in his sermons, fiction, and correspondence that touch upon the issue briefly but powerfully, using the affective language of sensibility to frame the practice of slavery in emotional terms. Excerpts and key phrases from Sterne occur in abolitionist contexts with some frequency in this period; imitations adopting Sterne's affective tone and phrasing also appeared. In fact, so widespread is Sterne's influence on abolitionist discourse in American popular media in this period that it would be impossible to document its many occurrences in the space of an essay; instead, after examining Sterne's antislavery texts, the focus of this study will be on a single significant passage from one of them and its many iterations within a single database.

Each of the four most prominent passages addressing slavery in Sterne occurs in a different source in his writings. The unlikely role of a rural English
parson as an advocate for American abolition most apparently begins in his
sermons, his primary exercise in writing from the time of his clerical appointment in 1741 to the composition of *Tristram Shandy* roughly seventeen years
later. One of these, "Job's account of the shortness and troubles of life, considered," addresses the issue at some length, relating a story from Plutarch, when
the Romans drove "one hundred and fifty thousand unhappy people . . . in one
day into captivity, to be sold to the highest bidder to end their days in cruel
anguish.——Consider how great a part of our species in all ages down to this,
have been trod under the feet of cruel and capricious tyrants, who would neither hear their cries, nor pity their distresses. ——Consider slavery——what
it is, ——how bitter a draught, and how many millions have been made to
drink of it."[2] Published with fourteen other sermons in 1760 in the wake of the
successful first two volumes of *Tristram Shandy*, "Job's account" goes on to
link the story to a typical vein of anti-Catholicism, "the history of the Romish
church and her tyrants, (or rather executioners)" (*S*, 100). Yet the issue of the
enslavement of Africans had been slowly moving to the forefront of cultural
discourse in England and America throughout the eighteenth century, and this
sermon's relevance likely was self-apparent to readers of the sermon collection (if perhaps less so to the Sterne's rural congregations).

The sermon does not lose sight that the enslaved multitudes are "people"
who utter "cries" and suffer "distresses" (sentient beings like the sermon's
audience) who are unnoticed by "cruel and capricious tyrants." The lack of
feeling on the part of the "tyrants" presumably forms a contrast with this
feeling audience, who are then asked simply to "Consider slavery——what
it is, ——how bitter a draught." As with the unique punctuation in Sterne's
fictions, the long dashes are neither arbitrary nor ornamental symbols,[3] and
the long pauses they signify urge the sermon's auditors (and later readers) to
ponder the simple and irreducible wrong being set before them.

Sterne's concept of slavery is here abstract and generalized. Markman Ellis
notes that it is uncertain whether "Sterne means slavery in the sense of the
system of coerced labour practised in the West Indies, or something else."[4]
The mention of slavery indeed does occur in the sermon after a series of historical instances of man's inhumanity to his fellow man, yet the obvious and
outstanding instance of slavery to midcentury Englishmen would have been
in the West Indies, where the practice peaked in the period 1740–1780;[5] this
particular sermon was composed and delivered in the 1740s or 1750s, and the
reference would have been more apparent still to the wider audience seeing
it in print during following decades. It seems unlikely that Sterne or his audiences could have considered the topic as a mere historical abstract.

References to slavery in Sterne's fiction were composed in the late 1760s—the last years of the author's life—and represent more complete and detailed arguments against the practice. In the last volume of *Tristram Shandy*, Corporal Trim relates the story of his ill-fated brother, Tom, who, courting a Jewish widow, arrives at her sausage shop to find there "a poor negro girl . . . flapping away flies" with "a bunch of white feathers slightly tied to the end of a long cane." Trim emphasizes that she was "not killing them," harkening to the earlier story of bighearted Toby catching and then releasing an irritating fly. Upon hearing Trim's description, Toby in fact immediately finds a kindred spirit in the servant and (interrupting Trim's story as usual), exclaims: "'Tis a pretty picture! . . . —she had suffered persecution, Trim, and had learnt mercy—."[6]

Within the space of a paragraph, the African servant is introduced and identified as one who had been treated unjustly, yet her reaction is of increased compassion. Most important, she is depicted primarily as a sympathetic individual acting on her own beliefs (that is, unwilling to inflict pain when she herself has suffered). Rather than merely serving as an object of pity for feeling readers, she exhibits a similar sensibility to theirs, and in doing so raises herself (and by implication potentially all enslaved Africans) above the status of objecthood to claim emotional equivalency with the readers themselves. The example of live-and-let-live seems to present a moral allegory for Sterne's readers as well, reiterating the "do unto others" ethic of reciprocity found in his body of sermons, most especially in Sermon 3, "Philanthropy recommended."[7]

Trim goes on to affirm that "the story of that poor friendless slut . . . would melt a heart of stone" and, to Trim's question about whether "a Negro has a soul," Toby answers, "I suppose, God would not leave him without one, any more than thee or me——." Trim then asks why "is a black wench to be used worse than a white one" and answers himself—suggesting he has learned Toby's point—stating, "only . . . because she has no one to stand up for her."[8] Toby leaps in with the final stroke of the moral lesson, stating that "'Tis that very thing . . . which recommends her to protection—and her brethren with her" (*TS*, 9.6.747–48).

The inclusion of the dehumanizing question as to whether Africans have souls seems to be a specific response to proslavery advocates who attempted to legitimize the trafficking in human beings with an array of biological and spiritual arguments centered on the denial of their humanity.[9] The servant's gesture of "mercy," as Toby recognizes, subtly refutes this claim, not only for the individual, but also for her race; her behavior, in fact, positions her within the ranks of subscribers to the culture of sensibility, as the parallel with Toby suggests. Thus, she is represented not as a mere object of pity but as an emotional as well as a spiritual equivalent to the readers themselves.

The passage continues in a clearly political vein with Toby's broader hypothesis about the arbitrary nature of military power. Having established the humanity of the servant (and with her all oppressed Africans), Toby responds with a charitable bravado not unlike the protection he extends over Le Fever, which is not without its didactic implications. Toby's consideration has a deeper basis still, again rooted in the ethic of reciprocity: "'tis the fortune of war which has put the whip into our hands *now*—where it may be hereafter, heaven knows!" (*TS*, 9.6.748). Ellis sees Trim's "moment of realisation" as a "conventional device of the sentimental," which leads a "character (and by association, the reader) to the adoption or formation of a sentiment or opinion in a moment of quiet insight" (70). In a sense, here Trim acts as a stand-in for the skeptical contemporary reader, beginning as a casual questioner of the humanity of Africans whose emotions, Sterne hopes, will recruit him as an advocate of the oppressed. The conversation between the two characters may well echo many taking place from midcentury onward, with Toby, who had by this time already garnered a level of literary celebrity,[10] taking a clearly abolitionist stand.

The discussion of slavery here is both more focused and more developed than its mention in the earlier sermon, possibly the result of Sterne's increased exposure to the institution through print media and during his six years of fame, his travels, and his occasional residence in London. What begins as a story about Trim's brother Tom and his unknown fate at the hands of the Inquisition—which, as Ellis points out, represents another tale of freedom and incarceration (68)—shifts its focus rapidly to the single figure of the African servant and eventually the subject of contemporary chattel slavery. The spontaneous discussion between Toby and Trim lightens the potentially heavy-handed preachiness that could accompany the subject, and its illustration through individual example literally puts a human face on the issue.[11] Brycchan Carey astutely identifies the story as "an excellent example of a sentimental parable" in which the servant "synecdochically represents the story of a multitude";[12] the idea of didacticism, of course, lies at the heart of a parable. Perhaps overrigorous in their analysis, other critics lament the sympathetic focus on the individual as a type of ownership that undermines the ostensible philanthropic appeal presented by the text. Inflating the idea of benevolence into manipulation, Shirley Samuels identifies a "sentimental gaze" that "appropriates and controls its objects of scrutiny" and that can act selfishly as "a form of social control."[13] Yet the text seems to be arguing the opposite: the perspective in Sterne's passage is broadened to include "all her brethren," and the implications of their captivity lead to the wider realization of the inhumanity of the practice, an inhumanity emphasized by the arbitrariness of power. It takes some twisting and emotional frigidity to make the implication of liberation into virtual captivity. As Carey observes, sentimental arguments work "by emotionally subverting the intellect," and bring us eventually to the "political dimension" of the scene (58), clearly one of sympathetic equality on several levels.

A Sentimental Journey, appearing a year after the last volume of *Tristram Shandy*, conveys Sterne's most significant and complex antislavery message. A passage within an agile, typically Sternean chain of associations begins with suspicions about Yorick being a spy and an at-first-acceptable, then re-pellent, prospect of imprisonment. Spurred by his encounter with the starling, Yorick apostrophizes, "Disguise thyself as thou wilt, still slavery! . . . still thou art a bitter draught; and though thousands in all ages have been made to drink of thee, thou art no less bitter on that account."[14] His imagination fired by the subject, Yorick asserts that he "was going to begin with the millions of my fellow creatures born to no inheritance but slavery; but finding, how-ever affecting the picture was, that I could not bring it near me. . . . I took a single captive and . . . look'd through the twilight of his grated door to take his picture" (*ASJ*, 97). Creating a parallel temporal reality by focusing on a single individual, Yorick forces himself as well as the reader to confront the captive's human qualities with careful and deliberate framing. His depiction centers on the character's physical and psychological distress (a "body half wasted away" and "sickness of the heart") in addition to his removal from domestic and social comfort (he had not "the voice of friend or kinsman" or "children" to comfort him [*ASJ*, 97]), revealing him stripped of his happiness and humanity. The narrator's compassion compels him to describe further the captive's psychological state, marked by "dismal days and nights," "a hopeless eye," and "a deep sigh," the last of which tellingly precedes Yorick seeing "the iron enter his soul." The captive, having proven himself to pos-sess the same feelings and domestic attachments as any sensitive reader of the time, becomes all the more tragic in his resignation. On two occasions, Yorick's vivid imagination carries him too far, preventing him from complet-ing his description, and the second time, he admits, "I could not sustain the picture of confinement which my fancy had drawn" (*ASJ*, 98), forcing him to conclude his imaginative exercise in compassion, but leaving an aposiopesis where readers are led to complete the picture—and consider its moral impli-cations—themselves.

The text preceding this description, as well as the passage itself, also en-gages readers, inviting them into a complex play of metaphor, reflexivity, and political positioning. Initially the starling's pleas of "I can't get out" displace Yorick's carefully wrought, logical conclusions about his own possible confinement (he states that "in one moment they overthrew all my systematic reasonings upon the Bastile" [*ASJ*, 96]) and his "tenderly awakened [affections]" pronounce the condemning apostrophe to Slavery. Here the conceptual yields to the specific, a description punctuated by the narrator's pauses, which themselves are created by the intensity of his own invocations. Yorick then returns to his personal priority: traveling to Versailles to obtain a passport to keep himself out of jail.

The presentation of the issue of slavery here is complicated both by Sterne's verbal playfulness (primarily with the mention of "*tint*" [*ASJ*, 96] in his apostrophe) and by Yorick's vulnerability to his own imaging of pathos, inviting critics to question the sincerity of the text. Broadly, the consistent recentering of the narrator over the sentimental subjects of the starling and captive and their subjectivization can be seen as reflecting poorly on Yorick's show of virtue; some have pointed out that the starling, in the end, is not freed, and the captive's described agonies are supplanted by Yorick's upwelling of emotion.

Yet these conclusions cannot displace or deny either the presence of an important issue in Sterne's time or its highly sympathetic treatment. The caged starling suggests obvious symbolic parallels with enslaved humans. Ellis asserts that it is "made a metonymic emblem of African slavery" (74). More specifically, Paul Moore observes that "when his passion has cooled, he [Yorick] likewise treats it [the starling] simply as a piece of property."[15] This shouldn't be surprising, though: in the end, the starling is a bird and not a person. Yorick's sympathetic identification with the starling does not magically make it human, and the emphasis on its repeated cry rather than its actual misery—an actor rather than sufferer—stresses its role as a herald, an awakener of conscience, rather than as a suffering individual. It is a vital point to consider the presentation of the starling as contrasted with the captive, a feeling individual. The starling serves as an emotional prompt on two counts—to remind Yorick of his own possible incarceration and by association of the broader issue of human captivity. Critical attempts to paint the bird as a symbol of slavery in fact are further complicated by Sterne's gesture to link himself to the starling, through the etymological link to his name, its attachment to his (by way of Yorick's) family crest, and the parallels between the bird's passage between patrons and Sterne's own adventures in English society.[16] The differences in the representation of the starling and the captive also explains the strong contrast in Yorick's responses to them: one is an intuitive and impulsive attraction, the other a poignant meditation.

The sentimentalization of the subject, more evident with the captive than in Sterne's other antislavery passages, has been a particularly contentious point of discussion. Yorick's process of envisioning his subject involves "shut[ting] him up in his dungeon" and viewing him "through the twilight of his grated door" (*ASJ*, 97). This process of visual isolation of the subject—which informs many of Sterne's character descriptions in his fiction and sermons—is labeled by Lynn Festa as an "oscillation between the sentimental and the ironic."[17] Arthur H. Cash, however, sees it as part of a larger pattern, a sign that Yorick "cannot be affected by abstract considerations and general ideas," needing instead individual examples (as with the monk) on which to focus his sympathy.[18] John Mullan seems to identify a similar quality with his observation that Yorick exercises "a sympathy which is not necessarily narcissistic and indulgent; it confesses itself to be inventive and purposeful: a necessary fiction."[19] This necessity is recognized by Festa as well, who perceptively observes that "one is ostensibly not meant to love *this* individual, but to love all slaves through him . . . one figure *must* stand in for another" (86). Finding the text "mawkish," Mullan nevertheless concedes that it is "progressive on the question of slavery by the standards of Sterne's culture" (194).

Others find that Yorick's narrative undermines the issue of abolition, an exercise of self-indulgence at best. Moore views Yorick's discussion as an act of "veiled sado-masochism" (45). Marcus Wood sees the narrative process in the passage as an "act of imaginative possession" that "exists in a troubled relation to the manner in which a real slave-owner can use the slave's body at any time, in any way." Using narrative to control fictional characters is hardly unique to this scene or to Sterne, of course; Dumas's restriction of the count of Monte Cristo to his cell, for instance, would seem to qualify him, in Wood's words, as an "authorial tormentor."[20] Yorick may touch on irony, as Festa notes, but to view the narrative description as exhibiting a "brutal and darkly humorous indifference" (18) as does Wood, a critical tormentor of sorts, exercises excessive determination over the text.

The narrative description of the single captive, in Robert Markley's perspective, "not only makes him a pitiable victim but also effectively isolates him from his fellow 'millions,' from any possibility of concerted and collective political action."[21] Of course, the "action" that needs to take place in Sterne's text is to rouse readers to an advocacy of abolition through political activity (rather than incite a revolution or uprising), a tested means of attaining change within a democratic system. Focusing on an individual out of a group for argumentative purposes is a widely used and accepted rhetorical technique, as Carey notes above, a device of synecdoche. Many of Sterne's rhetorical techniques lambasted by Markley and Wood are in fact standard devices of antiquity, and likely were part of Sterne's early education. Aristotle, for instance, catalogs the "argument by Example" in his *Rhetoric*, which may employ an "illustrative parallel."[22] For the purpose of arguments, Cicero notes in *De Partitione Oratoria*, "there is no object so pitiable as the unhappy man who once was happy,"[23] a strategy behind the inclusion of the captive's domestic history that forms a contrast with the emotional desolation of his current condition. Sterne may also have been acquainted with these techniques through homiletic handbooks that emphasized the work of classical rhetoricians, such as the *Art of Preaching: In Imitation of Horace's Art of Poetry* of the 1730s. Less essential than a specific source, though, is recognition of the traditional means of persuasion that Sterne artfully brought to bear in presenting the captive; in fact, Sterne's occasional ambiguities and mastery of language aside, the narrative attention on a single suffering individual as representative of a group in need of philanthropy is recognized even today as an effective approach to induce action from the viewer/reader, as is evinced by countless charity appeal advertisements.[24]

The validity of this approach, furthermore, was defended in Sterne's own time. In *The Theory of Moral Sentiments* (1759), Adam Smith considers the efficacy of Sterne's technique eight years before the passage featuring the captive was written. "We have no immediate experience of what other men feel," he says, except "by conceiving what we ourselves should feel in the like situation." Therefore "it is by the imagination only that we can form any conception of what are his situations."[25] He continues that "his agonies, when they are thus brought home to ourselves, when we have thus adopted and made them our own, begin at last to affect us, and we then tremble and shudder at the thought of what he feels" (12). Measured by Smith's standards, Yorick's description of the captive falls within an even more conventional (and effective) contemporary framework that, despite its emotional flourishes, in tone and structure is utterly typical in a historical literary context.[26]

The description of the captive, revealed detail by detail, creates a distance between Yorick and his subject, but it also induces readers into his sympathetic imagination slowly, so that they share what he "sees." In his advice to orators, Quintilian states that "when we desire to awaken pity, we must actually believe our own selves, and must persuade our minds that this is really the case."[27] Yorick's exercise of the imagination incapacitates him, not because he is frivolous in its exercise, but the opposite—he is overburdened by the gravity of the issue facing him.[28] The true horror of a human being enslaved is in many ways beyond words, beyond description, and accordingly Yorick is unable to maintain his narrative, creating an aposiopesis that enhances the moral outrage of the image more than a complete description would, not only in the absence of continuation but in shifting the burden of imagining the captive's distress to the reader.

In 1766, Ignatius Sancho, the self-described "coal-black jolly African," wrote to the famous author, complimenting his work. Sancho is himself an engaging figure of the period, and his life would stand as a testimony to the moral obligation to free captive Africans, even if he had never written to Sterne at all. Born into slavery, he served three spinster sisters who derisively named him after the Cervantes character and denied him an education. He went on to become butler to Lord Montagu, who encouraged his interests in reading and writing and whose bequeathal eventually facilitated Sancho's financial independence. Aside from establishing a shop in London, Sancho would gain wide acquaintance in London cultural circles, writing letters and composing music.[29]

In his letter to Sterne, Sancho shows a fondness for the author's style—Sukhev Sandhu credits him with a "studious creolisation of Sterne's aesthetic"[30]—particularly the sentimental mode, affectionately claiming, for instance, that he "would walk ten miles to shake hands with" Corporal Trim. He pointedly remarks he had been reading Sterne's sermons (evidently the first edition of the first volume, published in April 1760) and felt inspired by "Job's account of the shortness and troubles of life, considered," particularly the "bitter draught" passage cited above. He relates to Sterne, "I am sure you will applaud me for beseeching you to give one half hour's attention to slavery, as it is at this day practised in our West Indies.—That subject, handled in your striking manner, would ease the yoke (perhaps) of many."[31]

In his response, Sterne observes the "strange coincidence," as he "had been writing a tender tale of the sorrows of a friendless poor negro-girl, and my eyes had scarse done smarting with it, when your Letter of recommendation in behalf of so many of her brethren and sisters, came to me." After mentioning his work on the story of the "friendless poor negro-girl" in *Tristram Shandy*, Sterne's letter continues in a more philosophical vein:

> but why *her brethren?*—or your's, Sancho! any more than mine? It is by the finest tints, and most insensible gradations, that nature descends from the fairest face about St James's, to the sootiest complexion in africa: at which tint of these, is it, that the ties of blood are to cease? and how many shades must we descend lower still in the scale, 'ere Mercy is to vanish with them? . . . for my own part, I never look *Westward* . . . but I think of the burdens which our Brothers & Sisters are *there* carrying—& could I ease their shoulders from one ounce of 'em, I declare I would set out this hour upon a pilgrimage to Mecca for their sakes.[32]

Sterne accedes to Sancho's request to make an appeal on behalf of enslaved Africans—in fact, he claims to have already taken the issue under consideration—and logically argues against the possibility of delineation of humanity by skin color, reinforcing a Christian and sentimental idea of kinship among men. He also expresses deep sympathy for those laboring in the West Indies—not moving toward the practical abolishment of the practice but instead seizing on a hyperbolic gesture (the Anglican priest making an Islamic pilgrimage) if that would end the practice. He skillfully runs the thread of universal kinship, a sentimental trope, throughout his proclamation; initiated by Sancho, it is a shared value between the two that mirrors and underlies their sympathies.[33]

Some question exists as to whether Sterne was inspired by Sancho to write the two antislavery passages in his fictions or if he was actually working on them at the time, as he suggests in his response to Sancho.[34] For the purposes of this study, however, the source of Sterne's passages is secondary to the impact of the words themselves on the half century that followed. Cash observes that the letter "reveals how much [Sterne] had thought about the subject of slavery and the distinctions of race."[35] Although he finds an ambivalence in Sterne's description of "tints" (an odd echo, perhaps, of the reference in the apostrophe to Liberty in *ASJ*), which reveals "powerful remnants of racial difference," Ellis acknowledges a "powerful denial" of that difference as well (65). Carol Watts sees in Sterne's response "an enabling (for him) disavowal, producing an imagined kinship without barriers."[36] This kinship is represented, interestingly, in the equalizing atmosphere of London, where in the eighteenth century a black African man born a slave could become a middle-class shop owner and cultural figure.[37]

The very act of Sancho's writing to Sterne about this issue is revealing about the public perception of Sterne at the time. Ian Campbell Ross sees the gesture as "a telling indication of how the writer's much-criticised work was increasingly regarded by sympathetic contemporaries as a powerful exhortation to moral improvement and even practical social reform" (349–50). Given Sterne's wide renown from *Tristram Shandy* in the years before his death, his published sermons, and his amiable public persona—testified to by sales of his books (and of their imitations) as well as evidence of his celebrity, certainly known to the author himself—it is not difficult to imagine Sterne's public stature in Britain and America.[38]

Some key historical events are instructive when considering Sterne's reception in an abolitionist context in America between 1787 and 1831. For instance, in the 1780s, Connecticut, Massachusetts, New Hampshire, Pennsylvania, Rhode Island, and Vermont had all ended slavery (or initiated its gradual phasing out) and by 1805 New York and New Jersey had joined this list; accordingly, "bitter draught" (and likely antislavery sentiment in general) appears disproportionately in newspapers from these states (Harmer, 22, 51). In 1807, the trade in slaves was legally prohibited in the United States and Britain (Harmer, 52). Two slave uprisings in Louisiana territory required military intervention in 1810, a quiet period for "bitter draught" in the newspapers (Harmer, 22). The years 1819–1820 saw much discussion about the admittance of Missouri into the union as a slave state, and at least eight mentions of "bitter draught" occur in this period (Harmer, 22–23).

A tentative picture of Sterne's influence in the early republic can be sketched from the popularity of his books. While it is difficult to ascertain the number of copies of Sterne's work that arrived from England, the number of editions of his work that were published in America provides clues to his cultural perception. As on the other side of the Atlantic, *A Sentimental Journey* was his most popular title, with seven editions produced before 1800, followed closely by six editions of the *Beauties of Sterne*, all of which included the antislavery passages mentioned earlier. An appetite for specifically sentimental subjects in America is further suggested by two editions of the excerpt *The Sorrows of Maria* and three editions (including one published in Jamaica) of *Letters from Yorick to Eliza.* In contrast, before 1815, only three editions of Sterne's *Works* were published as well as single editions of his *Sermons* and *Letters*; no separate editions of *Tristram Shandy* were printed in the United States until the mid-nineteenth century.[39]

Sterne's antislavery passages were widely reprinted in the early republic, and key phrases found their way into printed discourse in a variety of formats. The sheer quantity of these reprints and shorter quotations prohibits their extensive exploration here; instead, a representation of Sterne's abolitionist influence will be suggested by an analysis of the appearances of his central statement on the topic, the apostrophe to Slavery and Liberty from *A Sentimental Journey*, as well as a key phrase from that passage, "bitter draught," in the context of slavery in America. As chattel slavery increasingly became the focus of public discussion, this passage appears to have gained propagandistic value; Watts acknowledges that it "became a touchstone" for proponents of abolition and women's rights into the early nineteenth century (176). These references in themselves form a substantial sampling that suggests an even wider sphere of Sterne's integration into abolitionist discourse. For instance, the apostrophe, sometimes accompanied by the episodes of the starling and the captive, appears in volumes of excerpts from varied works that enjoyed wide popularity in America in the late eighteenth and early nineteenth centuries; the titles of these books, such as *The speaker . . . selected . . . with a view to facilitate the improvement of youth*, suggest an undisguised didactic intent. Four of these collections incorporate the apostrophe to Slavery and Liberty, including *Lessons in Elocution . . . for the improvement of youth in reading and speaking*, which ran to fourteen editions over twenty years. Printed without further commentary that might reinforce its relevance to American slavery, the apostrophe could have been included merely as an example of effective writing; on the other hand, its inclusion in these collections might have been the result of not-so-subtle abolitionist intentions.[40]

The most widespread and creative use of the apostrophe (and the signal term "bitter draught") is in the pages of American newspapers, more conclusively suggesting its pervasiveness within the culture as a touchstone for rousing feeling against slavery. In newspapers accessible through the Early American Newspapers Series 1 database, the apostrophe, or "bitter draught" in reference to the enslavement of Africans, occurs nearly four dozen times between 1787 and 1831 in newspapers in eleven states and the District of Columbia.[41] While not a comprehensive examination of all newspapers of the period, or of all printed media for that matter (pamphlets and magazines are not included), these representative contributions from Sterne to American abolition are nonetheless significant.

The newspaper trade formed an important facet of life in the early United States, and, as Jeffrey L. Pasley observes, although dedicated abolitionist periodicals were not founded until the 1830s,[42] newspapers were particularly important in providing a broad venue for emergent abolitionist dialogue. They were especially influential as the only means of mass communication; at the turn of the century it was estimated that there were more than 180 newspapers in the United States (each with a mean circulation of about 600), a number that would swell to more than 680 titles nationwide by 1828.[43] While subscriptions were limited to the well-to-do and literate, newspapers were frequently found at public gathering places, where they would be read aloud; Pasley notes that "even a few newspaper subscribers were enough to spread the word to entire neighborhoods" (8).

Newspapers of this period were generally four pages (two sheets) in length, though a few ran to eight pages, printed one to three times weekly. Particularly outside of the larger urban papers, the type and quality of the content could be irregular, dependent on individual editorial priorities; Pasley asserts, for instance, that the "news" was delivered "in a desultory, haphazard fashion, printing letters written or lent to the editor, material from other newspapers, and raw government documents" (2). Thus editors and publishers were free to include items that might seem unorthodox in the twenty-first century, allowing for a broader, more expressive range of possible material.

The apostrophe appears in its entirety in American newspapers eleven times in the period of 1787 to 1831, both with and without the starling and captive passages, in a variety of contexts. It is often situated in a general, or more specifically literary, olio, sometimes occupying a newspaper's back page. Thus the apostrophe in the *National Aegis* (1805; a paper that will contain other references to Sterne) occupies the same page as Swift's "Meditations on a Broomstick" and an item entitled "Latest Parisian Fashions."[44] Sometimes the apostrophe appeared in an even more mixed format: on page 1 of the *Litchfield Republican* (1822), it coexists with a notice of the proclamation of a state holiday and a "Burlesque on Genealogy," and is followed on page 2 by the tender poem, "On the Death of an Infant Sister."[45] In the Georgetown *Olio* (1803), the apostrophe appears on the back page, just before an advertisement for a lost cow.[46] While these nonpolitical appearances may seem trivial or literary in their intent, one must recall both the significance of their very appearance in the limited space of newspaper columns and the emotional impact of the passage; even without further elaboration, the apostrophe carries a clear abolitionist message.

The intent of inclusion is more obvious, perhaps, in the New York *Washington Republican* (1809), where the apostrophe shares page 2 with political commentary, appearing between an antifederalist tract complaining of government money spent on "barren and unprofitable waters" (the Louisiana Purchase) rather than on fortifications and gunships, and an editorial expressing concern about rumors of revolutionary activities in the United States by "French hirelings."[47] This context casts the passage as a strong political statement, a principle embedded in Sterne's artful—and famous—rhetoric.[48]

While the use of the phrase "bitter draught" in relation to foul-tasting medicine dates back centuries, the specific application of the term as a metaphor for slavery appears to have originated with Sterne's writing, first in his sermon, "Job's account of the shortness and troubles of life, considered," and later in *A Sentimental Journey*. Apart from its original reference and as part of the often-reprinted apostrophe, the phrase often appears in a variety of abolitionist items in periodicals, from news reports to editorials and letters. Outside of the full reprints of the apostrophe cited above in this period, "bitter draught" appears in at least thirty-five different newspaper items in many shapes and sizes in abolitionist contexts. The term arises in a lengthy imitation and a brief toast, in news items and in letters, becoming something of a shared touchstone, each appearance functioning as a synecdoche for the apostrophe and, in a larger sense, for the sympathetic philosophy of *A Sentimental Journey*. Occasionally a few lines of the apostrophe are quoted, and Sterne—or simply "the celebrated writer"—is mentioned. All in all, a wide variety of texts advocating abolition will include this phrase from 1787 to 1831. Many of these texts also utilize rhetorical strategies similar to those in Sterne's own antislavery writings: the focus on the oppressed individual as well as an appeal to principle, the latter of which forms the core of the apostrophe itself.

The focus on the plight of the individual can vividly extend the sufferings of the subject to the reader; this generally is illustrated by a careful description, as in Sterne's passages depicting the captive. These portrayals emerge in reference to news items printed in northern newspapers reporting the inhumane punishment of slaves. A piece in the *Political Calendar* (1804) describes the "vengeance" of Hoffman, a slave owner, for a twelve-year-old slave's "laddish fault": hands and legs tied together, the individual was "suspended for two days without either meat or drink" after Hoffman "crammed down the throat of the wretched boy two table spoons full of *salt*," after which he whipped his victim and "applied to the boy's [*sic*] a mixture of *salt and brandy!*" The writer turns to the reader, asking "how greatly are we conscience struck . . . when we see it [slavery] thus 'undisguised,'" building on Sterne's premise. This item, which appeared on page 2 alongside national and international news, was also printed in the news sections of the *Salem Register* (1804) and the Hudson, New York, *Bee* (1805).[49]

The appeal of the individual is also central to a less visceral news item in the *Connecticut Mirror* (1830) that features two lines from the apostrophe as an epigraph. The text describes "a circumstance of a painful nature and which has excited much sympathy in the breasts of our citizens," when a Maryland man "arrived in quest of a fugitive slave." Some straightforward details of a hearing in which the slave is restored to the master are included, and the piece concludes with the observation that "there is something in the case of this unfortunate man . . . which is calculated to excite feelings of commiseration for his fate": his literacy, in the form of an intercepted letter, proved to be his undoing. The epigraph and the language of compassion provide an emotional contrast to the matter-of-fact tone of the legal proceedings, strongly suggesting the episode was seen through a Sternean lens of sympathy. The item is included with the news in the *Mirror*, and was reprinted on page 1 (with public notices and advertising) of the *New Bedford Mercury* less than a week later.[50]

Under the heading of "Melioration of Slavery," an item in the *New-Hampshire Gazette* (1812) reporting on Africans kidnapped for the purpose of "training for his majesty's navy" reflects on "*the wretched negro, whom unfeeling, accurs'd avarice had doomed to a life of toil!*" The writer asks, "*Will the lash cut less keen, exercised by the petty tyrant of a ship of war, than by a slave-driver of a West India planter? Ah no!*" and adds two lines from the apostrophe in conclusion.[51] Again, news reporting provides the platform for an emotional appeal, cemented further with the reference to Sterne.

Another means of humanizing a subject dehumanized by slavery is stressing broken domestic attachments, a rhetorical strategy briefly used by Sterne in the description of the captive: "in thirty years the western breeze had not once fann'd his blood . . . nor had the voice of friend or kinsman breathed through his lattice . . . —his children—" (*ASJ*, 97). A formal commentary in the *Baltimore Patriot* (1821) observes, "what can be said in extenuation of the Kidnapper, of the cold-blooded villain, who insidiously steals in the darkness of the night, to the lonely hut, the unprotected hut of the colored man, where slumber in fancied security, his wife and his children . . . he then seizes upon his defenceless victims, and drags them bound and manacled to his den, from thence they are quickly transferred to some negro vessel."[52] The victims' lack of defense renders their family unity both more precious and more fragile, further demonizing the "cold-blooded villain"—by extension anyone who tolerates the institution of slavery. The tone and pacing of this passage are familiarly Sternean, almost as if the scene could precede the tale of the captive itself.

The most effective use of this technique, which gained some currency in this period, underlines the humanity of the enslaved, not only evoking their familial attachments but also reminding the reader of parallels to his (or her) own family. The previous item in the *Baltimore Patriot* (1821) exclaims, "their hearts are torn . . . by as violent grief, when a child, a brother, or a sister, is kidnapped from them, as ours would be."[53] The *Concord Observer* (1819) includes a second-person appeal: "Reader, were you torn by ruthless hands from your country . . . never more to visit the dwelling of your parents—never to afford a momentary alleviation to a grief-worn father, a disconsolate mother, by informing them that their son yet lives; would you think yourself free . . . ?"[54] An essay entitled "The Traveller" from the Pennsylvania *Village Record* (1818) is more confrontational: "Let the slave-master not refuse to read and reflect upon what I have and what I shall advance. . . . I ask him to take [this] home with him, and read it whilst surrounded by his family . . . and when the partner of his life soothes his sorrows and his cares, let him think of the connubial happiness that he has marred—and when his children climb about his knees, and twine their arms around his neck; let him think of those children whom, prompted by sordid avarice, he has dragged from the embraces of parents equally affectionate with himself."[55] Here the sentimentalized and personalized illustration of family clashes with a harsh reality, creating a vivid emotional contrast that is as difficult to reconcile as the practice of slavery itself. So powerful is this approach that it was also pressed into action for antiabolitonist commentary in the *City of Washington Gazette* (1820): "the sale of human flesh . . . rend[s] asunder forever the ties of parents and children, brothers and sisters, husband and wife," the author insists, yet is a lesser evil when compared to the prospect of slaves "turned loose to steal, rob and murder, the certain consequence of emancipation."[56] This text performs a high-wire act, recognizing the strength of the argument of domestic sentiment in regard to abolition (that in turn acknowledges the intrinsic humanity of its subject), while simultaneously attempting to negate its weight; in the end, it more than anything else seems to validate the strength of the domestic appeal against abolition.

Using the apostrophe and the term "bitter draught" to pursue Sterne's influence on American abolitionism leads to evidence of another rhetorical strategy in newspaper texts: the focus on principle, or abstract value, rather than on the specific human traits of the individual subject. Simplest of all, perhaps, is the recording in the Worchester, Massachusetts, *National Aegis* (1820) of a toast made during an annual Fourth of July public banquet; a round of toasts in this time typically advertised political candidates and notable issues. One line of the apostrophe is followed by, "Thy principles are repugnant to the spirit of Republicanism. May the dealers in human flesh in consciousness of their own wrongs, turn from their impious traffick, and become the friends of oppressed humanity." (Other toasts on the occasion were addressed to Andrew Jackson and "The Patriots of South America.")[57] The passage from a fifty-year-old book was well known enough to identify broader sentiments about the increasingly vexing issue of slavery on the occasion. Other writings using "bitter draught" to build a moral argument against slavery include a letter to George Washington (reprinted from a Liverpool paper) in the New York *Time Piece* (1797); a response to an item in the Virginia *Farmer's Repository* (1819) accusing a writer of being "one of those gentry who had an interest in the captivity of those unfortunate Africans"; and a note in the *Cherry-Valley Gazette* (1818) lamenting "bloody minded" bounty hunters.[58]

As a single phrase, "bitter draught" appears profusely in American newspapers (at least six original pieces) between 1819 and 1820, when the term, rather than merely performing the role of an epigraph, is often integrated into the debate over Missouri's status as a free or slaveholding state before its admittance to the union. These opinion pieces, almost entirely from northern newspapers, use principles foremost in their disparaging of slavery. "Slavery alone, in whatever shape it exists, is indeed a 'bitter draught,'" a piece in the *Connecticut Mirror* (1819) intones, "but the bitterness of the draught is infinitely increased in all slave holding states."[59] An item under the heading of "Miscellany" in the *Providence Gazette* (1820) asserts, "But were they treated ever so humanely, they are still slaves, and slavery, however disguised, is 'a bitter draught.' It is a state from which the human heart instinctively recoils."[60] Arguing against "*the rights of the States*," *Poulson's Daily Advertiser* of Philadelphia (1820) exclaims, "Still Slavery! thou wilt remain to be a bitter draught, and furnish a standing jest to the revilers of our *free* and EQUAL government!"[61] Time and again, the phrase is seamlessly integrated into abolitionist discourse, reinforcing its role as a touchstone idea, at the same time possibly diminishing its Sternean origin.[62]

In pointing to Sterne's apostrophe, all of the mentions of "bitter draught" echo the more complete appeal of the apostrophe to Slavery and Liberty, and beyond that to the value assigned to the ideas of freedom and liberty in the early republic. By itself the term acts to provoke the individual conscience. The apostrophe is unambiguous in its consideration of the "thousands in all ages" who had been enslaved, a reflection that in itself is set into motion due to the repetition of the starling's phrase, "I can't get out." In a sense, the printed repetition of "bitter draught" shown in these examples mimics the starling's repeated complaint—it rouses its audience to a larger purpose.

The term was also utilized by proslavery advocates. An opinion piece in the *Connecticut Mirror* (1831) begins, "'Disguise slavery as you will,' says STERNE, 'it is a bitter draught.' This is equally true of both master and slave, at the present time, in our Southern states. Fear broods over the helpless inhabitants of Virginia, and South Carolina."[63] An item in the *Newport Mercury* (1828) follows a line of the apostrophe with the explanation that slaves "spend the night in revelry and feasting, while the master is stretched on a sleepless couch."[64] By appropriating the term, these writers seem to concede the influence and weight that Sterne's phrase carried, validating its influence in the contemporary slavery debate, and perhaps even attempting to dull its value by blurring the subject between slave and master. In addition, the term was versatile enough to be applied to a broad range of subjects: slavery at the Cape of Good Hope, the captivity of American sailors by Algerian pirates, indentured servants, and even marriage and taxation—all essentially leveraging the renown of Yorick's apostrophe.[65]

"Bitter draught" perhaps is most suitably situated in writings that effectively extend Sterne's philosophy of benevolence in creative expressions against slavery in this period. For example, a well-wrought imitation entitled "Prosperity and Humanity" reprinted from the London *Courier* that appeared at least twice in U.S. newspapers presses the familiar inhabitants of the Shandy parlor into service for the abolitionist cause. Walter's observations on ancient history lead to a discussion of English commerce, which in turn brings up the subject of the slave trade (via Dr. Slop, "with a sneer"), a notion that "touch[es] on the tenderest string in Yorick's soul." Slop tries to justify the practice, asking Yorick whether it is "the fulfilling of the Divine command" to enslave a "marked" race. "But what that mark was we are not informed" responds Yorick, "might it not have been a particular prominence of belly?" He continues in a serious tone: "we should not forget, that although their complexion is different to our own—their feelings are not. . . . I would more willingly become one of these children of affliction—be lashed like them—faint like them . . . wake to disappointment like them . . . than even speak to justify such dealing." Slop weakly counters that "they are happier than our poor," but Yorick then decisively declares that "whatever our poverty—there is something cheering in the faintest smile of freedom;—such is the structure of our mind."[66] Credibly borrowing Sterne's characters, the anonymous author refutes contemporary arguments in favor of slavery using the sentimental and principled voice of Yorick, also echoing the tone of Sterne's letter to Sancho; the masterful casting of Slop as a villainous proslavery agent, as unsympathetic as ever, further strengthens the link to Shandy Hall and Sterne's work.

Another imitation featured in the *Concord Herald* (1792), entitled "The Metabasist," begins with two lines from the apostrophe, followed by the narrator's uncle exclaiming, "*There are no slaves in heaven!*" A note reveals that this uncle "*was reading Sterne's works*" and smokes a tobacco pipe; his pattern of feeling-driven statements closely parallel those made by Uncle Toby, and serves as an emotional counterpoint in a conversation about slavery, arguing against an unnamed character who attempts to justify the institution through custom or scripture. The uncle's tone hits home on the subject; he exclaims, "as to your doctrine, that the Negroes are incapable of taking care of themselves, I cannot believe it to be true; I believe we had better let them try to take care of themselves, before we undertake to take care for them." The narrator departs, repeating to himself "*There are no slaves in heaven*" as he walks home, a simple but pithy thought that the writer seems to have intended to leave with the reader as well.[67] In a period when there were concerns about emancipation leading to widespread chaos, both these abolitionist pieces, extending Sterne's tone and philosophy of benevolence, express an optimism about humanity in general not discordant with the ideas behind the founding of the republic.[68]

Time and again, Sterne's texts utilize sentimental tropes that aimed, as Festa describes it, to "restore the humanity of the slave by emphasizing those aspects of the human that are inalienable, that have no equivalents" (153). In restoring this humanity, then, they fostered a sympathetic audience, furthering the cause of eradication of slavery in the United States. The popular applications of Sterne's texts and ideas to American abolition, and their pervasiveness, both argue for an understanding of the author in the late eighteenth and early nineteenth centuries as not only an advocate for the abolition of slavery, but an effective one at that. This conclusion is at odds with critics who view Sterne's works as largely egocentric and ineffective, such as Markley's claim that sentimentality is strictly "a form of moral self-promotion" (219) that "can neither interrogate nor change the socioeconomic injustices that its 'virtues' promote" (230). Stephen Ahern finds a similar lack of pragmatism in *A Sentimental Journey,* asserting that "Yorick persistently maintains a certain distance from the object of his gaze . . . in a strategy designed more to maximize pleasurable aesthetic response than to actually alleviate the misery at hand."[69] Yet the contemporary reception of Sterne's text in reference to abolition clearly contradicts this position; the appropriation of his sympathetic perspective into American abolitionist discourse, an example of a phenomenon labeled by Festa as a "migrat[-ion] across generic boundaries" (153), was as widespread as it was for a reason. Notwithstanding recent anachronistic analyses, the influence of Sterne's texts in the realm of actual (as opposed to theoretical) politics attests to their efficacy as emotional appeals in the real world.

A last example of Sterne's influence on U.S. abolition is found in the 1792 commonplace book of Anna Coale, the fourteen-year-old daughter of a Baltimore slaveholding family. Prominent on its first page, Coale wrote out the passage from *A Sentimental Journey* from Yorick's discovery of the starling to his description of the captive, and her transcription ends in midsentence, followed by a gap of four pages ripped out from the book. While we will never know the content of those missing pages, Coale was so affected by Sterne's words that she included them in a place of honor; as Catherine Kerrison notes, "something about them struck a chord within her, so she extracted them, carefully and deliberately copying them into a book she would read over and over again."[70] With Coale's inclusion of these words—and it is interesting to note that her father would include manumission of the family's slaves in his will—we can see a parallel to other instances of Sterne's abolitionist influences in America: readers appropriated Sterne's expressions of slavery, it seems clear, so as to feel the condition more acutely themselves. The historian Winthrop D. Jordan observes the "equalitarian" nature of sentimentality in abolitionist discourse that "assumed and played upon a sense of human sameness in feeling."[71] The bond of shared emotions is an undeniable part of the human condition; neither the callousness of the institution of slavery nor of determined literary critics can reduce the idea of sympathy to a sterile, purely political function. Abolitionist literature recognized the power of sentimental description—here distilled into Sterne's metonym "bitter draught"—and used it to build an effective sympathetic bridge between subject and reader, escalating a gradual political change toward the elimination of slavery.

NOTES

1. Sterne's biographers have presented different portraits of the writer in some respects, but are united in their view of his essentially provincial life before 1760. See Arthur H. Cash, *Laurence Sterne: The Early and Middle Years* (London: Methuen, 1975), and Ian Campbell Ross, *Laurence Sterne: A Life* (Oxford: Oxford University Press, 2001), 29–196. The living of Coxwold was added to Sterne's income in 1760 (Cash, 257).

2. Laurence Sterne, *The Sermons of Laurence Sterne: The Text*, ed. Melvyn New, vol. 4 of the Florida Edition of the Works of Laurence Sterne (Gainesville: University Press of Florida, 1996), 99; hereafter cited in the text as *S* followed by the page number. The second edition of the *Sermons* (also published in 1760) omitted this passage. This more emotionally charged version (cited as inspirational by Ignatius Sancho)

found its way into at least one American collection of *The Beauties of Sterne* (Phila-delphia: William Spotswood, 1789), which ran to ten editions. Melvyn New notes that both versions may have been derived "from William Wollaston, *The Religion of Nature Delineated*, 2nd ed. (1724)" (*The Sermons of Laurence Sterne: The Notes,* vol. 5 of the Florida Edition of the Works of Laurence Sterne [Gainesville: University Press of Florida, 1996], 140n89.18–30).

3. For more on the implications of Sterne's unique punctuation in the narrative voice, see Anne Bandry, "*Tristram Shandy* ou le plaisir du tiret," *Études Anglaises: Grande-Bretagne, États-Unis* 41, no. 2 (Apr.–June 1988): 143–54, and Roger B. Moss, "Sterne's Punctuation," *Eighteenth-Century Studies* 15, no. 2 (Winter 1981–1982): 179–200.

4. Markman Ellis, *The Politics of Sensibility: Race, Gender and Commerce in the Sentimental Novel* (Cambridge: Cambridge University Press, 1996), 56; hereafter cited in the text.

5. Harry Harmer, *The Longman Companion to Slavery, Emancipation and Civil Rights* (Harlow, Essex, UK: Pearson Educational, 2001), 9; hereafter cited in the text.

6. Laurence Sterne, *The Life and Opinions of Tristram Shandy, Gentleman*, ed. Melvyn New and Joan New, vol. 2 of the Florida Edition of the Works of Laurence Sterne (Gainesville: University Press of Florida, 1984), 9.6.747; hereafter cited as *TS* followed by volume, chapter, and page number in the text.

7. It is worth noting that the ethic of reciprocity (also called the Golden Rule) appears in many sermons of the period, which, in tandem with the sympathetic portrayal of the enslaved, may be seen as preparing audiences for more specific abolitionist arguments. For more on sentiment and Sterne's sermons, see Melvyn New, "The Odd Couple: Laurence Sterne and John Norris of Bemerton," *Philological Quarterly* 75, no. 3 (Summer 1996): 361–85.

8. Though the words "wench" and "slut" may carry strong negative connotations in the early twenty-first century, they had more neutral, or even affectionate, meanings in Sterne's era. The *OED* defines "wench" at the time as "a girl, maid, young woman" or "a female servant"; "slut" was more a term of disapproval, though the *OED* allows a "playful use, without the imputation of bad qualities."

9. As Ellis notes, "Trim's initial line of enquiry . . . refers to the contemporary debate about the status of Africans—both religiously and biologically" (70). J. R. Oldfield, in *Popular Politics and British Anti-Slavery* (Portland, OR: Frank Cass, 1998), attributes this growing awareness to several factors: a combination of increased literacy, the growth of newspapers, and sympathetic textual portrayals of slaves, including those in children's readers (9–40).

10. Some aspects of Sterne's texts drew criticism in his time, but the character of Uncle Toby was admired widely, and would go on to become a cult figure of sorts in the nineteenth century. See *Sterne: The Critical Heritage*, ed. Alan B. Howes (Boston: Routledge and Kegan Paul, 1974), 60, 76, and 140; W. G. Day, "Charles Robert Leslie's 'My Uncle Toby and the Widow Wadman,'" *Shandean* 9 (1997): 83–108; and W. B. Gerard, *Laurence Sterne and the Visual Imagination* (Burlington: Ashgate, 2006), 168.

11. An earlier passage in *Tristram Shandy* treats the subject of chattel slavery indirectly, suggesting more than is immediately revealed. At the end of volume 4,

Tristram asks, "now that you have just got to the end of these four volumes——one thing I have to *ask* is, how you feel your heads?" and then launches into the health benefits of "True *Shandeism*," which "makes the wheel of life run long and chearfully round" (*TS*, 4.32.401). He then considers, "Was I left like *Sancho Pança*, to chuse my kingdom, it should not be maritime—or a kingdom of blacks to make a penny of—no, it should be a kingdom of hearty laughing subjects" (*TS*, 4.32.402). The allusion, of course, is to *Don Quixote*, specifically (as per the Florida editors) the passage where Sancho considers means of exploiting his master's realms; if the territory includes the "Land of the Negroes," he would generate profit through slavery. See Melvyn New with Richard A. Davies and W. G. Day, *The Life and Opinions of Tristram Shandy, Gentleman: The Notes*, vol. 3 of the Florida Edition of the Works of Laurence Sterne (Gainesville: University Press of Florida, 1984), 334n402.1–4. The reference is from Cervantes, 2.27–28. Tristram's stated priorities here are of a whole with the rest of his work, which stresses the heart over the head (or the pocketbook, for that matter), and this statement, at the conclusion of a two-volume installment, carries particular weight.

12. Brycchan Carey, *British Abolitionism and the Rhetoric of Sensibility* (Basingstoke, Hampshire, UK: Palgrave Macmillan, 2005), 58; hereafter cited in the text.

13. Shirley Samuels, introduction to *The Culture of Sentiment: Race, Gender, and Sentimentality in Nineteenth-Century America* (New York: Oxford University Press, 1992), 5.

14. Laurence Sterne, *A Sentimental Journey through France and Italy* and *Continuation of the Bramine's Journal*, ed. Melvyn New and W. G. Day, vol. 6 of the Florida Edition of the Works of Laurence Sterne (Gainesville: University Press of Florida, 2002), 96; hereafter cited in the text as *ASJ* followed by page number.

15. Paul Moore, "Sterne, Tristram, Yorick, Birds, and Beasts," *British Journal for Eighteenth-Century Studies* 10.1 (Oct. 2008): 45; hereafter cited in the text.

16. For more on these parallels, see *A Sentimental Journey through France and Italy*, ed. Gardner D. Stout, Jr. (Berkeley: University of California Press, 1967), 205–6n37–40.

17. Lynn Festa, *Sentimental Figures of Empire in Eighteenth-Century Britain and France* (Baltimore: Johns Hopkins University Press, 2006), 31; hereafter cited in the text.

18. Arthur Hill Cash, *Sterne's Comedy of Moral Sentiments: The Ethical Dimensions of the "Journey"* (Pittsburgh: Duquesne University Press, 1966), 82.

19. John Mullan, *Sentiment and Sociability* (Oxford: Clarendon, 1988), 194; hereafter cited in the text.

20. Marcus Wood, *Slavery, Empathy, and Pornography* (Oxford: Oxford University Press, 2002), 16–17; hereafter cited in the text. Wood and other critics who pursue similar strategies also habitually label the servant a "slave" even though the term is not used in the text (indeed, she may be free), perhaps subconsciously employing a strategy to denigrate the character's dignity through rhetoric.

21. Robert Markley, "Sentimentality as Performance: Shaftesbury, Sterne, and the Theatrics of Virtue," *The New 18th Century: Theory, Politics, English Literature*, ed. Felicity Nussbaum and Laura Brown (1987; New York: Routledge, 1991), 226.

22. Aristotle, *The Rhetoric and Poetics of Aristotle*, trans. W. Rhys Roberts and Ingram Bywater (New York: Modern Library, 1954), 133.1393a.25, 133.1393a.29.

23. Cicero, *De Oratore Book III, De Fato, Paradoxa Stoicorum, De Partitione Oratoria*, trans. H. Rackham, Loeb Classical Library (1948; Cambridge, MA: Harvard University Press, 1992), 355.17.57–59.

24. See Marshall Myers, "The Use of Pathos in Charity Letters: Some Notes Toward a Theory and Analysis," *Technical Writing and Communication* 37.1 (2007): 8.

25. Adam Smith, *The Theory of Moral Sentiments*, ed. Knud Haakonssen (2002; Cambridge: Cambridge University Press, 2004), 11; hereafter cited in the text. Tim [J. T.] Parnell notes this passage from Smith in his edition of *A Sentimental Journey through France and Italy* (1968; Oxford: Oxford University Press, 2003), 237n61.

26. That Sterne was a writer of antislavery passages in the sentimental mode in his time, of course, is neither surprising nor unique. Novels like Sara Scott's *The History of Sir George Ellison* and poems like Thomas Day's "The Dying Negro" would appear in the 1760s and 1770s, creating highly sympathetic portrayals of enslaved Africans and arguing both explicitly and implicitly for the abolishment of slavery. Carey examines the techniques of these and similar texts in detail, identifying an emphasis on "ideas of common feeling and mutual sympathy" (38). While Sterne certainly represents this sympathetic bond in his texts, what distinguishes him from these writers (the quality of his prose aside) is his fame, which lent credence and familiarity to his abolitionist message. The effectiveness of the description of the captive is heightened by biblical allusions, especially for readers familiar with the original references. Stout suggests that Yorick's "choice of an imprisoned captive to exemplify slavery" is connected with Matthew 25:36–40, which begins, "I was in prison, and ye came unto me"; he further observes that part of this passage is "cited and paraphrased" in Sermon 3, "Philanthropy recommended" (201n9–10). Melvyn New points out another possible biblical reference, Hebrews 13:3: "Remember them that are in bonds, as bound with them; and them which suffer adversity, as being yourselves also in the body" (*ASJ*, 329–30n97.11ff). Additional likely biblical connections suggested by Tim Parnell include Proverbs 13:12 ("Hope deferred maketh the heart sick") and Psalm 105:18 in the Book of Common Prayer ("the iron enter into his soul") (237n61). These reminders of Sterne's occupational immersion in scripture inevitably add a dimension to Sterne's abolitionist ideas: that compassion in the eighteenth century is fundamentally and immediately identified with Christianity. This often-overlooked link, as a foundation to sentimental philosophy, adds an element of indelible genuineness to Sterne's passage.

27. Quintillian, *The Institutio Oratoria*, trans. H. E. Butler, Loeb Classical Library (1920; Cambridge, MA: Harvard University Press, 1963), 437.6.2.34–37.

28. While as a consequence Tristram or Yorick did not immediately lobby Parliament for cessation of the slave trade or board a ship to intervene in the slave trade, Yorick does carefully catalog elements of the captive's humanity in the passage, clearly implying the injustice of the character's imprisonment. As in the case of the African servant, an essential attribute of the captive is his equality as reflected in his ability to feel, a quality demonstrated by his affections for friends and family as well as his personal dejection under the circumstances; this in turn establishes a sense of

equivalence between the character (another synecdoche) and the reader, which argues on behalf of all those enslaved.

29. See James Walvin, "Ignatius Sancho: The Man and His Times," 94–113, and Jane Girdham, "Black Musicians in England: Ignatius Sancho and His Contemporaries," 116–25, both in *Ignatius Sancho: An African Man of Letters* (London: National Portrait Gallery, 1997). Ellis records an 1889 *Notes and Queries* mention of Sancho that relates that "Sancho's trade card celebrates his own brand of tobacco, and depicts two African boys" (John Pickford, "Ignatius Sancho," *Notes and Queries*, 7th ser., viii [1889]: 33). The tobacco itself is, of course, a product of slavery: as Ellis sees it, Sancho is "selling the produce of his enslaved compatriots to their enslavers" (58). Political ambiguity abounded, then as now.

30. Sukhev Sandhu, "An African Man of Letters," in *Ignatius Sancho: An African Man of Letters*, 53.

31. *Letters of the Late Ignatius Sancho, An African*, ed. Vincent Carretta (Edinburgh: Edinburgh University Press, 1998), 73–74; hereafter cited in the text. Sancho's *Letters*, first published posthumously in 1782, might be seen as influential on the American abolition movement as well. Interestingly, it was not published in the United States (though copies from England undoubtedly were imported), though the antislavery letter quoted above was included in the 1775 edition of Sterne's *Letters*, which was reprinted in America. Sandhu points out that "relatively few of [the] . . . letters deal with slavery or what might be called 'black issues'" (10) and that he was "by no means a slavish parrot of Sterne that he has often been cast as by critics" ("Sterne and the Coal-Black Jolly African," *Shandean* 12 [2001]: 20). At the same time, Sterne clearly had his impact on Sancho: Madeleine Descargues observes, "there is no need indeed for Momus's glass to see the omnipresence of Sterne in Sancho's heart" ("Ignatius Sancho's *Letters*," *Shandean* 3 [1991]: 162). In England at least the connection between volume 9 of *Tristram Shandy* and Sancho caused an upwelling of sympathy; as Wilbur L. Cross relates, the fashionable "courted the sentimental Negro" and would extend their delicacy of feeling to gently discouraging, rather than killing, flies (*The Life and Times of Laurence Sterne* [1925; New Haven: Yale University Press, 1929], 413–14).

32. *Laurence Sterne: The Letters*, ed. Melvyn New and Peter de Voogd, vols. 7 and 8 of the Florida Edition of the Works of Laurence Sterne (Gainesville: University Press of Florida, 2009), 8:504–5.

33. For a comprehensive discussion of the exchange, see Madeleine Descargues, "Ignatius Sancho's *Letters*," 145–66.

34. See Ellis, *Politics of Sensibility,* 62. This gesture has often been painted as particularly opportunistic (see below), although Sterne was likely revising with readability and audience in mind. Sterne felt these letters important enough for inclusion in the letter book, which was almost certainly based on the significance of the subject matter, with an eye to publication. The letter Sterne wrote to Sancho is important to consider in a reception context for the purposes of gauging its influence; in the eighteenth century the published correspondence of a man of letters was read alongside his other work; in this case, Sterne's letters ran to many editions. Sancho, too, undoubtedly influenced by Sterne, was a prolific man of letters, and his correspondence made its way into print; in the case of the correspondence with Sterne, both sides

were included. Thus Sterne's letter, published in 1775 in Sancho's volume as well as the new collection of letters compiled by his daughter Lydia, carried its own weight as an abolitionist text. With its feel of active history and mix of celebrity, Sancho's letter and Sterne's response represent an enticing combination to literary critics, an exchange addressing a political issue between contemporaries, both of whom had forged distinct and complex identities. Sterne, a self-confessed appropriator of texts (one recalls the passage on plagiarism in *Tristram Shandy* [*TS*, 5.1.408] copied from Burton's *Anatomy*), has been suspected of opportunism in this exchange; did he use Sancho's letter as inspiration for his two antislavery passages in his fictions (and slyly misrepresent this to Sancho)? While Sancho merely had been considered imitative of Sterne (and his style indeed may owe something to him), more recently critics like Ellis have argued for Sancho as Sterne's source for the captive passage (70–71ff). Carey sees that "an emerging consensus now suggests that Sancho's intervention was both an original and a radical gesture that strongly influenced Sterne" (57). Short of the discovery of additional documentation, it may be impossible to determine whether Sterne was spurred by Sancho to include the mention of slavery in one, or perhaps two, or his fictions, or whether he was in truth working on these antislavery statements when he received Sancho's letter.

35. Arthur H. Cash, *Laurence Sterne: The Later Years* (1986; London: Routledge, 1992), 254.

36. Carol Watts, *The Cultural Work of Empire: The Seven Years' War and the Imagining of the Shandean State* (Toronto: University of Toronto Press, 2007), 176; hereafter cited in the text.

37. Sancho's letters had an impact of their own, being reprinted four times in England. Ellis notes that Sancho's book was "read by many for its testimony to the writer's extraordinary biography" (59). Carey argues that the book "was constructed and deployed, both by Sancho himself and his editor, in the form of an epistolary novel of sentiment illustrating the immorality of slavery" ("'The Hellish Means of Killing and Kidnapping': Ignatius Sancho and the Campaign against the 'Abominable Traffic for Slaves,'" from *Discourses of Slavery and Abolition: Britain and its Colonies, 1760–1838*, ed. Brycchan Carey, Markman Ellis, and Sara Salih [Basingstoke, Hampshire, UK: Palgrave Macmillan, 2004], 82).

38. A study of Sterne's popular influence on the issue likely would be at least the length of a volume. Its reach is suggested by Sancho's comment, "You, who are universally read, and as universally admired" (73) as well as the English abolitionist Thomas Clarkson's remark that "in his account of the Negro girl . . . [Sterne] took decidedly the part of the oppressed Africans. . . . [and] procured a certain portion of feeling in their favour" (cited in Ellis, *Politics of Sensibility*, 69.)

39. These data were aggregated through the combined catalogs of the British Library and Yale University searched during November 2008 and are intended to provide an approximate rather than a comprehensive bibliography of American editions. See also Lodwick Hartley, "American Editions of Laurence Sterne to 1800: A Checklist," from *The Winged Skull: Papers from the Laurence Sterne Bicentenary Conference,* ed. Arthur H. Cash and John M. Stedmond (Kent, OH: Kent State University Press, 1971), 311–12.

40. These examples were located through the Early American Imprints (I and II) database; it is very likely additional titles including the apostrophe were published in this period.

41. The Early American Newspapers Series 1 database was formed around Clarence Brigham's authoritative bibliography, *History and Bibliography of American Newspapers, 1690–1820*, 2 vols. (Worcester, MA: American Antiquarian Society, 1947), and additional bibliographies. It includes more than one thousand newspapers published from 1690 to 1922. While it clearly is not a comprehensive record of American newspapers published within the chronological scope of this study, it provides a very useful sampling. It should be noted that numerous references to other antislavery passages from Sterne's work, such as the tale of the African servant, were apparent in this period, as well. The searches in this study were conducted in November 2008 and confirmed in March 2009.

42. Jeffrey L. Pasley, *"The Tyranny of Printers": Newspaper Politics in the Early American Republic* (Charlottesville: University of Virginia Press, 2001), 10; hereafter cited in the text.

43. Clarence Brigham, *Journals and Journeymen: A Contribution to the History of Early American Newspapers* (Philadelphia: University of Pennsylvania Press, 1950), 3–11.

44. "Liberty and Slavery," *National Aegis*, 23 October 1805.

45. "Liberty and Slavery," *Litchfield Republican*, 13 March 1822.

46. "Liberty and Slavery," *Olio*, 19 May 1803.

47. "Liberty and Slavery," *Washington Republican,* 16 September 1809.

48. Other appearances of the apostrophe in full, with and without the starling and captive episodes, include "The Starling," *Vermont Gazette*, 2 May 1791; "From Sterne," *National Intelligencer* (Washington, D.C.), 3 December 1800; "Liberty and Slavery," *Olio* (Georgetown, Washington D.C.), 19 May 1803; "The Starling," *Hive* (Northhampton, Massachusetts), 17 January 1804; "Liberty and Slavery," *National Aegis*, 23 October 1805; "Liberty and Slavery," *Newburyport Herald*, 29 October 1805; "Liberty and Slavery," *National Aegis*, 28 September 1808; "Miscellany: The Captive; From Sterne," *Republican Messenger* (Sherburne, New York), 4 December 1810; and "Liberty," *Providence Patriot*, 20 October 1827.

49. "Slavery," *Political Calendar*, 31 December 1804; *Salem Register*, 31 December 1804; and *Bee,* 8 January 1805.

50. "Disguise Thyself as Thou Will [*sic*], Still Slavery Thou Art a Bitter Draught," *Connecticut Mirror*, 22 May 1830, and "Disguise Thyself as Thou Will [*sic*], Still Slavery Thou Art a Bitter Draught," *New Bedford Mercury*, 28 May 1830. Both cite the *Kinderhook Herald* as their source, further evidence of the limited scope of the Early American Newspapers Series 1 database.

51. "Melioration of Slavery," *New-Hampshire Gazette*, 14 January 1812.

52. *Baltimore Patriot*, 19 November 1821.

53. Ibid.

54. "For the Observer," *Concord Observer*, 1 March 1819.

55. "The Traveller," *Village Record*, 24 June 1818.

56. "Missouri Question," *City of Washington Gazette*, 28 April 1820.

57. "Republican Celebration—at Dudley," *National Aegis*, 12 July 1820.

58. Edward Rushton, "Expostulatory Letter to George Washington . . . on his continuing to be a Proprietor of slaves," *Time Piece, and Literary Companion*, 26 May 1797, repr. pamphlet, Liverpool 1797; *Farmers Repository*, 18 August 1819; and *Cherry Valley Gazette*, 26 November 1818.

59. "Slavery," *Connecticut Mirror*, 16 August 1819.

60. "Miscellany," *Providence Gazette*, 31 July 1820.

61. "Slavery Versus the Constitution," *Poulson's American Daily Advertiser*, 24 January 1820.

62. An example of this diminishment is seen in a letter in the 8 December 1820 *American Farmer* that uses the phrase in context of "heavy clogs of several inches thick" worn by slaves in the field.

63. "Slavery," *Connecticut Mirror*, 17 December 1831.

64. "Miscellany," *Newport Mercury*, 2 February 1828.

65. "The Slaves. From Walks and Sketches at the Cape of Good Hope," *Reporter* (Brattleboro, VT) 5 May 1804; "Benevolence," *Boston Gazette*, 8 December 1794; "White Slavery," *Washington City Weekly Gazette*, 21 June 1817; "Disguise Thyself as Their Wife, Still Slavery thou Art a Bitter Draught," *Providence Gazette*, 31 January 1820; and "Anecdote," *New-York Journal*, 30 June 1774.

66. "Prosperity and Humanity," *Philadelphia Gazette*, 19 May 1797, and *Mercantile Advertiser* (New York), 7 October 1799; both repr. from *London Courier*, n.d.

67. "The Metabasist.—No. VII," *Concord Herald*, 8 February 1792.

68. See Andrew Burstein, *Sentimental Democracy: The Evolution of America's Romantic Self-Image* (New York: Hill and Wang, 1999).

69. Stephen Ahern, *Affected Sensibilities: Romantic Excess and the Genealogy of the Novel, 1680–1810* (Brooklyn, NY: AMS, 2007), 95.

70. Catherine Kerrison, *Claiming the Pen: Women and Intellectual Life in the Early American South* (Ithaca: Cornell University Press, 2006), 176.

71. Winthrop D. Jordan, *White Over Black: American Attitudes Toward the Negro, 1550–1812* (Chapel Hill: University of North Carolina Press, 1968), 369.

Chapter Eleven

Attribution Problems in Sterne's Ecclesiastical and Secular Politickings

W. G. Day

When Laurence Sterne resubmitted his manuscript of the first two volumes of *The Life and Opinions of Tristram Shandy, Gentleman* to Robert Dodsley in October 1759, he added a postscript to his cover letter in which he declared: "All Locality is taken out of the Book—the Satyr general,—Notes are added where wanted—& the whole made more saleable."[1] This evidence of revision was in response to Dodsley's initial rejection of the manuscript in June 1759. It is generally assumed that the suggestion of local satire is an indication that in its urtext *Tristram Shandy* had material similar to that found in *A Political Romance*, the pamphlet that had appeared in 1759 satirizing many dignitaries of the Minster Church of York.

In 1748 there arose a dispute between the dean of York, Dr. John Fountayne, and the archbishop, Matthew Hutton, about the right to appoint substitute preachers in the cathedral. Fountayne appears to have had right on his side by virtue of the long-standing tradition that the deans appointed such preachers; but Hutton, provoked and encouraged by an ecclesiastical lawyer, Dr. Francis Topham, saw this as an opportunity to assert his archiepiscopal authority. This quarrel is regarded as the stimulus for the writing of *A Political Romance* ten years later. The exchange of letters between the warring parties is preserved in a volume in the York Minster Library (shelf mark A2[1] h).[2] An ink inscription of the front cover reads: "1749/50 Correspondence between the Archbishop & Dean respecting the Appointment of a Residentiary" and another inked title on the spine reads: "Residentiaryship." It is noteworthy for the extent of material in Sterne's autograph: only the manuscripts of *A Sentimental Journey* and "Continuation of the Bramine's Journal" are more extensive.[3]

The manuscript is in four different hands, of which two can be securely identified: John Fountayne and Laurence Sterne. One of the other two is a legal hand. The volume starts in Fountayne's handwriting, which occupies folio 2a to partway down folio 19a. The material in this section is made up of a brief introduction to the dispute: a letter from Fountayne to the archbishop, dated 9 December 1749, a reply dated 12 December, and a further letter from Fountayne dated 16 December. From 19a to partway down 22a Sterne copies out a letter from the archbishop dated 19 December before Fountayne resumes copying, with a letter of 23 December that continues to the bottom of folio 25a. Sterne then writes out the archbishop's response of 26 December, which occupies 26a–29a. This letter has the first of a number of annotations by Fountayne, which is written on folio 28b. Fountayne resumes copying the main body of the correspondence with his own letter of 30 December, folios 30a–32a, and at the end of the letter writes "To this the AB^p wrote the following answer," which answer is in Sterne's hand and takes up folio 33a. Facing this on folio 32b is another brief note by Fontayne: "By ye same post Y^e AB^p wrote ye following Letter to Dr Sterne, a copy of wch was given to me by Dr Topham /," and there follows the archbishop's letter in Sterne's hand. A brief narrative in Fountayne's hand is found on 33b; a letter on 15 January written out by Fountayne is on 34a, and there is a further narrative link by the dean on 34b. From 35a–47a is Sterne's principal contribution to the volume: a letter from the archbishop to Dr. Topham on 13 January (35a–37a), Fountayne's response on 17 January (38a–42a), and the archbishop's reply on 20 January (42a–47a). This extensive section in Sterne's autograph is interrupted by one link supplied by Fountayne (37a) and the dean's frequent annotations, on occasion splenetic, on the facing versos (40b, 42b, 43b, 44b [twice], and 46b). This is the end of Sterne's contribution to the volume: 48a provides a further narrative link in Fountayne's hand, and from thence to the end of the correspondence (58a) the copying is carried out by an unidentified third person, with brief links in Fountayne's hand. Following the correspondence there is a gap of two leaves and then a section headed "The Repeal of Abp Rotherham's Decree," a key document in the dispute, which is written in a legal hand found nowhere else in the manuscript. Following a much larger blank section, the final six folios (83a–88a) are devoted to "The Copy of The Extracts refer'd to Page ye 17th." Of this the title, the correction to the first letter "B," and the spelling of "Praecentor" in the second line, are in Fountayne's hand, while the rest is in the hand of the unidentified third party.

This manuscript has been thought to be of some significance by Sterne's biographers: Arthur Cash says that Fountayne, distrusting Topham, who was acting as the archbishop's go-between, "started a volume of letters, copies of the correspondence which had passed among the principals in the quarrel. In this task he was assisted by Laurence Sterne, who copied many of the letters. Although Sterne played no public role in the coup, it looks as though he was advising the Dean."[4] Ian Campbell Ross is more positive in his assessment: "Fountayne, meanwhile, was evidently suspicious of the archbishop and his emissary and, with considerable foresight, began keeping a complete record of the correspondence passing between himself and Hutton. Among those who assisted him was Laurence Sterne. The record itself, unused at the time, was to prove significant a decade later, not only for Fountayne and the ecclesiastical power game but for Laurence Sterne's entire future as a writer."[5] Unfortunately, both biographers appear to have been misled by this collection of letters.

The first thing to notice is that initially Sterne's contribution is the copying of replies from the archbishop, rather than Fountayne's own missives. It is not until 38a that Sterne is found writing out one of the dean's letters, and this is the only occasion on which he is to be found copying an item originating from the dean's camp. This hardly suggests that Sterne was "advising" the dean, and is more indicative of the purely subservient role of a copyist. It is worth noting that Sterne does have a very legible hand and is ideally suited to the role of copying material to which reference may be needed. But the most telling evidence to suggest that the conventional biographer's view of the importance of this document is misconceived is to be found in an error that both Fountayne and Sterne make in their copying. On folio 7a Fountayne sets out his first letter in the war, a response to the archbishop's letter to Dr. Herring, the chancellor of the diocese and father-in-law to William Berdmore, whose elevation to the residentiaryship made vacant by the death of Dr. Samuel Baker was the starting point of the dispute. There is an introductory note, "Upon this I wrote the following Letter to the ArchBishop./" and the letter is headed "York Decem^r 9th 1749" as one would expect, except that the year has been corrected from "1758." Sterne makes a similar blunder on folio 38a. The headnote, as usual, is in Fountayne's hand: "Upon seeing this Letter from ye AB^p to Dr Topham I wrote to his Grace ye following Letter." On the next line "York Jan^{ry} 17th /" is in Fountayne's hand, and the date is completed by Sterne: "1749." That is Sterne's corrected date: initially he had written "1759." Both Fountayne and Sterne initially postdate material by a decade. There is only one logical explanation for this. One occasionally misdates material—writing the previous year's date on checks at the beginning of a new calendar year is an error most people will have experienced—but to date an item ten years into the future is almost inconceivable, and for two people to make the same error in the same record eliminates the "almost." This volume of letters must have been rather hastily put together in 1759 by Fountayne and a small group of helpers, including Sterne, as material to be used if necessary in the renewed hostilities between the dean and Dr. Topham. This was the dispute that generated the published exchange of letters between Fountayne and Topham, to which Sterne may well have contributed, and resulted in the appearance of *A Political Romance.*[6] The "Residentiaryship" volume may be ignored as evidence of Sterne's involvement in ecclesiastical politicking in the late 1740s and of his development as a writer. There is no evidence of any of this manuscript being indicative of a collaboration with Fountayne at the time; it is a collection of copies to which Sterne made no original contribution. That the material has been attributed to him is possibly the result of a desire on the part of certain Sterneans to add to his relatively limited corpus.

The same desire seems to have affected perceptions of Sterne's involvement in secular politics, where there are more complex problems. The part Sterne played in the by-election of 1741–1742 for the county of York, in which he supported the Independent Whig, Cholmley Turner, against the Country Party candidate, George Fox, was first explored by Lewis Perry Curtis, subsequently qualified by Cedric Collyer, and further contributions have been suggested by Kenneth Monkman; and the writings of these three scholars have colored the presentations of Sterne by his principal biographers, Arthur Cash and Ian Campbell Ross.[7] These attributions need to be looked at more closely. This is particularly the case with what has been thought to have been one of Sterne's most important early writings. In *The Politicks of Laurence Sterne* (1929) Curtis wrote, "To-day in the Minster Library there is preserved an octavo pamphlet of eight pages, of which the author is unrecorded. It bears the title *Query upon Query; Being an Answer to J.S.'s Letter Printed in the* York Courant, York: Printed in the Year 1741. This precious little brochure is Sterne's first book" (47). The pamphlet to which Curtis referred is still in the Hailstone Collection in the Minster Library (shelf mark Y/MA 143.1 L). It is a unique copy of a version of a text that exists in a surprising number of variants; indeed, of all the items attributed to Sterne, *Query upon Query* provides the most problems for an editor. Cedric Collyer first pointed out that, though there is some evidence to justify Laurence Sterne's involvement in the authorship of at least one of the versions, it appears that his uncle, Jaques Sterne, was also actively involved in the writing of other versions. It is now generally accepted that Curtis was not in possession of key manuscript material identified by Collyer, which would have led him to qualify his claim. However, whether the version Collyer identified as being by Laurence Sterne is indeed by him is questionable, and the evidence needs to be reviewed.

The history of the publication of the text known as *Query upon Query* is somewhat convoluted. It appears to have been initially printed in the *York Courant,* no. 837, for Tuesday, 27 October 1741, where it occupied the first two columns of the front page. Fortuitously, the Public Library at York has two files of the *York Courant* for 1741, and, most unusually, a collation of the two copies—the only recorded copies of the newspaper for that date—reveals that there are substantive differences between the texts of this item. This was an unexpected discovery, as R. M. Wiles pointed out that though there were variants in the inner formes of copies of the *York Courant*, the outer formes were identical.[8] For reasons that are not immediately clear, Caesar Ward, the printer of the *York Courant,* elected to revise parts of his front page on 27 October 1741.[9] Another version of the text appeared the following day in London in the *Daily Gazetteer* for Wednesday 28 October 1741; and a third version was printed in the *Leeds Mercury* of 3 November. It may be that other newspapers, of which we no longer have copies of the relevant dates, also printed this item.[10] And there is the pamphlet version.

Prior to Collyer's article, the attribution of *Query upon Query* to Laurence Sterne was based on a number of assertions in the *York Courant,* and it was assumed that these assertions also validated the attribution of earlier contributions. In the issue on 29 September 1741 (no. 833), Caesar Ward inserted a brief note: "When the Writer of a Letter sent Yesterday to the Printing Office, reflecting upon a worthy Clergyman in this County, and sign'd *J. Wainman*, thinks fit to substitute *his own Name*, it will be soon enough to insert it; in the mean Time it may be proper to inform the *Vicar*, who penn'd it, that the Printer of this Paper is not to be impos'd upon by *counterfeited Letters* from *Guisborough*, nor *fictitious Names* in *York*" (p. 3, col. 2).[11] That Sterne is the clergyman alluded to may be deduced from the reference to Guisborough, which is the nearest post town for Skelton Castle, where Sterne frequently went to visit his close friend John Hall-Stevenson. A slightly less allusive reference appeared at the conclusion of an unsigned letter from Leeds, dated October 31, in the *York Courant* for Tuesday 3 November 1741:

> I am sorry, Sir, that I have taken up so much of your Time and Paper, and promise never to trouble you again, since the four following Lines of Mr Pope will stand for a sufficient Answer to all that the Author of the last Queries has writ, or can write, on this Subject.
>
> > *Let L——y scribble——what! that Thing of Silk,*
> > *L——y that mere white Curd of Ass's-Milk?*
> > *Satire or Sense, alass! can L——y feel?*
> > *Who breaks a Butterfly upon a Wheel?*[12]

The "L——y" allows for the substitution "Lorry," the name Sterne was to use of himself in *A Political Romance* and that appears to have been a name by which he was known to several others. Part of the effect of this personal attack was to show that the Fox party was aware of the name of one of the leading collaborators in the Turner camp, while mocking the latter for their failure to identify "J.S.," who had become the principal thorn in their flesh.

The *York Courant* for Tuesday, 10 November 1741 (no. 839: p.1, col. 2) contained a piece acknowledged by Sterne, and with a headnote, which, in association with the items thus far described, may well have led Curtis and Monkman to some of their assumptions about the attribution of the various items written to support Cholmley Turner's candidature:

> *The following Letter is wrote by the same Gentleman that has wrote every Piece that has been inserted in this Paper in Vindication of Cholmley Turner, Esq;*
>
> To the PRINTER *of the* YORK COURANT.
>
> SIR,
>
> 'As J.S. in your last Courant has shown some Marks of Fear and Penitence in denying his Name, and promising never to offend again, it would be almost an Act of Cruelty to pursue the Man any farther; however since he has left the Field with ill Language in his Mouth, I shall send one Shot after him, which, I am confident, is too well founded to miss him.
>
> 'A certain nasty Animal in *Egypt*, which, I think, *Herodotus* takes notice of, when he finds he cannot possibly defend himself, and prey any longer, partly out of Malice, partly out of Policy, he lets fly backward full against his Adversary, and thereby covers his Retreat with the Fumes of his own Filth and Excrement.
>
> 'As this Creature is naturally very *impotent*, and its chief Safety depends on a plentiful Discharge on such Occasions, the Naturalists affirm, that Self-preservation directs it to a certain Vegitable on the Banks of the River *Nile*, which constantly arms it with a proper Habit of Body against all Emergencies. I am,
>
> *Yours*,   L.S.[13]

Having apparently broken his cover, and in such a vitriolic fashion, Sterne became the focal point for a sustained campaign of personal invective by the supporters of George Fox. But first there was a fairly reasoned piece in the *York Courant* on 24 November 1741 (no. 841, p. 3, col. 2) written by James Scott,[14] a clergyman at Leeds, whom the Turner supporters had wrongly identified as the principal Fox apologist.[15] The letter was addressed "*To* L.S. *at* York" and laid the blame for the misidentification squarely on Laurence Sterne. Subscribed, "*Leeds, Nov*. 19, 1741," the piece was signed "JAMES SCOTT." In a campaign that had been notable for its use of anonymous pieces, and squibs signed solely by initials, this was the first fully acknowledged identification. It was only a matter of weeks before Sterne himself was explicitly named in the increasingly bitter campaign. In the *York Courant* on 8 December 1741 (p. 4, col. 1):

York, *Dec. 8.*

A Printed Advertisement, by way of Letter to the Rev. Mr. *Scott* of *Leeds*, having been dispersed about the County last Week, wherein the Author, by what he calls a Chronological Argument, has urg'd, that a Passage in the *York Courant* of *Sept.* 25th, was the Occasion of his insinuating the said Mr *Scott* to have been the Writer of several Letters relating to the present contested Election; I think it proper, in Vindication of myself, to set his Chronology right; and to state the Matter of Fact as it *really* was.

On *Monday* the 28th of *September*, a Letter was brought to Me by a Person, who said he had it given him in the *Minster*, and had Orders to pay for its being inserted in the *York Courant*. Upon perusing the same, I observed that it contain'd several Scandalous and false reflections; and therefore return'd for Answer, that unless the Author would sign his Name, it should not appear in my Paper. Hereupon the Messenger went away, but instantly return'd with the said Letter, sign'd by the Name of *J. Wainman*; To this second Message I sent Word, that I knew the Hand-writing to be that of *Mr Lawrence Sterne, Prebendary* of St. Peter's, York; and that I was not to be imposed upon in that Manner.

But to come to the Chronology of the Matter. I do affirm, that the above Letter, in Mr Sterne's Hand-Writing, concluded thus, *I am, Rev. Sir, Yours*; for which Reason, in the next Day's *Courant*, I excused the Omission thereof in the following Manner:

When the Writer of a Letter sent Yesterday to the Printing-Office, reflecting upon a worthy Clergyman in this County, and sign'd J. Wainman, thinks fit to subscribe his own Name, it will be soon enough to insert it.

Now the Reader will hereby at once observe, that my saying in the Paper of *Tuesday, September* 29th, that I had refused a Letter signed, *J. Wainman*, reflecting on a worthy Clergyman in this Diocese, was owing to the said Letter's concluding with the Words, *I am, Rev. Sir, Yours*; and consequently that Mr *Sterne*, who, in his Letter sent to me, on *Monday, September* 28th, called *J.S. by the Stile of Rev. Sir*, could not borrow that Appellation from a Passage in the York Courant of the Day after. So much for that Gentleman's Skill in Chronology; but I would advise him next Time he abuses me to have a better Memory.

I can't help taking Notice of one Circumstance more, *viz.* on *Thursday* the 22nd of *October*, a Letter was brought to me in Vindication of Mr *Turner*, by Way of *Quære*, in which there were some Passages I made Objections to, whereupon the Messenger went away, and return'd again with those obnoxious Passages expunged, and I agreed to insert it in the next Paper: but the same Evening the abovementioned Mr *Sterne* came to me, and said, HE *had made some Mistake in the Letter which* HE *had sent me that Evening, and particularly by inserting the Word* NOT *superfluously*; whereupon I gave him his Letter, and he made some few Alterations in it, and ask'd me, *Why I had objected to any Expressions in it*? to which I gave him for Answer, *That they were not Arguments, but personal Abuses*; and I added these Words, *Mr* Sterne, *By an Expression therein, you seem to insinuate, as if* J.S. *the Letter-Writer in the* Courant, *was a Clergyman, I do assure you that he is not a Clergyman.*

As to the Compliments the Writer of the Advertisement, distributed last Week, is pleas'd to pay Me as Printer of the *York Courant*, I pass them over unnoticed as they deserve; and only add, that the above Assertions of mine are *strictly* and *truly* MATTER OF FACT; and upon this I stake my reputation.

CÆSAR WARD

This is an important document that claims that at least one of the political writings offered to the *York Courant* was in Sterne's handwriting, and moreover that the piece in question was signed with another name.

In the meantime "J.S.," who was still unidentified by the Turner camp, returned to personal assaults on Sterne, neatly reworking a passage from Pope's *Epistle to Dr. Arbuthnot* in the *York Courant* of 15 December 1741 (no. 844, p.1, col. 2):

> *Mr* Pope *against* L.S. *once more.*
>> A Wight, who reads not, and but scans and spells;
>> A Word-Catcher that lives on Syllables.
>> Who shames this Scribbler? break one Cobweb thro',
>> It spins the slight self-pleasing Thread a-new:
>> Destroy his Fib or Sophistry, in vain,
>> The Creature's at his dirty Work again,—
>> Thron'd in the Centre of his thin Designs,
>> Proud of a vast Extent of flimzy Lines.
>>> *From his humble Servant,*

J.S.

At this point a new party entered the fray, seriously complicating the secure identification of the authorship of the Turner pieces. Most of the material relating to this by-election is derived from the *York Courant*, a paper openly allied with the Country Party interest and opposed to Cholmley Turner's candidacy. In an effort to counter the influence of Caesar Ward's weekly, those supporting Turner, and chief among them Jaques Sterne, Laurence's uncle, had set up a rival newspaper, the *York Gazetteer*, of which, unfortunately, only a handful of copies are extant. In one of those rare survivals, for 15 December 1741 (no. 41, p. 3, col. 3—p. 4, col. 1), appeared a defense of Laurence Sterne:

York, *Dec.* 15. 1741.

WHEREAS *Cæsar Ward* in order to justify his Conduct with regard to Mr. Scot, has declar'd in his last Week's Courant, that the Letter subscrib'd, *I am, Rev. Sir*, Yours, was offer'd to him in the Hand-Writing of the Rev. Mr. Laurence Sterne; This is to acquaint the Publick, That I am desired by that Worthy Gentleman, to make use of his Name, and declare for him in a publick and Solemn Manner, That the Assertion of *Cæsar Ward* is a downright Falsehood; and that he (Mr. Laurence Sterne) neither Compos'd that Letter, nor transcrib'd it: The Letter (attested upon Oath and certified upon the back of it to be the same carried, to *Cæsar Ward*) is now lodg'd with Mr. Graves, Attorney in *Petergate*, where any Person, acquainted with Mr. Laurence Sterne's Hand, may see it.

As my Brother-Printer has staked his Reputation upon this Point, and has publickly lost it, I may justly hope to draw some Advantage to my Self from it; Since the Publick for the future can never depend upon his VERACITY, the only Substantial Qualification for one in our Business. 'Tis well however for him that he did not depose upon *Oath* what he has asserted upon his *Reputation*; for then he might have forfeited both It and his *Ears together*, which in all Senses wou'd totally have ruin'd him in the Capacity of News-Monger.

I am further authoriz'd by the Gentleman above-mention'd to declare in His name, and in the strongest manner I please, That *Cæsar Ward* did not assure him either at the Time he speaks of, or at any other time whatever, that J.S. the Letter-writer in the COURANT was not a Clergyman. My Brother, when he *invented* and printed this Falsehood, had to be sure forgot, that, but an Hour and a half before this pretended Declaration of His, when the Letter by way of Quære was carried to him by Mr. Graves and Mr. Emmanuel Gregson, he receiv'd it with the Reflection, That it was *"Vicar against Vicar.* This if requir'd will be attested upon both their Oaths.

And He will not *dare* to deny, that, even since Mr. Scott thought proper to disown the Brats laid to him, He has said to Gentlemen of Credit and Distinction, that the Author of those Letters, sign'd J.S. dated from Leeds, was really a Clergyman. And if a Clergyman, Mr. Scott has told us in the COURANT that it fixes it upon *Him*, so that it is left to *Him* and *Cæsar Ward* to settle it betwixt *themselves.*

JOHN JACKSON

This is a very specific denial and makes much of the existence of a document attested upon oath. Had the piece in question actually been in Sterne's hand, there could have been very serious legal consequences for Jackson, and so too for any others implicated in the matter. As Jackson says of Ward's reputation, "he might have forfeited both It and his *Ears together*," it being a conventional punishment for perjury to stand in the pillory and have one's ears cropped. It is possible, of course, that in order to justify this claim the Turner camp had had the letter in question rewritten by someone other than Sterne. This would assume that he had in fact been the original writer. The other possibility is that Sterne had indeed not written the disputed letter. Jackson, as printer of the *York Gazetteer*, made much of the necessity of veracity, writing in the issue on 15 December 1741, that it was "the only Substantial Qualification for one in our Business."[16] It is interesting and possibly indicative of the essential truth of Jackson's avowal that Fox's supporters appear to have ignored the *Gazetteer*'s provocation and simply continued with highly offensive personal attacks on Sterne, as can be seen from the *York Courant* on 5 January 1741/42 (no. 847, p. 3, col. 2):

A NEW YEAR*'s* GIFT *for* L——y.

> GRAVE Legends tell, nor is it yet deny'd,
> That old *St. Laurence* on a Grid-Iron fry'd;
> Our young *St. Laurence* is so wond'rous dry,
> I'll wager, that he'd sooner *burn than fry.*
> And, try to *roast* him—he's so lean and sallow,
> 'Tis Ten to One he drops *more T——d than Tallow.*

After a fractious campaign, the result of the poll for the county of York was declared on 26 January 1741/42: Turner polled 8005 votes as against the 7049 for Fox, a clear margin of victory and an increase on the number of votes Turner had gained in the previous election of 1734, when he had polled 7,879 votes. The completed election did not stop the Fox supporters from continuing their attacks on the man they held responsible for the successful canvassing. In the *York Courant* on 23 March 1742 (no. 858, p. 2, col. 2), an anonymous verse appeared that claimed that Sterne had given up politics:

L——Y*'s Reasons for writing no more* Gazetteers.

> Presuming that to wear the Lawn,
>   I had a just Pretence,
> I've scribbled now for one whole Year,
>   To baffle Common Sense.
>
> I've taken Pains by Logick Rules,
>   To prove myself an Ass;
> Not dreaming what a wondrous Change
>   Is like to come to pass.
>
> But now my Pen I've splinter'd quite,
>   And thrown away my Ink,
> For 'till I see which Side will win,
>   I'll neither write nor think

This was prescient in that Sterne himself declared an end to his politicking later that same year in the *York Courant* on 27 July 1742 (no. 867, p. 3, col. 1):

To the PRINTER *of the* YORK COURANT.

SIR,

'I find, by some late Preferments, that it may be not improper to change Sides; therefore I beg the Favour of you to inform the Publick, that I sincerely beg Pardon for the abusive Gazetteers I wrote during the last contested Election for the County of York, and that I heartily wish Mr Fox joy of his Election for the City.

Tempora mutantur, & nos mutemur in illis.

I am, Sir, your penitent Friend and Servant.

L.S.

What needs to be noted in all this journalism is the wording employed. Jackson's assertion that the disputed material of Caesar Ward's 8 December piece was not in Sterne's hand is a useful starting point. There are several possible explanations: that the letter was neither composed nor written by Sterne; that it was composed by Sterne, either on his own or in collaboration with others, but written out for publication by one of those others; that it was both composed and written by Sterne, in which case Jackson, in the heat of the election and having claimed that the facts he was asserting had been sworn before a notary, risked being accused of being a party to perjury. The distinction between composition and copying out was critical to the de-attribution of the "Residentiaryship" manuscript above and must also be considered here. In his very first implied assertion of the involvement of Sterne in the letter from Guisborough on 29 September, Ward had referred to "the *Vicar*, who penn'd it"; and on 10 November his headnote to the piece supporting Turner had read, "*The following Letter is wrote by the same Gentleman that has wrote every Piece that has been inserted in this Paper in Vindication of* Cholmley Turner, *Esq.*" In many ways this later item is the crux. It is an acknowledged piece, signed "L.S.," and if we assume that by writing "has wrote every piece" Ward intended to assert Sterne's responsibility for the composition of the Turner campaign pieces, then it would be reasonable to assume that the earlier pieces could also be attributed to Sterne. But the "Residentiaryship" manuscript should give us pause for thought.

The one piece of which we have multiple versions, *Query upon Query*, muddies the waters even more. There are four key versions,[17] two of which are dated 22 October 1741, within the text. Though it is possible to establish a chronological sequence of publication, albeit with certain caveats, priority of composition is another matter. On 27 October the lead piece in the *York Courant*, occupying the first two columns of page 1, was headed, "*The following Letter was sent on* Thursday *Night last to the Printer of this Paper, by the Friends of* Cholmley Turner, *Esq*; *and is inserted here at* their *Desire.*"

"Thursday *night* last" was 22 October, and this piece, if we are to believe Caesar Ward's headnote on 10 November cited above, was in the handwriting of Laurence Sterne. There are two settings of this letter, with substantive variants, and while it is possible to identify the order of printing, it is not possible to be sure that the corrections were made to accord with the original manuscript, rather than being authorial revisions sent while the item was in the press, though the relatively minor nature of the corrections inclines to the former. The following day, 28 October, the *Daily Gazetteer* in London printed a radically different version of the text. And on an undetermined day, though not before the morning of 28 October, appeared the pamphlet *Query upon Query*. To simplify slightly a complex problem, the layout of these principal texts can be tabulated:

1. Two *York Courant* versions: 6 preliminary paragraphs; 16 queries
2. *Daily Gazetteer* version: 11 preliminary paragraphs; 15 queries
3. *Query upon Query* pamphlet: 8 preliminary paragraphs; 19 queries

The different numbers of queries are the result partly of amalgamation and partly of introduction of new queries; the order of the queries also varies considerably. There are three clearly distinct texts here. Determining priority is difficult. The *York Courant* prints the earliest securely datable published version, and is claimed to be based on a manuscript delivered to the newspaper office on 22 October, the date within the text. Though the *Daily Gazetteer* version, which has no internal date, was published the following day, one has to allow for the time it would have taken to send the item to London in time for publication on 28 October. Dispatch from York on 22 October would fit this time scheme. The *Query upon Query* pamphlet is also internally dated 22 October, though there is no secure evidence of the day of publication.[18] This could mean that there were three distinct manuscript versions of the text possibly produced on the same day, which suggests that there may have been more than one person involved. And this is borne out by the fourth key version involved here.

There is an extant partial manuscript of this item—and it is not in the hand of Laurence Sterne. This manuscript, which is three paragraphs long, is textually closest to the pamphlet version, and also has marked similarities to the *Daily Gazetteer* piece. It was not the source of the *York Courant* lead. This manuscript is in the hand of Sterne's uncle, the precentor Jaques Sterne, who was heavily involved in the by-election, as he hoped by this political service to gain further ecclesiastical preferment. That Jaques Sterne was controlling the whole campaign can be seen from the letters he sent to the leading local Whig, Lord Irwin at Temple Newsam. One of the Tory squibs, which appeared in the *York Courant* over the letters "J.S.," was perceived as particularly damaging to the Whig interest, and Jaques Sterne wrote to Irwin claiming that "an Answer to Scott's Scurrilous Letter . . . will hurt them very much" and offering "if your Lordship wou'd have a serious one withal, one shall be given." This offer does not appear to have been taken up; however, a subsequent J.S. letter was the motivation for *Query upon Query*. In a letter to Irwin on 23 October, Jaques Sterne wrote, "As the Party build so much upon the mischief that Scots Letter in the York *Courant* this week wil do to Mr. Turner's cause, that they have order'd twelve thousand of them to be printed and dispers'd; and as the Printer wou'd not allow an answer to it in his paper the next week, unless it was sent to him before today, my nephew has given the enclosed, to stop the Poison till the Public can be obliged with a letter. Ward has consented to give it a place in his Paper, (all but the criticism upon his first letter) and I design to print 2 or 3 thousand of 'em."[19] In this letter the word "given" raises some problems. Jaques Sterne does not unequivocally attribute the *York Courant* piece to his nephew: "given" could equally imply the act of handing over the manuscript, which takes the argument back to the idea of Laurence Sterne being an amanuensis, rather than necessarily an author. However, having discovered this correspondence, Collyer's conclusion was that "the letter as it appeared in the London *Daily Gazetteer* is Sterne's original which he himself sent to that newspaper,"[20] a conclusion that is elaborated by Cash: "The original appeared in the London *Daily Gazetteer* on 28 October—apparently based upon a manuscript in Sterne's hand which he had sent to London at the time he gave copies to Ward and his uncle."[21] Ian Campbell Ross seems to incline toward the *York Courant* version, but wishes to retain a single sentence from the *Daily Gazetteer* as being "almost certainly by Sterne."[22] The difficulty with the latter argument is that the sentence in question appears for the first time in Jaques Sterne's manuscript. And the difficulty with the view of Collyer and Cash is that the extant partial manuscript accords very closely with the pamphlet version, and the *Daily Gazetteer* is textually much closer to the pamphlet than the *York Courant*.

If we were to accept Jaques Sterne's "given" as implying authorship, then the *York Courant* version would be the one that would have to be designated as by Laurence Sterne, with the subsequent printings being denominated collaborations. The more cautious editorial approach is to accept as the work of Laurence Sterne all those items in the *York Courant* in which his character is defended—that is, from the offensive note signed "L.S." on 10 November; and all the political campaigning prior to that date should be seen as, at best, the result of collaboration with his uncle, and possibly only the transcribing of his uncle's thoughts.

NOTES

1. *Laurence Sterne: The Letters*, ed. Melvyn New and Peter de Voogd, vols. 7 and 8 of the Florida Edition of the Works of Laurence Sterne (Gainesville: University Press of Florida, 2009), 7:97.

2. This is a vellum-covered notebook measuring 211 x 165 mm. and with 88 leaves, of which the first is blank and unnumbered, followed by numbered fols. to fol. 32, where both recto and verso of fol. 33 are numbered; then back to foliation only to fol. 50, when both recto and verso (except 53, versos of 54, 57, number omitted from 59) to end of first batch of text at 64, 65, 67, and 69 are blank and unnumbered, while 66 and 68 are numbered blanks. Fols. 61a–63a (numbered 70, 72, 74) contain "The Repeal of Abp Rotherham's Decree." Fols. 63b–82b are blank with versos numbered with even numbers. Fols. 83a–88a contain "The Copy of The Extracts refer'd to Page ye 17th" of which only 83a is numbered—114—and there is a final blank (88b).

3. The holograph manuscript of volume 1 of *A Sentimental Journey* is in the British Library, Egerton MS 1610; the holograph manuscript of *Continuation of the Bramine's Journal* is also in the BL, Add. MSS.34527.

4. Arthur H. Cash, *Laurence Sterne: The Early and Middle Years* (London: Methuen, 1975), 230.

5. Ian Campbell Ross, *Laurence Sterne: A Life* (Oxford: Oxford University Press, 2001), 185–86.

6. [Francis Topham], *A letter address'd to the Reverend the Dean of York; in which is given in full details of some very extraordinary behaviour of his, in relation to his denial of a promise made by him to Dr Topham* (York, 1758); [John Fountayne], *An answer to a letter address'd to the Dean of York, in the name of Dr. Topham* (York: T. Atkinson, 1758); and [Francis Topham], *A reply to the answer to a letter lately addressed to the Dean of York* (York, 1759). There is reason to suggest that Sterne may have collaborated on the second of these three pamphlets.

7. Lewis Perry Curtis, *The Politicks of Laurence Sterne* (London: Oxford University Press, 1929). C. Collyer, "Laurence Sterne and Yorkshire Politics: Some New Evidence," *Proceedings of the Leeds Philosophical and Literary Society* 7.1 (1952): 83–87. In two articles Kenneth Monkman suggested a number of further attributions to Sterne: "More of Sterne's *Politicks*, 1741–42," *Shandean* 1 (1989): 53–108; and "Sterne's Farewell to Politics," *Shandean* 3 (1991): 98–125. The validity of these attributions will be explored at greater length in the final volume of the Florida Sterne.

8. R. M. Wiles, *Freshest Advices: Early Provincial Newspapers in England* (Columbus: Ohio State University Press, 1965), 80–81, states that provincial newspaper printers would set and work off the outer forme first, then have page 2 in standing type, while page 3, which contained the latest news, would be the final piece of setting. Of the York Public Library files Wiles notes, "the first and fourth pages in one set are the same as those in the other set" (300n19). This proves to be not always the case. It is known that in 1746 the arrangement for printing the *York Courant* for publication on a Tuesday was that the outer forme was printed on a Saturday afternoon; new advertisements, which were found on page 3, could be set as late as Monday, as

was the latest news on page 2. See Wiles, 72–73, citing an advertisement printed by Ward on 9 December 1746.

9. The corrections to the *Query upon Query* version must have been made while it was in the process of printing, as measurements reveal that the first page was not reset. The substituted words were, in each case, of approximately the same length as those that replaced them: "conseqnently" was corrected to "consequently"; "adjoined" was replaced by "subjoined" and "adjoin'd" by "subjoin'd"; while the one correction to take advantage of a short line had "shews" replaced by "should be."

10. Though the poll for the county of York was a by-election and would not normally have generated a great deal of interest, the campaign was followed across the country. Walpole, who had been chief minister since 1719, was generally perceived to have a tenuous grip on his majority, and a defeat in what was the largest electoral division in the country might have toppled him from power. In addition to the London papers, the *Daily Gazetteer* and the *London Evening-Post*, a number of provincial papers ran items from the electioneering, including the *Leeds Mercury* and the *Nottingham Post.*

11. There are two editions of the paper, and this note only appears in the later one, which can be identified by the latest dated item in the "SATURDAY'S POST" section: in the earlier issue the most recent item is headed "*Cologne, Sept. 26*"; in the issue containing Ward's note is found an item dated "*Paris Sept 29.*"

12. There are two versions of this text, *York Courant,* no. 838: in one, 3, cols. 2–3; in the other 3, col. 2, with minor variants in accidentals. The earlier one is printed here.

13. This letter has been discussed by Melvyn New, "Two Notes on Sterne," *N&Q,* n.s., 16 (1969): 353–54.

14. Again, there are two issues with minor variants in the accidentals.

15. Collyer attributes the misidentification specifically to Jaques Sterne, ("Laurence Sterne and Yorkshire Politics," 84–85, 87), and thinks that the subsequent rupture between Sterne and his uncle may have been the result of the error of the uncle causing such vitriol to be poured upon the nephew.

16. Cited by Wiles, *Freshest Advices*, 193.

17. For the purposes of the argument here, the *Leeds Mercury* version has been discounted, as textual evidence suggests that it was derived from a printed source.

18. In a letter about the pamphlet version written to Lord Irwin and dated 28 October Jaques Sterne noted, "The Printer has disappointed me this morning." The pamphlet must therefore have appeared after the London *Daily Gazetteer* had been printed.

19. Cited in Collyer, "Laurence Sterne and Yorkshire Politics," 87.

20. Ibid., 85.

21. Arthur H. Cash, *Laurence Sterne: The Early and Middle Years*, 103.

22. Ian Campbell Ross, *Laurence Sterne: A Life*, 442n37.

Chapter Twelve

Sterne and the Miracle of the Fragment

Madeleine Descargues-Grant

Ever since Sterne's gloss on laughter as an addition of "something to this Fragment of Life" in his dedication of the second edition of *Tristram Shandy* to William Pitt,[1] the literary category of the fragmentary has won for itself a central, if elusive, place in Sternean criticism. It will be the purpose of this essay not so much to review this criticism, but to explore the seductiveness of the fragment as a form hatching within the text, in Sterne and in other writers. Fragments carry both paradigmatic and syntagmatic weight: they place the text in a series of other texts, vertically so to speak, but they also influence the narrative horizontally as they are incorporated into it. My exploration will first reflect on the fortunes of the fragment in the Augustan age, then examine the resonance of the notion and the term in a mostly Sternean corpus, elaborated with references to Shakespeare's *Troilus and Cressida*, Pope's *Dunciad*, and *Spectator* 85 by Addison.

Sterne wrote one separate fragmentary piece, which has come to be known as the "Rabelaisian Fragment." He also inserted real or so-called fragments into his two major works. Not surprisingly, his practice occasioned a profusion of imitators who thought their homage more aptly presented when entitled "Fragment(s)." In the wake of romantic and postromantic literary fashions, moreover, the word "fragment" became a catchword for such dissimilar performances as "Fragments in the Manner of Sterne"—paltry sentimental variations excusing themselves as based on the Maria theme of *Tristram Shandy* and *A Sentimental Journey*—or, nearly a century later, Paul Stapfer's fantastical "Fragment inédit."[2] It was even Sterne's fate to have his works artificially fragmented for the taste of the public, that is, anthologized and broken into more palatable pieces, as in the notorious example of *The Beauties of Sterne*.[3] Because of its polysemy, "fragment" is a slippery word with which to crack the code of Sterne's compositions.

Of course, the whole of *Tristram Shandy*, with its missing (or not) tenth volume, interpolated tales, displaced chapters, and typographical breakages, can be regarded as a compendious fragment of Tristram's life; and the same applies to Yorick's *Sentimental Journey*, with its unmistakably missing final period. Certainly the assiduous critic could identify dozens of "subfragments" scattered through Sterne's volumes. What I wish to do here is to concentrate only on those instances in the Sternean corpus where the word "fragment" is actually used by the author as a primary identification. The word can be simply present in a sentence or serve as a title. It will be useful at the outset to provide a list of my nine examples, from the "Rabelaisian Fragment" (1) to the fragments that may be collected from *Tristram Shandy*: (2) "Brother Didius . . . upon his backside;" (3.34.263); (3) "*The Fragment* [upon Whiskers]" (5.1.409–15); (4) "Now my uncle *Toby* . . . pieces of antiquity." (5.3.423); (5) "To those who call vexations . . . not to be able to see it." (7.30.625); and from *A Sentimental Journey*: (6) "A Fragment" (containing an anecdote about the town of Abdera)[4]; (7) "The Marquis d'E**** . . . how I envied him his feelings!" (107–8); (8) "The Fragment. Paris" (containing the story of the French notary) (134–35), "The Fragment. Paris" (136–39), "The Fragment and the Bouquet. Paris." (140); and (9) "The Case of Delicacy" (160–65).

One of these examples seems to me of particular significance, and this is (8) the episode of *A Sentimental Journey* situated in Paris, in which the word "fragment" is repeated in three consecutive titles, the fragment itself supplying at once a plot and a metanarrative, with Yorick playing the part of the reader. Nor is this the only feature that commands our attention. The remarkable proximity in the passage of a "sheet of waste paper" (134)—that is, the fragment itself—and of the butter that Yorick is eating for his breakfast establishes a thematic connection between Sterne's writing in the second half of the eighteenth century and the treatment of the notion of the fragment in texts from the Augustan age or even earlier. The complex idea of corruption, in the shape of degraded matter, and the simpler one of food are indeed two underlying metaphors that seem inseparable from the motif of the fragment for Pope, and even for Shakespeare. The food metaphor comes down to us from what can be considered as the biblical master trope of the fragment as nourishment in the episode of Jesus feeding the multitude. This episode is diversely told by Matthew, Mark, Luke, and John; the loaves of barley may be five or seven, and the fish may be a few and little or just two, but each time the breaking of bread and the leftover broken fragments are associated with the ideas of plenty and satiety. This could in turn be related to the doctrine of plenitude governing the Great Chain of Being, warranting, through God's own vigilance, that all species and all elements, down to the hairs on a man's head, form part of a meaningful whole.[5]

THE CLASSICAL FRAGMENT

Because fragmentation in a modernist sense has been such a central issue in twentieth-century criticism, including critical reflection on Sterne himself, I believe it useful to start with what very clearly distinguishes Sterne from the modernist aesthetic credo, according to which the fragmented world—a euphemism for the world without God—can only be made whole through art, whose mission it is to restore completeness. Such a divine mission on Earth, one gathers, might have been implied by Mallarmé when he declared that "the world is designed to reach its perfection in a book,"[6] a statement one can hardly imagine Laurence Sterne, an Anglican parson, would have endorsed. Mallarmé's book is a secular book, authorized by aesthetic judgment—an object in the cultural sphere. As such, it is far removed from the Book of Nature invoked by Christians throughout the Middle Ages for the metaphorical "reading" of God's creation. Sterne might play with the idea of a "work of redemption,"[7] he could count on writing and laughing it away to keep up his spirits, but he would not have confused writing a profane book and achieving salvation. For all his investment in literature, Sterne never proposed it (says Christopher Ricks) as "the be-all and end-all of human existence"; he was too conscious of "[t]he potential arrogance of literature—in its relation to the other arts, to the sciences, to religion, to life."[8] With this intellectual proviso in mind, we should be wary of overinterpreting Sterne's obsession with the fragmentary as secular epiphany, in the Joycean/Woolfian sense, and in the light of our own postmodern bewilderment in the diminished world we have inherited and that we continue to reduce to even smaller and more incomprehensible parts.

In order to do justice to the fragmentary in Sterne's writing, one needs rather to turn back to the classical age. As Alain Montandon has argued, Pascal's *Thoughts* are the turning point in matters concerning the literary status of the fragment: his confessedly uncompleted work is conditioned by his very vision of human life as "a mean between nothing and everything."[9] For Montandon, this amounts to a representation of life as "an incomprehensible fragment in the universe,"[10] a formula quite akin to Sterne's own "Fragment of Life." This philosophical conception of the fragmentary, let us remember, issues from the works of a Jansenist French Catholic, therefore one closer to Protestant notions of the centrality of God's grace, and hence tolerably compatible with the views of a Church of England cleric such as Sterne. It rests upon trust in a completeness that eludes the writer's human efforts: these can provide rhetorical glimpses into the sublime, but they can only aspire to the unachievable divine model found in the sublimity of the Bible.[11]

The fragmentary for Sterne, in other words, is characteristically human—
"all are from the dust, and all return to dust" (Eccles. 3:20)—as it is for the
French classical or the English Augustan ages. This dissociates it from the
fragmentary theorized as the ideal literary form by the romantic imagination,
in particular by the German romantics and Jean-Paul Richter, and indeed
from all later versions, including the modernist one. No transcendent function
is assigned by Sterne to fragments themselves. The relation of the fragment
with theology has to be sought, as Elizabeth W. Harries has cogently argued,
in the biblical intertext. Sterne's fragments and his way of using them "point
to the necessary incompleteness of our attempts to make sense of life's fragments and of life itself as a fragment, but also to the expanding and ultimately
liberating power of those attempts."[12]

The fragment as motif in the later eighteenth century is also "inextricably
bound up with our notions about the ancients," Harries observes in her study
The Unfinished Manner: "Relatively few ancient texts have come down to us
whole; we know many of them only as fragments or in fragments: isolated
lines or episodes, sometimes too discrete to be brought together into any form
that looks complete."[13] The interest in the fragmentary and the incomplete is
therefore inherently modern—"Only in the early Renaissance did it somehow
become possible to create fragments"[14]—and the preoccupation with the fragmentary comes with the "lateness" complex of the moderns. In the Augustans' eyes, the value of fragments is in any case ambivalent: they may be seen
either as precious (they are all that is left from the past) or as damaged (they
are broken, degraded material). This ambivalence is reflected in the treatment
given by at least one great Augustan, Alexander Pope, to the predominant
metaphors of gestation and digestion that conflate fragment and food in the
Dunciad. Besides the admiration for the ancients, the Christian intertext, as
we have indicated above, also enriches the metaphoric potential of the fragment. Whereas this metaphor is essentially negative in Pope's rhetoric, as it
was previously in Shakespeare's *Troilus and Cressida*, representing the degraded condition of modern culture and language, it gets a positive treatment
at the hands not only of Sterne in his *Sentimental Journey*, but also of Pope's
contemporary Joseph Addison, in the *Spectator*. One is familiar with the idea
that in Yorick's journey, the broken and the interrupted are associated with
good fortune, following the Shandean prejudice in favor of digressions. But
one cannot help wondering also if the coincidence that makes Addison and
Sterne consider fragments as choice morsels, in *Spectator* 85 and in "The
Fragment. Paris," respectively, might have to do with the engagement of
each author, separated though they are by decades, with the transformations
of print culture and of the market of literature. Both Addison and Sterne were
committed diversely to the serial mode of publication, and both sought means

to adapt to a new, broader readership in their manner of writing, recognizing the changes in readers' expectations and in what they themselves as authors could expect from their readers. The fragments around which they develop their microstories question the readers' motivation for reading and challenge their performance as readers. That might give a hint as to why both writers use the fragment as a pedagogical exercise in reading, and as an example of how to read, helping the relatively unpracticed to become more competent.

THE FRAGMENT IN STERNE

None has more weight than Rabelais to confirm the reading of *Tristram Shandy* in the Renaissance tradition of learned wit. It is therefore of particular interest to gauge Sterne's literary achievement when writing explicitly in the manner of the French writer, via a narrator called Longinus Rabelaicus. The "Rabelaisian Fragment" (1), possibly written just after *A Political Romance* and just before *Tristram Shandy*, is now read by critics as in some sense a germ for *Tristram Shandy* itself.[15] Melvyn New elaborated this diagnosis in 1972, tracing the palimpsest of the original "Fragment," under the bowdlerizations introduced by Sterne's daughter, and also the rewritings induced by Sterne's own "self-censorship [which] does suggest that [he] was aware of changing tastes and changing standards of decorum" (SRF, 1085). Tom Keymer contended more categorically that "the Fragment was unprintable from the start,"[16] with its flagrant obscenity. All in all, nevertheless, the "Fragment" is a successful exercise, in which the ingredients that flavor the writing—the "debt to and love for the French satirist," the "ear for the Rabelaisian vocabulary"—justly match their original (literary) purpose: "a satire on learning and sermon writing" (SRF, 1084, 1085, 1083).

But is it in fact more than a gifted pastiche, with its scatological comedy and its use of Rabelaisian idiom and onomatopoeia? Despite its vigorous and flavored style, the "Fragment" remains what it purports to be, "A Fragment in the Manner of Rabelais," effectively Sterne's "first attempt at what ultimately became *Tristram Shandy*," "cull[ed] for ideas as he writes his masterpiece" (SRF, 1085, 1086). While *A Political Romance* offers itself as a pamphlet in its own right, the "Rabelaisian Fragment" seems to be more intertext than text, and this is owing not only to its remaining unfinished. Whatever phrase comes alive in it does so with the prior reference to Rabelais or, better, the posterior reference to *Tristram Shandy* itself. Longinus Rabelaicus makes "an Exclamation, but taking Care to moderate his Voice at the same Time" (SRF, 1088), as Walter will during the conception of Tristram; he lays down the principles of the *Kerukopædia*, echoed later in the *Trista-pædia*, while

Homenas reflects on the exercise of pilfering and borrowing in the writing of sermons, adumbrating Yorick. But Tristram's interiority provides the ignition for the greater work, which combines the same ingredients with significant differences.

The "Fragment" proves that Sterne could quite convincingly write in the mode of Rabelais, qua respected figure from the Renaissance, as the first chapter puts it: "Shewing . . . What a Rabelaic Fellow, *Longinus Rabelaicus*, is" (SRF, 1088), a feat that perhaps does not add much, after all, to the creative translations of Urquart and Motteux. It also proves how different this emanation of Rabelais was from the ethos of the author Sterne, his Shandean self. It seems as if Sterne had tried out his voice in different registers to construct his fully fledged, hybrid persona, in which the proponent of learned wit described by D. W. Jefferson and the satirist identified by New coexist with the explorer of the sympathetic affections. The "Rabelaisian Fragment" is memorable for its genealogical interest and for the critical paraphernalia it has occasioned, *Tristram Shandy,* of course, being its most developed critical reading.

IN *TRISTRAM SHANDY*

Following the first, unforgettable use of the word in the phrase "this Fragment of Life" in the dedication of the second edition of the first two volumes to William Pitt, the reader meets the word "fragment" in volume 3, when Tristram launches into a discussion of the legitimacy of appropriating opinions as one does apples, simply picking them up, and calls Tribonius in support of Locke (2): "Brother *Didius, Tribonius* will say, it is a decreed case, as you may find it in the fragments of *Gregorius* and *Hermogenes*'s codes, and in all the codes from *Justinian*'s down to the codes of *Louis* and *Des Eaux*,—That the sweat of a man's brows, and the exsudations of a man's brains, are as much a man's own property, as the breeches upon his backside" (3.34.263). To identify Tribonius (for Roman emperor Justinian's chancellor Tribonianus), Gregorius, and company, New's annotations point us to the information Sterne would have found in Chambers' *Cyclopædia*, in the article "Civil Law," and again in "Code."[17] The discussion of property mentioning John's apple refers to Locke's *Two Treatises of Government* (264). New cites James Work's remark on Sterne's slapdash use of the sources: "*Des Eaux* appears to be a confused reference to Louis XIV's *Ordonnance des eaux et forêts* of 1669, a famous code designed to conserve and develop French forests, of which numerous erudite interpretations were written. This slip suggests that here, as in other known cases, Sterne derived his 'erudition' from marginalia rather than from the text" (265). New also traces in the passage an echo of the scattered rules of the *Kerukopædia* in the Rabelaisian fragment. The whole exercise suggests indeed a satire of pedantry and erudition maintained in the Rabelaisian spirit.

But what immediately follows bears on Walter's practical solution to the fragmentary state of ancient knowledge on noses—indeed, Slawkenbergius's tale is not far off: "he collected every book and treatise which had been systematically wrote upon noses, with as much care as my honest uncle *Toby* had done those upon military architecture" (3.34.265). This collecting hobbyhorse places the fragment in the realm of the compulsive and more generally of the affective, which the later part of this essay will explore in more depth. The whole context of chapters 34 to 38 is, in fact, contaminated metonymically by the fragment motif, bearing as it does on the collectioner's urge displayed by the two brothers, as if they are compelled to try to turn fragments, odd bits and pieces, into wholes, and to fail. Chapter 35 introduces Bruscambille and Slawkenbergius, before the text literally fragments itself to offer two major exhibits: the marbled page at the end of volume 3 and Slawkenbergius's tale at the beginning of volume 4. The opacity of the first, ironically suggestive of the very material on which classical fragments were often found, is matched by the inapplicability of the second to Walter's desperation and helplessness at the news of the crushing of his son's nose (4.2.327). In volume 3 of *Tristram Shandy*, far from enlightening their readers, fragments seem to obey a law of entropy and to make everything more scattered and disconnected, despite the futile efforts at reordering them.

Volume 5 provides good material for literary fragment seekers, opening as it does with the disquisition on the *"relicks of learning"* (5.1.408) spread as rubble in all modern texts, and continuing with the title *"The Fragment"* (3) to introduce the interpolated tale of the mishaps of the word "Whiskers" at the court of the queen of Navarre:

The Fragment.
* * * * * * * * * * *
* * * * * * * * * * *
* * *——You are half asleep, my good lady, said the old gentleman, taking hold of the old lady's hand and giving it a gentle squeeze, as he pronounced the word *Whiskers*—shall we change the subject? By no means, replied the old lady—. . . . I desire, continued she, you will go on. (5.1.409)

In this instance, the insertion of the fragment reads as an immediate visual commentary on the ancients-versus-moderns paradigm used with typical obliqueness by Sterne, first through his plagiarizing of Burton in an ironically performative discussion on plagiarism, then through his producing of a fragment of his own. This fragment, as shown above, is ostentatiously advertised as such by the generous portion of asterisks preceding the old gentleman narrator's cue: as if to illustrate the instability of ancient manuscripts and their degradation—a typographical sign mimicking Swift's *hic desunt multa* in *The Tale of a Tub*. Meanwhile, the so-called insertion provides the content of a chapter on whiskers and continues to tease the reader with a favorite theme, the gravity inherent in words, which inclines them to fall into the dirty rather than the clean path.

According to Richard A. Davies's investigations of historical sources, no connection between whiskers and Margaret's court life appears, though the court life was notoriously scandalous. Yet Sterne's invented fragment stumbles on some sort of truth: "However, the association of ideas does have its basis in a quirk of the Queen's that came to light during the nineteenth century: her fetish for hair which the French biographer of court-life of her age, Tallemant des Réaux, chose to hand down to posterity as one of Margaret de Valois's more interesting idiosyncracies."[18] The fragment here is worth noting for its ring of truth, despite—or perhaps because of—its fabrication and its offhanded treatment of historical chronicles: "nor had I ever seen the underwritten fragment" (5.1.409) is Tristram's cavalier introduction to his inserted piece, which may read as a warning to the naive. The ring of truth is in the narrative logic of *Tristram Shandy*, which makes its reader alert to the fact that whiskers, after the example of noses, are bound to be "dangerous" subjects.

Another sort of commentary on the productive use of textual fragments occurs in volume 5, when Toby misses the meaning of Walter's speech on the occasion of Bobby's death, owing to his inability to identify and locate his brother's lengthy quotation (4): "Now my uncle *Toby* knew not that this last paragraph was an extract of *Servius Sulpicius*'s consolatory letter to *Tully*.—He had as little skill, honest man, in the fragments, as he had in the whole pieces of antiquity" (5.3.423). Here, Toby is unable to place this broken piece in the puzzle of quotations issuing from his brother's mind. We can intuit a version of the continuous communication between writer and reader in this exchange between the two brothers. Walter we can cast in the role of the writer, his head charged with material and primed with ancient rhetorical models; Toby is the reader, doing his best to understand what is going on, despite his own "little skill" in the matter. The balance for the self-respecting writer or reader, it appears, must be found somewhere between Walter's excessive familiarity with ancient rhetorical models—indeed, his inability to extract himself from them and to make them yield meaning—and Toby's ignorant imperviousness to quotation, his inability to bridge (rhetorically, that is) the past and the present.

To complete this handful of examples from *Tristram Shandy*, the word "fragment" is, unsurprisingly, associated with antiquity and its monuments in volume 7 (5): the narrator's journey fatally exposes him to sights for "the curious and inquisitive" (1.4.5) tourist. And although Tristram "think[s] it very much amiss—that a man cannot go quietly through a town, and let it alone" (7.4.579–80), a warning that descriptions of monuments will be few and far between in his travel narrative, even he may occasionally wish to visit some renowned places. Unfortunately, all his attempts at sightseeing are frustrated, beginning with the permission refused "to take an exact survey of the fortifications" in Calais, a disappointment he soon makes good by acknowledging, "after all that is *said* and *done* . . . Calais was never upon any account so considerable from itself, as from its situation" (7.5.583). Predictably, a similar fate befalls him a little later, this time on his visit to Lyons: "there could not be a greater [vexation] than to be the best part of a day in Lyons, the most opulent and flourishing city in France, enriched with the most fragments of antiquity—and not be able to see it" (7.30.625). There is an unmistakable intimation of the vanity of the contemplation of architectural or sculptural fragments in the parodic treatment of the monument devoted to Amandus and Amanda that follows. Tristram's lucubrations on the "shrine" of the two lovers, which determine him to "go [on] a pilgrimage (though [he] had no other business at Lyons) on purpose to pay it a visit" (7.31.629), are brought to an abrupt ending: "When I came—there was no tomb to drop [this tear] upon. What would I have given for my uncle Toby to have whistled, Lillo bullero!" (7.4.643).

So much, one can half hear Sterne saying, for that precious fragment of antiquity. Even though he could (and would, especially in 1767, before the composition of *A Sentimental Journey*) be prey to fits of melancholy meditation inspired by Eliza Draper's miniature or by pictures "of the Sculptures upon poor Ovid's Tomb, who died in Exile, tho' he wrote so well upon the Art of Love,"[19] Sterne's Gothic inclinations were always blended with a healthy taste for the living rather than the dead. One remembers that Janatone's beautiful body, because she is alive, deserves more attention at the very beginning of the same volume 7 than "the great parish church" or the "fascade of the abbey of Saint Austreberte" (7.9.589).

In this series of examples, fragments, whether textual or architectural, serve mostly to confirm the narrator's authority. They lead him on a wild-goose chase when he (or any other character) seeks them out, and he is better off when he produces or forges them himself. Nowhere are they truly redolent of past literary grandeur and standards; never does Sterne intimidate us with past models. Nevertheless, the ability to identify the fragment is a cultural test (one that Toby fails), warranting the reader's wary participation in an intertextual game. Turning now to *A Sentimental Journey*—a work often said to be about reading as much as *Tristram Shandy* is about writing—should enable us to pursue this readerly game.

A SENTIMENTAL JOURNEY

The stone that obstructs Yorick's passage at the end of *A Sentimental Journey* (9) is a notable (and very material) example of the fragment. This is no inheritance from antiquity but a direct work of nature, produced by one of the many hazards that confront the traveler on his way: "mountains impracticable—and cataracts, which roll down great stones from their summits, and block his road up.—The peasants had been all day at work in removing a fragment of this kind between St. Michael and Madane" (160), which leads to Yorick's stopping at an inn. There is only one bedchamber, and when a lady and her maidservant arrive at the same inn, the English gentleman, being an English gentleman, can but share his room. Harries stresses the fact that, even though the obstacle represented by the massive stone is "but a pebble" (162) compared with "the mutual embarrassment of Yorick and a lady traveler when they discover that they must share the same small bedroom," the episode "leads to a connection, perhaps random and accidental, yet unmistakably there."[20] Indeed, *A Sentimental Journey* finishes with "The Case of Delicacy" and its well-known suspended ending, brought about by the fortunate fragment:

> So that when I stretch'd out my hand, I caught hold of the Fille de Chambre's
> END OF VOL. II. (165)

As in the third volume of *Tristram Shandy*, but this time with effects that reverberate in the narrative, the text is receptive to the interruptive and creative energy of the fragment as sign, and made richer (as is many a journey) by the digression. One can even suggest that the stone fragment functions literally as a "Fragment of Life," insisting as it does, in all its adventitiousness and unintelligibility, on a course of action that the narrative could not otherwise have supplied.

The episode of the old marquis in "The Sword. Rennes" (7) also associates the word "fragment" with an unpredictably positive outcome. "The Marquis d'E**** had fought up against his condition [decay, distress, and poverty] with great firmness; wishing to preserve, and still shew to the world some little fragments of what his ancestors had been—their indiscretions had put it out of his power" (107). Forced by poverty to go into commerce and to relinquish his sword, he is able, "in about nineteen or twenty years of successful application to business . . . to reclaim his nobility and to support it" (108). What is fascinating here, surely, is that it is the hazards of modern commerce (for which, read contingent narrative) rather than the symbolic sword (for which, read idealism) that restore the family fortunes, including the sword.

That protocapitalist victim of contingency, Robinson Crusoe, could not have organized things better.

A Sentimental Journey also contains two self-declared fragments. The first one, "A Fragment" (45), set in the town of Abdera (6), supports Yorick's motivation for hiring La Fleur—"He is always in love" (44)—with the authority of an anecdote that seems both classical and classic of its kind. This involves an endorsement of the passion of love, in which *Eros* and *Agape* are (con)joined: Yorick himself famously declares that "having been in love with one princess or another almost all my life . . . I hope I shall go on so, till I die, being firmly persuaded, that if ever I do a mean action, it must be in some interval betwixt one passion and another" (44). "A Fragment" then recycles the story of a representation of Euripides' *Andromeda*, found in Burton's *Anatomy of Melancholy*, to conjure up a striking picture: "The fire caught—and the whole city, like the heart of one man, open'd itself to Love" (45). Typically, John Ferriar, who first noted that Burton himself had borrowed from Lucian, remarked, "Burton has spoiled this passage by an unfaithful translation. Sterne has worked it up to a beautiful picture, but very different from the original in Lucian, with which, I am persuaded, he was unacquainted."[21] It seems an apposite fate for the fragment, which, of all the examples so far examined, can boast the most authenticity, that it should turn out to be a mere reflection of an original ignored by Sterne. This textual episode might well be seen as a fable on the inevitable loss of originals in the age, which compensated by inventing "originality."

But the most significant use of the fragment motif is certainly in the triple chapter "The Fragment. Paris" (134, 136) / "The Fragment and the Bouquet. Paris" (140) 8). This is when "the simple irreparability of the fragment" (140) is at its most tantalizing for Yorick and for the reader, since it is also an episode in which the narrator joins the reader in poring over a page. Yorick's "deep attention" (135) is exercised by the few lines printed on a piece of wastepaper (protecting his breakfast butter), which he treats as a gripping enigma.

With this fragment we seem to return to Rabelais, the hallmark of old wholesome, pithy writing—now lost: "It was in the old French of Rabelais's time, and for ought I know might have been wrote by him" (134). But the tone and the subject of the story bear no resemblance with the "Rabelaisian Fragment"; they rather remind one of the promise by Trim in *Tristram Shandy* of "The Story of the king of Bohemia and his seven castles" (8.19.683–91), which remains a kind of protonarrative gesture and never gets actually told: a "poor notary," sent to the devil by his wife, embarks on a nocturnal ramble in Paris, only to lose his hat in the windy night and to lament his fate ("to be born to have the storm of ill language levell'd against me and my profession wherever I go—to be forced into marriage by the thunder of the church to a tempest of a woman"), until a voice calls out for "the next notary" (138), a quality that he happens inevitably to be invested with. He offers his services and is presently begged by an old gentleman to record his "uncommon" story: "I have nothing to bequeath which will pay the expence of bequeath-ing, except the history of myself . . . ; the profits arising out of it, I bequeath to you for the pains of taking it from me—it is a story so uncommon, it must be read by all mankind" (137–39). Needless to say, this story is itself on the rest of the wastepaper, two other sheets of which have been wrapped around a bouquet presented by La Fleur, Yorick's servant, to a demoiselle. At Yorick's request, La Fleur runs to the Count de B****'s house, where she works, to get the sheets back:

> In a very little time the poor fellow came back quite out of breath, with deeper marks of disappointment in his looks than could arise from the simple irrepara-bility of the fragment—*Juste ciel!* in less than two minutes that the poor fellow had taken his last tender farewel of her—his faithless mistress had given his *gage d'amour* to one of the Count's footmen—the footman to a young semp-stress—and the sempstress to a fiddler, with my fragment at the end of it—Our misfortunes were involved together—I gave a sigh—and La Fleur echo'd it back again to my ear—
> —How perfidious! cried La Fleur—How unlucky! said I. (140)

If before we had been struck by the loss of originals (see above), here we are struck by the risk of a seepage of meaning, along with the fragment's ad-ventures: redirected or misdirected, it seems caught in a maddened version of "the ring of pleasure" (65). Sterne's fragment leads us on its debased trajec-tory, from the wrapping of Yorick's butter to that of La Fleur's bouquet. But Sterne's comic perspective requires a happy middle (if not a happy ending), and it is the rescue of the salvaged piece of wastepaper that now attracts our attention: "When I had finish'd the butter, I threw the currant leaf out of the window, and was going to do the same by the waste paper—but stopping to read a line first, and that drawing me on to a second and a third—I thought it better worth; so I shut the window, and drawing a chair up to it, I sat down to read it" (134). What he reads and translates is the aforementioned story of the notary, narrated in "The Fragment. Paris" (136–39), itself supposed to intro-duce the "uncommon" story of the old gentleman, which will never get told.

Yet as he is toiling at his table, Yorick is delighted by an accidental addi-tion to his breakfast: "La Fleur had left me something to amuse myself with for the day more than I had bargain'd for." The association of fragment and food is fresh and delicious here, by virtue of the contiguity of fragment and butter: "[La Fleur] had brought the little print of butter upon a currant leaf;

and as the morning was warm, and he had a good step to bring it, he had begg'd a sheet of waste paper to put betwixt the currant leaf and his hand—" (134). The fragment seems endowed metonymically with nourishing qualities, like the print of butter itself, and with the fragrant subtlety of the currant leaf. This joyful synesthesia combines the pleasures of smell and touch, taste and gaze as well as the more intellectual promises of text in a sensual encounter with the world, an encounter that fulfills every sense and is therefore in every sense fulfilling—a miracle of completeness—one of those moments when Yorick is "positive [he has] a soul" (151).

THE FRAGMENT AND FOOD

In itself, the connection between fragment and food is not new. As I touched on earlier, it goes back to Christ's breaking of bread at the Last Supper and to the quantity of fragments left after the miracle of the loaves and the fishes to feed the multitude. But the availability of the Christian reading of the notion tends to be obscured, from the Renaissance onward, in a typically modern sense of the inadequacy of language, which is associated with the Fall and the curse of Babel. Therefore the connection is often established negatively; the fragment endures a fall of its own. As such, it belongs to a rhetorical series that can be found in Shakespeare, one case in point being *Troilus and Cressida*. In a famous scene toward the end of the play, after witnessing Cressida's dallying with Diomedes, who has taken her in exchange to the Greek camp, Troilus memorably despairs of the coherence required for the established meaning that must lie at the heart of a faithful relationship:

> The bonds of heaven are slipp'd, dissolv'd, and loos'd;
> And with another knot, five-finger-tied,
> The fractions of her faith, orts of her love,
> The fragments, scraps, the bits, and greasy relics
> Of her o'er-eaten faith are given to Diomed. [22]

These degraded fragments conceded to a new lover, comparable to the bits of food left by greedy eaters, are the sign of the loss of wholeness and indicate the corruption of faith and meaning. In the richness of its negative precision, this description emphasizes an important characteristic of the fallen fragment: it is always used to recuperate what would otherwise have been thrown away, even to salvage what has already been disposed of. What profit can one make of this, and of what worth is such secondhand material? For Troilus, Cressida's recycled love, by losing its undivided quality, is not love anymore. In the sexual context, pleasure is denied if it is impinged upon by someone else; the consummation is broken, satisfaction is impossible. The fragment evokes here, by means of the food metaphor, the loss of wholeness without which the world itself is meaningless. In a similar situation Othello exclaims, "Chaos is come again."[23] But this very meaninglessness, engendered by the division and the corruption of meaning, is a fertile topic for the eighteenth century: it is the main source of inspiration of the goddess Dulness in Pope's *Dunciad*.

Corrupted meaning is precisely what Augustan satirists accuse hack-writers of trading in when they write potboilers. Dunces gnaw at old bones for want of new inspiration. They show unrelenting zest in scavenging only to feed themselves. At a time when, "[d]irectly and indirectly, the livelihoods of journalists, artists, poets, architects, designers and tutors all lay in the palms of the Great," in the words of Roy Porter,[24] this was the common lot. Consequently, self-respecting writers wanted to make it clear that they owed their success to their competence and talent, and not to their servility and promptitude to oblige. The notion of writing with strictly utilitarian motivations was detestable to them as it represented a threat to their literary identity. Later in the century, in 1767, one year before his death, Sterne wrote to a correspondent, "I was once such a puppy myself, as to pare, and burn, and had my labour for my pains, and two hundred pounds out of pocket.—Curse on farming (said I) I will try if the pen will not succeed better than the spade." But this frank admission has to be weighed against his prouder declaration, albeit tongue-in-cheek, in a 1760 letter, at the beginning of his literary career: "I wrote not to be *fed*, but to be *famous*."[25]

The major sin of hacks was that in doing just the reverse, they plagiarized their betters. By offering the same recycled stuff to an undiscriminating public, they also put writing on a level with eating, or rather with voracity. As Pope says, they were condemned to compete for "solid pudding against empty praise."[26] The fault, of course, is not in eating itself but in eating indiscriminately, ravenously, or to excess: in being governed by one's appetite. In Sterne's sermon, "Our conversation in Heaven," the "voluptuous epicure, who knows of no other happiness in this world, but what arises from good eating and drinking," is punished by his lack of proportion. He cannot have access to spiritual forms of pleasure: "represent to him that saints and angels eat not . . . —why, the only effect would be, that the fat glutton would stare a while upon the preacher, and in a few minutes fall fast asleep."[27]

In Pope's *Dunciad* we find another description of gluttony, in this case as a metaphor for Cibber's plagiarism:

> Next, o'er his Books his eyes began to roll,
> In pleasing memory of all he stole,
> How here he sipp'd, how there he plunder'd snug

And suck'd all o'er, like an industrious Bug.
Here lay poor Fletcher's half-eat scenes, and here
The Frippery of crucify'd Molière.
(726)

Such feats of stealing, sipping, sucking, and plundering are performed for the benefit of "nameless Somethings" and "Nonsense," "Where things destroy'd are swept to things unborn" (723, 731) in the words of Dulness herself (as mediated by Pope). The result of debased writing is that words lose the substance and the nutritive value that is found in old classic texts. So speaks Dulness again:

In ancient Sense if any needs will deal,
Be sure I give them Fragments, not a Meal;
What Gellius or Stobæus hash'd before,
Or chew'd by blind old Scholiasts o'er and o'er.
The critic Eye, that microscope of Wit,
Sees hairs and pores, examines bit by bit:
How parts relate to parts, or they to whole,
The body's harmony, the beaming soul,
Are things which Kuster, Burman, Wasse shall see,
When Man's whole frame is obvious to a *Flea*.
(779)

The perverse goddess ensures that this is how fragmentary texts, seen as fragments of food, return to literal waste. This demented assembling and disassembling of the same incomplete bits of meaning takes place in Grub Street, the street of dirt, where Smithfield, the meat market, is held. Therefore the modern English word "grub," a low colloquial term for food, even fast food, is very faithful to its original meaning in Pope.

But strikingly, it is through the celebration of meaninglessness and fragmentation that the invocations of Dulness in *The Dunciad* are paradoxically most effective in conjuring up meaning and wholeness—just as the "universal Darkness" that descends in the last line of the poem is actually the evidence of a new dawn: the *Dunciad* itself. Integrity of sense is invoked in the negative, so to speak, which reminds us that in the end, the distribution of meaning is governed by rhetorical credibility. In other words, the fragment, a broken, incomplete piece of something, can, when handled by Pope's synthetic imagination, help the reader regain what has been lost: the ideal whole, the great mythical, primitive unity of words and things. This has been effected, for the fragment, by a kind of cultural re-insertion.

It is in the spirit of this cultural shift that I now wish to explore the association of fragment and food, material and spiritual, in a *Spectator* essay by Addison, offering common points with Yorick's experience: "I once met with a Page of Mr. *Baxter* under a *Christmas* Pye. Whether or no the Pastry-Cook had made use of it through Chance, or Waggery, for the defence of that Superstitious *Viande*, I know not; but, upon the Perusal of it, I conceived so good an idea of the Author's Piety, that I bought the whole Book. I have often profited by these accidental Readings, and have sometimes found very Curious Pieces that are either out of Print, or not to be met with in the Shops of our *London* Book-sellers."[28] This statement by Addison in *Spectator* 85 does not make it absolutely clear whether the Christmas pie, "that Superstitious *Viande*," has to be defended by or against Baxter. Metonymy permitting, is Baxter defending the pie from the heat of the oven, or is a mischievous pastry cook defending his tempting pie from the Puritan divine's austere remonstrations against the pleasures of the flesh, especially at Christmas? What it does make clear is the other function of the metonymy: the fragment as medium, bearing a degraded message, speaks nevertheless for the message, for reading and for literature. Indeed, in its perverted condition, the page of a book (turned into wrapping paper) can still forcefully reveal the book it was. To the eye of a hungry reader, it is even potentially a most captivating text.

Such an avid reader is Yorick, in *A Sentimental Journey*, discovering his fragment of text under the butter-bearing leaf. But Addison in 1711 had already provided a comparable insight into the potential of the fragment as food, in its material and spiritual acceptations. Mr. Spectator in the aforementioned paper is thrilled to examine "the several printed Papers which are usually pasted upon [walls]. The last Piece that I met with upon this Occasion, gave me a most exquisite Pleasure." In fact all pleasures are blended, sensual and intellectual, including that of quiet playful impertinence: "I have lighted my Pipe more than once with the Writings of a Prelate." Fragmentation is not synonymous with loss of meaning here. It suggests the process of the systematic recycling of meaning through the intelligent reader's interpretation: "I remember, in particular, after having read over a Poem of an Eminent Author on a Victory, I met with several Fragments of it upon the next Rejoycing-day, which had been employed in Squibs and Crackers, and by that means celebrated its Subject in a double Capacity"—revealing at the same time a spectacular performative "Capacity" (361–62).

Addison, as essayist, has some reason to prioritize the part before the whole; so has Sterne, on whose finished or unfinished *Tristram Shandy* no critic can pretend to have the last word. This might help us understand why these two reader/writers are especially fascinated by fragments, why they are able to treat an incomplete part of a writing as the choicest morsel. But how is it that these may be privileged revelations of a fuller substance, when conversely they signify the loss of an ideal whole? By what miracle can they seem to multiply their worth and provide their tasters with a special gratification?

In order to suggest answers to these questions, I will first turn to Addison to review the fortunes of the fragment. "It is the Custom of the *Mahometans*, if they see any printed or written Paper upon the Ground, to take it up and lay it aside carefully, as not knowing but it may contain some Piece of their *Alcoran*. I must confess I have so much of the *Mussulman* in me, that I cannot forbear looking into every Printed Paper which comes in my way, under whatsoever despicable Circumstances it may appear" (360–61). His attention to fragments makes him stumble on something worthwhile, quite the contrary of Pope's "nameless Somethings," as he yields to his particular hobby of "examin[ing] the several printed Papers which are usually pasted upon [the walls of some houses]." This is the ballad "Two Children in the Wood," "a plain simple Copy of Nature, destitute of all the Helps and Ornaments of Art," an example of the highest sort of poetry (that is, the sublime) through its very poverty of expression. This quality allows the reader's feelings to develop fully: "because the Sentiments appear genuine and unaffected, they are able to move the Mind of the most polite Reader with inward Meltings of Humanity and Compassion" (361–62). In the modest piece he studies on the wallpaper, Addison sees a treasure that nobody else (no critic at least) had discovered before him—or so he says—though it was available to all, and he grounds in it a new Lockean conception of aesthetics based on sensations and feelings as well as on the response of the reader.

Addison's readiness to perceive a whole vision of the world through a detail goes with his compulsive disposition: he "cannot forbear looking" and acknowledges an "inquisitive Temper, or rather impertinent Humour of prying into all sorts of Writing." He reveals the collector in himself; over the years he has gathered a number of miscellaneous items made of printed paper: "when my Friends take a Survey of my Library, they are very much surprised to find, upon the Shelf of Folio's, two long Band-boxes standing upright among my Books, till I let them see that they are both of them lined with deep Erudition and abstruse Literature. I might likewise mention a Paper Kite, from which I have received great Improvement; and a Hat-Case, which I would not exchange for all the Beavers in *Great Britain*" (361). In like manner, in *A Sentimental Journey*, Yorick is obsessed with his buttered fragment, whose opacity increases his reader's interest: "it was moreover in a Gothic letter, and that so faded and gone off by damps and length of time, it cost me infinite trouble to make any thing of it—I threw it down; and then wrote a letter to Eugenius—then I took it up again, and embroiled my patience with it afresh—and then to cure that, I wrote a letter to Eliza.—Still it kept hold of me; and the difficulty of understanding it increased but the desire" (134). "Cure" and "desire" are the master words of this charmingly neurotic ritual.[29] An artist in procrastination such as Sterne can be trusted to know what he is speaking about. The mode of gratification he describes in the study of the fragment is analogous with that provided by fetishism, not taken here as pathological but as a pattern enacted in the fulfillment of desire in general. Satisfaction is achieved, as it were, metonymically, by overestimating a detail. The piece, the part is given the power to evoke what cannot be present otherwise, namely, wholeness. The pleasure taken in the fragment is the grasping of the part for the whole, or the fixation on the veil, which is and is not what it hides; for the briefest of instants, it is a triumphant denial of the absence of the missing object of our wishes. It is also a successful resolution of the grieving for the completeness that cannot be possessed.

Mr. Spectator and Yorick are not repelled by the incomplete quality of fragments or by the various usages these have been subjected to by other readers before them: like Lazarus in another biblical context, they are happy enough to take what is left. More important, they demonstrate what a serious game can be played with discarded fragments. Because of the diversity of their origins, these can suggest unexpected compositions and liberate new meanings, just as a meal cooked with leftover pieces from other meals can be the occasion for the most delicious picnic. In both cases one has to respect the distinctive flavor of each piece and identify it carefully to make the most of it: preserving what is left and enhancing what is found, with a *gourmet*'s passion and expectation. The pleasure of the fragment is not untroubled though, as is testified to by the definitive interruption suffered by the old gentleman's story, despite the willingness of the notary, "inflamed with a desire to begin" (139); just as Yorick is desirous to know what follows, like readers "reading for the plot," in Peter Brooks's expressive title.

The use of the fragment motif by Addison and even more conspicuously by Sterne lays bare the crude motivation of reading: the desire to know what happens next. The notary's misfortunes command all the more attention from Yorick's viewpoint, as they allow him to meet the possessor of a story—which both he and we will not be told. One can assume that, like in the *Thousand and One Nights*, it is the telling that makes sense and keeps life going. Plot here has to be taken in its starkest definition as investigated by Paul Ricoeur (not in the restricted sense it acquired through the development of the realist novel in the nineteenth century), that of a simple formal principle of configuration, establishing a basic coherence, which is necessary to the human mind. As such, it becomes, as Ricoeur says, "the intelligible whole that governs a succession of events in any story," or, as Brooks puts it, "the dynamic shaping force of the narrative discourse."[30]

Lovers of fragments such as Addison and Sterne will not complain that their pleasure is too little or too suspended in medias res, just as the texts that yield it, which have no definitive origin or ending. They—the lovers and the texts—do not obey the law of linear development found in the bildungsroman. This law has mortal implications since it is only when you reach the end—of the text, of reading, of life—that the whole structure makes sense. This may by contrast enhance the seduction of the fragment as form—more properly, as formal subversion, as a continuous questioning of formal conventions, especially assumptions regarding regularity and completeness. Compared with fully developed narratives, fragments are aleatory expressions. They are chance pieces, rescued by their readers from oblivion and from the destructiveness of time; they just would not *be* without the warm reading that brings them back to life again, miraculously.

Thus, broken pieces can be ennobled, in an echo of Christ's miracle as related by Matthew: "And He took the seven loaves and the fish and gave thanks, broke *them* and gave *them* to His disciples; and the disciples *gave* to the multitude. So they all ate and were filled, and they took up seven large baskets full of the fragments that were left" (Matt. 15:36–37; italics added). Fragments become sufficient (as communion itself is given in small pieces of bread); the material is transformed. This has implications for the creative use of the fragment motif by Sterne and Addison. In their perspective, a fragment may be used not only to reconstitute a previously written text—and fragments need not belong to a distant past to be precious. The conjuring up of what was once written may even be a mere pretext, since the deciphering of fragments serves in fact to activate the very mechanism of storytelling, rather than to reconstitute a preexisting story.

Sterne's use of the formal possibilities of the fragment never depends upon authorizing his writing with the invocation of an established truth. It is likewise free from the temptation to endow the fragment with aphoristic meaning. Yet the fragment chez Sterne has an uncanny appeal, and the practice of reading and discrimination may confer on certain passages a special, almost talismanic value, as they find themselves at the very core of the motivation of reading, where the desire for someone else's untold story impels the reader forward.

The genetic code of DNA offers itself as a tempting further metaphor here, and one that respects the etymology of the fragment: a broken piece—as such useful or useless, depending on the capacity for imaginative response in the reader. A fragment of DNA can be used, precisely, to identify the whole, often for forensic, but also for more creative purposes—including the science-fiction possibility of regerminating a species from a fragment rescued from fossilization. We would do well not to recycle the story of Yorick's skull in this connection, but the materials provided by this unique receptacle continue to motivate the curious reader, so often invoked by writers of the age.

Who is this curious reader, one may ask, if not the one who follows the thoroughfares and byways of a text, in an endless search for provisional truth? No one has applied himself to the task better than the dedicatee of this volume, whose scrupulous example has made Sterne's works quite undissociable from his own (in)formative and indefatigable enterprise. We hope that this fragment may be added, with no derogation from such an example, to the ongoing criticism of Sterne and to the steady accumulation of Sterneana.[31]

NOTES

1. *The Life and Opinions of Tristram Shandy, Gentleman: The Text*, ed. Melvyn New and Joan New, vols. 1 and 2 of the Florida Edition of the Works of Laurence Sterne (Gainesville: University Press of Florida, 1978), preface; all subsequent references to *Tristram Shandy* cite Sterne's original volume and book numbers followed by the Florida edition page number and will appear in the text.

2. Isaac Brandon, "Fragments in the Manner of Sterne 1797," *Sterneiana,* vol. 21 (New York: Garland, 1974); Paul Stapfer, "Fragment inédit," in *Laurence Sterne: Sa personne et ses ouvrages: Etude précédée d'un fragment inédit de Sterne* (Paris: G. Fischbacher, 1882), 16–52.

3. "I intended to have arranged [the most distinguished passages] alphabetically," the editor explains in the third edition, "till I found the stories of *Le Fever*, the *Monk*, and *Maria*, would be too closely connected for the *feeling reader*, and would wound the bosom of *sensibility* too deeply: I therefore placed them at a proper distance from each other." *The Beauties of Sterne*, 3rd ed. (1782), v–vi, quoted in Alan B. Howes, ed., *Sterne: The Critical Heritage* (Boston: Routledge and Kegan Paul, 1974), 257.

4. *A Sentimental Journey through France and Italy and Continuation of the Bramine's Journal: The Text and Notes*, ed. Melvyn New and W. G. Day, vol. 6 of the Florida Edition of the Works of Laurence Sterne (Gainesville: University Press of Florida, 2002), 45; hereafter cited in the text by page number.

5. See Matt. 15:36–37, Mark 8:6–8, Luke 9:16–17, and John 6:11–13. Elizabeth Harries uses John's version persuasively and invokes the metaphorical meaning of Jesus's injunction to his disciples to "gather up the fragments that remain, that nothing be lost," which she applies dynamically to Sterne's novels as the disciples' baskets in which he "'gathered up the fragments' of learning and of the quotidian that came his way." Elizabeth Wanning Harries, *The Unfinished Manner: Essays on the Fragment in the Later Eighteenth Century* (Charlottesville: University Press of Virginia, 1994), 51. My own purpose is to reflect on the notion of literal as well as spiritual food, associated to fragments in each Gospel, and to address the metonymic connection of fragment and food in literature, and account for its lasting power.

6. Stéphane Mallarmé, *Œuvres complètes*, ed. Henri Mondor and G. Jean-Aubry (Paris: Gallimard, 1945), 872.

7. "He has communicated a Manuscript to us, that he means soon to publish. It is stiled a *Sentimental Journey through Europe*, by Yoric [*sic*]. It has all the Humour and Address of the best Parts of *Tristram*, and is quite free from the Grossness of the worst. There is but Half a Volume wrote of it yet. He promises to spin the Idea through several Volumes, in the same chaste Way, and calls it his *Work of Redemption*." Richard Griffith, *A Series of Genuine Letters between Henry and Frances*, vol. 5 (London, 1770), quoted in *Sterne: The Critical Heritage*, 185.

8. Christopher Ricks, "Introductory Essay," in *Tristram Shandy*, ed. Melvyn New and Joan New (Harmondsworth: Penguin, 1997), xv, xiv.

9. Blaise Pascal, *Thoughts*, ed. Charles W. LL. D. Eliot, trans. W. F. Trotter (New York: Collier and Son, 1909), 28. Accessed online at http://etext.lib.virginia.edu/toc/modeng/public/PasThou.html.

10. Alain Montandon, "Le Fragment," in *Les Formes brèves* (Paris: Hachette, 1992), 81.

11. "The inexpressibility or inaccessibility of the divine so often encountered in the sermons manifests itself in the sublime silences which suggest an origin they cannot convey." Christopher Fanning, "'The Things Themselves': Origins and Originality in Sterne's Sermons," *Eighteenth Century: Theory and Interpretation* 40 (1999): 41.

12. Harries, *The Unfinished Manner*, 52.

13. Ibid., 12.

14. Ibid.

15. Melvyn New, "Sterne's Rabelaisian Fragment: A Text from the Holograph Manuscript," *PMLA* 87 (1972): 1083–92; hereafter cited in the text as SRF.

16. Introduction to *A Sentimental Journey*, ed. Thomas Keymer (London: J. M. Dent, 1994), xvi.

17. *The Life and Opinions of Tristram Shandy, Gentleman: The Notes*, ed. Melvyn New with Richard A. Davies and W. G. Day, vol. 3 of the Florida Edition of the Works of Laurence Sterne (Gainesville: University Press of Florida, 1984), 226, 264–65; hereafter cited in the text by page number.

18. Richard A. Davies, "'The Fragment' in *Tristram Shandy V, 1*," *English Studies* 57 (1976): 523.

19. *A Sentimental Journey through France and Italy and Continuation of the Bramine's Journal*, 201.

20. Harries, *The Unfinished Manner*, 54.

21. Quoted from *A Sentimental Journey through France and Italy and Continuation of the Bramine's Journal*, 282.

22. *Troilus and Cressida*, 5.2.157–59.

23. *Othello*, 3.3.93.

24. Roy Porter, *English Society in the Eighteenth Century* (1982; London: Penguin, 1990), 71.

25. *Laurence Sterne: The Letters*, ed. Melvyn New and Peter de Voogd, vols. 7 and 8 of the Florida Edition of the Works of Laurence Sterne (Gainesville: University Press of Florida, 2009), 8:619; 7:116.

26. Alexander Pope, *The Poems of Alexander Pope*, ed. John Butt (1963; London: Methuen, 1984), 723; hereafter cited in the text.

27. *The Sermons of Laurence Sterne: The Text*, ed. Melvyn New, vol. 4 of the Florida Edition of the Works of Laurence Sterne (Gainesville: University Press of Florida, 1996), 279.

28. *The Spectator, 1711–1714*, ed. Donald F. Bond (Oxford: Clarendon, 1965), 1:361; hereafter cited in the text. Richard Baxter (1615–1691), Nonconformist clergyman, acted as army chaplain with the Puritans under Cromwell, was appointed a royal chaplain at the Restoration, then driven out of the Church of England by the Act of Uniformity in 1662. The Act of Indulgence in 1672 permitted him to return to London, where he divided his time between preaching and writing. Other mentions of Baxter by Addison in the *Spectator* include no. 598: "I could not but smile upon reading a Passage in the Account which Mr. *Baxter* gives of his own Life, wherein he represents it as a great Blessing, that in his Youth he very narrowly escaped getting a Place at Court" (5:44); also no. 445, about "*The last Words of Mr.* Baxter" (4:63).

29. There is a remarkable example of what I am describing as "neurotic" or "fetishistic" reading in a novel by William Golding worth citing here. A young man on board ship receives a long-awaited letter from a young woman he has met and fallen peremptorily in love with. The letter itself is conventional enough; but the man's interest is caught, and his desire quickened, by the fact that there are lines from another unblotted sheet on the reverse of the letter (the lines turn out to be a quotation from Pope); and he is further tantalized by a fragmentary phrase, ambiguous, "pressed through a previous page by a lead or silver point" (*Close Quarters* [London: Faber and Faber, 1987], 216).

30. See Paul Ricoeur, *Temps et récit*, vol. 2, *La Configuration du temps dans le récit de fiction* (Paris: Seuil, 1984), and Peter Brooks, who refers to Ricoeur as he develops his own theory in *Reading for the Plot* (New York: Knopf, 1984), 13.

31. The modest testimony offered by J. C. T. Oates is worth remembering. His collection of Sterneana, he tells us, was achieved by chance. He had first been hunting for a seventeenth-century minor author whose works were "almost impossibly rare and, for me, quite impossibly expensive; . . . it was soon borne in upon me that this was not the right tree up which to bark. Nor indeed . . . did I appear to be in the right century. I moved on to the eighteenth." And here fortune smiled on his endeavor: "It was while I was making myself familiar with the contents of my library that I discovered a cache of Sterne and Sterneana bequeathed by an early addict." Oates disclaimed the role of critic—"I hold it to be no part of the book-collector's province to be a critic as well"—but his hobbyhorsical industry forms part of our research, and when he says,"I accept with gratitude such crumbs as fall my way from the tables of the philosophers of book-collecting," we recognize in him a true devotee and disciple of the fragment. See "On Collecting Sterne," *The Book Collector* 1, no. 4, 1, 6, 11.

Chapter Thirteen

The Centrality of Sterne in the Culture of Modernity, or Melvyn New and the Rewriting of the West

Donald R. Wehrs

In four decades of extraordinary scholarship, Melvyn New has helped move Laurence Sterne from an eccentric position within the story of Western modernity to one of centrality. This achievement goes beyond championing a favorite author and being the dominant spokesman for half of a two-sided scholarly debate (as many accounts of post-1960s Sterne criticism would have it), in which Sterne is either a backward-looking Renaissance Christian humanist satirist *or* an isolated pioneer of modernist irony or postmodern indeterminacy. On the contrary, Professor New's critical and editorial work places Sterne *both* alongside Lucian, Erasmus, and Montaigne, on the one hand, *and* alongside Nietzsche, Proust, and Levinas, on the other. Sterne becomes a central relay station in the production of literary modernity, his discourse highlighting integral links between modern literature's ethical vocation and its cultivation of delight in disorientation by associating the value of literature with its production of unease, detachment from opinions through attachment to people, and openness to immediacies that may shipwreck one's darling schemes or capsize a cherished self-image. By self-consciously combining aspects of Shakespeare and Cervantes, Sterne bequeaths to his successors, beginning with Goethe, a new idea of what literature should do. Rather than using fable and rhetoric to present to the imagination what an understanding clarified of error should "see," some conjunction of the true, the good, and the beautiful that should orient sense, literature instead should induce ethical disorientations that prompt sensibility of, behind and before metaphysics' conceptualizing "grasp," behind and before cultural-historical meanings, a more fundamental orienting sense, one that intimates the ethical insufficiency of both metaphysics of presence and the modern forms of *constructed*, egocentric value, meaning, and identity that seek to replace it. Professor New's appreciation of how Sterne exposes the folly and violence of both dogmatic systematizing and narcissistic self-approval informs his unease with criticism's tendency, especially under the aegis of theory, to lapse into both conditions.

Underlying such unease, as underlying the disorienting sense of Sternean prose, is the primacy of the ethical—in Professor New's case, the question of what being responsible in the face of the Holocaust entails, and what literature has to do with that responsibility. Having been born a Jew in 1938, New observes, contributed mightily to "the disaster of European Jewry" becoming "the one inescapable event defining [his] intellectual horizon."[1] While noting that such a focus was unique neither to himself nor to Jews, but rather shaped postwar "liberalism" and the "antiauthoritarianism" of the post-1968 academy, New suggests that in his case it yielded a "contrarian" style of thinking in which any drift toward "total agreement," conducive of narcissistic self-approval, set off warning signals "of something amiss."[2] Thus New challenged the expression of postwar liberalism in Sterne criticism—epitomized for New by John Traugott's 1954 book, which treats Sterne, New argues, as "'one of us,' a modern existentialist, alienated and absurd, but confronting the abyss with sentiment and fellow-feeling."[3] New highlights by contrast Sterne's reliance upon authority and distrust of individualism, arguing that "*Tristram Shandy* joins works like *A Tale of a Tub* and the *Dunciad* as one further effort to stem the eighteenth century's ever increasing enthusiasm for human self-sufficiency."[4] In following decades New challenged theory's embrace of "antiauthoritarianism" as a sufficient professional and political good, both by pointing out its performative contradiction (how theories of indeterminacy rest upon determinate theorizing)[5] and by posing a question that exposes the naïveté of imagining that unmasking moralistic discourse might render determinate moral judgments unnecessary: "if every construct tells a lie, and truth is only in the ineffable, ungraspable present, what do we tell the children?"[6]

Theory's marginalization of such questions reflects what philosophic discourse calls intellectualism or theoreticism—the positing of an abstract rationality disjunctive with embodied subjectivity. Such intellectualism is the original target of the satiric traditions upon which Sterne draws to challenge, New argues, modernity's "enthusiasm for human self-sufficiency." Traceable to Plato, and central to his attack upon poetry and rhetoric, intellectualism is recuperated in modern philosophy by Descartes, who separates "eloquence" and "poetry" from (abstract) rationalism ideally pursued in isolation from other people.[7] Constructive, regulative thought should resemble the activity of "a single architect" or "some prudent legislator" whose solitary ordering mirrors "the condition of the true religion, whose rules were laid down by God alone."[8] The literary traditions upon which Sterne draws, by contrast, equate abstract rationalism with cloud-cuckoo-land. Through absurd dialogues and scenarios, Aristophanes, Lucian, and Rabelais demand instead that ideas assume, at least in poetic and rhetorical thought experiments, material shape and consequences. Satire thus exposes how not just anything may be thought, and how dependent thought is upon bodily frames of reference to which vulnerabilities and anxieties are necessarily annexed.[9] Both points are central to Sterne's presentation of Walter's and Toby's respective efforts at self- and world-construction—and both inform New's suspicion that contemporary theory tends to replicate their folly.

Within ancient, medieval, and Renaissance contexts, however, such satire assumes, in the words of the epigraph for the first two volumes of *Tristram Shandy*, that "Men . . . are tormented with the Opinions [*dogmata*] they have of Things, and not by the Things [*pragmata*] themselves."[10] Clearing away false thought born of prideful dogmatic consistency is sustained in its geniality, in its political optimism, by expectation that delight in folly's self-revelation will open us to real presence (or sufficient "right seeing" to make thinking and living well possible). Satire not only disabuses common sense; it frees understanding for the kind of metaphysical contemplation without which common sense, unable to escape thought's distortions by bodily senses, would resolve itself into low animal cunning. Skepticism toward various schools' claims to conceptual adequacy need not challenge notions of understanding (*nous, intellectus*) resting upon what Hans Blumenberg calls theological trust that "the soul *and* its objects . . . belong to *one* world . . . in which existential fulfillment is guaranteed if what is planned to go together does come together."[11] Becoming sensible to the insufficiency of our conceptual grasp makes present to us, paradoxically, the metaphysical principles structuring a cosmos whose intelligibility is the trace of the transcendence from which we emerge and toward which we aspire to return.

But by Sterne's time, New argues, literary simulations of presence have become problematic in ways that place literary meaning in crisis. In an essay originally published in 1976, he notes that eighteenth-century fiction uses "the concept of an intrusive and particular providence with great regularity," even though "the conditions under which" belief in such a concept "could be sustained in the eighteenth century were radically different from the conditions of the fourteenth."[12] Eighteenth-century fiction's generic perplexity rests upon wishing, at once, to present for understanding's contemplation a "God-ordained, God-contrived world in which virtue is rewarded and vice punished," and to articulate a narrative concordant with a "secular vision" of human motivation and chance predicated upon experience and the deliberations it regulates.[13] While this issues in a splendid incoherence—the "self-sustained world of the modern novel" woven upon/over the "God-sustained world of the romance" so as to juxtapose, not reconcile, varying senses of sense and understanding (*nous*)[14]—it also establishes the possibility of a grim double bind.

In a 1979 essay New raises the prospect that the novel's "self-sustained world," its revolt against romance's evocation of metaphysical presence, may culminate in Pynchon's self-consuming, paranoiac narrative structures. That Pynchon's fictive worlds intimate "that something has gone incredibly wrong in modern life" casts doubt upon contemporary theory's faith in "antiauthoritarianism" as moral panacea.[15] Indeed, theory's optimism that antifoundationalism will somehow make present what is needed to guide humans toward goodness and happiness mirrors the theological trust of premodern skepticism and satire. By contrast, in Pynchon, "[t]he tension between design and accident, pattern and fragment, is played out against a grave suspicion that the fragments cannot be ordered in any way that could satisfy our need to understand the structure of life."[16] New implies that such *need* is not simply residual nostalgia for "metaphysics." Subsequent research suggests its bodily basis in neurobiological bonds between feelings of well-being and confidence that one is oriented properly in relation to one's environment.[17] In *V.*, where all promise to present V. for our understanding's contemplation is delusion and trickery, the narrative blocks orienting sense so thoroughly that no "paraclete" can offer comfort, for "the true voice of the artist is simply the measure of the apocalypse, the holocaust to come."[18]

If divestiture of presence seems to drain literature of solace, receptivity to presence would seem, on the part of writers and readers, wholly anachronistic. New reminds us that romance's authority and coherence depend upon belief in its underlying metaphysics. Faith that love governs the world for the best is uncompromised by the implausibility of Heliodorus's *An Ethiopian Story*, or Tasso's and Sidney's displacing Heliodorus's Apollo in favor of the Christian God in their retellings. In scriptural hermeneutics, the truth made present guarantees the truth of the narrative events related: "the attribution of miraculous intervention fostered belief among those for whom God's sustaining presence was a reality. Less real, then, were attempts to retell events without that presence."[19] Validating miracles and divine intervention were part of traditional historiography because events without presence appeared unreal. Similarly, plausibility in romance was dispensable because of "the priority of the Word over the world."[20] By the eighteenth century, however, such modes of narrative become impossible in ways that are historically irreversible: "What happened to eighteenth-century fiction was not the invention of a new mode of narration but the imposition of a new worldview," even though its own, and our own, furtive commerce with romance suggests that "we have still not found a way of storytelling totally free from a longing for the past certainties of an immanent and sustaining God."[21] For New, such loss is not just a historical fact. It is a moral necessity: "Unlike those who today still accept the reality of an intervening god, I find the notion, in view of twentieth-century Jewish experience, appalling."[22] The question for New becomes, what does literature *do* that evades Plato's charge that poets lie without colluding with the big lie that is Platonic-Christian metaphysics?

At first it might seem that Professor New's early work's very success in grounding Sterne's narrative in Swiftian satire and latitudinarian theology weds Sterne's fiction to historically irretrievable confidence that once delusions of self-sufficiency are cleared away, the reasonableness of Anglican moderation, sociability, and institutional authority will become present to sense. New's own identification of such confidence with unwarranted assumptions and rhetorical sleights of hand suggests that what Sterne affirms is so time-bound that to contextualize it is to objectify it along the lines that Hans-Georg Gadamer associates with traditional historicism: the literary text's value becomes its service "as a source," its "conveying knowledge of the historical context, just like the other silent relics of the past."[23] New's 1970s and early 1980s account of the crisis facing literary meaning in modernity implies that even if *Tristram Shandy*'s critical project remains relevant as long as humans hunger after romance and presence, Sterne's alternative to intellectualist folly—"the use of reason to control pride and acknowledge one's limitations; the use of reason to argue against pride the necessity for authority"[24]—might be so rooted in particular ideological contexts that its explication tends to corroborate Plato's charge that literature uncritically reflects "common opinion," *doxa*.

New is able to evade this critical impasse by showing how Sterne's satire against the intellectualism peculiar to the modern West yields an orienting sense irreducible to recuperated metaphysics and so points literature a way out of the double bind he describes. Noting intricate intertextual bonds between *Tristram Shandy* and *A Tale of a Tub*, Professor New points out that Tristram's declaration, "When a man gives himself up to the government of a ruling passion,—or, in other words, when his HOBBY-HORSE grows head-strong,—farewell cool reason and fair discretion!" echoes "Swift's famous remark" that "when a Man's Fancy gets *astride* on his Reason, when Imagination is at Cuffs with the Senses . . . the first Proselyte he makes, is Himself."[25] While Swift targets the imperialistic, antisocial bent of abstract rationalism generally, he is particularly concerned with how delusions of self-sufficiency in modernity involve not contemplating but projecting a world. After asking, "what Man in the natural State, or Course of Thinking, did ever conceive it in his Power, to reduce the Notions of all Mankind, exactly to the same Length, and Breadth, and Heighth of his own?" he singles out Descartes, who "reckoned to see before he died, the Sentiments of all Philosophers, like so many lesser Stars in his *Romantick* System, rapt and drawn within his own *Vortex.*"[26] Starting from a Lucianic exposure of the antisocial madness of seeking perfected contemplative understanding in abstracting oneself from sense and other people,[27] Swift moves to expose the madness of making one's own "Vortex" or System the object of "rapt" contemplation, the force toward which others necessarily gravitate. Modern subjectivity becomes "at Cuffs with the Senses" in aspiring to *construct* the equivalent of presence, to accord the mind's own products a role akin to the beatific vision.[28] Subjectivity aspires to the self-sufficiency not of just any god, but of the god traceable to nominalist theology.

Late medieval nominalist theology argued that the distinction between God's absolute power (what He might do, abstractly considered) and his ordained power (what he chose to do through Creation) meant that the created world was not obliged to reflect Neoplatonic-Aristotelian metaphysics discernible to understanding's (*nous's*) contemplation. Rather, the created world, as the product of unconstrained Sovereign Will, possesses an internal logic—a rationality predicated upon will—that only empirical inquiry could discern. Such premises, Hans Blumenberg argues, provide the philosophical underpinnings of modern scientific inquiry.[29] Louis Dupré and Ullrich Langer, building on Blumenberg's work, trace how nominalist conceptions of God as subject, constrained only by what his freedom willed, restructures Western reflection upon human subjectivity.[30] Tracing how the "modern self" emerges from a "rationalist philosophy . . . severed from those sources that once provided its content," Dupré notes that selfhood, now narrowed to "individual solitude, . . . reduces the other to the status of object," so that "theoretical egocentrism inevitably leads to a moral one."[31] Just as God comes to be identified with unconstrained voluntarism, so the subject "ordains" his own identity through a Sovereign Will that, like Descartes' architect and legislator, and like Swift's "mad" system-maker, mirrors the unconditioned will of a voluntarist God. [32] Langer points out that once "the will is conceived of more and more as not determined by the *intellectus* [*nous*] or by its objects as final cause, but instead as an essentially free power *ad oppositum*," the rational and the good become relative to an intentional "world" "created" from an act of will whose unconditionality means that the "reasons for a decision can never be sufficient to explain the decision," indeed, are "irrelevant to the decision,"[33] making decision, in effect, hobbyhorsical.

The identification of self with will, and the will's freedom with noncontradiction, stands behind such characters as Don Quixote, Othello, Coriolanus, and Leontes, who conceive themselves as incarnations of their own ideas, and so expect others to be "rapt" and "drawn into their vortices." Don Quixote sustains the world his will brings into creation through reimagining experience in ways that preserve the principle of noncontradiction, as his explanation of defeat by the windmill exemplifies: "aquel sabio Frestón . . . ha vuelto estos gigantes en molinos por quitarme la gloria de su vencimiento" ("that magician Frestón . . . changed the giants into windmills in order to deprive me of the glory of overcoming them").[34] Through having multiple characters mirror Quixote's madness, Cervantes depicts the "infectious" nature of the new form of subjectivity he represents, while dramatizing its antisocial, dogmatic propensities in such scenes as when Quixote and Cardenio come to blows upon disagreeing over whether Queen Madásima of *Amadis of Gaul* was guilty of adultery with master Elisabat (*Quijote,* 232/ *Quixote,* 194).[35]

These aspects of Quixote clearly lie behind the portrait of Walter Shandy, who, Tristram tells us, had so much of what is "known by the name of perseverance in a good cause,—and of obstinacy in a bad one," that his mother "knew 'twas to no purpose to make any remonstrance" (1.17.50), that "The Hero of *Cervantes* argued not the point with more seriousness,—nor had he more faith,—or more to say on the powers of Necromancy in dishonouring his deeds" (1.18.58) than did Walter in expounding his theory of names, for "he was systematical, and, like all systematick reasoners, he would move both heaven and earth, and twist and torture every thing in nature to support his hypothesis" (1.18.61). As Professor New points out, by the time of Swift and Sterne, the consequences of such subjectivity, in terms of religious and civil war, ideological fanaticism and political oppression, were painfully evident; Augustan satire and latitudinarian theology conceived themselves, in part, as therapies against its further ravages.[36] Indeed, the totalitarian potential of conditioning reason and morality upon will and freedom is glimpsed in Mrs. Shandy's foreknowledge that any words contradicting his favorite schemes would only bounce off Walter, so determined is he to "twist and torture every thing in nature" to fit his ideas.

Long before Zîzêk identified the narcissistic pleasure of ideological consistency for its own sake, in a 1975 essay New explored how Orwell, prompted by anti-Semitism's imperviousness to rational refutation, asks why people so frequently "swallow absurdities on one particular subject while remaining sane on others,"[37] a propensity of Quixote. Linking Orwell's question to Hannah Arendt's analysis of the political logic of concentration camps, New suggests that the will to willfulness culminates in aspiring to annihilate "good and evil, right and wrong," to conjure away anything external to power (here, the state's): "The function of the camps, then, is to demonstrate, to those *temporarily* outside, the absolute power of the state to render everyone superfluous, nonexistent, nonhuman."[38] Totalitarianism's performative contradiction—the need to display total power requires an "outside" to be seized: absent Jews, the state will have to "invent" some—makes state terror voraciously open-ended.

Nonetheless, in personal, especially erotic life, such contradiction offers, New suggests in a 1988 essay on Proust and Sterne, some hope of escaping the system's totalizing logic: "For Sterne and Proust both, the aggressive act of possession is simultaneously an act of loss; and for both, that loss had to do with the fact that desire has become an intellectual (verbal) pursuit rather than a sexual one; an act of memory rather than of presence."[39] The central paradox Proust explores, one consistent with the totalitarian shadow hanging over modern sensibility, is that Marcel is made prisoner to his own compulsion to "imprison" Albertine, to know and control her utterly, a project whose impossibility Proust's narrative charts: Marcel's conceptual schemas can "hold" Albertine no more than his apartment can contain her. By contrast, Sterne's *A Sentimental Journey*, delineating similar dynamics in Yorick's interactions with a series of female "fugitives," is, according to New, "more hopeful" in suggesting, in the place of impossible presence, "the value of nonverbal communication," the "puzzlement" of sexual appetite's conjunction with "our desperate need for connection with the other," and the surrender of illusions of mastery in experiencing modification by the other not as an assault upon will, but as erotic delight.[40]

In tracing Sterne's alternative to the tyrannizing potential of modern subjectivity, Professor New discloses Sterne's improvisation of an ethical agency for literature disjunctive with romance's fictive picturing of presumed metaphysical truths. The Anglican satiric model Sterne adapts from Swift reaffirms the Augustinian notion that *cupiditas* so deflects the senses into antisocial directions and so darkens understanding that attributions of self-sufficiency to good conscience appear culpably naive. Correlating Swift's "On the Testimony of Conscience" sermon with Sterne's "The Abuses of Conscience Considered" sermon, New links the former's satiric exposure of the hack writer's self-engrossed willfulness with the latter's depiction of Tristram as a highly problematic conjunction of Walter and Toby—both of whom create worlds through will (theories, the bowling green sieges) that condition what, within those worlds, counts as rationality and goodness. In contrast with Shaftesbury's writings, "[t]he crux of both Swift's and Sterne's sermons is that the testimony of conscience cannot be trusted" because "conscience is abused by our other interests."[41] Thus, the intense attention to concupiscence in *Tristram Shandy*, the constant veering of language toward bawdiness, not only reflects the travestying of intellectualist delusions, but also highlights how concupiscence shapes mental and moral perception much as the curvature of light shapes physical perception: "[o]ur imaginations [are] caught, Eugenius points out, by the crevice Toby stares at in II.vii," and "delicacy and concupiscence" are "simply two aspects of the same unreason," for a vicious dialectic of appropriativeness and defensiveness repels us from genuine sociability, exemplified in Tristram's "final failure with Nannette,"[42] where the "cursed slit" in her petticoat (7.63.650) makes present to Tristram his own *cupiditas* and so his exposure to that of others.

Latitudinarian Anglican rejections of will-constructed subjectivity as neither orthodox nor sensible cannot merely return to prenominalist metaphysics of presence. The conscience that is untrustworthy, as Sterne's imagery of a judge deciding a case illustrates (2.17.164), is conscience viewed as an object of reflection by an onlooker whose putative abstract rationality presumes a philosophically untenable forgetting of the body and a religiously untenable forgetting of sin. Such critique forecloses contemplating presence, as New explains in a 1992 essay linking *A Tale of a Tub* with Thomas Mann's *The Magic Mountain* and a 1993 essay on Swift and Sterne. The *Tale*'s "gift of three coats" constitutes "a primal religious truth," on which the father's will already comments: "Hence, from the outset the gift calls forth commentary, and the commentary plants the seeds for assertion and counterassertion, persuasion and the need to convert others to one's own understanding of the gift's disposition."[43] Swift's success in painting the dogmatic irrationalism of Peter and Jack obscures the tension between acknowledgment that the primal truth cannot be recovered, consistent with "the early shoots of the higher criticism," and Swift's desire to associate Martin with a doctrinal truth that "eschew[es] commentary": "Martin's position, despite its privilege, is indeed part of a 'scholastic dispute,' even perhaps a cunning rhetorical ploy."[44] Martin's proximity to Peter and Jack betrays how easily the definition of a mad projector, "a man persuaded first of his own truth and in turn persuading others," might fit Christ: "the pathos of the center, the finite regression of language in the face of conflicting ideologies," leads Swift to recognize that "his irony had diminished his own position as well as his enemy's," and so reduces Martin from the originally intended role of conduit through which true doctrine is made present to largely silent counterpoint to Peter's and Jack's voluble certitudes.[45]

New notes that Sterne seems to have recognized a similar "pit he had dug for himself" in his efforts, in anti-Methodist polemics, to distinguish enthusiasm from inspiration, and suggests that Sterne's perception, in the Rabelaisian fragment of Slawkenbergius's tale, of "a particularly mechanical operation of the intellect whereby each argument comes into existence only as a counter to the preceding," yields the conclusion that since the "vulgar look too high" and statesmen "too low," truth always falls away into an enigmatically silent, absent "middle."[46] Similarly, in *The Magic Mountain*, Hans Castorp is rendered disillusioned and indecisive by the mutually undermining, internally limiting arguments of Settembrini and Naphta, both of whom create worlds out of will to which reason and goodness are subordinate. Irony against dogmatism is a necessary but insufficient response, as Mann indicates by having Hans become, for a time, enthralled by Mynheer Peeperkorn, whose incoherent portentousness, epitomized by speaking gravely before a waterfall that drowns out his words, creates an illusion not of best commentary but rather of "awful presence—an uncanny and frightening foreshadowing of the total breakdown of thought and intellect, criticism and commentary coming to Germany ten years later."[47] The implication, New suggests, is that presence's intellectual impossibility does not diminish its psychic "hold." Indeed, one might further argue that becoming sensible of the willfulness deforming all claims to represent presence may only strengthen their powers of enchantment—a phenomenon to which not only the emergence of Nazism and other totalitarian enterprises, but also the rise of fundamentalisms attest.

Instead of surrendering modernity to subjectivities displacing contemplative presence with enacting will, Sterne makes embodied, disorienting ethical experience, rather than speculative/spectular metaphysics, the conditioning context of rational and moral deliberation. Delineating this turn, Professor New is led through gender criticism to Levinas's ethical challenge to the metaphysics of presence and its various modern substitutes—a challenge whose consequences for literary study constitute "something new under the sun."[48] In distinguishing the "hopefulness" of *A Sentimental Journey* from *The Captive*'s rueful pessimism, New suggests that "[p]erhaps Sterne's major insight into the nature of human desire is the idea that the most satisfying human union is achieved when the female penetrates and the male receives," a notion bearing some relation to "the model of Christian love constantly before" Sterne as a clergyman, one in which "Christ the incarnate God . . . enter[s] us, male and female both" and "male and female both . . . receiv[e] Christ," which allows an overturning of patriarchal ideology—epitomized by Walter—to become imaginable.[49] New reads Yorick's journey as moving away from "the sentimental" understood as "evasion of desire," with "desire" no longer denoting *cupiditas* but rather its opposite—something exterior to (self- and world-creating) will, with "terms" and a "right" of its own.[50] Such externalized desire presses upon us a longing for "connection" with others culminating in finding one's "soul" in the other's "moving" us beyond will and its representations, for "the exchange of sexual roles (aggressor and recipient, active and passive)" constitutes the foremost, most bodily immediate articulation of a "need for human connection," which is the signature secondary means by which "grace" acts in and through nature.[51]

Commenting on Yorick's account of feeling the *grisset*'s pulse, New observes the pattern of imagining "movement from self to other . . . first as a silent sexual balance . . . followed by the male surrender of aggression (pursuit) to the female, who 'penetrates' his reins."[52] In a 1990 essay on gender criticism, New argues that such scenes are representative of how "Sterne initiates a feminist discourse, if that is what stands in opposition to the phallocentric one."[53] For Sterne, sexual vulnerability to a desire exterior to will links delight to receptivity and exchange, the intellectual correlative of which is delight in aesthetic nuances and nondogmatic "dancing" habits of mind. Goethe and Nietzsche, New notes, view such attributes as central to Sterne's achievement and aspire to make them their own.[54] They read Sterne as pointing the way to an alternative modernity that understands truth not only to be external to will but also to demand "courting"—indirection, tentativeness, flexibility, lightness of touch, and sense woven into sensibility.

In his 1994 study New notes how Sterne's articulation of the "paradox" that people "except in rare, fleeting moments of acute self-consciousness, believe far more than they can ever know, and evaluate their surroundings based on those beliefs in a never-ending process of mismeasurement, misevaluation, and maladjustment" informed Goethe's association of antidogmatic restlessness with the confluence of aesthetic and ethical imperatives, as well as Nietzsche's ideal of "self-overcoming" and association of conventional morality with dogmatic "mismeasurement."[55] Similarly, Sterne's suspicion of "Toby's stability, his monolithic hobby-horse, his self-satisfaction in the rightness of his cause," informs Goethe's depiction of egocentric sentimentalism from Werther to "the beautiful soul" of *Wilhelm Meisters Lehrjahre* to the utopian communities of *Wilhelm Meisters Wanderjahre*, and shapes Nietzsche's apprehension that "good conscience" constitutes perhaps a "far more dangerous threat to morality" than Walter's irritable lurching from one theory to another: New cites *Zarathustra*: "With whom does the greatest danger for the whole human future lie? Is it not with the good and just?—with those who say and feel in their hearts: 'We already know what is good and just, we possess it too; woe to those who are still searching for it!'"[56]

Yet Goethe's characters tend to divide between those who forfeit inner freedom through deference to others and those who conserve it at the price of ethical obtuseness or insouciance; similarly, the "dancing," iconoclastic Nietzsche contrasts with the Nietzsche for whom "will to power" recuperates nominalist subjectivity in a biophysics that resembles metaphysics.[57] By contrast, Sterne's "feminist," antidogmatic discourse is rooted in a latitudinarian piety, itself rooted in Cambridge Platonism's seemingly regressive efforts to salvage premodern thought.[58] Paradoxically, this theological-metaphysical context helps Sterne to imagine modification of self as both a chastening of egoism and an increase in freedom and joy, which moves his "feminist" discourse toward what contemporary, academic "feminist" discourse has notable difficulty articulating—an ethics that does not construe the good as "whatever empowers women" in ways that lapse into Nietzschean or liberal-individualistic variants of nominalist subjectivity.[59] Behind Anglicanism stands Erasmian theology generally, and behind Sterne's imagining of ethical self-modification stands Erasmus's account of nature and grace, mediated especially, Professor New notes in 1996 essay, by the late Cambridge Platonist John Norris.[60]

As I have argued elsewhere,[61] Erasmus understands grace to inform nature on the material level. Being (creation, nature) is constituted by God's love (as opposed to unconditioned will) so that there is nothing anterior to the ethical. Because such informed nature engenders within us a practical rationality (*phronêsis*) that, unlike Luther's "prudence of the flesh," directs us toward sociability and love, grace need not, as in Luther, overturn "the flesh's" (cojoined body and soul's) naturally sinful egoism through a metaphysical equivalent of sheer force.[62] Acting in a manner resembling discursive persuasion or perfected pedagogy rather than physical violence, Erasmian grace moves affections so as to realize, contrary to the drift of concupiscent intentionality, a wondrous but nonetheless not unnatural transformation of nature: "The impelling grace of God stimulates the desire in thousands of ways to lead it to justification, egging on a person's latent, feeble impulse. . . . [W]e owe this very intention to the grace which arouses and assists it and which will finally perfect it."[63] So understood, the operation of grace becomes an imaginable narrative sequence. Moreover, in thinking of grace-inflected natural sense perfecting itself in responsiveness to what lies beyond itself, and thinking of grace itself as ethically committed to preserving the freedom of the other ("egging on a person's latent, feeble impulse" is far from forcing another into essential identity with oneself), Erasmus suggests that what makes the self redeemable is its grace-informed susceptibility, "in thousands of ways," to modification by the sensible.

It is this redemptive mutability of sense that Professor New finds central to Sterne's paraphrasing of Norris in his fiction and sermons. While Tristram's observation that "[n]o man thinks right whilst he is in" his body, given its bending of the mind to self-love (7.13.593), echoes Norris's arguments that the Pythagoreans were "in a Qualified and Corrected Sense" justified to argue along these lines, Norris does not merely repeat Platonic claims that understanding entails leaving the senses behind; rather, he insists that "the senses and the passions, in themselves are good; only errors in understanding and judgment, the desire after the wrong objects, make them seem otherwise."[64] Like Erasmus on grace, Norris argues that the senses and passions "are not to be suppressed but directed, not contained but educated. That reason is, half of it, sense [Tristram's words (7.13.593)] is to be seen as God's gift, but only if our vision of perfection in heaven is not shaped by the imperfect sensations of this world."[65] Norris, again concordant with Erasmus, notes the convergence of natural sense and revelation in correlating Plato's definition of God as "goodness" with scripture: "For when it defines God, it does not say he is Wisdom or Power, but that he is Love. Not Loving, but Love it self."[66] Making love, rather than power or will, unconditioned, Norris makes rationality answerable to ethics in a way that allows grace-inflected senses to imitate Christ's "pity and compassion."[67] They constitute media whose refinement through experience follows from ongoing conversation between "sense" as common sense, "sense" as reflective understanding (for Norris, gaining a better grasp of the "innate ideas" through which God and morality are impressed upon us through nature), and "sense" as unconditioned ethical responsiveness to others.[68] After noting that "[t]hrough Christ (the Logos, Truth) . . . the senses and passions, originally designed to make possible our interaction with both the Good and God (and they are one and the same for Norris), can be redeemed,"[69] New suggests that Sterne not only affirms such propositions in his sermons but seeks to dramatize their actuality in his fiction.

Exploring how fiction might reform sense so as to estrange subjectivity from concupiscence leads New to place Sterne in dialogue with Levinas. In the preface to his 2001 collection of essays on Levinas and the eighteenth century, New notes that Levinas "questions . . . whether, when we hold the world of reason to be a *suspect* construct, we are totally impaled on our own suspect reasoning," for when ideology denies ethics the "status of reason," it compromises its own appeals to reason.[70] Before such an impasse, Levinas poses the "deceptively simple" question, "Whence comes the urge to question injustice?" prompting a further question: why does this *urge* escape the "suspect finalities of ideologies"?[71] Levinas answers that metaphysics is no more first philosophy than will is the first attribute of subjectivity: "*In the form* of the relationship with an other . . . there occurs a transcendence, a departure from being and thus *impartiality*."[72] As in Sterne's depiction of the senses' responsiveness to images of others in distress (for him, the means by which grace acts in and upon nature), to be unsettled from "rest" or "inner peace," to be pushed out of objective neutrality—as New puts it, "'de-posed' by the face of the other, for-the-other"[73]—sets reason *in motion*. If we allow *lived* experience of the unconditioned ethical to displace abstract rationalism, putting aside intellectualism in favor of the testimony of sensory immediacy, common sense, and our consequent "sense" of understanding that the ethical is not something added on to human subjectivity, but constitutive of it, then we are led to a literary theory calling upon us not simply "to disturb the text, but to be disturbed by it as well. . . . [W]e demonstrate responsibility to the text by welcoming the disturbance, displacement, and disorientation of ourselves *in response* to the text."[74]

Returning to the relationship between Sterne and Proust in 2001, New confesses to being struck by "how heavily" his 1988 readings "were influenced by . . . Levinas's *Totality and Infinity* (and Derrida's 1964 essay 'Violence and Metaphysics'), [his] only familiarity with Emmanuel Levinas in the mid-1980s."[75] Indeed, New's pivotal interpretation of desire as exterior to will, as having a "right" of its own that mandates the preservation of the other's otherness, is cognate with Levinas's extraordinary separation of desire from need, and thus from the appropriative/assimilative erotology governing Western reflection upon subjectivity from Plato to Heidegger. For Levinas, desire "toward the *absolutely other*" is incommensurate with desire derived from need, which "would characterize a being indigent and incomplete or fallen from its past grandeur. It would coincide with the consciousness of what has been lost; it would be essentially a nostalgia, a longing for return."[76] By contrast, Levinasian desire "desires beyond everything that can simply complete it"; it is a "desire without satisfaction which, precisely *understands* [*entend*] the remoteness, the alterity, and the exteriority of the other."[77] Ethical disruptions, modifying will and its representations, thus both traumatize and delight. Placing us in contact with what is irreducible to our ideas, they spare us a Godless universe by *blocking* the kind of self-sufficiency that need-predicated desire imagines to constitute happiness.[78] In taking the other as a reflection of oneself, one reduces the other to an object of consciousness; one betrays the separateness integral to ethical identity. In confusing consciousness or reflection with selfhood, one lapses into intellectualism and its estrangement from the sense through which ethical life is experienced.

New charts in Sterne's movement from the *Bramine's Journal* to *A Sentimental Journey* an increasingly self-conscious coming to terms with the ethical insufficiency of the erotology buttressing both metaphysics of presence and willful subjectivity's efforts to *construct* presence: "For in *Sentimental Journey*, as if to comment on the increasingly evident failure of *Bramine's Journal* to create the world as Sterne wanted it to be (a failure, indeed, to create—Godlike—the object of his desire as an entity standing before him), he rethinks the male-female relationship as a recomposition of the self in which the woman, in infinite desirability, is imagined as neither mirrored nor doubled, but as other, always happily either just out of reach, unpossessed, or attainable only through a surrender of the self to uncertainty and the transient caress . . . , rather than the assertion of self as knowledge and the permanent grasp."[79] The redemptive mutability of the senses through attunement to the differences of others both socializes desire (makes it noncolonizing) and places sense and understanding in a dialogue that, like ethics and Levinasian desire, renounces the "rest" of complacency and the "peace" of possession. Whereas Sterne loses Eliza "in the process of binding her so closely to himself, imprisoning her in the miniature around his neck," Yorick discovers in the Marquesina F***, "the other whose presence (present) is fleeting and momentary, . . . the moment in which his journey fulfills itself. She and he both move on; after all, what they are doing initially is clearing space precisely so that the other can move on."[80]

Sterne's struggle to free himself not from Anglican piety, but from a conceptualizing of presence (being) traditionally equated with the good, links ethical disorientations wrought by literature with discoveries of orienting sense behind and before cultural-historical meanings. Thus Sterne dramatizes what Levinas argues: that "before Culture and Aesthetics, meaning [*signification*] is situated in the Ethical, presupposed by all Culture and all meaning. Morality does not belong to Culture: it enables one to judge it."[81] Propelling the antidogmatic mobility of Sternean discourse is "the antecedence of sense to cultural signs," which is both the consequence and mechanism of erosion of the "[t]he Ego['s] . . . dogmatic naïveté before the Other who asks of it more than it can do spontaneously."[82] Prompting such "erosion" in readers by dramatizing its logic in fictional worlds, Sterne consolidates the entwinement of ethical sense and literary signification that Shakespeare and Cervantes pioneer.

As New points out, Sterne dramatizes how images no less than words, and often better, surprise affect out of subordination to egoism and ideology.[83] If Professor New suggests that Walter, Toby, and Tristram belong primarily in the world of satire, that they embody dead-end possibilities for modern subjectivity, his reading of Yorick suggests the creation of a character, who, like those of Shakespeare and Cervantes (Yorick is introduced through allusions to both), opens us to the world of the novel—*if* understood not as the generic analogue of nominalist-inspired modern subjectivity, but its alternative.[84] Yorick, entering literature via an account of his death, is defined by a material contingency, a being-before-death, that links subjectivity's embodiment to its nonresemblance to the nominalist God. "Last things"— death, judgment, justification, the black page—ineluctably accompany Yorick as a character (we are reminded of his death each time he appears).[85] Anglican doctrine regarding the soul's accountability before God underlies Sterne's presentation of "being-toward-death," not in terms of existential anguish or Heideggerian authenticity but in ways evocative of Levinasian being-toward the Other. Yorick rides a horse resembling Rocinante because "[e]xperience had taught [him] that benevolence could just as effectively be dispensed from a slow-moving nag as from a hard-charger."[86] Unlike Quixote, he knows he looks ridiculous, but the ethical takes precedence over will to self-construction. Consequently, Yorick habitually articulates ethical sense, as through his "Abuses of Conscience" sermon, through insisting that preaching divest itself of egotism (4.26.377), and through praising Trim's "practical" interpretation of doctrine (5.32.470–71), a process culminating in characterizing Shandean dysfunctional modernity as a story about "A COCK and a BULL" (9.33.809). Such a judgment, conditioning reason and sensibility upon the ethical, makes life in time consequential, thus pushing Yorick into novelistic realms where the self's gradual modification by others allows the work of grace to consecrate everyday experience with ultimate significance.[87]

The implications of such a reformed sense of the novel for reforming literary theory are explored in New's 2005 study of Sternean currents in Dickens's *Dombey and Son*.[88] Noting that Levinas associates art with "images of the objects of the real world," which would seem to recuperate Plato's critique, New observes that Levinas instead suggests that art "darkens" being— self-creating subjectivity as codified by Heideggerian phenomenology—by virtue of "substitut[ing] images for objects, where images are precisely not concepts, ideas, or powers."[89] Simulating through images immediacies not yet given the "perspective" of cognitive mastery of an object, art opens imagination to affect and thus transformations evocative of grace: "Levinas's musing on rhythm and image may suggest . . . that we can profitably return" to scenes in Sterne and Dickens that address "their artistry to the senses rather than to the understanding" so as to "learn to read the play of rippling shadows on the wall as incarnating a truth other than the truth of dialectical reasoning."[90] Such reeducation in reading opens us to perceiving in Dickens's supposedly "sentimental" scenes ethical critiques of "the egoism of the *conatus*, that is, the Hobbesian-Malthusian universe," and so "teach[es] us how to admire . . . the skillfulness of Dickens's images of *caritas* and grace."[91] Thus, "Miss Tox's overwhelming passivity and self-abnegation" constitutes an "image" of "ethics based on responsibility," as does Florence's asking forgiveness of the father who has always neglected and devalued her.[92]

To discern what literature *does* in the culture of modernity entails becoming sensible of the affective agency of images. This demands a reformed criticism allowing us to "use our eyes and ears, our sensibilities, prior to any urge to redefine the moment in conformity to our own thoughts," so as to see in the image of Florence's remarkable suspension of judgment in favor of love "a touchstone for the *realistic* novel."[93] By offering us extraordinary images of such criticism, Melvyn New provides both the tools and the inspiration for scholarship not entirely unworthy of his own.

NOTES

1. Melvyn New, introduction to *Telling New Lies: Seven Essays in Fiction, Past and Present* (Gainesville: University Press of Florida, 1992), 7.

2. Ibid., 7–8.

3. Melvyn New, "The Introduction Polemical," in *New Casebooks: The Life and Opinions of Tristram Shandy, Gentleman*, ed. Melvyn New (London: Macmillan, 1992), 3. New's remarks concern John Traugott, *Tristram Shandy's World: Sterne's Philosophical Rhetoric* (Berkeley: University of California Press, 1954).

4. Melvyn New, *Laurence Sterne as Satirist: A Reading of "Tristram Shandy"* (Gainesville: University of Florida Press, 1969), 2–3.

5. See esp. Melvyn New, "Sterne and the Narrative of Determinateness," in *Critical Essays on Laurence Sterne*, ed. Melvyn New (New York: G. K. Hall, 1998), 127–39; repr., *Eighteenth-Century Fiction* 4 (1992): 315–29.

6. New, introduction to *Telling New Lies*, 11.

7. Martha C. Nussbaum, *The Fragility of Goodness: Luck and Ethics in Greek Tragedy and Philosophy* (Cambridge: Cambridge University Press, 1986), 146–47; "The *Republic*: True Value and the Standpoint of Perfection," 136–64; Plato, *Republic*, esp. books 2–3, in Plato, *The Collected Dialogues*, ed. Edith Hamilton and Huntington Cairns (Princeton: Princeton University Press, 1963), 605–61; and René Descartes, *"Discourse on Method" and "Meditations,"* trans. Laurence J. Lafleur (New York: Bobbs-Merrill, 1960), 7. Compare with Plato, *Republic* V (476a–480), in *Collected Dialogues*, 715–20.

8. Descartes, *Discourse on Method*, 10–11.

9. Much the same points are stressed in recent cognitive science. See Patrick Colm Hogan, *Cognitive Science, Literature, and the Arts: A Guide for Humanists* (New York: Routledge, 2003), 107–8; Gilles Fauconnier and Mark Turner, *The Way We Think: Conceptual Blending and the Mind's Hidden Complexities* (New York: Basic Books, 2002), 24.

10. Melvyn New with Richard A. Davies and W. G. Day, *The Life and Opinions of Tristram Shandy: The Notes*, vol. 3 of the Florida Edition of the Works of Laurence Sterne (Gainesville: University of Florida Press, 1984), 37.

11. Hans Blumenberg, *The Legitimacy of the Modern Age*, trans. Robert M. Wallace (Cambridge: MIT Press, 1983), 243. For the easy commerce between skepticism and fideism in ancient and Renaissance thought that post-Enlightenment sensibilities find puzzling, and for this tradition's relevance to Sterne, see Melvyn New, *Tristram Shandy: A Book for Free Spirits* (New York: Twayne, 1994), 28–45; J. T. Parnell, "Swift, Sterne, and the Skeptical Tradition," in *Critical Essays on Laurence Sterne* (New York: G. K. Hall, 1998), 140–58, repr., *Studies in Eighteenth-Century Culture* 23 (1994): 220–42; and Donald R. Wehrs, "Sterne, Cervantes, Montaigne: Fideistic Skepticism and the Rhetoric of Desire," in *New Casebooks: Tristram Shandy*, 133–54, repr., *Comparative Literature Studies* 25 (1988): 127–51.

12. New, "'The Grease of God': The Form of Eighteenth-Century English Fiction," in *Telling New Lies*, 28, 33; repr., *PMLA* 91 (1976): 235–44.

13. New, "'The Grease of God,'" 34, 35.

14. Ibid., 42.

15. New, "Profaned and Stenciled Texts: In Search of Pynchon's *V.*," in *Telling New Lies*, 61; repr., *Georgia Review* 33 (1979): 395–412.

16. New, "Profaned and Stenciled Texts," 61.

17. See esp. Antonio Damasio, *Looking for Spinoza: Joy, Sorrow, and the Feeling Brain* (Orlando, FL: Harcourt, 2003); Patrick Colm Hogan, *The Mind and Its Stories: Narrative Universals and Human Emotions* (Cambridge: Cambridge University Press, 2003), 45–121; and Keith Oatley, *Best Laid Schemes: The Psychology of Emotions* (Cambridge: Cambridge University Press, 1992). Also see Charles Taylor's discussion of the inherently spatial and narrative structure of subjective senses of orientation in *Sources of the Self: The Making of Modern Identity* (Cambridge, MA: Harvard University Press, 1989), 3–52.

18. New, "Profaned and Stenciled Texts," 63.

19. New, "Modes of Eighteenth-Century Fiction," in *Telling New Lies*, 69; repr., *Literature and Criticism: A New Century Guide* (London: Routledge, 1990), 505–17. See Augustine, *On Christian Doctrine*, trans. D. W. Robertson, Jr. (Indianapolis: Bobbs-Merrill, 1958), 3.10–15 (pp. 87–93); and Joerg O. Fichte, *Chaucer's "Art Poetical": A Study of Chaucerian Poetics* (Tübingen: Gunter Narr Verlag, 1980), 22–36.

20. New, "Modes of Eighteenth-Century Fiction," 70. See Brian Stock, *After Augustine: The Meditative Reader and the Text* (Philadelphia: University of Pennsylvania Press, 2001), esp. 24–37; and Giovanni Boccaccio, *On Poetry: Being the Preface and the Fourteenth and Fifteenth Books of Boccaccio's "Genealogia Deorum Gentilium,"* trans. Charles G. Osgood (New York: Liberal Arts Library, 1930), 47–51.

21. New, "Modes of Eighteenth-Century Fiction," 76.

22. New, introduction to *Telling New Lies*, 8.

23. Hans-Georg Gadamer, *Truth and Method*, 2nd ed., trans. Joel Weinsheimer and David G. Marshall (New York: Crossroads, 1989), 198. The burden of Gadamer's argument is that historicist hermeneutics, even when aspiring to open itself to the experience (*Erlebnis*) expressed in texts, as in Dilthey, lapses into conceiving the text as a content of consciousness to be assimilated into a historicized variant of contemplative *nous* (i.e., a variant of Hegelian *Geist*). Gadamer advocates the alternative of what he calls "historical consciousness": "Historical consciousness no longer simply applies its own criteria of understanding to the tradition in which it is situated, nor does it naively assimilate tradition and simply carry it on. Rather, it adopts a reflective posture toward both itself and the tradition in which it is situated. It understands itself in terms of its own history. *Historical consciousness is a mode of self-knowledge*" (235). See 173–242. Recent critical reassessments of New Historicism argue that it often recycles one or another of the failings of the old historicism as identified by Gadamer. See, for example, B. J. Sokol, *A Brave New World of Knowledge: Shakespeare's "The Tempest" and Early Modern Epistemology* (Madison, PA: Fairleigh Dickinson University Press, 2003); Thomas McAlindon, *Shakespeare Minus Theory* (Aldershot: Ashgate, 2005); and Arthur F. Kinney, *Shakespeare and Cognition: Aristotle's Legacy and Shakespearean Drama* (New York: Routledge, 2006).

24. New, *Laurence Sterne as Satirist*, 28.

25. Laurence Sterne, *The Life and Opinions of Tristram Shandy, Gentleman*, vol. 1 of the Florida Edition of the Works of Laurence Sterne, ed. Melvyn New and Joan New (Gainesville: University of Florida Press, 1978), 2.5.106. Citations to *Tristram Shandy* (hereafter in the text) are to original volume and chapter number followed by the Florida edition page number. Concerning Swift, see New, *Laurence Sterne as Satirist*, 17; *Tristram Shandy: The Notes*, 141.

26. Jonathan Swift, *A Tale of a Tub*, in *The Writings of Jonathan Swift*, ed. Robert A. Greenberg and William Bowman Piper (New York: Norton, 1973), 348.

27. See Lucian, *Philosophies for Sale*, in *Lucian II*, trans. A. M. Harmon (New York: Loeb Classical Library, 1915).

28. For epitomizing examples, see Dante, *The Banquet*, trans. Christopher Ryan (Saratoga, CA: Anma Libri, 1989), 4.12.153–54; 4.28.196; Dante Alighieri, *Convivio*, ed. Giorgio Inglese (Milano: Biblioteca Universale Rizzoli, 1993), 4.12.266–67; 4.28.330; Dante, *Paradiso*, 2.119–41; 33.

29. See Blumenberg, *The Legitimacy of the Modern Age*, 37–226, 343–75.

30. Louis Dupré, *Passage to Modernity: An Essay in the Hermeneutics of Nature and Culture* (New Haven: Yale University Press, 1993), 42–144; Ullrich Langer, *Divine and Poetic Freedom in the Renaissance: Nominalist Theology and Literature in France and Italy* (Princeton: Princeton University Press, 1990), 3–24, 84–148. Also see Heiko A. Oberman, "*Via antiqua* and *via moderna*: Late Medieval Prologomena to Early Reformation Thought," in *From Ockham to Wyclif*, ed. Anne Hudson and Michael Wilks (Oxford: Basil Blackwell, 1987), 445–63; and Francis Oakley, *Omnipotence, Covenant, and Order: An Excursion in the History of Ideas from Abelard to Liebniz* (Ithaca, NY: Cornell University Press, 1984).

31. Dupré, *Passage to Modernity*, 119. Also see Taylor's discussion of Descartes and moral philosophy in *Sources of the Self*, 143–58.

32. Dupré, *Passage to Modernity*, 140. Also see Taylor's discussion of Lockean subjectivity in *Sources of the Self*, 159–76; Langer, *Divine and Poetic Freedom in the Renaissance*, 84–148.

33. Langer, *Divine and Poetic Freedom in the Renaissance*, 129–30.

34. Miguel de Cervantes, *Don Quijote de la Mancha*, ed. Martín de Riquer (Barcelonia: Editorial Juventud, 1955), 82; Miguel de Cervantes, *Don Quixote*, trans. Samuel Putnam (New York: Modern Library, 1949), 64. References will henceforth be cited parenthetically.

35. Cervantes develops this aspect of Lucianic satire in "El licenciado Vidriera" and "El coloquio de los perros," in Miguel de Cervantes, *Novelas ejemplares*, vol. 2, ed. Harry Sieber (Madrid: Cátedra, 1982), 43 74, 299 359.

36. See New, *Laurence Sterne as Satirist*, 7–69; "Swift and Sterne: Two Tales, Several Sermons, and a Relationship Revisited," in *Critical Essays on Jonathan Swift*, ed. Frank Palmeri (New York: G. K. Hall, 1993), 164–86; *Tristram Shandy: A Book for Free Spirits*, 46–66.

37. New, "Orwell and Antisemitism: Toward *1984*," in New, *Telling New Lies*, 119; repr., *Modern Fiction Studies* 21 (1975): 81–105. New cites *The Collected Essays, Journalism and Letters of George Orwell*, ed. Sonia Orwell and Ian Angus (New York: Harcourt, Brace and World, 1968), 3:335. See Slavoj Zîzêk, *The Sublime*

Object of Ideology (London: Verso, 1987) and *The Plague of Fantasies* (London: Verso, 1997); and Slavoj Zîzêk and Renata Saleci, ed., *Gaze and Voice as Love Objects* (Durham, NC: Duke University Press, 1996).

38. New, "Orwell and Antisemitism," 124. New draws on Hannah Arendt, "The Concentration Camps," *Partisan Review* 15 (July 1948).

39. New, "Proust's Influence on Sterne: Remembrance of Things to Come," in New, *Telling New Lies*, 142; repr., *MLN* 103 (1988): 1031–55.

40. New, "Proust's Influence on Sterne," 156, 147, 151, 157.

41. New, *Laurence Sterne as Satirist*, 16.

42. Ibid., 128, 183.

43. New, "Jonathan Swift, Thomas Mann, and the Irony of Ideology," in New, *Telling New Lies*, 171.

44. New, "Jonathan Swift, Thomas Mann, and the Irony of Ideology," 171, 172.

45. New, "Swift and Sterne," 169, 170, 171.

46. Ibid., 175, 180, 182–83.

47. New, "Jonathan Swift, Thomas Mann, and the Irony of Ideology," 186. Concordant with New's argument, T. J. Reed identifies Mann's reaction to the June 1922 assassination by right-wing youths of Walter Rathenau, the Jewish financier who had organized Germany's war economy and reluctantly agreed to serve the Weimar Republic, as the pivotal event alerting him to what antirationalist nationalism portended. This, in turn, Reed argues, radically altered the direction of *The Magic Mountain* (*Thomas Mann: The Uses of Tradition* [Oxford: Oxford University Press, 1974], 288–316).

48. Melvyn New, "Preface: Something New Under the Sun," in *In Proximity: Emmanuel Levinas and the Eighteenth Century*, ed. Melvyn New with Robert Bernasconi and Richard A. Cohen (Lubbock: Texas Tech University Press, 2001), xi–xxiv.

49. New, "Proust's Influence on Sterne," 145.

50. Ibid., 151.

51. Ibid., 155, 156, 157, 158.

52. Ibid., 145.

53. Melvyn New, "Job's Wife and Sterne's Other Women," in *Out of Bounds: Male Writers and Gender(ed) Criticism*, ed. Laura Claridge and Elizabeth Langland (Amherst: University of Massachusetts Press, 1990), 69.

54. New, *Tristram Shandy: A Book for Free Spirits*, 13–14, 16–17.

55. Ibid., 44, 13. For Goethe, New cites *Sterne: The Critical Heritage*, ed. Alan B. Howes (London: Routledge and Kegan Paul, 1974), 433–35; for Nietzsche, *Human, All Too Human: A Book for Free Spirits*, trans. R. J. Hollingdale (Cambridge: Cambridge University Press, 1986), 310. Also see Jeffrey Morrison's account of the prominence of disorienting immediacy in Goethe's account of aesthetic experience in *Winckelmann and the Notion of Aesthetic Education* (Oxford: Clarendon Press, 1996), 211–43.

56. New, *Tristram Shandy: A Book for Free Spirits*, 88; Friedrich Nietzsche, *Thus Spoke Zarathustra*, trans. R. J. Hollingdale (Harmondsworth: Penguin, 1961), 229. On Wilhelm Meister's traumatic recognitions of his unintended effects upon others, see Donald R. Wehrs, "Levinas, Goethe's *Wilhelm Mesiters Lehrjahre*, and the Compul-

sion of the Good," in *In Proximity*, 215–42, repr., *The Eighteenth Century: Theory and Interpretation* 40 (1999): 261–78. The "beautiful soul" resolves experience into ideas with a completeness that, while "beautiful," is static, self-limiting, and self-enclosing. See Goethe's discussion of his character's model, his elderly relation Susanna von Klettenberg, in Johann Wolfgang von Goethe, *Dichtung und Wahrheit* (Frankfurt am Main: Insel Verlag, 1975), 378–80, 570, 681, 702–5. For Goethe's delineation of the totalitarian potential of utopian idealism, see Johann Wolfgang von Goethe, *Wilhelm Meisters Wanderjahre oder die Entsagenden* (Frankfurt am Main: Insel Verlag, 1982), esp. 413–18. For "self-overcoming," see Friedrich Nietzsche, *Thus Spoke Zarathustra*, in *The Portable Nietzsche*, ed. and trans. Walter Kaufmann (Harmondsworth: Penguin, 1954), first part, prologue 4, 126–28; and *Beyond Good and Evil, "The Free Spirit,"* 35–56, the homage to Goethe in *Twilight of the Idols*, trans. Walter Kaufmann, in *The Portable Nietzsche*, "Skirmishes of an Untimely Man, 49–51," 553–56.

57. See Hans-Georg Gadamer, "On the Course of Human Spiritual Development: Studies in Goethe's Unfinished Writings," in *Literature and Philosophy in Dialogue: Essays in German Literary Theory*, ed. Robert H. Paslick (Albany: State University of New York Press, 1994), 31–66; Friedrich Nietzsche, *The Will to Power*, trans. Walter Kaufmann and R. J. Hollingdale (New York: Vintage, 1967), 272–86, 322–66; *Beyond Good and Evil: Prelude to a Philosophy of the Future*, trans. Walter Kaufmann (New York: Vintage, 1966), "What is Noble," 201–37.

58. See New, *Laurence Sterne as Satirist*, 9–10, 32–33; also Taylor, *Sources of the Self*, 249–51.

59. The tendency of academic feminist discourse to divide between analytical critique and advocacy has motivated efforts to chart a feminist ethics—most notably Luce Irigaray's *An Ethics of Sexual Difference*, trans. Carolyn Burke and Gillian C. Gill (Ithaca: Cornell University Press, 1993) and Kelly Oliver's *Family Values: Subjects Between Nature and Culture* (New York: Routledge, 1997). Yet the relationship between analyzing thwarted agency, advocating expanded agency, and an ethics acknowledging the conditioned nature of will and freedom remains elusive.

60. See Melvyn New, "The Odd Couple: Laurence Sterne and John Norris of Bemerton," *Philological Quarterly* 75, no. 3 (1996): 361–85.

61. Donald R. Wehrs, "Touching Words: Embodying Ethics in Erasmus, Shakespearean Comedy, and Contemporary Theory," *Modern Philology* 104, no. 1 (2006): 1–33.

62. See Erasmus, *Ecclesiastes*, in *Opera Omnia* (henceforth cited as *ASD*), 5-4 (Amsterdam: North-Holland, 1977), 368; Erasmus, *A Declamation on the Subject of Early Liberal Education for Children*, trans. Beert C. Verstraete, in *Collected Works of Erasmus* (henceforth cited as *CWE*, vol. 26, ed. J. K. Sowards (Toronto: University of Toronto Press, 1985), 311; and *De Pveris Statim ac Liberaliter Institvendis*, in *ASD*, vol. 1-2 (Amsterdam: North-Holland, 1971), 39. Also see Martin Luther, *Lectures on Romans: Glosses and Scholia*, ed. Hilton C. Oswald, in *Luther's Works* (*LW*), vol. 25 (Saint Louis, MO: Concordia, 1972), 350; and Anders Nygren, *Agape and Eros*, trans. Philip S. Watson (New York: Harper & Row, 1969), 716–21. On the influence of nominalist theology upon Luther, see Dupré, *Passage to Modernity*, 204–6.

63. Erasmus, *Hyperaspistes*, book 2, trans. Clarence H. Miller in *CWE*, vol. 77, ed. Charles Trinkaus (Toronto: University of Toronto Press, 2000), 732.

64. New, "The Odd Couple," 366, 373.

65. Ibid., 373.

66. See Erasmus, *Enchiridion militis christiani* (*Handbook of the Christian Sol-dier*), trans. Charles Fantazzi, in *CWE,* vol. 66, ed. John W. O. O'Malley (Toronto: University of Toronto Press, 1988); *Antibarbari*, trans. Margaret Mann Phillips, in *CWE,* vol. 23, ed. Craig R. Thompson (Toronto: University of Toronto Press, 1978); and Margorie O'Rourke Boyle, *Christianizing Pagan Mysteries: Erasmus in Pur-suit of Wisdom* (Toronto: University of Toronto Press, 1981). Also see John Norris, *Reason and Religion; or The Grounds and Measures of Devotion*, in John Norris, *Treatises Upon Several Subjects, 1698* (New York: Garland, 1978), 79.

67. New, "The Odd Couple," 374.

68. See Norris, *Reflections upon the Conduct of Human Life*, in Norris, *Treatises Upon Several Subjects*, 161–262; *Cursory Reflections upon a Book call'd An Essay Concerning Human Understanding*, appended to John Norris, *Christian Blessedness, 1690* (New York: Garland, 1978). See esp. Norris's account of the fifth beatitude in Norris, *Christian Blessedness*, 122–43.

69. New, "The Odd Couple," 374.

70. New, "Preface: Something New Under the Sun," xiv; Emmanuel Levinas, "Ideology and Idealism" (1973), in Emmanuel Levinas, *Of God Who Comes to Mind*, trans. Bettina Bergo (Stanford, CA: Stanford University Press, 1998), 4; cited in New, "Preface: Something New Under the Sun," xiv.

71. New, "Preface: Something New Under the Sun," xv; Levinas, "Ideology and Idealism," 9.

72. Levinas, "Ideology and Idealism," 9; cited in New, "Preface: Something New Under the Sun," xv.

73. New, "Preface: Something New Under the Sun," xvi.

74. This claim, which Levinas derives from phenomenological analysis, is cor-roborated by cognitive research, as I discuss elsewhere. See Wehrs, "Touching Words"; "Moral Physiology, Ethical Prototypes, and the Denaturing of Sense in Shakespearean Tragedy," *College Literature* 33, no. 1 (2006): 67–92; "Somatic Marking, Ethical Sense, and Practical Reason: The Political Economy of Literary Universals from Richardson and Austen to Dostoyevsky and Grass," *Conscious-ness, Literature and the Arts* 6, 2 (2005), accessed at www.aber.ac.uk/tfts/journal. I have sketched some connections between Sternean narrative and Levinasian thought in Donald R. Wehrs, "Levinas and Sterne: From the Ethics of the Face to the Aesthetics of Unrepresentability," in *Critical Essays on Laurence Sterne*, 311–27, repr., *In Proximity*, 141–65. Also see Elizabeth Kraft, "Laurence Sterne and the Ethics of Sexual Difference: Chiasmic Narration and Double Desire," *Christianity and Literature* 51 (2002): 363–85; and New, "Preface: Something New Under the Sun," xvi–xvii.

75. New, "Reading Sterne through Proust and Levinas," in *In Proximity*, 112.

76. Emmanuel Levinas, *Totality and Infinity: An Essay in Exteriority*, trans. Al-phonso Lingis (Pittsburgh: Duquesne University Press, 1969), 33.

77. Levinas, *Totality and Infinity*, 34; also see Emmanuel Levinas, "Meaning and Sense," in *Emmanuel Levinas: Basic Philosophical Writings*, ed. Adriaan T. Pep-

erzak, Simon Critchley, and Robert Bernasconi (Bloomington: Indiana University Press, 1996), 51–52.

78. See Emmanuel Levinas, *Otherwise Than Being, or Beyond Essence*, trans. Alphonso Lingis (Pittsburgh: Duquesne University Press, 1981), 140–52; "God and Philosophy," in *Basic Philosophical Writings*, 129–48.

79. New, "Reading Sterne through Proust and Levinas," 120–21.

80. Ibid., 131.

81. Levinas, "Meaning and Sense," 57.

82. Ibid.

83. See Melvyn New, "William Hogarth and John Baldessari: Ornamenting Sterne's *Tristram Shandy*," *Word & Image* 11, no. 2 (1995): 182–95; also see New's discussion of the image of the prisoner and the starling in "Reading Sterne through Proust and Levinas," 131–32, and "Proust's Influence on Sterne," 146–51.

84. See New, *Laurence Sterne as Satirist*, 146, 153, 187, 203–4; *Tristram Shandy: A Book for Free Spirits*, 65–66, 87–88. In "'The Grease of God,'" New objects to a novel-centered teleology for literary history, if the novel is understood, as in Erich Auerbach's *Mimesis: The Representation of Reality in Western Literature*, trans. William R. Trask (Princeton: Princeton University Press, 1953), as the generic expression of modernity's drive toward self- and world-construction. Thus Auerbach's account of Shakespeare's pivotal role in the creation of modernity is tied to Auerbach's "obvious enthusiasm for 'self-orientation,'" and for "nineteenth-century liberal values" (32), which we might describe as political inflections of subjectivity modeled upon nominalist theology.

85. See Melvyn New, "Sterne in the Future Tense," *Shandean* 11 (1999–2000): 63–69.

86. New, *Laurence Sterne as Satirist*, 79.

87. See New, *Laurence Sterne as Satirist*, 110, 139, 144–46, 205; *Tristram Shandy: A Book for Free Spirits*, 89–112; "Three Sentimental Journeys: Sterne, Shlovsky, Svevo," *Shandean* 11 (1999–2000): 126–34.

88. Melvyn New, "Taking Care: A Slightly Levinasian Reading of *Dombey and Son*," *Philological Quarterly* 84, no. 1 (2005): 77–104, repr., in *Levinas and Nineteenth-Century Literature: Ethics and Otherness from Romanticism through Realism*, ed. Donald R. Wehrs and David P. Haney (Newark: University of Delaware Press, 2009), 236–63.

89. New, "Taking Care," 81–82.

90. Ibid., 83–84. The argument here may be compared with Jenefer Robinson's discussion of the agency of "non-cognitive affective appraisals" in literary communication in *Deeper Than Reason: Emotion and Its Role in Literature, Music, and Art* (Oxford: Clarendon Press, 2005), esp. 28–135, 154–94.

91. New, "Taking Care," 88, 89.

92. Ibid., 90, 91, 95.

93. Ibid., 95, 98.

Index

abolitionist movement: historical context, 80, 83n11, 190–91; newspapers' role in, 192–98; principle of, 195–98; sentimental mode in antislavery writings, 199, 202n26; and Sterne's "bitter draught" passage, 182, 189, 190–93, 196–97, 199; and Sterne's captive passage, 185–88, 192, 193–95, 199, 202n26; and Sterne's starling passage, 185–86, 192, 197, 199; widespread influence of Sterne on, 181

The Abuse of Casuistry (Jonsen and Toulmin), 48, 50, 51–52, 57, 61–62, 66

abyss, 164, 177n4

Adamic myths, 170

Addison, Joseph, 223, 226–27, 238–39, 240–41

The Adventurer: Bathurst essays, 54; Johnson essays, 56

The Adventures of Roderick Random (Smollett), 73–82

Aeolists, 148–49

aesthetics, 6–7

Ahern, Stephen, 198

Anatomy of Melancholy (Burton), 233

Anglican rationalism, 156n15

Antony and Cleopatra (Shakespeare), 8

Apologia Pro Vita Sua (Newman), 66–68

apostrophe to Slavery and Liberty, 191–93, 194, 195–97

Aquinas, Thomas, 51, 62

Arendt, Hannah, 251

asceticism, 145

Asfour, Amal, 33, 36, 37, 39, 40–41

Astley, Thomas, 77, 80–81

Atkins, John, 73, 80–81

Augustine, St., 51, 56, 62–64, 68

authorship, attribution of, 53–55, 68

autonomy, 130–31

Barrell, John, 36–37, 40

Bathurst, Richard, 54

Battestin, Martin C., 111, 124

Baudelaire, Charles, 18

Baxter, Richard, 67, 119, 238, 244n28

Beasley, Jerry, 74

Belsey, Hugh, 42

Benjamin, Walter, 164–65

Bennett, Arnold, 24n11

Bentley, Richard, 10, 11, 15–16, 19

Bermingham, Ann, 33–34, 38

Beyond Good and Evil (Nietzsche), 146–47

About the Contributors

Martha F. Bowden is professor of English at Kennesaw State University. She has edited the novels of Mary Davys, *The Reform'd Coquet, Familiar Letters Betwixt a Gentleman and a Lady, and The Accomplish'd Rake* (1999) and published *Yorick's Congregation: The Church of England in the Time of Laurence Sterne* (UDP, 2007). She is at present investigating the depiction of the seventeenth and eighteenth centuries in contemporary historical fiction.

Taylor Corse is associate professor of English at Arizona State University. He has written extensively on John Dryden, Alexander Pope, Aphra Behn, Anne Conway, Francis Mercury van Helmont, and other authors from the Restoration and eighteenth century. He is currently at work on a study of English and Italian literary culture in the late seventeenth century.

W. G. Day is Eccles and Fellows' librarian at Winchester College, UK, where he was previously head of the English department. He has collaborated with Melvyn New on two volumes of the Florida Edition of the Works of Laurence Sterne, *Tristram Shandy: The Notes* (vol. 3) and *A Sentimental Journey and Continuation of the Bramine's Journal* (vol. 6). He is the review editor of the *Shandean*.

Madeleine Descargues-Grant is professor of English literature at Valenciennes University (Nord de France). Her first book on Sterne, *Correspondances* (1994) was a literary study of Sterne's letters. She has contributed to the *Shandean* and to the ongoing international critical dialogue on Sterne, including frequent exchanges with Melvyn New, whom she met at the York conference on "Sterne in Modernism and Post-Modernism" (1993). She has published many articles on eighteenth-century literature, in French and in English, and a book on essays and sermons, *Prédicateurs et journalistes* (2004) addressing the writings of Swift, Addison, Fielding, and Sterne. She has also edited a book on the English sources of the French *Encyclopaedia* (2005) and coauthored *Tristram Shandy: Laurence Sterne* with Anne Bandry (2006).

W. B. Gerard is associate professor of English at Auburn University Montgomery. His *Laurence Sterne and the Visual Imagination* (2006) explores the interpretive functions of the many illustrations of Sterne's texts, which have been cataloged further in a four-part series in the *Shandean* (2005–2008). He is editor of *Divine Rhetoric: Essays on the Sermons of Laurence Sterne* (UDP, 2010) and coeditor of *The Scriblerian and the Kit-Cats*. He studied under Melvyn New at the University of Florida from 1998 to 2002 and is one of the coeditors of this volume.

Elizabeth Kraft is professor of English at the University of Georgia. She is the author of several essays and monographs on eighteenth-century topics. Her most recent projects include a collection of essays, *On Second Thought: Updating the Eighteenth-Century Text*, coedited with Debra Taylor Bourdeau (UDP, 2007) and *Sir Charles Grandison* in the Cambridge Edition of the Works of Samuel Richardson, coedited with Melvyn New and Derek Taylor.

Joseph G. Kronick graduated with a BA from the University of Florida, where he studied with Melvyn New. He did his graduate work at UCLA (PhD, 1981), and has since taught at Louisiana State University. He is the author of *American Poetics of History: From Emerson to the Moderns* (1984) and *Derrida and the Future of Literature* (1999). He has written on nineteenth- and twentieth-century American writers and on philosophy and literature. He has published essays on a number of writers, including Emerson, Hawthorne, Poe, Henry Adams, Ezra Pound, Wallace Stevens, Don DeLillo, Stanley Cavell, Hegel, Nietzsche, and Heidegger. More recently, he has written on the ancient quarrel and modern theory.

James E. May is associate professor of English at the Pennsylvania State University's DuBois campus. He edited "The Life of Young" for the Yale Edition of the Works of Samuel Johnson, compiled the Henry Pettit Edward Young Collection at the University of Colorado Boulder (1989), and contributed bibliographical and textual studies to *Papers of the Bibliographical Society of America*, *Studies in Bibliography*, and *Swift Studies*. For more than a decade he has provided "Scriblerian Transferred" surveys of rare books and manuscript sales to the *Scriblerian*, compiled section 1 of *The Eighteenth Century: A Current Bibliography*, and edited the *Eighteenth-Century Intel-*

ligencer. He is now editing the letters between Edward Young and Samuel Richardson and completing a descriptive bibliography of the writings of Edward Young published in English before 1776.

Frank Palmeri is professor of English at the University of Miami, the author of *Satire in Narrative* (1990), and *Satire, History, Novel: Narrative Forms, 1665–1815* (UDP, 2003), and editor of *Critical Essays on Jonathan Swift* (1993) and *Humans and Other Animals in Eighteenth-Century Britain* (2006). He is currently working on the influence of eighteenth-century conjectural history in the formation of the social science disciplines.

Eric Rothstein is Edgar W. Lacy professor emeritus of English at the University of Wisconsin. British literature, 1660–1800, has been the focus of most of his articles and of his six books, the most recent of which is *Gleaning Modernity: Early Eighteenth-Century Literature and the Modernizing Process* (UDP, 2007). His latest work has largely dwelt on the development of modernity, and on cultural historiography more broadly.

E. Derek Taylor, an associate professor of English at Longwood University and a coeditor of this volume, studied under Melvyn New at the University of Florida from 1994 to 2000. His essays on eighteenth-century literature and intellectual history have appeared in *Notes and Queries*, *Eighteenth-Century Fiction*, *Journal of the History of Ideas*, *Studies in Bibliography*, and *Mary Astell: Reason, Gender, Faith* (2007). He coedited with Melvyn New an edition of Astell and John Norris's *Letters Concerning the Love of God* (2005) and is currently collaborating with New and Elizabeth Kraft on an edition of *Sir Charles Grandison*, forthcoming in the Cambridge Edition of the Works of Samuel Richardson. His book *Reason and Religion in "Clarissa"* was published in 2009.

Robert G. Walker, a coeditor of this volume, was a graduate student under Melvyn New at the University of Florida from 1969 to 1974. He is the author of *Eighteenth-Century Arguments for Immortality and Johnson's "Rasselas"* (1977), as well as more than twenty-five articles and notes on both eighteenth-century and modern literature for journals that include the *Huntington Library Quarterly, Philological Quarterly,* the *Sewanee Review, English Studies,* and *Age of Johnson.* His most recent essays are on Arthur Koester, James Boswell, and Curzio Malaparte.

Donald R. Wehrs is professor of English at Auburn University where he teaches comparative literature, eighteenth-century studies, and postcolonial literature. He is author of *Islam, Ethics, Revolt: Politics and Piety in*

Francophone West African and Maghreb Narrative (2008); *Pre-Colonial Colonial Africa in Colonial African Narratives: From "Ethiopia Unbound" to "Things Fall Apart," 1911–1958* (2008); *African Feminist Fiction and Indigenous Values* (2001); and coeditor, along with David P. Haney, of *Levinas and Nineteenth-Century Literature: Ethics and Otherness from Romanticism through Realism* (UDP, 2009). He has published essays on eighteenth-century British literature, postcolonial fiction, Shakespeare, Hardy, and critical theory.